PLEASE UNDERSTAND ME II

TEMPERAMENT

CHARACTER

INTELLIGENCE

David Keirsey

Foreword

"The point of this book," writes my old friend David Keirsey, "is that people differ from each other, and that no amount of getting after them is going to change them." The point is also, David might have added, that the important differences between us are our natural birthright, arising in just a few distinctive patterns. Recognizing these patterns can vastly enrich our sense of who we are, of who others are, and of how much we can learn from one another about the problems of life.

No person that I know of has studied temperament in action more persistently and more brilliantly than Keirsey, and no one is in a better position to speak to us about it. Keirsey has been "people watching" for almost fifty years, and his interest in temperament as an organizing principle stretches back almost as far. If *Please Understand Me* was a valuable report on his progress to that time (1978), *Please Understand Me II* serves to present a report on what he has worked out in the interim twenty years, and also the valuable addition of his ideas about the relationship of temperament to intelligence.

I have known David for almost thirty years now. During those years I have had the pleasure of teaching and writing and learning with him, and the even greater pleasure of arguing with him. Our time together has been filled with logical discourse and theoretical speculation, and, at the same time, good, old-fashioned hair-splitting debate (including the use of devious debate tactics and other trickery to see if we could catch the other napping). We are both Rationals, and as you read this book you will understand why we Rationals treasure collecting various skills, exercising ourselves with logical investigation, but also finding delight in argumentation, logical trickery, and (I confess) terrible jokes—as long as they are clever plays on words. You will also see, by the way, why non-Rationals will—each temperament for its own reasons—find what is so rewarding for us Rationals to be intolerable!

What I find remarkable about Keirsey's empirical investigations is which of the many problems in psychology he has chosen to investigate—intelligence, madness, personality—each a very complex problem, and each with a checkered history. And I find his treatment of each unique. His theory of intelligence is like no other, nor is his theory of madness, nor is his theory of personality. Each is unique, true, but far more important, each is useful to practitioners, something that cannot be said, at any rate with much conviction, of any other extant theory of intelligence, or madness, or personality.

From David's study of temperament I have learned that the great personal differences between me and those around me were not an indication that there was something wrong with me—or with them. I have learned that the apparent deficiencies in a person's characteristic ways of dealing with the world are offset by natural strengths in different areas. We don't require that a great painter be a wise teacher, nor that a trusted accountant be a brilliant physicist. We all, according to our temperament, have our areas of distinction and our areas of struggle. Both deserve to be respected for what they are. So it is with temperament: different temperaments naturally show us different patterns of intelligent behavior.

Perhaps most important, I have learned that we must not judge either ourselves or others harshly when our (or their) values, preferences, and style of experiencing and dealing with the world are different. There is room for us all, and a need for us all. I am grateful that David has decided to offer us *Please Understand Me II*, and I feel certain that its readers will be fascinated and pleased with it.

Ray Choiniere

Acknowledgments

Stephen Montgomery, himself an author of note, served as my editor not only for the first edition of *Please Understand Me,* twenty years ago, but for its recent revision. Without his help over the years I would never have finished the revision, given my penchant for continuously revising my revisions. He was even more than helpful, going as he did far beyond editing, by doing much of the composition. And even more than that, he did a tremendous amount of research over the years and in the remotest places. For instance, it was he who detected what Plato and Aristotle had to say about the different roles the four temperaments of Hippocrates played in the social order. And of course his years of research that went into his four volume set, *The Pygmalion Project,* are embedded throughout *Please Understand Me II.*

Then there was my family, my son and daughters and their spouses, and of course my wife. They were always there to veto my more wayward speculations and to catch me in my many errors of omission and commission.

And my former colleagues and students in the counseling department at California State University Fullerton have been of great help in reviewing the many drafts of the revision and in suggesting things that ought to be inserted or deleted.

I wish especially to thank and to commend my colleague, psychologist Ray Choiniere, for his monumental study of the temperament of our forty American Presidents. In return for helping me complete my book on madness and temperament, I helped him complete his book, *Presidential Temperament.* The findings of our collaborative study of the Presidents are included in the new version of *Please Understand Me.* And that is not all. Besides his years of research on our many Presidents, his years of work on madness and temperament, Choiniere has been a constant companion for me, assisting me in many ways in conceptualizing *Please Understand Me II.*

David Keirsey

Contents

If a man does not keep pace with his companions, perhaps it is because he hears a different drummer. Let him step to the music which he hears, however measured or far away.

—Henry David Thoreau

1
Different Drummers

If you do not want what I want, please try not to tell me that my want is wrong.

Or if my beliefs are different from yours, at least pause before you set out to correct them.

Or if my emotion seems less or more intense than yours, given the same circumstances, try not to ask me to feel other than I do.

Or if I act, or fail to act, in the manner of your design for action, please let me be.

I do not, for the moment at least, ask you to understand me. That will come only when you are willing to give up trying to change me into a copy of you.

If you will allow me any of my own wants, or emotions, or beliefs, or actions, then you open yourself to the possibility that some day these ways of mine might not seem so wrong, and might finally appear as right—for me. To put up with me is the first step to understanding me.

Not that you embrace my ways as right for you, but that you are no longer irritated or disappointed with me for my seeming waywardness. And one day, perhaps, in trying to understand me, you might come to prize my differences, and, far from seeking to change me, might preserve and even cherish those differences.

I may be your spouse, your parent, your offspring, your friend, your colleague. But whatever our relation, this I know: You and I are fundamentally different and both of us have to march to our own drummer.

As in the original *Please Understand Me*, the point of this updated and expanded edition is that people are different from each other, and that no amount of getting after them is going to change them. Nor is there any reason to change them, because the differences are probably good.

We differ from each other in fundamental ways. We differ in our

1

thoughts, in our feelings, in our wants and beliefs, and in what we say and do. Differences are all around us and are not difficult to see, if we look. Unfortunately, these variations in action and attitude trigger in us an all-too-human response. Seeing others as different from ourselves, we often conclude that these differences are bad in some way, and that people are acting strangely because something is the matter with them.

Thus, we instinctively account for differences in others not as an expression of natural diversity, but in terms of flaw and affliction: others are different because they're sick, or stupid, or bad, or crazy.

And our job, at least with those we care about, is to correct these flaws, much as the mythical sculptor Pygmalion labored to shape his perfect woman in stone. Like Pygmalion, we labor to remake our companions in our own image. After all, are we not ourselves, even with our flaws, the best models for how humans should think, feel, speak, and act? Remember the line in *My Fair Lady* (based on Shaw's play *Pygmalion*), when Henry Higgins wonders why Eliza Doolittle can't simply "be like me?"

But our Pygmalion Project cannot succeed. The task of sculpting others into our own likeness fails before it begins. Ask people to change their character, and you ask the impossible. Just as an acorn cannot grow into a pine tree, or a fox change into an owl, so we cannot trade our character for someone else's. Of course we can be pressured by others, but such pressure only binds and twists us. Remove a lion's fangs and behold a still fierce predator, not a docile pussycat. Insist that your child or your spouse be like you, and at best you'll see his or her struggles to comply—but beware of building resentment. Our attempts to reshape others may produce change, but the change is distortion rather than transformation.

Temperament Theory: Lost and Found

That people are highly formed at birth, with fundamentally different temperaments or predispositions to act in certain ways, is a very old idea. It was first proposed in outline by Hippocrates around 370 B.C., and the Roman physician Galen fleshed it out around 190 A.D. The idea continued in the mainstream of thought in medicine, philosophy, and literature up through the 19th century.

On the other hand, the idea that people are born without predispositions and are therefore largely malleable appears to be an early 20th century notion. Ivan Pavlov saw behavior as nothing more than mechanical responses to environmental stimulation. John Watson, the first American behaviorist, claimed he could shape a child into any form he wanted by conditioning it, provided that the child is put in his charge while yet an infant.

Many investigators around the turn of the century also believed that people are fundamentally alike in having a single basic motive. Sigmund Freud claimed we are all driven from within by instinctual lust, and that what might seem to be higher motives are merely disguised versions of that instinct. Although many of Freud's colleagues and followers took issue with him, most retained the idea of a single motivation. Alfred Adler, another Viennese physician, saw us striving for superiority. Harry Sullivan, an American physician, put forth social solidarity as the basic motive. Finally, existentialist psychologists, men such as Carl Rogers and Abraham Maslow, had us all seeking after self-actualization. In spite of their differences about what it might be, they all agreed that everyone had a single fundamental motive.

Then, in 1920, a Swiss physician named Carl Jung disagreed. In his book *Psychological Types* he wrote that people are different in essential ways. He claimed that people have a multitude of instincts, what he called "archetypes," that drive them from within, and that one instinct is no more important than another. What is important is our natural inclination to either "extraversion" or "introversion," combined with our preference for one of what he called the "four basic psychological functions"—"thinking," "feeling," "sensation," "intuition." Our preference for a given function is characteristic, he wrote, and so we can be identified or typed by this preference. Thus Jung presented what he termed the "function types" or "psychological types."

About this time, a number of other investigators revived the long practiced study of personality that philosopher John Stewart Mill had called "ethology," and what psychologist Henry Murray would much later call "personology." But their books, along with Jung's *Psychological Types*, gathered dust in college libraries, while psychology came to be dominated by Freudian psychodynamics on the one hand, and Pavlovian conditioning on the other. Behavior was explained as due to unconscious motives or to past conditioning, or to both. The idea of inborn differences in human action and attitude was all but abandoned.

Breakthroughs in the behavioral sciences often come from outside the field, and Jung's ideas were given new life almost by accident. At mid-century Isabel Myers, a layman, dusted off Jung's *Psychological Types* and with her mother, Kathryn Briggs, devised a questionnaire for identifying different kinds of personality. She called it "The Myers-Briggs Type Indicator." Largely inspired by Jung's book, the questionnaire was designed to identify sixteen patterns of action and attitude, and it caught on so well that in the 1990s over a million individuals were taking it each year. Interest in personality typology was restored in both America and Europe. (By the way, the test had been around as a research tool since the early 1950s, and the Japanese became interested in it in 1962, the year of publication of Myers's book, *The Myers-Briggs Type Indicator*.)

Let us suppose that people are not all the same, and that their patterns of attitude and action are just as inborn as their body build. Could it be that different people are intelligent or creative in different ways? That they communicate in different ways? That they have different mating, parenting, and leading styles? That they desire to learn different things at school?

That they will, if given the chance, excel at different sorts of work? Could it be that such popular sayings as "to each his own," "different strokes for different folks," and "do your own thing" express something that can be put to good use in everyday life?

There is much to be gained by appreciating differences, and much to be lost by ignoring them or condemning them. But the first step toward seeing others as distinct from yourself is to become better acquainted with your own traits of character. Of course, the best way to determine your traits of character is to watch what you actually do from time to time and place to place and in different company. There is no substitute for careful and informed observation. But self examination is quite foreign to most people, and so devices like this questionnaire can be useful in getting you started asking questions about your preferred attitudes and actions.

The Keirsey Temperament Sorter II

Decide on answer **a** or **b** and put a check mark in the proper column of the answer sheet on page 10. Scoring directions are provided. There are no right or wrong answers since about half the population agrees with whatever answer you choose.

1 When the phone rings do you

_✓_(a) hurry to get to it first   __(b) hope someone else will answer

2 Are you more

_✓_(a) observant than introspective   __(b) introspective than observant

3 Is it worse to

__(a) have your head in the clouds   _✓_(b) be in a rut

4 With people are you usually more

__(a) firm than gentle   _✓_(b) gentle than firm

5 Are you more comfortable in making

__(a) critical judgments   _✓_(b) value judgments

6 Is clutter in the workplace something you

_✓_(a) take time to straighten up   __(b) tolerate pretty well

7 Is it your way to

__(a) make up your mind quickly   _✓_(b) pick and choose at some length

8 Waiting in line, do you often

_✓_(a) chat with others   __(b) stick to business

9 Are you more

__(a) sensible than ideational   _✓_(b) ideational than sensible

10 Are you more interested in

__(a) what is actual   _✓_(b) what is possible

11 In making up your mind are you more likely to go by

__(a) data   _✓_(b) desires

12 In sizing up others do you tend to be

__(a) objective and impersonal   _✓_(b) friendly and personal

13 Do you prefer contracts to be

_✓_(a) signed, sealed, and delivered   __(b) settled on a handshake

14 Are you more satisfied having

__(a) a finished product   _✓_(b) work in progress

15 At a party, do you

_✓_(a) interact with many, even strangers   __(b) interact with a few friends

16 Do you tend to be more

__(a) factual than speculative   _✓_(b) speculative than factual

17 Do you like writers who

__(a) say what they mean   _✓_(b) use metaphors and symbolism

18 Which appeals to you more:

__(a) consistency of thought   _✓_(b) harmonious relationships

19 If you must disappoint someone are you usually

__(a) frank and straightforward   _✓_(b) warm and considerate

20 On the job do you want your activities

__(a) scheduled   _✓_(b) unscheduled

21 Do you more often prefer
__(a) final, unalterable statements ✓(b) tentative, preliminary statements

22 Does interacting with strangers
✓(a) energize you   __(b) tax your reserves

23 Facts
__(a) speak for themselves   ✓(b) illustrate principles

24 Do you find visionaries and theorists
__(a) somewhat annoying   ✓(b) rather fascinating

25 In a heated discussion, do you
__(a) stick to your guns   ✓(b) look for common ground

26 Is it better to be
__(a) just   ✓(b) merciful

27 At work, is it more natural for you to
__(a) point out mistakes   ✓(b) try to please others

28 Are you more comfortable
✓(a) after a decision   __(b) before a decision

29 Do you tend to
__(a) say right out what's on your mind   ✓(b) keep your ears open

30 Common sense is
✓(a) usually reliable   __(b) frequently questionable

31 Children often do not
__(a) make themselves useful enough   ✓(b) exercise their fantasy enough

32 When in charge of others do you tend to be
__(a) firm and unbending   ✓(b) forgiving and lenient

33 Are you more often
__(a) a cool-headed person   ✓(b) a warm-hearted person

34 Are you prone to
__(a) nailing things down　　　　　　__(b) exploring the possibilities

35 In most situations are you more
__(a) deliberate than spontaneous　　　__(b) spontaneous than deliberate

36 Do you think of yourself as
__(a) an outgoing person　　　　　　　__(b) a private person

37 Are you more frequently
__(a) a practical sort of person　　　　　__(b) a fanciful sort of person

38 Do you speak more in
__(a) particulars than generalities　　　__(b) generalities than particulars

39 Which is more of a compliment:
__(a) "There's a logical person"　　　__(b) "There's a sentimental person"

40 Which rules you more
__(a) your thoughts　　　　　　　　　__(b) your feelings

41 When finishing a job, do you like to
__(a) tie up all the loose ends　　　　　__(b) move on to something else

42 Do you prefer to work
__(a) to deadlines　　　　　　　　　　__(b) just whenever

43 Are you the kind of person who
__(a) is rather talkative　　　　　　　　__(b) doesn't miss much

44 Are you inclined to take what is said
__(a) more literally　　　　　　　　　__(b) more figuratively

45 Do you more often see
__(a) what's right in front of you　　　__(b) what can only be imagined

46 Is it worse to be
__(a) a softy　　　　　　　　　　　　__(b) hard-nosed

47 In trying circumstances are you sometimes
__(a) too unsympathetic   ✓(b) too sympathetic

48 Do you tend to choose
__(a) rather carefully   ✓(b) somewhat impulsively

49 Are you inclined to be more
✓(a) hurried than leisurely   __(b) leisurely than hurried

50 At work do you tend to
✓(a) be sociable with your colleagues   __(b) keep more to yourself

51 Are you more likely to trust
✓(a) your experiences   __(b) your conceptions

52 Are you more inclined to feel
__(a) down to earth   ✓(b) somewhat removed

53 Do you think of yourself as a
__(a) tough-minded person   ✓(b) tender-hearted person

54 Do you value in yourself more that you are
✓(a) reasonable   __(b) devoted

55 Do you usually want things
✓(a) settled and decided   __(b) just penciled in

56 Would you say you are more
__(a) serious and determined   ✓(b) easy going

57 Do you consider yourself
✓(a) a good conversationalist   __(b) a good listener

58 Do you prize in yourself
__(a) a strong hold on reality   ✓(b) a vivid imagination

59 Are you drawn more to
__(a) fundamentals   ✓(b) overtones

60 Which seems the greater fault:
__(a) to be too compassionate   ✓(b) to be too dispassionate

61 Are you swayed more by
✓(a) convincing evidence   __(b) a touching appeal

62 Do you feel better about
__(a) coming to closure   ✓(b) keeping your options open

63 Is it preferable mostly to
✓(a) make sure things are arranged   __(b) just let things happen naturally

64 Are you inclined to be
✓(a) easy to approach   __(b) somewhat reserved

65 In stories do you prefer
__(a) action and adventure   ✓(b) fantasy and heroism

66 Is it easier for you to
__(a) put others to good use   ✓(b) identify with others

67 Which do you wish more for yourself:
__(a) strength of will   ✓(b) strength of emotion

68 Do you see yourself as basically
__(a) thick-skinned   ✓(b) thin-skinned

69 Do you tend to notice
__(a) disorderliness   ✓(b) opportunities for change

70 Are you more
__(a) routinized than whimsical   ✓(b) whimsical than routinized

Answer Sheet

Enter a check for each answer in the column for **a** or **b**.

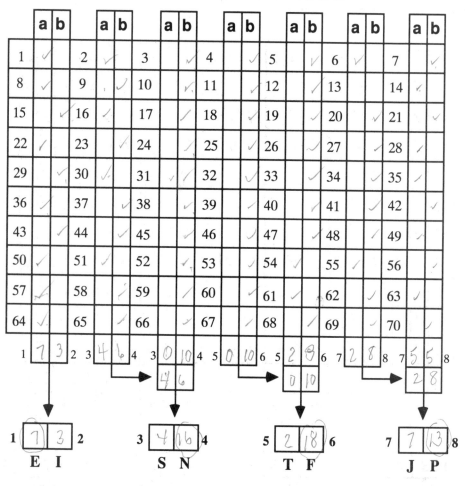

Directions for Scoring

1. Add down so that the total number of **a** answers is written in the box at the bottom of each column (see next page for illustration). Do the same for the **b** answers you have checked. Each of the 14 boxes should have a number in it.

2. Transfer the number in box No. 1 of the answer grid to box No. 1 below the answer grid. Do this for box No. 2 as well. Note, however, that you have two numbers for boxes 3 through 8. Bring down the first number for each box beneath the second, as indicated by the arrows. Now add all the pairs of numbers and enter the total in the boxes below the answer grid, so each box has only one number.

3. Now you have four pairs of numbers. Circle the letter below the larger numbers of each pair (see sample answer sheet below for an illustration). If the two numbers of any pair are equal, then circle neither, but put a large X below them and circle it.

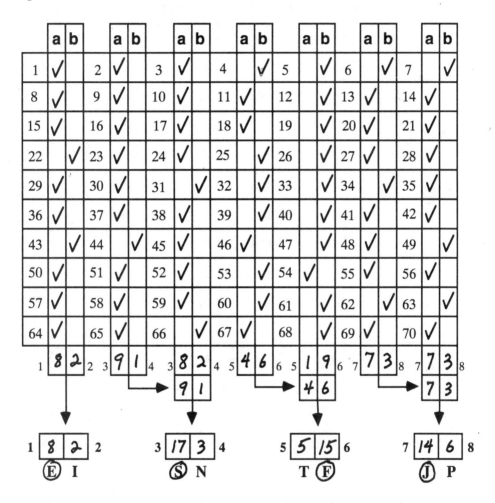

The 16 Combinations

You have now identified your type. It should be one of the following:

Four SPs [Artisans]
  ESTP [Promoter, pg. 63]
  ISTP [Crafter, pg. 66]
  ESFP [Performer, pg. 69]
  ISFP [Composer, pg. 71]

Four SJs [Guardians]:
  ESTJ [Supervisor, pg. 104]
  ISTJ [Inspector, pg. 107]
  ESFJ [Provider, pg. 110]
  ISFJ [Protector, pg. 112]

Four NFs [Idealists]:
  ENFJ [Teacher, pg. 149]
  INFJ [Counselor, pg. 152]
  ENFP [Champion, pg. 155]
  INFP [Healer, pg. 157]

Four NTs [Rationals]:
  ENTJ [Fieldmarshal, pg. 196]
  INTJ [Mastermind, pg. 199]
  ENTP [Inventor, pg. 201]
  INTP [Architect, pg. 204]

If you have an X in your type label you should read the two portraits indicated, and choose the one more like you. For example, if your type label was ESXJ, then reading both ESTJ and ESFJ portraits may help you choose one or the other as more like you. Or perhaps your type label was XNFP. Here again reading both INFP and ENFP portraits may help you decide which type seems more like you. You will find individual portraits on the page number indicated in the list above, and extra scoring forms on pages 346 and 347.

However, if an X appears in the S-N scale (or even if the two scores are nearly equal) it is advisable to disregard the Temperament Sorter and turn to the Keirsey FourTypes Sorter on page 348. By completing this questionnaire you may be able to identify your basic temperament type—NF, NT, SP, SJ—and you can then scan the four variants of whichever type is indicated. By the way, having family or friends take the FourTypes Sorter can be a fascinating and enjoyable way to promote discussion on the topic of personality differences.

What the Myers-Briggs Letters Mean

Instead of naming her sixteen types of personality with descriptive words, Myers elected to label them with a combination of letters, chosen from four pairs of alternatives, E or I, S or N, T or F, J or P, as indicated above. The letters represent the following words:

E = Extraverted	or	I	= Introverted
S = Sensory	or	N	= Intuitive
T = Thinking	or	F	= Feeling
J = Judging	or	P	= Perceiving

Myers found these words in Jung's *Psychological Types,* but in adopting them she put her own spin on them. So let us consider what Myers actually meant in using Jung's words in *The Myers-Briggs Type Indicator.*

E = Expressive	or	I	= Reserved
S = Observant	or	N	= Introspective
T = Tough-minded	or	F	= Friendly
J = Scheduling	or	P	= Probing

Thus, if we look closely at her type descriptions, we discover that by "extraverted" Myers meant having an "expressive" and outgoing social attitude; by "introverted" she meant having a "reserved" and seclusive social attitude.[1] By "sensory" Myers meant being highly "observant" of things in the immediate environment; by "intuitive" she meant being "introspective," or highly imaginative of things seen only with the mind's eye.[2] By "thinking" she meant being "tough-minded" or objective and impersonal with others; by "feeling" she meant being "friendly," or sympathetic and personal with others.[3] By "judging" she meant given to making and keeping "schedules"; while, in the case of "perceiving" Myers apparently failed to notice that her mentor Jung had said that sensation and perception are identical, so she went her own way and opposed "perceiving" to "judging."[4] However, little harm was done because when Myers said "perceiving" she actually meant looking around for alternatives, opportunities, and options, hence "probing" or exploring.

Myers regarded the eight letters and the traits they represent as the parts or elements of personality, independent of one another. In her view ESTJs, for example, are eager to express their views to others (E), are sensibly observant of their environs (S), are tough-minded (T), and are judicious in scheduling activities (J). In contrast are the INFPs, who maintain a quiet reserve (I), are introspective (N), are friendly (F), and are given to probing for options (P). Or take another pair, the ISFPs and ENTJs. Myers saw ISFPs as reluctant to exhibit themselves socially (I), as sensually observant (S), as friendly (F) and as opportunistic (P). On the other hand, the ENTJs are socially outgoing (E), are introspective (N), are tough-minded (T), and are given to making scheduling judgments (J). So here is a rather simple and literal way to spell out some easily observed differences between people. It is probably the apparent simplicity of this scheme that has caught the attention of millions of people around the world.

Myers presented all of her types as effective people. But we are effective in different ways, and are at our best when contributing what she called our special "gifts differing." For example, in some situations, such as those requiring the marshalling of forces, the ENTJ will be more effective than his or her opposite, the ISFP. But in different circumstances, such as when artistic composition is called for, the ISFP is in a much better position to succeed than the ENTJ. And this reversibility is thought to hold for all eight pairs of opposites. It is the social context that determines which kind of personality will be more effective.

The Contribution of Isabel Myers

During the last thirty years of her life, Isabel Myers handled the problem of individual differences with a freshness of vision not unlike that of the child (in the Hans Christian Anderson tale) who innocently exclaimed, "the emperor has no clothes on!" One reason Myers could do this was that she was not weighted down by the long history of bickering among anthropologists, biologists, psychologists, and sociologists on the question of human nature.

What we do, she proposed, comes from what we have in mind. And what we have in mind is a matter of character, for different characters usually have different things in mind. No need to worry, she implied, about the knotty problems of logic, of epistemology, of linguistics, or, for that matter, about the problems facing anthropologists, biologists, psychologists, and sociologists. After all, human differences confront us at every turn and are clear and present to the layman. Therefore it is the layman who must deal with those differences, here and now, and in as straightforward a manner as possible. That is just what Myers did. Her solution was to figure out what different kinds of people have in mind.

Well now, is this too simple a way to approach the very difficult problem of identifying individual differences in personality? Of course it is. But only if the purpose is to define and explain the problem of individual differences to the satisfaction of behavioral scientists. But maybe it isn't too simple if the very practical purpose is that of devising a tool for identifying different kinds of personality. Myers confined her efforts to that very practical purpose, so her definitions and explanations are very few and these few are very brief. And let it be noted that all previous attempts by behavioral scientists to devise useful tests of personality had failed. The Grey-Wheelwright Type Schedule failed, though, like The Myers-Briggs Type Indicator, it was based on Jung's *Psychological Types*. And The Allport-Vernon Study of Values, though based on Spränger's *Types of Men*, identified six types, rather than four, thereby missing Spränger's main point, and so failed to be useful. But the Myers-Briggs questionnaire did not fail, and set the stage for people around the world to get a word portrait of themselves and of their companions.

Looking Back

I must comment about the way the work of Isabel Myers struck me when I first encountered it in 1956. I remember vividly, even after forty or so years, when a visiting psychologist from Educational Testing Service handed me my psychological type portrait upon my completion of the Myers-Briggs questionnaire. The portrait said that I was an INTP who is

> primarily interested in the principles underlying things rather than the things themselves ... is inwardly absorbed in current analysis or problem ... is persevering and markedly independent of external circumstances ... wants to state the exact truth—and keeps it so exact and so complicated that few can follow ... takes in the possibilities, values facts mainly in relation to theory, is good at pure science, research, mathematics, and the more complicated problems of engineering ... with non-technical interests, makes the scholar, teacher, abstract thinker in economics, philosophy, psychology, etc. ... as a teacher cares more for the subject than for the

students ... likely to have insight, ingenuity, quickness of understanding, intellectual curiosity, fertility of ideas about problems ... more interested in reaching solutions than in putting them into practice.

Wow! Here I was, only five years out of graduate school, working as a corrective interventionist for schools and trying very hard to figure out how to apply what I had learned about people in making myself useful to school children and their parents and teachers and administrators, these people having all sorts of difficulties getting along with each other. And along comes a little old lady from Princeton New Jersey, Isabel Myers, to tell me about myself, about who I was and what I was good for. Oh, I already knew some of that stuff about myself, but I didn't know that I was a kind or type of person, and that therefore there had to be others just like me. Indeed, looking back on my graduate studies I realized that my two best friends in the psychology department were just like me, and the one professor I admired was just like me, and was my friend and mentor for my twenty years of graduate studies. Wow, again!

I also understood for the first time why I felt so different from everybody else, including my parents, brothers, and friends, and why I was so very different from my fellow fighter pilots in the Marine Corps. All those years growing up I hadn't been sure whether there was something wrong with me or with all these other people, but I was sure that I had never met anyone like me until after the war when I began studying psychology at school. It was then that I met two of them who turned out to be my friends for life. At the time I didn't realize they were like me, only that we saw eye to eye on most everything we were interested in.

The Debt to Isabel Myers

Myers must have accomplished her feat of developing Jung's distinctions into sixteen type portraits by dint of considerable observation of people in action, as well as a great deal of imaginative speculation. Salvaging the useful parts of Jung's cumbersome and self-contradictory theory of psychological types and making it available to scientist and layman alike was quite a feat. So the debt owed Isabel Myers by students of human conduct is truly enormous.

Had she not devised her personality inventory and its accompanying portraits of personality, I for one, long immersed in my studies of personology, would not have been able to connect her portraits to earlier ones. For I was later to find that the four groups of personality types described by Myers corresponded nicely with the four personality types of several predecessors, especially those of Eric Adickes, Eduard Spränger, Ernst Kretschmer, and Eric Fromm, all of which could be traced back to the ideas of Plato, Aristotle, and Galen.

How to Proceed

As I said at the beginning of this chapter, we are all different from each other, which means that our most effective route through the rest of this book is likely also to be different. Let me make some suggestions.

Chapter 2, I must say, is a bit on the abstract side, focusing on the theory and history of temperament and character studies, and many readers might want to skim it or save it for later, after they have gotten better acquainted with the actions and attitudes of the four temperaments presented in the other chapters.

In any event, after Chapter 2 readers are invited to go their separate ways, turning directly to the chapter on their specific temperament: Chapter 3 (pg. 32) for the Artisan SPs, Chapter 4 (pg. 75) for the Guardian SJs, Chapter 5 (pg. 116) for the Idealist NFs, and Chapter 6 (page 161) for the Rational NTs. At the end of each temperament chapter are the role variant portraits, and readers might at this point want to read about their fellow SPs, SJs, NFs, or NTs—this will add details and round out their own portraits. And maybe a glance at the role variants of their opposites might provide an interesting and enlightening contrast. As explained in Chapter 2, Artisans and Idealists (SPs and NFs) are opposites, as are Guardians and Rationals (SJs and NTs).

With a firm grasp of their character style, readers can move on to the last three chapters which discuss how the four temperaments play three key social roles: Mating in Chapter 7, Parenting in Chapter 8, and Leading in Chapter 9. However, each of these chapters is also divided into sections pertaining to the four temperaments, so here again readers might want to read the brief introductory material and then turn to the pages on their particular roles as mate, parent, or leader.

But remember: no matter how you proceed, whether you read in a traditional way, first page to last, or skip around at your pleasure, whether you read for comprehensive knowledge or for personal insight, your choice depends largely upon your temperament.

2

Temperament and Character

Once upon a time, in the land of Oz, four individuals set out on a strange and dangerous journey. Each of them was lacking something vital to his or her nature, and each wanted to find the great Oz and ask him for his help.

Lion was lacking courage. Although a powerful, magnificent beast, he had grown cowardly and lost his self-respect, and he wanted the Wizard to give him back his nerve. "As long as I know myself to be a coward I shall be unhappy," he said.

Dorothy was afraid she had lost her way home. "Toto," she said to her little dog, "I don't think we're in Kansas any more." Though never really lost at all, Dorothy felt stranded and alone, and she wanted Oz to return her to the security of her Aunt and Uncle's farm. "There's no place like home," she said.

Tin Woodman believed he had no heart. As tender and sensitive as he was, he felt stiffened with rust and unable to love, and he wanted Oz to help him feel a warm, loving heart beating in his chest. "No one can love who has no heart," he said.

Scarecrow thought he had no brain. Although the most ingenious of the four, he considered himself witless and worthless, and he wanted Oz to make him smart. "Brains are the only things worth having in this world," he said.

Arm-in-arm, these four very different characters set off to the Emerald City to seek the Wizard's help.

Courage, Home, Heart, Brain—Baum in his *Wizard of Oz* characters managed to catch the essence of four personalities, four distinct patterns of attitude and action that have been observed again and again in human beings for over two thousand years. These are also the four groupings that

17

Myers seems to have had in mind when she discussed similarities among certain of her sixteen types, and so let us start with her observations.

Myers's Four Groups

Crossing paths with Isabel Myers got me in the habit of typewatching way back in 1956. Myers completed her book *The Myers-Briggs Type Indicator* in 1958 and published it in 1962, though Educational Testing Service had been using her questionnaire, the MBTI, for some years doing personality research in numerous colleges and high schools around the country, and this is where I first encountered her work.

I soon found it convenient and useful to partition Myers's sixteen types into four groups, which she herself suggested in saying that all four of what she referred to as the "NFs" were alike in many ways and that all four of the "NTs" were alike in many ways—although what she called the "STs" seemed to me to have very little in common, just as the "SFs" had little in common. However, four earlier contributors, Adickes, Spränger, Kretschmer, and Fromm, each having written of four types of character, helped me to see that Myers's four "SJs" were very much alike, as were her four "SPs." Bingo! Typewatching from then on was a lot easier, the four groups—SPs, SJs, NFs, and NTs—being light years apart in their attitudes and actions. This, then, is what Myers had to say about the four groups:

The SPs

Myers had SPs probing around their immediate surroundings in order to detect and exploit any favorable options that came within reach. Having the freedom to act on the spur of the moment, whenever or wherever an opportunity arises, is very important to SPs. No chance is to be blown, no opening missed, no angle overlooked—whatever or whoever might turn out to be exciting, pleasurable, or useful is checked out for advantage. Though they may differ in their attitude toward tough-mindedness (T) and friendliness (F) in exploring for options, and though some are socially expressive (E) and some reserved (I), all of them make sure that what they do is practical and effective in getting what they want.

Consistent with this view Myers described SPs as "adaptable," "artistic," and "athletic"—as very much "aware of reality and never fighting it"—as "open-minded" and ever "on the lookout for workable compromises"—as knowing "what's going on around them" and as able "to see the needs of the moment"—as "storing up useful facts" and having "no use for theories"—as "easygoing," "tolerant," "unprejudiced," and "persuasive"—as "gifted with machines and tools"—as acting "with effortless economy"—as "sensitive to color, line, and texture"—as wanting "first-hand experiences" and in general "enjoying life." So SPs, as seen by Myers, are very much like one another and very much different from the other types, the SJs, NFs, and NTs.

The SJs

Myers had SJs, like SPs, observing their close surroundings with a keen eye, but for an entirely different reason, namely that of scheduling their own and others' activities so that needs are met and conduct is kept within bounds. Thus for SJs, everything should be in its proper place, everybody should be doing what they're supposed to, everybody should be getting their just deserts, every action should be closely supervised, all products thoroughly inspected, all legitimate needs promptly met, all approved ventures carefully insured. Though SJs might differ in being tough-minded (T) or friendly (F) in observing their schedules, and though they can be expressive (E) or reserved (I) in social attitude, all of them demand that ways and means of getting things done are proper and acceptable.

And so Myers described the SJs as "conservative" and "stable"—as "consistent" and "routinized"—as "sensible," "factual," and "unimpulsive"—as "patient," "dependable," and "hard-working"—as "detailed," "painstaking," "persevering," and "thorough." This too is a clear-cut pattern of action and attitude, highly unlike that of the SPs, NFs, and NTs.

The NFs

On the introspective side, Myers had NFs as friendly to the core in dreaming up how to give meaning and wholeness to people's lives. Conflict in those around them is painful for NFs, something they must deal with in a very personal way, and so they care deeply about keeping morale high in their membership groups, and about nurturing the positive self-image of their loved ones. Indeed, while they might differ from each other on how important judging schedules (J) or probing for options (P) is in acting on their friendly feelings, and while their social address can be expressive (E) or reserved (I), all NFs consider it vitally important to have everyone in their circle—their family, friends, and colleagues—feeling good about themselves and getting along with each other.

Thus Myers, an INFP herself, saw her fellow NFs as "humane" and "sympathetic"—as "enthusiastic" and "religious"—as "creative" and "intuitive"—and as "insightful" and "subjective." Again this is a distinct picture of attitude and action, showing NFs to be very much like each other and greatly different from SPs, SJs, and NTs.

The NTs

Also on the introspective side, Myers had NTs as tough-minded in figuring out what sort of technology might be useful to solve a given problem. To this end, NTs require themselves to be persistently and consistently rational in their actions. Though they may differ in their preference for judging schedules (J) or probing for options (P) as they tackle problems, and though they can seem expressive (E) or reserved (I) around others, all NTs insist that they have a rationale for everything they do, that whatever they do and say makes sense.

So Myers described the NTs as "analytical" and "systematic"—as "abstract," "theoretical," and "intellectual"—as "complex," "competent" and "inventive"—as "efficient," "exacting" and "independent"—as "logical" and "technical"—and as "curious," "scientific," and "research-oriented." Here again is a unique and easily recognizable configuration of character traits, the NTs a breed apart, starkly different from SPs, SJs, and NFs.

Temperament, Character, Personality

Before I trace the history of these four underlying forms of personality, and set the Myersian groups into this larger and more ancient context, let me try to clarify the nature of temperament and character. What, we might ask, is this thing called "temperament," and what relation does it have to character and personality? There are two sides to personality, one of which is temperament and the other character. Temperament is a configuration of inclinations, while character is a configuration of habits. Character is disposition, temperament pre-disposition. Thus, for example, foxes are predisposed—born—to raid hen houses, beavers to dam up streams, dolphins to affiliate in close-knit schools, and owls to hunt alone in the dark. Each type of creature, unless arrested in its maturation by an unfavorable environment, develops the habit appropriate to its temperament: stealing chickens, building dams, nurturing companions, or hunting at night.

Put another way, our brain is a sort of computer which has temperament for its hardware and character for its software. The hardware is the physical base from which character emerges, placing an identifiable fingerprint on each individual's attitudes and actions. This underlying consistency can be observed from a very early age—some features earlier than others—long before individual experience or social context (one's particular software) has had time or occasion to imprint the person. Thus temperament is the inborn form of human nature; character, the emergent form, which develops through the interaction of temperament and environment.

I want to emphasize that temperament, character, and personality are configured, which means that, not only are we predisposed to develop certain attitudes and not others, certain actions and not others, but that these actions and attitudes are unified—they hang together. Thus, the SPs base their self-image on artistic action, audacity, and adaptability to circumstance, these three traits evolving together of necessity. Furthermore, these three traits, developing together as if out of a single seed, preclude the emergence of a self-image based on, say, empathy, benevolence, and authenticity, which are characteristics of the NFs. In the same way, the SJs base their self-image on reliability, service, and respectability, these three traits emerging together as a unified structure of personality. And again, the unfolding of these three traits together weighs against developing a self-image based on ingenuity, autonomy, and willpower, which is characteristic of the NTs.

This notion of four distinct temperaments, inborn and unified, calls into question two major points of view in 20th century behavioral science. The first can be called the theory of hierarchical motivation. Abraham Maslow, a leading proponent of this theory, held that we are all motivated by a number of needs which displace each other as we satisfy them. We ascend, he said, from physical needs (food, clothing, shelter) to safety needs (security, protection, assurance), then on to social needs (love, friendship, belonging), and next to the need for self-esteem (valuing self, self-worth, pride). And a few of us—not really very many, he suggested—are able to arrive finally at what he called the "self-actualizing" stage of development, no longer motivated by the primary physical needs, nor by needs for safety, belonging, and self-esteem. Maslow seemed to believe that the fully-realized, enlightened, self-actualized personality is everyone's highest goal in life, and implied that those people who don't make it nevertheless have a latent need for self-actualization, which will break forth as a full-blown motive once they satisfy their more primary needs.

It certainly makes sense to say that in normal development many of us arrange our lives so that we satisfy our need for sustenance, for safety, for social ties, and that we then turn our interest to achieving self-esteem.

But beyond this point temperament theory counsels us to part company with Maslow and other hierarchists. For if people are fundamentally different, born with different needs and inclinations, then they might not all share the desire to take Maslow's last step into self-actualization. Perhaps not even most of them. Of course all must have self-esteem. Maslow was right in this. But as it turns out, most people base their self-esteem on something else entirely. Only those of one particular temperament, Myers's NFs, are concerned with becoming self-actualized—finding their true selves—and value themselves more in the degree they achieve this aim.

Thus it is not that self-actualization is a step beyond self-esteem; rather, it is but one path to self-esteem. There are other paths. Freud, for instance, was right when he said that physical pleasure is the way. But not for everybody, as he supposed, and not as an end in itself, but as a means to self-esteem. Those of the SP temperament prize themselves more when they live sensually and hedonically. Harry Sullivan was also right. The security of social status is important—for some at least, and in the service of self-esteem. Those of the SJ temperament hold themselves in higher regard when they attain a reputation as pillars of society. Likewise, Alfred Adler was right in that the quest for powers motivates us—some of us—and those of the NT temperament look upon themselves with pride as their technological powers increase. It is unfortunate that Maslow, himself an NF, saw the aims of the other three character types as merely arrested attempts at the NF goal of self-actualization.

The other point of view challenged by the four types theory says that not only do all of us have the same goals, but we also go through the same stages of growth and development. Reading the leading writers on maturation, we are counseled that all mature persons have certain attitudes and certain habits, and that all must take the same developmental steps to get there. Such a position was taken, sometimes explicitly and always implicitly, by investigators such as Gesell, Ilg, Ames, Erikson, Piaget, Sheehy, and Levinson, to name some of the more prominent contributors.

But this way of defining maturity will not do. A mature NF is strikingly different from a mature SP. Likewise, a mature NT is astonishingly different from a mature SJ. Just as the fox matures differently from the beaver, so does the dolphin mature differently from the owl. Just as the Lion wanted Courage to get on with life, so Dorothy wanted Security, the Tin Woodman wanted a Heart, and the Scarecrow wanted Brains. To use the same criteria of maturity for all kinds of creatures is to miss the entire point of this essay. Imagine a mother fox schooling a young beaver in the art of sneaking into a chicken yard and making off with a fat hen, and picture also the little beaver's astonished paralysis upon receiving such guidance. This, of course, is unimaginable, but as parents many of us encourage our offspring to emulate us, to be chips off the old block, to follow in our footsteps. The Pygmalion Project ascends to its greatest heights and generates its greatest intensity in pointing the young toward our own conception of maturity. None of the temperaments are above wanting to validate their own style, and so set about, unconsciously and involuntarily to be sure, to sculpt their young into the image of themselves.

Temperament will out in maturation as in all other domains of life, and so, again, we are asked to think of temperament as inborn, innate, inherent, and of character as exactly configured, as precisely patterned, as definitively systemic. SP or SJ, NF or NT, our traits of character entail each other and are bound together by a common origin and a common destiny. And it is not until these traits have developed that we can be said to have acquired our mature character, to have become a full-blown specimen of what we were meant to be, just as the tiny acorn becomes the mighty oak tree.

Let us now turn to a brief look at the history of those rather neglected studies of ethology, characterology, and personology.

Historical Overview

In the first part of the 20th century a good many writers essayed their views on temperament and character. Four of these, Adickes, Kretschmer, Spränger, and Fromm, agreed with each other, implicitly at least, in how they defined temperament and character types, and differed from men such as Apfelbach, Bulliot, James, MacDougal, Roback, and Sternberg, who elected their own categories.

Adickes, Kretschmer, Spränger, and Fromm saw the usefulness of an ancient belief that came primarily from the early Greeks and Romans. It was the Roman physician Galen[1] who, developing the ideas of Hippocrates, proposed (around 190 A.D.) that it is neither the stars nor the gods that determine what we want and what we do; rather, it is the balance of our bodily fluids, the four "humors," as they were called. If our blood predominates Galen called us "Sanguine" or eagerly optimistic in temperament; if our black bile or gall predominates, then we are "Melancholic" or doleful in temperament; if our yellow bile predominates, then we are "Choleric" or passionate in temperament; and if our phlegm predominates, then we are "Phlegmatic" or calm in temperament. Thus, for the first time, in the West at any rate, our physiology was said to determine our attitudes and actions, and not the deities or the heavenly bodies. As Shakespeare would put it, writing many centuries later, "The fault, dear Brutus, is not in the stars but in ourselves." We might smile at this early view of human physiology, but at the same time we must acknowledge it to be a major departure from what had gone before. Our predispositions, said Galen, come in four styles, and from within and not from without.

Nearly six hundred years before Galen, Plato[2] had written in *The Republic* of four kinds of character which clearly corresponded with the four temperaments attributed to Hippocrates. Plato was more interested in the individual's contribution to the social order than in underlying temperament, and so he named the Sanguine temperament the *"iconic"* (artisan) character, endowed with artistic sense, and playing an art-making role in society. He named the Melancholic temperament the *"pistic"* (guardian) character, endowed with common sense, and playing a caretaking role in society. He named the Choleric temperament the *"noetic"* (idealist) character, endowed with intuitive sensibility, and playing a moral role in society. And he named the Phlegmatic temperament the *"dianoetic"* (rational) character, endowed with reasoning sensibility, and playing the role of logical investigator in society.

A generation later, Aristotle[3] defined character in terms of happiness, and not, as his mentor Plato had done, in terms of virtue. Aristotle argued that there are four sources of happiness: "The mass of men," he said, find happiness either in "sensual pleasure" (*"hedone"*) or in "acquiring assets" (*"propraietari"*), while some few find happiness either in exercising their "moral virtue" (*"ethikos"*) or in a life of "logical investigation" (*"dialogike"*). Not surprisingly, Aristotle (a Rational himself) regarded logical investigation as bringing the truest happiness because it is the most self-sufficient, and the least dependent on external conditions.

In the Middle Ages the four temperaments theory appears to have been largely forgotten, if not disregarded,[4] only to be rediscovered, like so many Classical ideas, in the European Renaissance, when interest in science and the physical nature of mankind revived. Thus, we see Geoffrey Chaucer (in 1380) describing a Doctor of Physic as knowing "the cause of every malady, And where they were from, and of what humour."

Also Paracelsus,[5] a mid-sixteenth century Viennese physician, proposed four totem spirits which symbolized four personality styles, and which ran parallel to the temperament types of Galen and the character types of Plato. Paracelsus characterized human beings as "Salamanders," impulsive and changeable; as "Gnomes," industrious and guarded; as "Nymphs," inspired and passionate; and as "Sylphs," curious and calm.

Although the ever-skeptical French essayist Montaigne cautioned his readers (in 1580) that "a man should not rivet himself too fast to his own humors and temperament," the playwrights of the period certainly made use of the ancient theory. Shakespeare points out dozens of times what he called the "spirit of humours" in his enormous gallery of characters: a soldier's sanguine appetite or a Countess's sorrowful melancholy, a lover's impassioned choler or a physician's phlegmatic detachment. Moreover, Shakespeare's contemporary Ben Jonson developed a whole style of play he called the "Comedy of Humours," creating his characters according to a formula he articulated in 1599: "Some one peculiar quality Doth so possess a man, that it doth draw All his affects, his spirits, and his powers In their confluctions, all to run one way."

The same in other fields. When William Harvey discovered the circulation of blood in 1628, he argued that blood was simply the most sovereign of the four humors, and he came to look on the Sanguine temperament with special favor. And philosophers of the 16th, 17th, and 18th centuries, Bruno in Italy, Hume in Scotland, Voltaire and Rousseau in France, Kant in Germany, took the idea of four humors as a matter of course, as part of the air they breathed. For instance, in his *Dialogues Concerning Natural Religion* (1755), Hume spoke of the "usual phlegm" of a character having an "accurate philosophical turn" of mind. Moreover, when Hume described (in *An Inquiry Concerning Human Understanding*, 1748) how one comes to see a "degree of uniformity and regularity" in mankind's "temper and actions," he made a remarkably accurate statement of the characterologist's method. Hume credited Aristotle and Hippocrates with teaching him to base his observations of humanity on "experience acquired by long life and a variety of business and company," and concluded:

> By means of this guide we mount up to the knowledge of men's inclinations and motives from their actions, expressions, and even gestures, and again descend to the interpretation of their actions from our knowledge of their motives and inclinations. The general observations, treasured up by a course of experience, give us the clue of human nature and teach us to unravel all its intricacies.

19th century novelists, from Jane Austen and the Brontës to George Eliot and Tolstoy, had these four patterns of human attitude and action clearly in mind when they framed their characters. In *War and Peace*, for example, Tolstoy divides the members of a lodge of Freemasons into what he described as "four classes" of character: some looking for social "connections" and opportunities, some interested in the lodge's "external form and ceremony," some seeking a "fully understood path for themselves," and some occupied exclusively with "the scientific secrets of the order."

Even some early 20th century writers demonstrated detailed knowledge of the roots of temperament and character theory. D.H. Lawrence not only saw human nature as organized around "four poles of dynamic consciousness," but he actually described a ruddy, sanguine character in his novel *Sons and Lovers* (1913) as Paracelsus' Salamander.

But in the behavioral sciences what had been the prevailing current of thought for centuries—that temperament determines character—gradually decreased to a tiny trickle in the latter part of the 19th century, owing mainly to the ideas of two men, Sigmund Freud and Ivan Pavlov. Freud reduced mankind to mere animal, nothing more than a creature of blind instinct. Similarly, Pavlov reduced mankind, not to animal, but to machine, its actions nothing more than mechanical response to environmental stimulation. And the 20th century was nearly swept away by these two new theories, both of which suggested that all humans are fundamentally alike and only superficially different. The ancient idea of the human as a vital organism animated by four different spirits was all but forgotten.

Even so, the four-temperaments theory found a few champions in Europe and America in the first half of the 20th century. With social field theory invading the behavioral sciences, Adickes, Kretschmer, and Spränger revived the idea that mankind is designed on four distinctive configurations. In 1905 Adickes[6] said that mankind could be divided into four "world views"—Innovative, Traditional, Doctrinaire, and Skeptical. In 1914 Spränger[7] wrote of four "value attitudes" which distinguish one personality from another—Artistic, Economic, Religious, and Theoretic. And in 1920 Kretschmer[8] proposed that both normal and abnormal behavior can be understood in terms of four "character styles" similar to those of Adickes and Spränger—Hypomanic, Depressive, Hyperesthetic, and Anesthetic.

Other, more familiar voices were advancing similar ideas at this time. Rudolph Dreikurs, a disciple of Alfred Adler, pointed out in 1947 what he called four "mistaken goals" which different kinds of people pursue when their self-esteem declines too far for safety—Retaliation, Service, Recognition, and Power. Also in 1947 Eric Fromm,[9] looking at both negative and positive sides of personality, as did Kretschmer, attributed four different "orientations" to the four styles—Exploitative, Hoarding, Receptive, and Marketing.

In summary, it must be said that the above is only the barest outline of the history of temperament and character theory. By the early part of the 20th century close to five thousand reports on temperament and character had been identified (See especially Roback's *A Bibliography of Character and Personality,* published in 1927.) The table below lists a small portion of this long history. If we scan the variety of contributors and the many characteristics they have attributed to the four temperaments, we are able to see how true-to-type the four classifications have remained over the centuries.

Plato c340 B.C.	Artisan	Guardian	Idealist	Rational
Aristotle c325	Hedonic	Proprietary	Ethical	Dialectical
Galen c190 A.D.	Sanguine	Melancholic	Choleric	Phlegmatic
Paracelsus 1550	Changeable	Industrious	Inspired	Curious
Adickes 1905	Innovative	Traditional	Doctrinaire	Skeptical
Spränger 1914	Aesthetic	Economic	Religious	Theoretic
Kretschmer 1920	Hypomanic	Depressive	Hyperesthetic	Anesthetic
Fromm 1947	Exploitative	Hoarding	Receptive	Marketing
Myers 1958	Probing	Scheduling	Friendly	Tough-minded

Each successive contributor looked at the four types from slightly different but related angles, such that it is not at all difficult to see how an Artisan (SP) is likely also to be hedonic, sanguine, innovative, aesthetic, and probing, or how a Guardian (SJ) is also likely to be proprietary, melancholic, industrious, traditional, and scheduling. Nor is it difficult to see how an Idealist (NF) is also likely to be ethical, inspired, doctrinaire, hyperesthetic, and friendly, or how a Rational (NT) is also likely to be dialectical, curious, skeptical, theoretical, and tough-minded.

And so the idea that individuals are predisposed to develop into one of four different configurations of attitude and action has survived for well over two thousand years. Surely this idea would not have been employed for so long, by so many people, in so many countries, had there not been some sort of widely shared recognition of its usefulness. As a personologist I must say that I have long found this history to be quite compelling.

The Basic Dimensions of Personality

That the characteristics of the four temperaments are this consistent over time is no accident, but seems to reflect a fundamental pattern in the warp and woof of the fabric of human nature. Indeed, I would argue that the four types are most likely derived from the interweaving of the two most basic human actions, how we communicate with each other, and how we use tools to accomplish our goals. Clearly, what sets human beings apart from the other animals are two advantages we have over them—words and tools. And what sets us apart from each other is the way we use words and tools. The great majority of us are predominantly concrete in our word usage, the rest predominantly abstract. And about half of us are utilitarian in our choice and use of tools, the other half cooperative.

Abstract versus Concrete Word Usage

In considering human differences some investigators have focused on differences in linguistic orientation, others on differences in cognitive orientation; both, however, are concerned with the human imperative that bids us locate ourselves in our social context as we take action. On the linguistic side Kurt Goldstein and Ernst Cassirer thought of humans as talking animals. In his *Abstract and Concrete Behavior*, Goldstein had some people talking more abstractly than concretely and others talking more concretely than abstractly. Similarly, in his *Essay on Man* Cassirer had some talking more analogically than indicatively, others talking more indicatively than analogically. In other words, some people are prone to send symbol messages, others to send signal messages—signals pointing to something present to the eye, symbols bringing to mind something absent from view.

As for cognition, Myers in *The Myers-Briggs Type Indicator* had some of us oriented by intuition or introspection, the rest by sensory perception or observation. Similarly David Riesman, in *Individualism Reconsidered*, spoke of "inner-directed" and "outer-directed" orientations. And Eric Adickes, in his *Character and Worldview*, saw some as "heteronomous" or other-directed in orientation, and others as "autonomous" or self-directed in orientation.

Thus our thoughts and the words that reflect them keep us oriented to reality by telling us who we and our companions are, and what we and they are to do. Thoughts of course are not observable, but words are, so some inspection of the kinds of words we choose may be useful.

Abstract words can be used in slightly different but related ways—analogical, categorical, fictional, figurative, general, schematic, symbolic, and theoretical. Likewise, concrete words can be used in slightly different but related ways—detailed, factual, elemental, empirical, indicative, literal, signal, and specific. To illustrate the relationships between these terms I have linked them together with overlapping Venn diagrams, as follows:

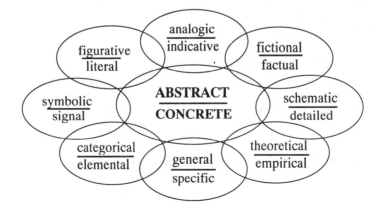

The diagram suggests that an analogy, for example, is both fictional and figurative, a figure of speech both symbolic and analogic, a symbol both figurative and categorical, and so on, all different forms of abstract speech. Likewise, an indicative expression is both factual and literal, a factual expression both indicative and detailed, a detail both factual and empirical, and so on, all concrete in some manner. Thus both words, 'abstract' and 'concrete,' have many, but related, uses, and we are wise to keep this in mind as we compare and contrast those who are more prone to abstract speech with those more prone to concrete speech.

Cooperative versus Utilitarian Tool Usage

Human beings are far more than word-using animals. Indeed the prolif-eration of our words came only when there was a proliferation of our tools. As tools differentiated there was a reciprocal differentiation of words, neither getting ahead or falling behind the other.

Nearly everything we do to implement our goals requires several kinds of tools used both simultaneously and successively. No matter where we look we see tools in every direction, inside or outside our homes and throughout our communities. The house itself is an enormously complex tool. Everything in it is a tool—chairs, tables, books, computer, television, phone, radio, pictures, lamps, rugs, boxes, on and on and on. Our vehicles are tools as are our roads and bridges and walkways and even our clothes. Civilization itself is created and maintained by tools. We distanced ourselves from the other animals and made ourselves supreme among them by fash-ioning a fantastic array of tools. Indeed, it is this array of tools that enables us to pursue goals not dreamed of in centuries past.

No matter what our goals, however, we do not necessarily choose the same tools to reach them. And this is where our character takes a hand. Some of us prefer to use tools that have been approved by our membership groups. Others will use the best tools for the job whether or not they have been approved. Let us think of the former as cooperative in going after what they want, and the latter as utilitarian in their pursuit of goals.

To put it simply, the Cooperators try to get where they want to go by getting along with others, that is, by being law-abiding and accommodating with those around them, so that they are in full accord with the agreed-upon rules and mores of the social groups they belong to. In contrast, the Util-itarians tend to go after what they want in the most effective ways possible, and they choose tools that promise success with minimum cost and ef-fort—whether or not they observe the social rules.

Not, mind you, that the habitually cooperative persons don't care about useful and effective tools. Certainly they do, but they consider the ef-fectiveness of tools as secondary to whether they should be used, or how they will be regarded by others—in other words, whether they are socially acceptable, or morally correct. In the same way, it is not that the habitually utilitarian persons refuse to cooperate with their social groups, but they see pleasing others and observing rules as secondary considerations, coming only after they have determined how well their chosen tools will work in accomplishing their ends. It's a matter of priorities. Most of us learn to get along with others most of the time, and most of us opt for effective action, but our first instinct is to pursue our goals according to our habit of cooperating or utilizing.

By intersecting the rows and columns in a four-cell matrix (see below), the four types of character can be clearly seen in relation to each other:

Words
Abstract   Concrete

	Abstract	Concrete
Cooperative	**NF** Cooperator	**SJ** Cooperator
Utilitarian	**NT** Utilitarian	**SP** Utilitarian

Tools

Note that SPs are utilitarian like NTs and concrete like SJs, and are not like NFs in either way. NFs, on the other hand, are cooperative like SJs and abstract like NTs, and again, unlike SPs in either way. So each temperament has two complementary types and one opposite, when it comes to the way they communicate their messages and the way they implement their goals.

Observing people's uses of words and tools gives us a convenient and remarkably accurate way of determining their temperament. Thus, having first noticed that a person is, say, habitually concrete in speech, and then noting that he or she is habitually cooperative in getting things done, we have determined the person we watch to be Plato's Guardian, Aristotle's Proprietary, and Myers's SJ. And so it goes with typewatching, our observations of concrete or abstract word usage and cooperative or utilitarian tool usage enabling us to determine whether we are watching or interacting with an SP Artisan, an SJ Guardian, an NF Idealist, or an NT Rational.

These two dimensions of personality are the very foundation of my type definitions, and will be referred to throughout this book.

Psychological Functions vs Intelligent Roles

This idea of defining personality differences by sticking to what can be observed—words and tools—sets Myers's and my view of personality rather far apart. Remember that Myers's concept of types was heavily influenced by Jung's *Psychological Types*, a book in which he presented the purely hypothetical notion that there are four "psychological functions": "sensation," "intuition," "feeling," and "thinking." Positing introversion and extraversion as the fundamental attitudes that separate personalities, Jung (with Myers following suit) defined eight types by combining extraversion and introversion with the four psychological functions, thus creating four function types—Thinking Types, Feeling Types, Intuiting Types, and Sensing Types, each with two variants.

I must say I have never found a use for this scheme of psychological functions, and this is because function typology sets out to define different people's mental make-up—what's in their heads—something which is not observable, and which is thus unavoidably subjective, a matter of speculation, and occasionally of projection. A good example of the difficulties such guesswork can introduce is the way in which Jung and Myers confound introversion with intuition, saying that the introverted types are the ones "interested in ideas and concepts," while the extraverted types are "interested in people and things." In my view, which is based on close observation of people's use of words, the intuitives are the ones primarily interested in ideas and concepts, while the sensing types are those primarily concerned with concrete things. Indeed, after forty years or so of typewatching, I have not found any SPs or SJs who were more inclined to discuss conceptual matters (abstractions) than to discuss factual matters (concretions). The sensing types are more perceptual than conceptual, while the intuitive types, NFs and NTs, are more conceptual than perceptual.

To take some of the guesswork out of temperament theory, I base my type definitions on what people do well, their skilled actions—what I call their "intelligent roles"—which are observable, and which thus can be defined more objectively. (For those interested in the specific differences between Jung's and Myers's function types and my intelligence types, see note 10 in the Chapter 2 Notes at the end of the book.) Let me point out that during most of the 20th century intelligence was also thought to be in the head, defined as "the ability to think abstractly," and of late, as "cognitive ability." But this has never been a very useful way of defining intelligence. Common sense tells us that intelligence is being smart in what we do. In other words it is not how well we think, but how well we act in a given role. If our behavior is adaptive to circumstances, so that we act effectively in such circumstances, then we can be said to be intelligent in those circumstances. Other circumstances are likely to call for different kinds of action, and hence different intelligent roles.

The reason for Myers's and my differences is that we start from widely different premises. Myers unwittingly adopted Jung's 19th century elementalism, which assumed that personality could be pieced together from independent elements. On the other hand I was imbued with the 20th century organismic wholism of men such as Karl Bühler, Kurt Goldstein,

George Hartmann, David Katz, Wolfgang Köhler, Kurt Koffka, Kurt Lewin, Max Wertheimer, and Raymond Wheeler, to name the more prominent organismic psychologists. So I have long believed that personality, like anatomy, comes about not by an integration of elements, but by differentiation within an already integrated whole, emerging gradually as an individuated configuration. I claim an organism never becomes integrated because it is always integrated. It differentiates by a process of evolution into the mature form it is meant to become. Thus, in the view of organismic wholism, traits of character emerge just as cells do, by a process of differentiation, with the traits clinging together, cohering—not by association, but by a common origin and a common destiny. The tiny acorn, a fully integrated organism from the start, looks forward to the stately oak tree it is destined to become.

The next four chapters will examine the four integrated configurations of personality separately and in some detail—first the SP Artisans, then the SJ Guardians, next the NF Idealists, and last the NT Rationals—defining their many traits of temperament and character, including their intelligent roles and their role variants.

3

Artisans

Don't be afraid....Taste everything....Sometimes I think we only half live over here. The Italians live all the way.

This was the creed of the young Ernest Hemingway, after returning home from his tour in Italy as a volunteer ambulance driver for the Red Cross in World War I. Hemingway was still on crutches, convalescing from a shrapnel wound, but the experience of the war had whetted his appetite for excitement, and shown him how thrilling and necessary it was for him to "taste everything" and to "live all the way." And so, for forty more adventurous, creative years, Hemingway boxed, he ran with the bulls in Pamplona, he hunted lion and buffalo on the Serengeti Plain, he fished for trout in Idaho and marlin off Cuba, he skied, he boated, he survived a car wreck in London, a hurricane at Key West, two plane crashes in Africa. And of course he wrote, not only some of the century's most gripping novels and short stories, but he also dashed off hundreds of articles and dispatches from every war he could get himself assigned to, making him the most famous and daring war correspondent of his time.

In the mid 1970s I wrote of Myers's SPs as "Dionysians," after the Greek fertility god Dionysus. Reborn in the spring of every year, Dionysus would return from the underworld to release the land from the death-grip of winter, exciting his followers to shake themselves free of the cold, to feel the blood coursing in their veins, and to make the land fruitful in flora and fauna. For the "Artisans" (as I now call them), life's cup is to run over, people are to be enjoyed, games are to be played, resources are to be expended. To be human is to be generous, to spend and sow freely, impetuously, spreading bounty like scattering seed.

In recent years I have come to think of the Dionysians as fox-like. There have been many such characters in history—the Desert Fox (General Erwin Rommel), the Red Fox of Kinderhook (President Martin Van Buren), the Gray Fox of Hyde Park (President Franklin Roosevelt), the Gray Fox of Arlington (General Robert E. Lee), the Swamp Fox (General Francis Marion)—and the wily President Lyndon Johnson, who once quipped "I'm just like a fox." Foxes have got to be the craftiest of the mammalian predators, and human foxes, such as those mentioned, have got to be the most practical of the human predators, every one of them smart like a fox. Foxes thrive around the world on the edges of civilization while most other predators gradually become extinct. Foxes thrive because they are so effective at hunting (and even at scavenging), rarely wasting their time on prey that cannot be easily caught—Aesop's Reynard Fox, remember, turned up his nose at those "sour grapes" on the trellis just beyond his reach. At the same time, foxes are known for their skill in avoiding capture, and just as foxes are one of the cleverest and nimblest of the canines, so the Artisans are the cleverest of the humans—clever tactically, that is, clever at getting what they want and remaining one step ahead of those who would restrain them. Tennessee Williams wrote that "We of the artistic world are...the little gray foxes and all the rest are the hounds."

Thinking back, I have to say that I've been asked over and over again for years why I have championed the Artisans more than I have the other types. Well, both of my parents were Artisans, as were my brothers and many of my friends and fellow fighter pilots in the Marine Corps. I still have some very good friends among the Artisans, and I continue to admire their artistic capabilities. In addition, much of my work for thirty or so years as a family therapist was focused on those Artisan children who gave their parents and teachers a hard time by not doing their assignments and being noisy and restless at school. So my long association with and understanding of Artisans of all ages has enabled me to be more useful to them than to others of different temperament. I think Artisans ought to be enjoyed for what they are instead of condemned for what they are not, something that can also be said of the other three temperaments.

Plato's Artisans

The term 'Artisan' is the English equivalent of Plato's Greek word '*eikoniké*' otherwise 'icon-maker,' 'image-maker,' or 'arti-factor.' Artisans, as suggested by the word 'artifact,' tend to become masters in the making of solid, practical things, and thus in Plato's *Republic* the Artisans' social function is to fashion those sensory images, ornaments, and objects that are useful in daily living. Art is much more, however, than the so-called "fine arts"—music, literature, dance, sculpture, drawing, painting—and must include theatrical arts, martial arts, industrial arts, athletic arts, medical arts, indeed any activity in which successive actions are free variables rather than fixed constants. Words such as 'artist,' 'artisan,' and 'artifactor,' have the same root as words such as 'rational,' 'rationale,' and 'reason,' the IndoEuropean root 'ar' and its reversed form 'ra' both having to do with fitting things together. Thus Artisans and Rationals have something very important in common: they are both fitters, the Artisans having a practical and technique-oriented way of fitting things together, the Rationals a pragmatic and technology-oriented way of fitting things together.

Plato's pupil, Aristotle, said that happiness is "the highest realizable good" and that some men find happiness more in "sensuous living" (*hêdonê*) than in "proprietary acquisition" (*propráietari*), in "ethical musing" (*ethikê*), or in "theoretical dialogue" (*dialogikê*). The "Hedonics," as Aristotle called them, pursue the pleasures of the senses. Hedonism is the doctrine holding that only what is pleasant or has pleasurable consequences is intrinsically good, and that behavior is motivated by the desire for pleasure and the avoidance of pain. In Aristotle's view, then, Plato's Artisans pursue the arts more for the sensual pleasure involved than from any strong desire to make money, to make an ethical statement, or to expound a theory.

The Roman physician Galen considered these Artisans to be exceedingly optimistic, so he called them the "Sanguines." In choosing the word 'sanguine' Galen was referring to a certain "humor" or fluid—in this case blood—that at the time was thought to dominate Artisan behavior, making them excitable and intemperate, as in the modern phrases "getting your blood up," or "hot-blooded." But Galen's interests lay primarily on the negative side of temperament, on the problems associated with one's balance of humors, and so he saw the over-optimistic Sanguines as different from, but temperamentally no worse than, the somber Melancholics, the irascible Cholerics, or the taciturn Phlegmatics.

The Renaissance physician Paracelsus likened the Artisan type to the Salamander. Paracelsus' Salamander is a mythical, lizard-like creature, believed capable of changing color to blend in with its surroundings. Thus Paracelsus regarded the Artisan as a changeable or inconstant person, and indeed they are capable of mimicking anyone they approach, often convincing others that they are just like them. Perhaps it is this capacity to change themselves to resemble the other that makes Artisans such good actors. Also it may be that this changeability explains their disinterest in their own identity, something their opposite, the Idealist, cannot comfortably exist without. For Artisans, "all the world's a stage" and they the players, taking on part after part, now hero, now villain, with equal facility and equal delight. So the guiding spirit of the Artisan is the mythical Salamander, whispering in the Artisan's ear what part is best played at any given moment in any given context.

The name Adickes gave to the Artisan type was the "Innovator," hence one given to changing things and on the lookout for something new and different. So the changeling of Paracelsus was for Adickes an agent of change in a constant search for novelty, so different from the Guardian who seeks to avoid change and to urge observance of tradition and custom.

Spränger referred to this character as the "Aesthetic" type, which, though similar to Plato's Artisan, focused on the perception of beauty rather than the construction of the beautiful. The Artisan makes works of art, while the Aesthetic experiences artistic works sensuously. In a way Spränger is echoing Aristotle's concept of the Hedonic type who focuses on pleasure. Indeed, what we have here is a sort of artistic trinity—Plato's type the producer of art, Aristotle's type taking pleasure in art, and Adickes's type sensitive to art, these three ideas looking forward to what psychologist Marvin Zuckerman called the "Sensation Seeking Personality."

Kretschmer was first to take a careful look at the dark side of character. So he named the Artisans "Hypomanics," thinking of them as recklessly impulsive. Certainly Kretschmer was echoing Galen in seeing Artisans as exuberant and over-optimistic, but he was saying much more, namely that the kind of irrational behavior that some Artisans engage in is more a matter of temperament than something over which they have control. If Artisans are forced by untoward circumstances to become recklessly impetuous they tend to do so as if compelled by irresistible urges which overcome their will. So in Kretschmer's view what some call madness is determined in large part by temperament and not by illness.

Fromm had many names for the Artisans, but he emphasized one of the negative traits that he attributed to them—exploitiveness. Fromm's term 'Exploiters' looks forward to Myers's notion that Artisans are opportunists, ever on the lookout for advantages or payoffs. On the positive side of temperament Fromm saw Plato's Artisans as "active," "initiators," "claiming," "proud," "impulsive," "self-confident," and "captivating."

Myers named Plato's Artisans the "Sensory Perceptive" types or "SPs" and said of them that they are "adaptable," "artistic," "athletic"; are very much "aware of reality and never fight it"; are "open-minded," "know what's going on," are ever "on the lookout for workable compromises," are "able to see the needs of the moment," "store up useful facts"; are "easy going," "tolerant," "unprejudiced," and "persuasive"; "act with effortless economy," "don't get wrought up," are "gifted with machines and tools"; are "sensitive to color, line, and texture," "want first-hand experiences," and in general "enjoy life." Now this is a very clear-cut pattern of action and attitude, quite different from the SJs, and, as will be shown, starkly different from NFs and NTs. Though apparently unaware of the contributions of her predecessors, Myers was clearly able to identify the more salient traits that characterize Plato's Artisans.

The Concrete Utilitarians

These different views of Plato's Artisans, whatever they are called, all have something in common: they all characterize this type as concrete in communicating messages and utilitarian in implementing goals. So in beginning our consideration of the habits of action and attitude of the SPs, let's look at their quadrant in the matrix of character at the right.

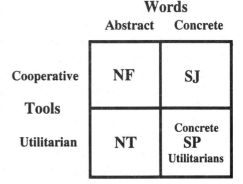

| | Words | |
	Abstract	Concrete
Cooperative **Tools** **Utilitarian**	NF	SJ
	NT	**Concrete** **SP** **Utilitarians**

As indicated, the foundation of the SP character, setting them apart unmistakably from the other three personalities, is their unique combination of concrete word usage with utilitarian tool usage, and thus I want to add another name to the list and call them the "Concrete Utilitarians." Although they share concrete word usage with the SJs and utilitarian tool usage with the NTs, their words are noticeably different from those of the SJs, and their tools are noticeably different from those of the NTs. Notice also that they have nothing important in common with the NFs, who are the very opposite of SPs in their habits of using tools and words.

Concrete Word Usage

The communication of Artisans can be said to be concrete in that they are apt to talk mostly of what is going on at the moment and what is immediately at hand. Most SPs spend little time considering things that cannot be observed or handled. This means that they are likely to take things literally rather than figuratively and, when making comparisons, to use similes more often than metaphors. Their everyday speech is typically filled with details and devoid of planning, and they are more inclined to be specific rather than to generalize. Also they speak less of categories or classes of things and more of actual, individual things themselves, and in general they tend to be more experiential than theoretical in thought and speech. Indeed, the abstract commands little of their attention, content as they are to do without definitions, explanations, fantasies, principles, hypotheses, and the like. They usually consider such topics a waste of time, interesting to others perhaps, but not to them.

Many of our greatest poets and orators have been Artisans, from Lord Byron and Dylan Thomas to Winston Churchill and Ronald Reagan. Why? Why are not the Idealists in the forefront, instead of only a few, along with but a handful of Rationals? It has to be conceded that the Artisans have captured most of the top spots in this domain because of their sensitivity to harmonic coherence, or what sounds good. The Artisans' ear for sound is incomparable. Their consciousness is sensuous, highly attuned to audible consonance, and, if they wish, dissonance. It may be said that paragraphs written by Artisans are in effect songs, as when, for example, Churchill stirred his countrymen during the darkest moments of World War II with his eloquent, rhythmical language: "We shall defend our island, whatever the cost may be, we shall fight on the beaches, we shall fight on the landing grounds, we shall fight in the fields and in the streets, we shall fight in the hills; we shall never surrender!"

It might be added that, more than the other types, Artisans are comfortable in their bodies, and they frequently use their hands to help their speech along, almost always accompanying their spoken words with distinctive hand gestures. The most common gesture is a pawing motion, with the palm down and slightly bent, the thumb held loosely next to the fingers. More aggressive gestures include the closed fist used to pound home one's point, the index finger used to jab one's point across, and the index finger apposed mid-joint by the thumb, used to peck at an opponent.

But spoken or written, Artisan language is filled with concrete words, indicativesthat indicate or that point to things seen and felt. Gully Jimson, an Artisan painter in Joyce Cary's novel, *The Horse's Mouth*, claims he can feel a painting with his eyes:

> You feel all the rounds, the smooths, the sharp edges, the flats and hollows, the lights and shades, the cools and warms. The colors and textures. There's hundreds of little differences all fitting together.

And Ernest Hemingway, much like the Artisan hero in his novel, *A Farewell to Arms*, wanted to avoid figurative language (the language of inference and interpretation, of metaphor and symbol), trusting only descriptive words to present his perceptions as sensually and realistically as possible.

> There were many words you could not stand to hear and finally only the names of places had dignity. Certain numbers were the same way and certain dates and these with the names of the places were all you could say and have them mean anything. Abstract words such as glory, honor, courage, or hallow were obscene beside the concrete names of villages, the numbers of roads, the names of rivers, the numbers of regiments and the dates.

Here Hemingway was artificially flattening his vocabulary and simplifying his sentences in order to catch the tone of war-time disillusionment. Much of everyday Artisan speech is far more lively, more filled with vivid, unorthodox terms, though not much more abstract. SPs like to use colorful phrases and current slang in their speech, and they pick up hip phrases quickly ("I'm outta here," "no way," "ya know what I'm saying?"). When they reach for images, they tend to use quick, sensory adjectives ("slick," "cool," "sharp"), or they say what things are like, using rather striking similes, "drunk as a skunk," "like taking candy from a baby," "goes like a bunny."

Utilitarian Tool Usage

In implementing their goals, or as they say, "going for it," Artisans are primarily interested in what works, what fits, and only secondarily in what meets with social approval. As I've said, the root of the word 'art' means "to fit together," and SP artists even call their productions "works of art," all of which suggests that a thing must be useful to interest an Artisan, immediately useful, concretely useful, otherwise who needs it? If some action doesn't fit your intention and advance you toward your goal, then why do it? NTs share this utilitarian, whatever-works mindset with SPs, but functional utility in the concrete differs from functional utility in the abstract. SPs do not map out the relationship between means and ends as do NTs. Artisans simply and without hesitation give the chosen operation a try, put it to the test, give it a whirl or a shakedown cruise. If it works it is used, if it doesn't it is set aside without a second thought.

Because of their utilitarian character, Artisans will strike off down roads that others might consider impossible, tackling problems, making deals, clearing hurdles, knocking down barriers—doing whatever it takes (authorized or unauthorized) to bull their way through to a successful outcome. One prominent State Department negotiator has exhibited all of these SP traits in his roller-coaster career:

> He has yelled at Foreign Ministers and cursed at a President. He has negotiated agreements of immense consequence on the fly, making them up as he goes along...betting on himself and the deal in hand at two o'clock in the morning. He has politely negotiated with killers and, by his own account, at least one psychopath....He has shamelessly and effectively exploited the media...in order to promote American policy aims and to intimidate those who stood in his way.

No high-flown speculation for the Artisan, no deep meaning or introspection. Leave to others the protocol, the scientific inquiry, the inward search. SPs focus on what actually happens in the real world, on what works, on what pays off, and not on whose toes get stepped on, what principles are involved, or why things happen.

The Tactical Intellect

What Artisans do most and best is work on their immediate environs in a tactical way. Tactics is the art of making moves to better one's position in the here and now, whether those moves are dabbing oils on canvas, flying in rough weather, dishing off the basketball on a fast-break, or skirmishing on the battlefield. Indeed, SP battle leaders are no different from SP painters, pilots, or point guards: they are always scanning for opportunities, always looking for the best angle of approach, and so are able to come up with that particular action which at the moment gives them the greatest advantage, and that brings success. Robert E. Lee, George Patton, and Erwin Rommel were all brilliant SP tactical leaders, able to notice the smallest details in their immediate surroundings, the slightest changes in both foreground and background, which allowed them to grasp the moment and to exploit fully whatever resources were at hand. With their ear to the ground and their finger on the pulse of battle, they could spot an opening, sniff out an opportunity, and taste a victory.

Tactical intelligence, however, need not be confined to the gym, the cockpit, the art studio, or the battlefield. Artisans are the great performers, stars such as Judy Garland, Louis Armstrong, Marlon Brando, Bob Hope, and Gene Kelly. They also make gifted business and political leaders—John DeLorean and Rupert Murdoch, for example, and Winston Churchill, Theodore and Franklin Roosevelt, John F. Kennedy and Lyndon Johnson, just to name a few. Moreover, the Artisans' keen perception makes them the natural scroungers or foragers among the four temperaments, those with an uncanny ability to locate any and all available resources, and to turn some sort of profit on them. Films such as *Stalag 17*, *The Great Escape*, and *Empire of the Sun* depict the incredible skill of the Artisan scroungers as prisoners of war.

But whether on the battlefield or the stage, in the corporate suite or the political arena, SPs are busy making maneuvers with equipment of all sorts, from paint brushes to basketballs, jet planes to tanks—even singers, dancers, and actors call their voice or their body their "instrument," and comedians describe their skill with an audience as "working the room." Artisans can handle their equipment in an expediting or an improvising way—or both—but they are interested first, last, and always in working with equipment.

Interest, Practice, Skill

Now, skills are acquired by practice. No practice, no skill; much practice, much skill. Any skill will wither on the vine and gradually fade away in the degree it is starved of practice, and the same skill will increase precisely in the degree it is given exercise in practice. The neural cell is no different from the muscle cell in this. Use it or Lose it is Nature's inviolable law.

Moreover, there is a feedback relation between interest and ability. We improve in doing things we're interested in doing, and have greater interest in things we do well. Interest reinforces skill, skill reinforces interest, and neither seems to be the starting point. So the Artisans' lifelong interest in tactical action fuels their daily exercise of tactical skills, and as tactical skill increases so then does interest in it, precisely and exclusively measured by the amount of practice.

Naturally, we all have our short suit as well as our long suit in the things we do well. Whatever our long suit, we are not totally without talent in our short suit—it is merely shorter.

In the following graph, which shows the natural variation in the development of Artisan intelligence, notice that the tactical intelligence of SPs is usually far advanced over their diplomatic intelligence. This disparity occurs because of the Artisans' constant practice of tactical operations and inconstant practice of diplomatic operations, since the SPs are frequently interested in tactics and rarely interested in diplomacy. Note also that their strategic and logistical intelligence lag behind tactics but outdo diplomacy, owing to the middling amount of practice usually given them.

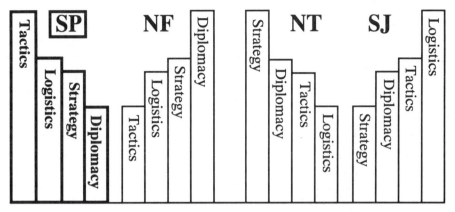

There's a reason why the SP profile is the mirror image of the NF profile. SPs are concrete like SJs and so are likely to practice some of those concrete logistical operations that SJs tend to be so good at. Also, SPs are utilitarian like NTs, and so are likely to practice some of those utilitarian operations involved in strategic planning. Thus, depending on circumstances, logistical and strategic intelligence are likely to develop almost equally, giving the SPs two second suits. But having nothing in common with NFs, SPs tend to neglect diplomatic operations, which usually come in a distant fourth in the race for intellectual development.

Tactical Role Variants

While all the Artisans have tactical intelligence in common, they differ in the kinds of tactical roles they like to practice. In broad terms, Artisans are interested in playing the role of what I call the "Operator" or the "Entertainer," and these give rise to four tactical role variants, the "Promoter" (ESTP), the "Crafter" (ISTP), the "Performer" (ESFP), and the "Composer" (ISFP), all Artisans in their own right, but differing significantly in their artistry. The following chart presents the SP tactical roles and role variants, alongside their most skilled intelligent actions:

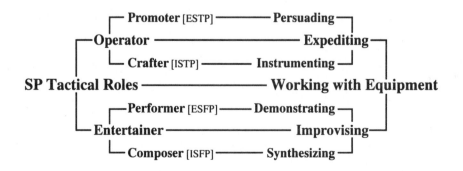

Tactical Operators

The Operator Artisans are particularly interested in acting expediently, that is, in using whatever maneuvers or instruments it takes to advance their current enterprise or project. Oddly enough, the word 'expedient' is derived from the activity of freeing a foot that is caught in a trap (ex = out + ped = foot). But the word has gradually come to suggest the clever moves of someone in a situation calling for timely tactics, mainly to increase chances of success, and only rarely to decrease the possibility of failure. These tough-minded Operators are masters of the expedient use of anything that can be adapted to their immediate intentions, which is to say they instinctively know where they want to go and the fastest way to get there. These are also the directive SPs, which means that, in order to get what they want, they are not at all shy about telling others what to do.

Operators make their moves in two roles, acting either as the expressive Promoter or the reserved Crafter.

Promoters put boundless energy into persuading others to buy into their ventures. With all their charm, these "smooth operators," as they are called, are well able to advertise, announce, boost, convince, entice, induce, lure, publicize, publish, proclaim, talk up, tempt, sway, and wheel and deal. All of these might be thought of as tactical actions to advance the Promoter's enterprises, be they in sales, property development, politics, show-business production, or industrial negotiation—any occupation that calls for winning others' confidence.

Crafters, on the other hand, focus on the tool, implement, mechanism, or instrument employed to get a job done. These quiet, often solitary Operators know about, and know how to use, whatever equipment will effectively accomplish the task at hand. Action of this kind is tactical by its very nature, requiring awareness of those instruments and resources that are close by, available, and how they can be modified to serve the purpose, no matter how they are conventionally defined, or what their intended use. Thus Crafters, depending on their experience, can skillfully do such things as sail boats, do surgical procedures, drive race cars, handle power and hand tools, operate earth movers, forklifts, and cranes, pilot aircraft, work gadgets, steer vehicles, wield weapons, and so on, their skills spreading across the ever widening spectrum of operant equipment.

Tactical Entertainers

Other Artisans are drawn toward improvising works of entertainment, and these friendly, informative Entertainers are able to use effortlessly whatever materials they find to wing it, to play it by ear, to fly by the seat of their pants—to make things up as they go along—far more comfortable sharing their creations with others than directing their actions. Like Operators, Entertainers have the tactical ability to notice every sensual detail of their surroundings and to react spontaneously, adapting something on the spot, on the spur of the moment. They can hit upon ways of utilizing what's at hand to suit their current artistic intention, and they can do this without pre-planning. In other words, their style is to jerry-build or jury-rig things in front of them rather than to pre-configure and devise things out of the blue. The latter is called engineering, an activity requiring NT strategic rather than SP tactical intelligence. It is true, however, that improvising and engineering resemble each other in that both are methods of fitting things together. However, Entertainers use creatively whatever bits and scraps of material are actually present and immediately available, whereas Engineers envision and build whatever components are necessary for a system to operate as designed.

Entertainers come up with their works of art in either the expressive role of Performer or the reserved role of Composer.

Performers improvise in front of others, and so they get good at demonstrating, displaying, showing, presenting, staging, enacting, or exhibiting their artistic skills. Putting on a show for others to watch with pleasure is an extraordinarily demanding task. The most obvious examples of virtuoso Performers are of course the great Artisan actors, singers, dancers, and comedians. But these outgoing Entertainers also excel in less glamorous occupations, in retail sales, real estate, elementary and secondary teaching, public relations, politics—wherever skillfully handling an audience is part of the job description.

Composers use their talents to fashion pleasurable works rather than to stage shows for others. Often working alone, the reserved Entertainers make arrangements, combinations, groupings, mixtures, and the like, exercising their improvisational skills by spotting parts or ingredients and then fitting them together into pleasing forms. The most obvious examples of virtuosity in this synthesizing process are some of the great musical composers. But skilled Composers excel in all aesthetic endeavors, painting, choreography, directing films, writing songs, poems, or novels, cooking, fashion designing, interior decorating, landscaping, perfumery—any occupation calling for the attentive blending of sights, sounds, tastes, textures, or fragrances.

Comparing the Tactical Role Variants

While every Artisan plays these four roles with skill, they do not play them all with equal skill. What distinguishes Artisans from one another is the structure of their intellect—their profile of tactical roles. Some Operators, for instance, are better as Promoters of enterprises, while others are better as Crafters manipulating instruments, even though persuading and instrumenting skills often go hand-in-hand. Just so, some Entertainers are better as Performers puting on shows, while others are better as Composers of works, even though Performers are often successful at composing, and Composers often perform their own works with great skill. To get a clearer picture of the differences in likely tactical development among the Artisans, let us consider the following chart:

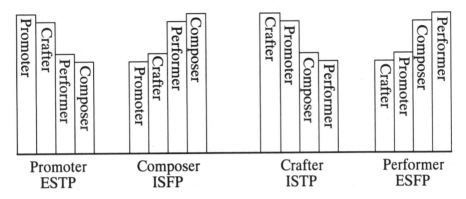

| Promoter
ESTP | Composer
ISFP | Crafter
ISTP | Performer
ESFP |

Note that Promoters (ESTPs) and Composers (ISFPs) are mirror images of each other, as are Crafters (ISTPs) and Performers (ESFPs). Thus the Promoters are usually ready, willing, and able to talk up their enterprises, while they are less inclined to fashion works of art. The reverse holds for the Composers, who are likely to create entertaining works with increasing energy, while they would find it more difficult to boost enterprises. Just so, the Crafters are quite willing and able to run all sorts of machinery, but less so to stage a performance. And last, the Performers are the best of all in putting on a show of some kind, though not the best at operating tools. However, even with their long and short suits, Artisans will tend to practice, and thus will develop, any one of these four tactical roles well above those strategic, logistical, or diplomatic roles of the other types.

Complete portraits of the four Artisan role variants can be found at the end of this chapter, beginning on page 63.

It must be said that tactical intelligence, in any of its forms, is so much more observable than the other kinds! Strategic, logistical, and diplomatic intelligence, if observable at all, are hard to see or hear for what they are. But not tactical intelligence, shouting as it does into our ears and parading itself before our eyes, so that we cannot help noticing it. Think about it: who are the most famous artists, entertainers, athletes, warriors, politicians, and entrepreneurs—all visibly persons of effective action—if not Artisans?

The Interests of Artisans

Everyone has interests, but not everyone has the same interests. Remember that we are interested in doing what we do well, and tend to do well in what we are interested in doing. The interests of Artisans are diametrically opposite of those of Idealists and quite different from those of Guardians and Rationals. These differences are most easily seen when placed side by side for comparison, as in the following chart:

Interests	Artisans	Guardians	Idealists	Rationals
Education	**Artcrafts**	Commerce	Humanities	Sciences
Preoccupation	**Techniques**	Morality	Morale	Technology
Vocation	**Equipment**	Materiel	Personnel	Systems

At school the Artisans typically head for the arts and crafts, and steer clear of the humanities and sciences. Later on, when looking for work, some will study commerce, and can become quite successful in business and industry. But SPs are rarely interested in building morale, or in worrying about morality, and even have some aversion to technology. When they go to work, if they are lucky, they get to work on or with tools and equipment.

Educational Interest in Artcrafts

In school Artisans tend to be interested in artcrafts, where they can practice the required techniques. SPs can appear to be dull, and even bored, when asked to study business (particularly clerical matters), or the humanities, or science and technology, but give them the opportunity to practice any of the arts or crafts and watch them shine. Parents and teachers only rarely give SP children permission, or opportunity, to follow their artistic interests, but this has always been the case, as the Italian Renaissance artisan Benvenuto Cellini reminds us:

> [at] the age of fifteen, I put myself, against my father's will, to the goldsmith's trade with a man called Antonio, son of Sandro....a most excellent craftsman and a very good fellow to boot, high-spirited and frank in all his ways. My father would not let him give me wages like the other apprentices; for having taken up the study of this art to please myself, he wished me to indulge my whim for drawing to the full. I did so willingly enough; and that honest master of mine took marvellous delight in my performances.

Remember, however, that artcraft must not be limited to the so-called fine arts, such as painting and sculpture, or the performing arts, such as music and dance, but in fact includes the athletic, culinary, literary, martial, mechanical, theatrical, and industrial arts, not to mention what Donald Trump called the "Art of the Deal" in big business. Artisans have a natural ability to excel in any of these arts—a Pete Sampras service game in tennis or a Chuck Yeager supersonic test flight is just as artistic as a Rembrandt painting or Beethoven symphony.

Preoccupied with Techniques

Artisans don't spend much time worrying about morality or morale, and they have only a passing interest in devising technology (the concerns, respectively, of the Guardians, Idealists, and Rationals.) But they are always interested, even preoccupied, with the acquisition of technique. In regard to this distinction between SP technique and NT technology, it is necessary to understand that, although the two resemble each other in a superficial manner, they are fundamentally different. Both are derived from the root 'tech,' which means they have to do with effective building, but they are entirely different ways of builiding Technology is the theoretical study of method, technique the empirical perfecting of method. And this is where the Artisans shine. No matter what the cost in time, energy, hardship, peril, or expense, they must perfect their repertoire of techniques.

This is most easily observed in artists and athletes, who give over their lives to mastering the techniques of painting or sculpting, of playing musical instruments, of throwing, catching, kicking, and so on. Watch surfers. They will spend hours daily—and for years—in perfecting their technique of riding the waves. Many then take up wind-surfing, or riding the waves with a sail attached to their surfboard, so that they can develop the technique of doing somersaults directly into the waves! No matter the SP's activity, however, technique is the main issue. Whether it be a President's technique of speechmaking, the business tycoon's technique of making deals, or the skip loader's technique of earthmoving, it is the mastery of technique that draws the SPs like moths to a flame.

Vocational Interest in Equipment

Artisans are happiest when working with any and all sorts of equipment. Apparatus, implements, machines, and instruments captivate them; they are things to be used—employed, deployed—and the SPs cannot not operate them. They must drive the bulldozer, pilot the plane, steer the boat, fire the gun, toot the horn, wield the scalpel, brush, or chisel. Something about equipment strikes a chord in the character of the SPs, extending the reach, augmenting, amplifying, and sharpening the effects of the many techniques they increasingly acquire and perfect. Listen as a truck driver interviewed by Studs Terkel describes the excitement of being behind the wheel of a big tractor and semi-trailer:

> The minute you climb into that truck, the adrenaline starts pumping. If you want a thrill, there's no comparison, not even a jet plane, to climbing on a steel truck and going out there on the expressway. You'll swear you'll never be able to get out the other end of that thing without an accident. There's thousands of cars, and thousands of trucks and you're shifting like a maniac and you're braking and accelerating and the object is to try to move with the traffic and try to keep from running over all those crazy fools who are trying to get under your wheel.

Even in ancient times, long before industrial civilization, Artisans must have been the chief hunters and the finest warriors. The sling, the club, the spear, the bow and arrow: these equipped the SP tribesmen for their deadly art. And is it not so even today, for who but the Artisan is first to enlist when war comes, and who but the Artisan best wields the weapons and the machines of modern warfare?

The Orientation of Artisans

We are born into a social field and we live out our lives in that field, never, for long, stepping outside of it into isolation. Of course, we can be disoriented for short periods of time, owing to a shock or a danger. But we soon reorient ourselves and return to our ordinary waking social frame of reference. Indeed, we are the most social of all the animals, our sociability ending in massive and complex societies. Whatever we think or feel, say or do, occurs, must occur, in the iron crucible of social reality. We are oriented always from a certain angle, a slant, a standpoint, something Adickes spoke of as our built-in *"Weltanschauung,"* or "worldview."

But different personalities have different perspectives, viewing time and place as well as past, present, and future differently. Consider the following chart in making these comparisons:

Orientation	Artisans	Guardians	Idealists	Rationals
Present	**Practical**	Dutiful	Altruistic	Pragmatic
Future	**Optimistic**	Pessimistic	Credulous	Skeptical
Past	**Cynical**	Stoical	Mystical	Relativistic
Place	**Here**	Gateways	Pathways	Intersections
Time	**Now**	Yesterday	Tomorrow	Intervals

Here it is claimed that Artisans are practical about the present, optimistic about the future, cynical about the past, their preferred place is here in the middle of the action, and their preferred time is now. How different are the other temperaments in the way they view these things. So let us look closely at these five dimensions of orientation so that we will not be surprised when our Artisan friends prove, for example, to be less dutiful, or altruistic, or pragmatic than we are.

Practical in Looking Around

All of us look upon ourselves as practical. Even those of us who identify ourselves as Idealists feel that nothing is more practical than being diplomatic in interacting with others, just as the Guardians regard the observing of traditions a very practical thing to do. And of course the Rationals consider efficiency in action the very essence of practicality. But often to be practical it is necessary to be decidedly undiplomatic, or to wink at tradition, or to forget, for the moment, about being efficient. And these departures are quickly made by the Artisan, while the others are reluctant to do so.

In a sense Artisans are born to be practical, to get what they want by any means necessary, and if necessity requires a measure of rudeness, or flaunting convention, or being wasteful of effort, well, so be it. Their question is always, "What's it good for?" "What do you get out of this?" "What's in it for me?" "Where's the payoff?" "Why bother?"—or just plain "So what?" Being practical is what it means to be utilitarian in the concrete sense. The abstract utilitarianism of the Rational is different from the concrete utilitarianism of the Artisan in that the Artisan is looking for maximum effect, the Rational for maximum efficiency. Artisans will spend whatever amount of effort is necessary to get what they want; Rationals will not, since they require that the most result is gotten with the least effort. Getting results is more of a theoretical issue with Rationals, a more practical issue with Artisans.

Optimistic in Looking Ahead

Artisans are the supreme optimists. The past is water under the bridge, so forget it. The distant future is a long way off, so don't waste time planning for it. But the next moment? Here the SPs shine with a natural confidence that things are going to turn their way. SPs feel lucky: the next roll of the dice, the next move, shot, or ploy will be a lucky one, never mind that the last few have failed. What comes next is bound to be a break, a windfall, some smile from Lady Luck. And once on a roll or a hot streak, SPs believe their luck will hold, and they will push it to the limit.

Along with their optimism, Artisans have an incorrigible belief that they lead a charmed life, which makes them easily the most devil-may-care of all the types. And which can get them into trouble. SPs are more subject to accidents and downturns than other temperaments, injuring themselves through inattention to possible sources of setback, defeat, or loss. SPs often live a life of violent ups and downs, winning a fortune one day and gambling it away the next, trusting the fickle goddess Fortune as she spins her wheel.

Cynical in Looking Back

We all have times when things don't turn out well, when we lose, take a hit, are in the wrong place at the wrong time. Each type has its own way of coping with such negative outcomes, of explaining them or rationalizing them. SJs, for example, tend to take a stoical view, often believing that difficulties, when they come, are inevitable, fated, that nothing could have been done to avoid them, perhaps even that they are the will of some deity. SPs, on the other hand, look upon mishaps in a cynical manner, which means that they don't see life as having some larger pattern to it. Artisans view life as chancy, risky, a leap in the dark, a crap-shoot—and they would have it no other way. When luck smiles on them they ride the streak, and when their luck turns sour they simply shrug their shoulders, sloughing off adversity with an attitude of "that's life," "that's the breaks," or "that's the way the ball bounces." No doubt it was some hardened soldier who came up with the expression *"c'est la guerre."*

Artisans can be cynical about human motives as well. They harbor no illusions about people being noble or saintly—"come off it," says the SP, no matter how virtuous we think ourselves, we all have feet of clay, we are all ultimately corruptible and self-serving. With their cynical take on people's intentions, Artisans know to look a gift horse in the mouth and to check on their wallet when someone is trying to give them something. And a great source of chagrin for SPs is to be naive and fall for a trick, to be taken, duped, to be a sap or a sucker.

Such cynicism gives SPs a huge tactical advantage over the other more trusting and gullible types, who can become easy marks for Artisans. Listen as P.T. Barnum recalls how cleverly he manipulated the American public with one of his famous hoaxes (and notice how he expresses himself in feeding images):

> The public appetite was craving something...the community was absolutely famishing. They were ravenous. They could have swallowed anything, and...I threw them, not a 'bone,' but a regular tidbit, a bon-bon, and they swallowed it in a single gulp.

In another area of show business actor and film director Clint Eastwood explored the aesthetics of cynicism in his Italian-made "spaghetti westerns," then later in his popular *Dirty Harry* movies, with his sardonic take on the world reaching its zenith in his 1990s films, *White Hunter, Black Heart, A Perfect World,* and *Unforgiven.* After Eastwood's artful display of cynicism, American movies would never be the same. Indeed, the philosophy of the cynic, albeit eschewed by those Guardians and Idealists who strongly advocate cooperation, is as morally correct for Artisans as the stoicism, mysticism, and relativism are for the other types.

The Place is Here

Artisans do not care to take tickets at the gate, or sit in the bleachers, or referee the game. They must be in the game, at the very center of things where the action is. Just as their time is now, their place is here, and so they can be said to live in the "here-and-now." Their time and space are inseparable, and it is this unity of time and space that makes their precision of motion in the arts, especially the athletic arts, understandable. How is it possible, for instance, for baseball players to hit a one hundred mile-per-hour fastball? Or for basketball players to hit so small a target from so far away? Of course they must swing their bats and shoot their jump shots daily, and for long hours. But other types could do that and still not attain the SPs' prowess. While others attempt their motions they are all too often concerned about what is going on elsewhere, or at some other time. The Artisans' only concern is what is happening here at this very moment, and this makes them the masters of timing and graceful movement.

Arthur Hailey captured the here-and-now expertise of the Artisan in this scene of troubleshooting from his novel, *Airport:*

> 'Mister, there's spilled gasoline around here. You'd better get that cigar out.'
> ...Patroni ignored the instruction, as he ignored almost all smoking regulations. He waved his cigar toward the overturned tractor-trailer. '...son, you'd be wasting everybody's time, including mine and yours, trying to get that hunk of junk right side up tonight. You'll have to drag it clear so traffic can move, and to do that you need two more tow trucks—one on this side to push, two over there to pull.' He began moving around, using his electric lantern to inspect the big articulated vehicle from various angles. As always, when considering a problem he was totally absorbed. He waved his cigar once more, 'The two trucks together'll hitch onto three points. They'll pull the cab first, and faster. That'll overcome the jackknifing. The other truck...'
> 'Hold it,' the state trooper said. He called across to one of the other officers....'Hank, there's a guy here sounds like he knows what he's talking about.'

The Time is Now

Far more than the rest of us, Artisans live and act in the present. After all, they tell us, "tomorrow never comes" and yesterday is "water over the dam." To an SP, there's no time like the present, so we'd better make the most of it, better seize the day, strike while the iron is hot, or get while the getting's good. Watch a thorough-going SP athlete in action. He or she acts to a great extent in the now, focusing easily on this time, not that time, on this stroke, not the last one or the next one.

Others may grouse and groan about their errors, or worry that the next shot might fail, but less so the Artisans. They do not mourn their losses as their concrete cousins the Guardians do; they do not dissect and redesign their mistakes as their abstract cousins the Rationals do; nor do they live in anticipation of mistakes as their abstract opposites the Idealists do. What SPs do is keep their eye on the ball and so are able, more than the others, to hit it at precisely the right instant. Oblivious to the past and the future, they can concentrate all their powers on a clear and present opportunity. And so more often than not they win.

However, there's a price to pay for living so intently in the moment. Since Artisans do not reflect very much on their errors or analyze their mistakes to any great extent, it is difficult for them to learn from their errors, and so they can become caught in a loop, repeating their mistakes. Here, however, their talent for going with what works usually saves them. SPs instinctively repeat those acts that bring them success, and so they do indeed learn from positive experience.

The Self-Image of Artisans

All of us have a concept of ourselves composed of things we believe about ourselves. Three aspects of our self-image or self-concept are of particular importance in determining how well we regard ourselves: self-esteem, self-respect, and self-confidence. Thus the self-image is a triangular affair, the three bases of self-regard vitally affecting each other. For example, when our self-esteem diminishes, this decrement tends to undermine our self-respect and self-confidence. Likewise, as we lose self-respect, it becomes more difficult for us to maintain our self-confidence and self-esteem. And it works the other way too—the more we prize ourselves the more we respect ourselves and the greater our self-confidence.

But different types of personality base their self-image on entirely different things. Since having a good opinion of oneself is one of the keys to happiness, and often to success, it is well that we pause for a moment to compare the four temperaments on this important aspect of personality:

Self-Image	Artisans	Guardians	Idealists	Rationals
Self-Esteem	**Artistic**	Dependable	Empathic	Ingenious
Self-Respect	**Audacious**	Beneficent	Benevolent	Autonomous
Self-Confidence	**Adaptable**	Respectable	Authentic	Resolute

Thus, to feel good about themselves Artisans must regard themselves as artistic, audacious, and adaptable, while other attributes, empathy and benevolence, for instance, contribute little to their self-image. I believe that these three attitudes —artistry, audacity, adaptability— are mutually reinforcing, as suggest-

The Self-Image of Artisans

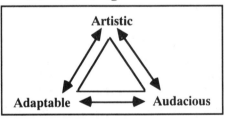

ed by the figure at the right, such that they wax and wane together. Perhaps this is so even though they independently characterize the self-esteem, self-respect, and self-confidence of the Artisans.

Still, whether interdependent or independent of one another, the three attitudes toward the self deserve careful examination, so let us look at them one at a time.

Self-Esteem in Artistry

Artisan self-esteem is greatest when they see themselves and are seen by others as artistic in expediting and improvising productions. Most Artisans enjoy presenting themselves as graceful in action, their sense of pride stemming from their ability to act fluidly, beautifully, and with effortless freedom. John Updike captures this pride-of-performance when his character

Rabbit Angstrom stops to shoot baskets with some playground teenagers:

> As they stare hushed he sights squinting...setting his feet with care, wiggling the ball with nervousness in front of his chest, one widespread white hand on top of the ball and the other underneath, jiggling it patiently....Then the ball seems to ride up the right lapel of his coat and comes off his shoulder as his knees dip down, and it...drops into the circle of the rim, whipping the net with a ladylike whisper. [That his touch still lives in his hands elates him. He feels liberated.] 'Hey!' he shouts in pride....'Luck,' one of the kids says....'Skill,' he answers.

On the other hand, the Artisans' greatest source of embarrassment is in performing some action poorly or awkwardly, any lapse of what dancer Martha Graham calls "the physical use of the body in action." When Graham became too old to dance with the fluid gracefulness which was her trademark, she was frustrated by the loss of her masterful technique:

> I wonder where all the loveliness, all the awareness of the magic of the body, has gone....What I miss some days...is the eagerness to meet life, the curiosity, the wonder that you feel when you can really move—to work toward a perfect first or a perfect fifth position. There becomes an excitement, an avidity, a forgetfulness of everyone about you. You are so completely absorbed in this instrument that is vibrant to life.

It is a mistake to confuse the artistic action of the Artisans with the efficient action of the Rationals. Efficiency is measured by the proportion of input to output. The action that gets the most result for the least effort is efficient, and NTs take pride in their efficiency. In contrast, graceful action boosts the SPs' self-esteem regardless of the effort they put into the performance. Artisans will expend whatever effort is required to adorn an activity, styling and restyling their performance, pushing their artistry to its limits, failing again and again until fluency has been reached. And in this they can be quite wasteful of effort, at least in the eyes of the NT. For example, witness how tap-dance prodigy Savion Glover, as he choreographs a number with his dance troupe, is far more concerned with embellishing his moves than with running his rehearsal efficiently:

> As Glover takes the members of Real Tap Skills through the steps in rehearsals, he improvises as he goes....[He] paces and taps in front of the mirror, hearing phrases, repeating them, building up a tapestry of intricate sound, which sometimes frustrates the dancers of Real Tap Skills, who struggle to keep up with him. 'Let's go again,' he says, and they stolidly assume their positions and start over.

Self-Respect in Audacity

Artisans see themselves, and wish to be seen by others, as bold, daring, venturesome—audacious. General Patton is credited with saying that it is *"l'audace, toujour l'audace"* that wins battles. The SPs' self-respect depends upon their ability to act fearlessly, to look danger in the eye and defeat it under any circumstances. Boldness is a virtue to cultivate, and like the lion in *The Wizard of Oz*, Artisans feel guilty if they are cowardly, if they are yellow or chicken out. Hemingway often wrote about what his biographer Carlos Baker called "his favorite subjects of bravery and cowardice":

> Courage, he believed, was a matter of dignity....A man without inner dignity was an embarrassment. Ernest knew from personal experience 'what is was to be a coward and what it was to cease being a coward.' Now, in the presence of actual danger, he found that he did not care what happened. 'I knew it was better to live it so that if you died you had done everything that you could do about your work and your enjoyment of life up to that minute.'

With this eagerness to live boldly "up to that minute," Artisans are the world's great risk-takers. They delight in putting themselves in jeopardy, taking chances, facing hazards, whatever form their endangerment might take. Even if it means they must walk away from a good job or a settled life, they might very well pay that price. SPs say that "life is too short," that they must "make hay while the sun shines," and that "he who hesitates is lost." SPs do not hesitate; on the contrary, they often find risk-taking so irresistible that they court it again and again, pushing ever closer to the edge. It is likely that most skydivers, race drivers, and mercenary soldiers are SPs who have become compulsive in risking themselves.

Not that all risks are death-defying. The most successful Wall Street wheeler-dealers and corporate high-rollers are usually Artisans, as are many surgeons and defense lawyers, political negotiators, trouble-shooters—and comedians. Johnny Carson, for example, developed a brand of humor based on risque jokes and stories. Even in college, hosting fraternity shows, Carson's quips were brash and slightly off color, or as biographer Laurence Leamer puts it:

> Johnny's...best jokes were usually about sex, not bawdy burlesque stories, but witty allusions. He gave thousands before him the feeling that here was a daring young man.

Generally speaking, however, the SP gravitates toward jobs where bold physical action is involved, not only in the performing arts and athletics, but in construction work, jobs where heavy machinery is employed, in the building operations for dams and skyscrapers, for freeways and mines, in operations for pitting human force against the forces of nature, such as working the oil fields and logging, in loading freight, in driving ambulances, motorcycles, and aircraft, in detective work, police work, soldiering, fire and rescue work. All these are SP occupations which require bold action and a considerable amount of physical courage.

Unfortunately, cultural stereotyping provides male Artisans far more than female Artisans the opportunity to express their attraction to risk. Perhaps the influence of the feminist movement will eventually make this style of life more socially acceptable for females; nonetheless, current realities still exclude the SP female from most typical SP occupations, in spite of the fact that half of the SPs are women. True, a few women have entered professional athletics (golf, tennis, and now basketball), also heavy construction and the military, and some have succeeded as trouble shooters; but the action occupations, involving precision, endurance, strength, boldness, and timing, remain largely in the hands of men. The majority of women still enter three traditional occupations, nursing, teaching, and clerical work, none of which is likely to give the female Artisan much chance to build her self-respect.

Self-Confidence in Adaptability

Artisans may well pride themselves on their artistry, and respect themselves for their boldness, but they base their self-confidence on their ability to adapt spontaneously to changing circumstances, to alter and shape their behavior in the moment, in order to operate effectively in the most unstable situations. Paracelsus, as noted earlier, saw this type as guided by the Salamander, a mythical creature capable of changing its appearance so as to blend in with its immediate surroundings. And, indeed, of all the styles Artisans are best able to respond quickly and flexibly to a changing environment.

This is why Artisans work so well in a crisis; new situations demand new actions, and earlier commitments often have to be abandoned—with regret, perhaps, but still abandoned. Today is today, and yesterday's arrangements must give way in the face of more urgent demands. SPs hate to be bound by rigid, pre-established laws—by the SJ's rules and regulations, by the NF's ethical concerns, or by the NT's laws of logic. SPs will go along with such conventions for a time, lying low and not rocking the boat, but only until a crisis occurs, and then they spring into action.

Of course Artisans are not always successful in dealing with crises. They have successes and failures like everyone, perhaps more than most people. But win or lose, they are always adaptable, pliable, and have the ability to roll with the punches and land on their feet, surviving setbacks which might leave other types permanently immobilized. Jennie Churchill, Winston Churchill's extraordinary mother, showed this knack of adapting to survive. She lived with a vivacity which is rare, even in SPs, and Ralph Martin caught her style when he wrote of a low point in her life:

> For Jennie, the year 1895 began bitter and bleak. After a lingering illness, her husband had died of syphilis, raving mad. Only weeks before, her lover, unwilling to wait any longer, had married. Her sons, Winston and

Jack, both had problems which required her full attention. Physically and emotionally she felt drained....So here was Jennie with the man who had loved her most now married to someone else, little money, not even a home of her own....And yet, such was the inner resource and resilience of this woman that her life soon took on an excitement and vitality such as she had never dreamed of. As her friend, Lady Curzon, said in a letter to her, 'You are the only person who lives on the crest of a wave.'

The Values of Artisans

Different people value different things, but even in our values temperament plays a decisive role. Even though we may wish to value something, if it is not in our nature to do so, we cannot. We may will, but we cannot will to will. Different types differ in their preferred mood, in what they put their trust in, what they yearn for, what they seek, what they prize, and what they aspire to. It is perhaps in our values that the patterns of personality are most easily discernible, moreso than in other domains, such as the self-image or the forms of intelligence. To appreciate these differences let us study the following chart:

Value	Artisans	Guardians	Idealists	Rationals
Being	**Excited**	Concerned	Enthusiastic	Calm
Trusting	**Impulse**	Authority	Intuition	Reason
Yearning	**Impact**	Belonging	Romance	Achievement
Seeking	**Stimulation**	Security	Identity	Knowledge
Prizing	**Generosity**	Gratitude	Recognition	Deference
Aspiring	**Virtuoso**	Executive	Sage	Wizard

I think that Artisans typically enjoy being excited, trust their impulses, yearn to have impact on others, often seek stimulation, prize generosity, and aspire to virtuosity. These value preferences are radically different from those of other temperament. Therefore is will serve us well if we study these six kinds of value in the case of Artisans lest we are surprised (and perhaps annoyed) to find them, for instance, less security-minded, less sagacious, or less hungry for achievement than we are.

Being Excited
Artisans like being excited and insist on being excited, especially when things get dull. They are excitable as children and they never seem to get less excitable as they grow up. They enjoy being turned on and can tolerate a lot of excitement for long periods of time. Unlike the other three temperaments, the SPs' public performances even improve the more excited they get. Not that this excitement is always displayed openly. Artisans at their milling machine or crawling on the World Wide Web, working on their

paintings or taking batting practice, are just as keyed up, high-strung, and show the same restless energy.

This excitability is what enables Artisans to be oblivious to pain or fatigue, depending, of course, on what they're doing. If they're caught up in some artistic activity, grasped by the action itself—as by a magnet—then they are too excited to feel pain or fatigue. The rest of us get tired and sore in our efforts, but the Artisans are not making effort in our sense; rather, they are acting in the heat of excitement, and so need not endure anything. SPs climb the mountain for the thrill of it—because it's there—not to get to the top or the other side. Action is for the high, the rush, not for something else. Some say that Artisans, during their excited actions, are dedicated, but this is neither dedication, commitment, nor devotion. It is, rather, a kind of repetition compulsion, making them continue the action that has caught them in its energy field.

Moreover, Artisans (especially the sociable ones) lend an electricity to the environment and to the people around them. SPs tend to live life at the level of a gourmet feast, and they bring to work and to play a sense that something delicious is about to happen. Wherever they go, the atmosphere takes on a glow, seems brighter, more colorful—charged with an excitement that others often admire and even envy. Auntie Mame defies a disapproving world, urging her friend to take some risks: "Yes! Life is a banquet, and most poor sons-of-bitches are starving to death! Live!" And her friend catches the SP fever, responding, "Yes! Live, live, live!"

Excitability has its price, however, which is that Artisans can easily become bored. Boredom is one of the most painful conditions SPs can experience, and if it continues for long they are likely to do almost anything to end it. A friend of Leonard Bernstein remembers the brilliant young musician in his student days at Harvard as "endlessly energetic and...needing constant variety":

> He was magnetic, outgoing, fun-loving, surrounded himself with many friends and had an abundance of acquaintances, from all walks of life....He became bored if made to have a regimental existence. He had a fascination with unique people and artistic projects, and needed to have many projects going on at once.

Similarly, John F. Kennedy hated boredom above all else, as White House correspondent Nancy Dickerson recalls:

> To Jack, the cardinal sin was boredom; it was his biggest enemy, and he didn't know how to handle it. When he was bored, a hood would come down over his eyes and his nervous system would start churning. You could do anything to him—steal his wallet, insult him, argue with him—but to bore him was unpardonable.

Very likely the SP's love of excitement is why Kennedy pulled strings to get himself assigned to the dangerous PT boats during World War II, only to have his boat crushed by a Japanese destroyer.

Artisans, of course, are capable of all the moods. Besides being excited, they can be calm, concerned, or enthused like other types. In old age, particularly, some SPs seem to calm down a bit, but this may be because they have lost some of their steam, or because they have gained some control over their impulses. But even with their best years behind them, Artisans still prefer to be excited—to be hot, turned on, to be a live wire—and the other moods of calm, concern, and enthusiasm tend to be short-lived.

It may seem strange to distinguish between enthusiasm and excitement, especially when dictionaries present them as synonymous. But they are quite different attitudes. To be <u>en</u>thused is to be aroused by something inside—an idea, an image, a goal. To be <u>ex</u>cited is to be stimulated by something outside—a game, a contest, a challenge, an opportunity. Thus the prevailing mood of the SPs is opposite that of the NFs, with SPs frequently and easily becoming excited, but only slowly and rarely becoming enthused; and with NFs frequently and easily showing enthusiasm, but only slowly and uneasily getting excited.

Trusting Impulses

Artisans are impulsive. They like being that way. To be impulsive, spontaneous, is to be really alive. SPs trust their impulses without reserve, enjoy feeling them well up within; and they love discharging them, like setting off an explosion. They even feel uneasy if they don't have impulses. At one time or another all the types feel these sudden urges to act, but the others try to control them, looking ahead to what they think of as more valuable goals. SJs, NFs, and NTs discipline their impulses in the name of duty, ethics, or reason, behavior which would only make the SP feel bound and confined. Joe Namath, professional football player (and one-time famous bachelor), was more interested in playing the field than in committing to marriage:

> I have no desire to have children, so why get married? Ladies, for the most part, want to get married and have children. Most have been conditioned that way. I can't handle it. Inside of me I get a little crazy. I start feeling locked in if I have to be somewhere at a certain time and then I worry if I'm not there, she'll worry. Man, the biggest burden I ever had was love.

Life for an Artisan means having impulses and acting spontaneously on those impulses. Since an impulse, by definition, is ephemeral, the SP must live in the immediate moment. Action cannot be saved for tomorrow. The young Hemingway suddenly quit his job and volunteered to drive ambulances in World War I, but he became impossibly "bored with sightseeing" in France while waiting for his assignment and wrote his sister, "I wish they'd hurry up and ship us off to the front." For SPs, to wait is psychological death, no matter how dangerous the action.

Other types often find it hard to understand why an Artisan wants to live so impulsively; but to an Artisan, a life of action in the moment, which disregards long term goals, is life at its freest and most intense. This is not to say that SPs do not have goals and ties just like the rest of us. They do, of course, only their goals are fewer and more tentatively held. And if the ties become too numerous or too binding, then the SP is likely to become restless and get the urge to take off for elsewhere. Artisans, of all the types, are most likely to answer the call to wander, and they can sever social or family ties more easily than others, even though they may be aware of the distress such behavior causes those close to them. The SP can abruptly abandon either an activity or a relationship, walking away without a backward glance. At mid-life particularly, the Artisans' need for freedom from constraints may be so intense that they can become unusually impatient. A stifling career is suddenly discarded; family responsibilities are dropped, sadly, even painfully, but still with little regret. Although the SP himself created these ties, now they seem a suffocating burden. Gauguin, in his early forties, turned away from his wife and children and sailed off to Tahiti, where he produced many paintings, some held to be masterpieces, though he left broken trust behind.

Artisans must do whatever their impulse dictates and continue the action as long as the urge compels. When the impulse lets up, when they no longer feel like racing, painting, playing, or whatever, then they can stop. Under stress, SPs will sometimes claim that they have to behave in a particular way, that they can't help themselves. Thus they may admit to being "compulsive gamblers," for example, or "compulsive drinkers," and are likely to be labeled as such by therapists who encounter them. But while compulsions are experienced by the other types as burdensome and onerous (NTs can be compulsive, too), the SPs' compulsions are almost all exciting and not at all burdensome.

Yearning for Impact

Social impact is vital for Artisans, even for those who appear to shrug their shoulders and turn away from society. Artisans need to be potent, to be felt as a strong presence, and they want to affect the course of events, if only by defying, shocking, or mocking the establishment. For an Artisan, to be without impact, to make no difference in human affairs, is like being deprived of oxygen. More than other types, the SP is subject to what Karl Bühler, one of the great Gestalt psychologists, called "function lust," that is, a craving for impressive action, a longing to perform some conspicuous function in their social context and so make their mark. SPs hunger to have a piece of the action, to make a splash, to make something happen, to hit the big time, whether in the world of art or corporate business, on the battlefield or ball field, on stage or in the political arena. This is why so many professional politicians are SPs: the world of politics allows not only for maneuvering, excitement, and risk—but for powerful social impact. In his Presidency, and in his life, Teddy Roosevelt lived by a motto that speaks for all his fellow-Artisans: "Get action; do things...create, act, take a place wherever you are; get action."

Seeking Stimulation
Artisans spend a good deal of their time seeking stimulation because they need it. As much as possible, they live in their five senses, and they seem to like their music a little louder than the other types, their clothes a little more colorful, and their food and drink a little stronger. Marvin Zuckerman, an American psychologist, spoke of this type as the "Sensation-Seeking Personality," a name that British playwright Alan Ayckbourn seems almost to have had in mind when one of his comic heroes, Norman Dewers, rather drunkenly begs his brother-in-law to join him on a holiday:

> no, not a holiday—that sounds so damn conventional. I want us just to go....And see things. And taste things. And smell things. And touch things...touch trees—and grass—and—earth....Let's be able to say—we have seen and experienced everything.

Artisans believe that variety is the spice of life, and they want their lives to be filled with new sensations and experiences. In family life, Artisans are eager to try different vacation spots, to buy new cars, new clothes, to change houses, to try out new foods, new places to eat, or even to vary the dinner hour, wanting to eat whenever the impulse strikes. This tends to be upsetting to the more conservative types, SJs particularly, and can lead to difficulty when an SP marries.

The same at work: if their job has little variety or unpredictability, in other words, little that is stimulating about it, the Artisan becomes disinterested. But as the range of possibilities and emergencies increases, so does the SP's eagerness to take on the task. In fact, when a job becomes too dull and routine, SPs have been known to create a sensation—just to liven things up a little. Not that Artisans refuse to do what they're supposed to do, or in the prescribed way, or even to do it over and over again. They may or may not, depending on how they feel at the moment. But they will turn the job into play if they can, and if they must repeat an action, they will either make it variations on a theme, or they will tune out and reduce it to an automatic way of operating, their *modus operandi*, or M.O., a habit pattern which Artisans often resort to.

Prizing Generosity
Child-like in other ways, perhaps Artisans are most child-like in the life-long pleasure they get out of giving. They never really lose the sense of fun that accompanies fortuitous generosity—not giving because some-

thing is owed to them or by them, but giving that is done spontaneously, for no reason other than having fun. For SPs giving out of duty isn't fun at all, but impulsive giving is very gratifying. For example, Artisan men are the most likely of all the types to bring flowers, candy, and whatnot to their girl friend or spouse, while Artisan women are the most likely to throw a party for spouse or child or parent just for the fun of it, and are just as delighted when this is done for them. Of course other types, especially Guardians, are pleased to give gifts, but not to the same extent or frequency of pleasure experienced by Artisans. Santa Claus, the elfin spirit of the Guardians, is known to give only to the deserving, but Dionysus, the spiritual guide of the Artisans, is pleased to give of his bounty to all who come to the party, whatever their just deserts may or may not be.

This impulsive generosity can be expensive at times, as seen in a story about one of Elvis Presley's whims. Presley had parked his custom-made Cadillac near a car lot, and when he returned he found a total stranger with her head in his car, looking it over longingly. Elvis asked the woman if she liked it, and then offered, "This one is mine, but I'll buy you one." He caught the stranger by the arm, took her to the nearby car lot, and told her to pick one out. After she had selected a gold and white model, Presley learned that it was the woman's birthday, so he handed her the keys to the car, wished her happy birthday, and told his aide to write her a check so that the woman could "buy some clothes to go with the car." And Frank Sinatra, according to John Lahr's *New Yorker* profile, "has always been known among his friends for impulsive, awesome acts of generosity—those grand gestures that Sicilians call *la bella figura*." For instance, one time when his friend actor George Raft was under indictment by the IRS, Sinatra sent him a blank check with a note saying, "To use if you need it."

Aspiring to be a Virtuoso

Aspiration is more of a dream than an ambition, something one would be if only one could, something seen as almost out of one's reach, such that those who make it to that level of expertise wonder how they got there. In the case of Artisans, they so covet skill in technique that they tend to aspire secretly to becoming some sort of virtuoso of performance, the aspiration becoming less secret as the technical mastery increases. Scratch an SP, find a would-be virtuoso, who, short of virtuosity, can attain surprising proficiency in some art form.

Now, it's one thing to dream of being a virtuoso—an ace in one's field—and quite another actually to become one. After all, a virtuoso is the ultimate technician, capable at times of perfect artistic execution, showing skill so great as to be unimaginable. Take figure skating. How Olympic skaters perform those incredible turns and leaps so flawlessly is beyond imagination, even though it is clear that such skill requires daily practice for years on end. Most of us, were we somehow to practice that much, still would not develop such extreme prowess. No, it is something in the Artisans' temperament that puts virtuosity barely within their reach but not the reach of others. After all, those of other type aspire to other things—wizardry, wisdom, executive status—and so cannot aspire at the same time to virtuosity.

Virtuoso performers in the fine arts, or on stage and screen, are apt to be Artisans, but we must not forget that virtuosity in performance can be achieved, or at least sought, by any of the SPs: not only the figure-skater, but the surfer, the chef, the sculptor, the surgeon, the racer, the mountain-climber, the gambler, the politician, the fighter-pilot, even the con artist and the gunslinger of the Old West. Indeed, the gunslinger could draw his long-barreled revolver, cock it, aim it, and fire it, hitting unbelievably small moving targets, without sighting down the barrel. He was able to perform this feat in less than one-fifth of a second—so swiftly that the motion of his hand could not be seen. The fast draw of the gunslinger is just as incredible as the bowing and fingering of the violinist, the twirling of the ice-skater, or the triple somersaults of the high board diver—all feats of the same character type.

The Social Roles Artisans Play

There are two kinds of social roles, those that are allotted to us by virtue of our position in our social milieu, and those that we reach out and take for ourselves. It is impossible not to play a role in all of our social transactions. We perforce play offspring to our parents, siblings to our brothers and sisters, and relatives to our extended family members. On the other hand we choose to play mate to our spouse, parent to our offspring, superior to our subordinate, subordinate to our superior, friend to friend, and so on. Allotted or embraced, we have no choice but to enact our roles, since interaction with others can never be role-free.

Three of our social roles are of special significance in the context of the study of personality: mating, parenting, and leading. In these three roles the temperaments differ in important ways, important, that is, in the effects their ways of mating, parenting, and leading have on their mates, offspring, and followers. Let us consider a chart which shows the different ways in which mating, parenting, and leading roles are played:

Social Roles	Artisans	Guardians	Idealists	Rationals
Mating	**Playmate**	Helpmate	Soulmate	Mindmate
Parenting	**Liberator**	Socializer	Harmonizer	Individuator
Leading	**Negotiator**	Stabilizer	Catalyst	Visionary

Note the striking difference between enacting the Playmate role in the case of the Artisans, and the Helpmate, Soulmate, and Mindmate in the other three types of personality. These different roles will require lengthy and complex study and so a chapter on mating (Chapter 7) is provided.

Chapters on parenting roles (Chapter 8) and leadership roles (Chapter 9) are also furnished. Even so, a few remarks on each of the Artisan's social roles can at least give outlines of how they are played.

The Playmate

The spousal role the Artisan is something to behold. The most hedonic of all, the Artisans seek to lighten up their spouses, and in taking the role of Playmate, devote themselves to giving pleasure and excitement to their mates. The vast majority of Artisans end up, if they do not start out, with Guardian mates. One reason is that together the Artisans and Guardians comprise about 85% of the population, so there is little chance of either of them even encountering, let alone marrying, either Rationals or Idealists. Another reason is that marriage between Artisans tends to be rather unstable and is often terminated after a few months or years, so the second time around the divorced Artisan goes for a Guardian. And a third reason is that SPs and SJs complement each other very nicely, for reasons to be discussed in Chapter 7. To say the least, marriage to an Artisan can be exciting and fun, and never boring, whatever the temperament of his or her mate.

The Liberator Parent

Wanting freedom for themselves, it is quite natural that Artisans would want freedom for their kids. Not that they let their kids get away with abusing their privileges, but Artisans are apt to encourage their kids to test the limits of their surroundings, so that they can do things on their own as early as possible—shoved out of the nest as soon as they're ready to fly. In line with liberating their kids, SP parents are likely to see to it that they get to learn how to do lots of concrete operations such as using hand tools, building things, running vehicles, playing games, and participating in sports or theater. In short, Artisan parents are likely to be less concerned than other types about socializing, individuating, or bonding with their children, and more concerned with encouraging them to become free spirits with enough gumption to take off and sample the world's waiting pleasures.

The Negotiator Leader

Negotiating is a kind of bargaining or dealing in such a manner that the negotiator is able to resolve a strained and trying situation. Effective negotiators make do by using whatever is at hand at the moment, and to their advantage. It must be the opportunism of the SPs—always on the lookout for an edge—that sets them up as good negotiators. That's it: an edge. Artisans can spot things that give them an edge where others can't, at least not with the same ease and accuracy. By the way, that's why SPs make good trouble shooters in corporations and institutions, but more about this in Chapter 9. For now, suffice it to say that when taking on a leadership role, the Artisan has no peer in negotiating tense situations.

Matrix of Artisan Traits

The matrix below collects and highlights the terms used in this chapter to define the personality of the Artisans. For ease of comparison, I have placed these terms in parallel with those used to define the other three personalities.

The Traits of Temperament and Character

Communication Implementation Character	┌─ Concrete ─┐ Utilitarian **Artisan**	Cooperative **Guardian**	┌─ Abstract ─┐ Cooperative **Idealist**	Utilitarian **Rational**
Language	**Harmonic**	Associative	Inductive	Deductive
Referential	**Indicative**	Imperative	Interpretive	Categorical
Syntactical	**Descriptive**	Comparative	Metaphoric	Subjunctive
Rhetorical	**Heterodox**	Orthodox	Hyperbolic	Technical
Intellect	**Tactical**	Logistical	Diplomatic	Strategic
Directive Role	**Operator**	Administrator	Mentor	Coordinator
• Expressive Role	• **Promoter**	• Supervisor	• Teacher	• Fieldmarshal
• Reserved Role	• **Crafter**	• Inspector	• Counselor	• Mastermind
Informative Role	**Entertainer**	Conservator	Advocate	Engineer
• Expressive Role	• **Performer**	• Provider	• Champion	• Inventor
• Reserved Role	• **Composer**	• Protector	• Healer	• Architect
Interest				
Education	**Artcraft**	Commerce	Humanities	Sciences
Preoccupation	**Technique**	Morality	Morale	Technology
Vocation	**Equipment**	Materiel	Personnel	Systems
Orientation				
Present	**Practical**	Dutiful	Altruistic	Pragmatic
Future	**Optimistic**	Pessimistic	Credulous	Skeptical
Past	**Cynical**	Stoical	Mystical	Relativistic
Place	**Here**	Gateways	Pathways	Intersections
Time	**Now**	Yesterday	Tomorrow	Intervals
Self-Image				
Self-Esteem	**Artistic**	Dependable	Empathic	Ingenious
Self-Respect	**Audacious**	Beneficent	Benevolent	Autonomous
Self-Confidence	**Adaptable**	Respectable	Authentic	Resolute
Value				
Being	**Excited**	Concerned	Enthusiastic	Calm
Trusting	**Impulse**	Authority	Intuition	Reason
Yearning	**Impact**	Belonging	Romance	Achievement
Seeking	**Stimulation**	Security	Identity	Knowledge
Prizing	**Generosity**	Gratitude	Recognition	Deference
Aspiring	**Virtuoso**	Executive	Sage	Wizard
Social Role				
Mating	**Playmate**	Helpmate	Soulmate	Mindmate
Parenting	**Liberator**	Socializer	Harmonizer	Individuator
Leading	**Negotiator**	Stabilizer	Catalyst	Visionary

It might prove useful to take time to study this matrix and thumb back to it from time to time, in order to get a sure grip on the complex configuration of the Hedonic Artisan Personality, as well as to get a feel for its uniqueness and radical difference from the Proprietary Guardians, the Ethical Idealists, and the Dialectical Rationals.

Artisan Role Variants

These "Concrete Utilitarians" as I like to call them—Plato's Artisans, Aristotle's Hedonics, Galen's Sanguines, Myers's SPs—have a tightly configured personality, so that each trait of character entails the other traits. This means that Mother Nature does not permit Artisans, any more than other types, to pick and choose their traits. If their environment enables them to develop a given trait it can only be one that is predetermined by their temperament.

While it is useful to think of each of the four temperaments as a single, unified pattern of attitudes and actions, individual members of each temperament clearly differ from one another. Thus, all the Artisans seem to have a gift for tactical artistry, but some (the tough-minded SPs) are drawn to the directive role of Operator, while others (the friendly SPs) take up the informative or reporting role of Entertainer. These two divisions can be further broken down to reflect an expressive or a reserved social attitude, with the Operators tending to play the role variants of Promoter or Crafter, and the Entertainers playing Performer or Composer.

The Promoter [ESTP]

Promoting is the art of putting forward an enterprise and then of winning others to your side, persuading them have confidence in you and to go along with what you propose. Of all the Artisans, ESTPs seem especially able to advertise or publicize their endeavors in this way, and to maneuver others in the direction they want them to go. In a sense, they are able to operate people with much the same skill as ISTPs operate instruments, machines, vehicles, and other tools. It might be said that people are instruments in the hands of these Promoters, and that they play them artistically.

As a variant of Plato's Artisans and Aristotle's Hedonics, the ESTPs are little different from other SPs in most respects. Like all the Artisans they are concrete in their communication and utilitarian in their use of tools. They are interested in learning about arts and crafts, are preoccupied with technique, and work well with equipment. In orientation they tend to be practical, optimistic, cynical, and focused on the here and now. They want to be seen as artistic, audacious, and adaptable. Often excited, they trust their impulses, yearn for impact, seek sensation, prize generosity, and aspire to virtuosity. Intellectually, they are prone to practice tactics far more than logistics, strategy, and especially diplomacy. Further, with their tough-minded nature they tend to play the directive role of Operator more easily than the informative role of Entertainer, which takes a more friendly or soft-hearted character. And because of their expressiveness and sociability they prefer to be a Promoter boosting enterprises than an Crafter handling instruments. To visualize ESTP intellectual development consider the following graph which depicts the most probable profile of their tactical roles:

The Tactical Roles of the ESTP		
Promoter	**Operator**	
Crafter		
Performer	**Entertainer**	
Composer		**Promoter**

There are lots of Promoters, maybe ten or so percent of the population, and life is never dull around them. Witty, clever, and fun, they live with a theatrical flourish which makes even the most routine events seem exciting. Not that they waste much time on routine events. Promoters have a knack for knowing where the action is. They always seem to have tickets to the hot show or big game (or can get them when others can't), and they usually know the best restaurants, where the headwaiters are likely to call them by name. To be sure, ESTPs have a hearty appetite for the finer things of life, the best food, the best wine, expensive cars, and fashionable clothes. And they are extremely attentive to others and smooth in social circles, knowing many, many people by name, and knowing how to say just the right thing to most everyone they meet. None are as socially sophisticated as they, none as suave and polished—and none such master manipulators of the people around them.

Promoters are so engaging with people that they might seem to possess an unusual amount of empathy, when in fact this is not the case. Rather, they are uncanny at reading people's faces and observing their body language, hypersensitive to the tiniest nonverbal cues that give away the other's attitudes. ESTPs keep their eyes on their audience, ever on the lookout for signs of assent or dissent, and with nerves of steel they will use this information to achieve the ends they have in mind—which is to sell the customer in some way. Winning people over with this kind of brinkmanship might seem exhausting to others, but Promoters are exhilarated by working close to the edge. Indeed, a theme of seeking excitement through taking risks runs throughout their lives.

Promoters can be hard-nosed utilitarians, willing to do whatever it takes to achieve their goals, and it is this utilitarianism that allows them to be such capable troubleshooters and negotiators. Concerned more with what works than with traditions or moral niceties, they can keep their cool in crises and operate freely, since they do not stand on ceremony, do not worry much about justifying their actions, and are fully aware of all expedients that can be put to immediate use. Thus ESTPs are invaluable as hired gun administrators who can pull troubled companies or departments out of the red very quickly, and with style. Thus, too, they make the very best negotiators, willing to put anything and everything on the table, which gives them a tactical edge over opponents who might hold some asset or procedure as sacred and thus non-negotiable.

Promoters can be sharp entrepreneurs, able to swing deals and kick-start enterprises in a way no other type can—although they ordinarily have little patience with following through and mopping up. This impatience can obscure their extraordinary talents, since people lose sight of their contributions and focus on the little things they've left undone, criticizing their weaknesses rather than appreciating their strengths. Few companies or institutions use this type of Artisan as they should be used. But neither does this type always succeed when they strike out on their own, because their unwillingness to bother with follow-up details may cause an otherwise excellent project to fail. Whenever possible, ESTPs need careful, methodical assistants who will take care of completing their operations.

If the promotional, entrepreneurial capabilities of Promoters are used to constructive ends, an institution—or a nation—is fortunate for their presence. ESTPs are without peer as deal-makers, sales promoters, arbitrators, and negotiators, just as they make bold defense lawyers, aggressive industrialists and real estate developers, and flamboyant show-business producers. And Promoters have been some of America's most charismatic political leaders, including Andrew Jackson, Teddy Roosevelt, Franklin Roosevelt, John Kennedy, and Lyndon Johnson. On the other hand, if their desire for excitement is not met constructively, they may channel their energies into antisocial activities such as those of the con artist.

Although nothing is too good for their friends, Promoters are rarely interested in heartfelt, long-term commitments with their mates, and at times give their family responsibilities second priority. All relationships are essentially conditional for ESTPs, with their eye on what they have to gain by their investment. As long as there is a social or sexual payoff for them, they can be captivating mates, giving freely and generously to their spouses, and bringing fun and surprise to their relationships. Concerning matters of personal sympathy and family commitment, however, they can be less generous, and their mates may in time come to feel like possessions or negotiable commodities.

In their role as parents, ESTPs are energetic and spontaneous, much like their children. They will arrange lavish birthday parties for their children, with the latest toys and equipment in abundance. They will push their children to take up competitive sports and to play hard at them—"nice guys finish last" they say. And they are proud to have their children tackle exciting, even dangerous activities, surfing, skiing, racing, rock-climbing, and so on, and will often participate with them. However, while they entertain and play with their children, they can be impatient with weakness or timidity in their children, and are all too often unavailable for the personal chat or the quiet moment of sharing.

Charming, confident, popular, these tough, outgoing Artisans carry on amusing repartee with friends and colleagues, the laughter surrounding them as they recount from their endless supply of quips, anecdotes, and jokes. At the same time, these smooth Operators are usually something of a mystery to others. While they live in the moment and lend excitement—and unpredictability—to all their relationships, they rarely let anyone get really close to them. They have a low tolerance for anxiety and are apt to leave relationships that are filled with interpersonal tensions. Promoters understand well the maxim, "He who travels fastest, travels alone," although they are not likely to be lonely for long, since their boldness and sense of adventure tends to make ESTPs highly attractive to many other people.

The Crafter [ISTP]

The nature of the ISTPs is most clearly seen in their masterful operation of tools, equipment, machines, and instruments of all kinds. From microscopic drill to supersonic jet, from tiny scalpel to giant crane, a tool is any piece of equipment that extends or varies human powers—vehicles, lifters, cutters, and weapons are just four of the many categories of the tools that surround us. Most of us use tools in some capacity, of course, but these Crafters (as much as ten percent of the population) are the true masters of tool work, with an innate ability to command tools and to become expert at all the crafts requiring hand tool skills. Even from an early age they are drawn to tools as to a magnet—tools fall into their hands demanding use, and they must manipulate them. Indeed, if a given tool is operated with a precision that defies belief, that operator is likely an ISTP.

As a variant of Plato's Artisans and Aristotle's Hedonics, the ISTPs are little different from other SPs in most respects. Like all the Artisans they are concrete in the way they use words and utilitarian in the way they use tools. They are interested in learning about arts and crafts, are preoccupied with technique, and work well with equipment. In orientation they tend to be practical, optimistic, cynical, and focused on the here and now. They want to be seen as artistic, audacious, and adaptable. Often excited, they trust their impulses, yearn for impact, seek sensation, prize generosity, and aspire to virtuosity. Intellectually, they are prone to practice tactics far more than logistics, strategy, and especially diplomacy. Further, with their tough-minded nature they tend to play the directive role of Operator more readily than the informative role of Entertainer, which takes a friendly or fond-hearted character. And owing to their reserve and love of solitude they seem more drawn to be a Crafter wielding instruments than a Promoter boosting enterprises. To visualize ISTP intellectual development consider the following graph depicting the most probable profile of their tactical roles:

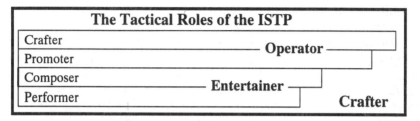

The Crafter's tool artisanship is masterful, but it is also born of impulse rather than of deliberate purpose. For these Artisans, action is more enjoyable—and more effective—if it is unplanned, serving no purpose other than the doing. ISTPs prefer their actions to be spontaneous and unfettered; they want to follow their own lead, and to have their own impulses not subject to rules, regulations, or laws. Indeed, Crafters can be fiercely insubordinate, seeing hierarchy and authority as unnecessary and even irksome. It is not so much a matter of going against regulations as it is simply ignoring them, and not allowing them to influence execution. ISTPs must be free to do their thing, varying each next move as the urge strikes them, and they are proud of their ability to make the next move skillfully. In a sense, Crafters do not work with their tools, but play with them on impulse and not on schedule. If an externally imposed schedule coincides with their impulse, fine; if not, so much the worse for the schedule.

Crafters also seek recreation on impulse, taking off at any time just because they feel like it to play with their toys. The surgeon shifts his schedule in order to get in a round of golf, or the carpenter is late to the job site because the surf was up or the fish were biting. Such urges to escape routine and to play can be irresistible and overpowering, and we are advised not to try to stop the ISTP who feels like doing something.

Not only impulsive, Crafters are fearless in their play, risking themselves again and again, despite frequent injury. Of all the types, these Artisans are most likely to pit themselves, or their technique, against chance or odds. There can be no end to the ways they seek thrills in their recreation, daring disaster for the fun of it. They thrive on excitement, especially in the form of fast motion—racing, sky diving, or water-skiing, for instance. This desire for the rush of peak experiences also makes them more subject to boredom than any other type, their need for stimulation driving them to faster and faster pace. Strangely, however, Crafters are not bored while doing their thing, even though there may be long stretches when nothing happens, as during travel, surfing, hunting, or fishing.

In general these hard-bitten, soft-spoken Artisans communicate through action, and show little interest in developing verbal skills. Their lack of expressiveness makes them seem like loners at school and on the job, and even though they hang around their own kind in play, they base their companionship on their mastery of tools, and their conversation is sparse and terse. Indeed, this lack of interest in communication is often mistaken by physicians and teachers as "learning disability" or "dyslexia," both questionable notions of medics and academicians. Let ISTPs handle equipment of any complexity and power and see how fast they learn to use it, and how precisely they speak of it.

With their concrete, artisan intelligence, Crafters are not in the least interested in the clerical, humanities, and science curricula that abound in modern American schools, and this often gets them into trouble, because they refuse to do their assignments. Ordinary school work is, after all, mere preparation for something the ISTPs figure they're never going to do anyway. Crafters do not wish to prepare—for anything—and they are careful to make this clear to their would-be instructors. All too often this refusal to sit still and cooperate gets them labeled as "minimally brain damaged," or "hyperactive," or as having "attention deficit disorder," and they are prescribed stimulant narcotics to drug them into apparent obedience. Such labels are purely fictional, and this experimental narcotherapy is likely criminal. Certainly ISTPs are active, but only in their stubborn insistence upon getting to do something interesting, something that allows them to test their mettle. They'll work in a tool-centered curriculum.

In spite of poor schooling many Crafters manage to develop their tactical skills on their own. Gifted with their hands and eyes, Crafters make wonderful tradespeople, carpenters, mechanics, plumbers, furniture makers, weavers, jewelry smiths, and so on. They are the very best pilots of all manner of vehicles, trucks, trains, planes, boats, and they also make incomparable surgeons, artists, athletes, musicians—and warriors. Born hunters, Crafters are from an early age fascinated by weapons of all kinds, and soon learn to wield their weapons with lethal virtuosity, taking pride in their prowess. Warriors good and evil can be seen as weapons artists, not only the marksmen among soldiers and police, but also the mob hit man and the gunslinger of the American West. This is not to say that all warriors are ISTPs, or that all ISTPs are weapons experts, but that the weapons virtuoso is more frequently than not an ISTP.

Crafters are hard to get to know. On the one hand, they are egalitarian and can be fiercely loyal to their friends, teammates, and sidekicks. They will give their friends the shirt off their back, and will often give generously of their time and tool skills to help their friends with building projects or mechanical jobs, house remodeling, for example, or repairing their cars or boats. On the other hand, these Artisans are lone wolves who will not be tied to schedules and commitments, and thus they cannot always be counted on to follow through on their offers of assistance. They might show up, or they might not, as the impulse strikes them, and their friends are best off not expecting them until they see them.

This combination of generosity and waywardness is especially difficult for the members of a Crafter's family. ISTPs can treat their mates royally, with ardent attention and beautiful gifts of their handiwork, and they can be great buddies with their children and patiently teach them their tool skills. But they can also forget their family and go off with their friends for extended periods of time, taking a road trip from family responsibilities. These Crafters need their freedom to seek adventure, flying their plane, sailing their boat, racing their motorcycle, and mates who wish to keep them happy are wise to give them a long leash.

The Performer [ESFP]

Performing is putting on a show or demonstration of some kind to entertain others, and ESFPs are the natural performers among the types, people for whom it can truly be said "all the world's a stage." Playful and fun-loving, these expressive Artisans' primary social interest lies in stimulating those around them, arousing their senses and their pleasurable emotions—charming them, in a sense, to cast off their concerns and lighten up. Such Performers radiate warmth and festivity, and whether on the job, with friends, or with their families, they are able to lift others' spirits with their contagious good humor and their irrepressible joy of living.

As a variant of Plato's Artisans and Aristotle's Hedonics, the ESFPs are little different from other SPs in most respects. Like all the Artisans they are concrete in their communication and utilitarian in their use of tools. They are interested in learning about arts and crafts, are preoccupied with technique, and work well with equipment. In orientation they tend to be practical, optimistic, cynical, and focused on the here and now. They want to be seen as artistic, audacious, and adaptable. Often excited, they trust their impulses, yearn for impact, seek sensation, prize generosity, and aspire to virtuosity. Intellectually, they are prone to practice tactics far more than logistics, strategy, and especially diplomacy. Further, with their friendly nature they tend to play the informative role of Entertainer over the tough-minded, directive role of Operator. And with their outgoing expressiveness they lean more toward pleasing others as a Performer than as a Composer. To visualize ESFP intellectual development consider the following graph depicting the most likely profile of their tactical roles:

The Tactical Abilities of the ESFP		
Performer	Entertainer	
Composer		
Promoter	Operator	
Crafter		Performer

Performers are plentiful, something over ten per cent of the population, and that is fortunate, because they bring joy to so many of us. They love the excitement of playing to an audience, and they try to generate a sense of showtime wherever they are. They aren't comfortable being alone, and seek the company of others whenever possible—which they usually find, for they make wonderful playmates. Lively, witty conversationalists, they always seem to know the latest jokes and stories, and are quick with wisecracks and wordplay—nothing is so serious or sacred that it can't be made fun of. Performers also like to live in the fast lane, and seem up on latest fads of dress, food, drink, and entertainment, the chic new fashion, the in nightclub, the hot new musical group. Energetic and uninhibited, ESFPs create a mood of eat, drink, and be merry wherever they go, and life around them can have a continual party-like atmosphere.

The Performers' talent for enjoying life is healthy for the most part, though it also makes them more subject to temptations than the other types. ESFPs are inclined to be impulsive and self-indulgent, which makes them vulnerable to seduction, giving in easily to the wishes of others, or to the desire of the moment. Pleasure seems to be an end in itself for the Performers, and variety is the spice of life, and so they are open to trying almost anything that promises them a good time, not always giving enough thought to the consequences. Most often, they will do what they feel like in the moment rather than what is good for them in the long run, chalking it up to experience, or blaming someone else, if things don't turn out well.

Performers do quite well when life is easy for them, and they don't let themselves get too caught up in what they call "sticky" situations. Their tolerance for anxiety is the lowest of all the types, and they will avoid worries and troubles by ignoring the unhappiness of a situation as long as possible. "Always look on the bright side," is their motto, and if forced to endure a tense, complicated situation (at work, for example, or in a love relationship), they will not make waves or put up a show of resistance. They will let themselves appear outwardly concerned—and then go their own way to do what they enjoy.

ESFPs are the most generous of all the types, and second only to the ISFPs in kindness. They haven't a mean or stingy bone in their body—what's theirs is yours—and they seem to have little idea of saving or conserving. These Artisans view life as an eternal cornucopia from which flows an endless supply of pleasures that require no effort on their part to create or to insure. Essentially communal in outlook, they give what they have to one and all without expectation of reward, just as they love freely, and without expecting anything in return.

Performers are emotionally expressive and affectionate people, virtually unable to hide their feelings or hold their tongue. With their emotions so close to the surface—their heart forever on their sleeve—they tend to fall in love easily, impetuously, and always as if for the first time. Intent on pleasing everybody, Performers can appear fickle, even promiscuous, to other types, when in truth they are simply, and rather innocently, sharing with others from the bounty of life.

Although they are often popular with their classmates because of their good-hearted clowning and cutting up, Performers are not deeply interested in school or scholastic pursuits, caring little about preparation, schedules, and grades. Unlike the ISTPs, ESFPs are not usually hostile to their teachers, and will go along with the classroom agenda in a friendly way, though the work they hand in rarely shows the kind of effort the teacher hopes for. Performers put up with school, finding fun where they can, in sports, in music, in the school play, and especially in fooling around with their friends. But, as with all the Artisans, the traditional school is largely a waste of time for Performers, who want knowledge only so that they can do practical things in the here and now.

In the matter of career, ESFPs enjoy entertaining people and are thus drawn to the performing arts, thriving on the excitement of being on-stage, in the limelight. But even in less glamorous pursuits, they prefer active people jobs over solitary, technical occupations, and thus they avoid science and engineering and gravitate toward business, where they are apt at selling, particularly at selling tangible goods. Performers can be extremely effective real estate agents, for example, because they are continuously and effortlessly scanning both clients and listings, gathering information to help them fit people to properties. These Artisans love working with people, and are outstanding at public relations, their sociability and adaptability making them easy to get along with and fun to be around. They can be effective teachers, especially at the elementary level, and are also good at working with people in crisis, a talent which often leads them into social work, where they are very sensitive to the pain and suffering of others, particularly small children. ESFPs are childlike themselves, and perhaps this is why they seem so finely attuned to children's feelings.

Performers—sociable and outspoken Artisans—make exciting and entertaining (though somewhat unpredictable) mates and parents, which may give their families a good deal of anxiety. They love to spend money on fun things (like clothes, jewelry, sports cars, vacation trips, and so on), and they will impulsively use up their credit card limits, and more, without giving much thought to family necessities. ESFPs are happiest when their home is filled with people all having a good time, led by the ESFP who weaves his or her way through the party, welcoming, teasing, laughing. In such a generally festive atmosphere, family problems will not be allowed to make their appearance. Performers prefer to walk by the graveyard whistling, often refusing to recognize their mate's dissatisfactions or their child's need for stability. Performers make warm, generous, loving friends to their mates and children, but should not be expected to take these relationships much more seriously than that.

The Composer [ISFP]

Although ISFPs excel in what are called the "fine arts," composing must not be thought of as only writing music, but as bringing into synthesis any aspect of the world of the senses. More than the other Artisans, Composers have a sure grasp of what fits and what doesn't fit in any and all kinds of artistic works, and so when an especially gifted painter, sculptor, choreographer, film director, song writer, playwright, poet, novelist, chef, decorator, or fashion designer shows up, he or she is likely an ISFP.

As a variant of Plato's Artisans and Aristotle's Hedonics, the ISFPs are little different from other SPs in most respects. Like all the Artisans they are concrete in their communication and utilitarian in their use of tools. They are interested in learning about arts and crafts, are preoccupied with technique, and work well with equipment. In orientation they tend to be practical, optimistic, cynical, and focused on the here and now. They want to be seen as artistic, audacious, and adaptable. Often excited, they trust their impulses, yearn for impact, seek sensation, prize generosity, and aspire to virtuosity. Intellectually, they are prone to practice tactics far more than logistics, strategy, and especially diplomacy. Further, with their friendly nature they tend to play the informative role of Entertainer more comfortably than the tough-minded, directive role of Operator. And with their quiet reserve they prefer playing the part of a Composer than a Performer. To visualize ISFP intellectual development consider the following graph that depicts the most probable profile of their tactical roles:

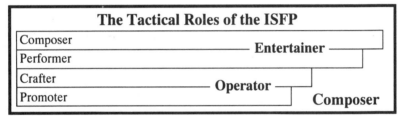

Composers are just as plentiful as the other Artisans, say nine or ten per cent of the population. And like the other Artisans, they have a special talent for tactical artistry, such talent differing radically from that possessed by Idealists, Rationals, and Guardians. As the word 'tactical' implies, Artisans know their way around in the world, their senses finely tuned to concrete reality. However, while the Crafters are attuned to the tool and its uses, the Composers are attuned to sensory variation, which gives them an extraordinary ability to work with the slightest nuances of color, tone, texture, aroma, and flavor. This observant sensuality seems to come naturally to the ISFPs, as if inborn.

While a few of these Artisans become world famous, Composers in general are very difficult to observe, making this type probably the least understood of all. Perhaps such misunderstanding comes from their tendency not to express themselves verbally, but through action. Like the ISTPs, ISFPs are usually not interested in developing facility in speaking or conversation. The spoken word, after all, is not as handy as the tool, and Composers prefer to have their fingers on their compositional tools and through them feel the pulse of life. That pulse must be felt—by touch, in the muscles, in the eyes, in the ears. This insistence on the senses being so closely attuned to concrete reality can, in some ISFPs, occasion a breach with language, such that they give up rather easily in their attempts to express themselves verbally. But this reluctance in speech is not so much a lack of ability as disinterest. If Composers find a medium of expression, some art form, then they will express their character quite eloquently via that medium. If not, it simply doesn't come out, and no one knows them, their reticence leaving their character all but invisible. Again, in those rare cases where remarkable skill is achieved, such as in the virtuoso, ISFPs can become celebrities, but their nature is still far from visible.

Although Composers often put long, lonely hours into their compositions, we must not assume that they are working on their art in the sense of careful planning and dutiful execution. On close observation, ISFPs prove to be just as impulsive as the other Artisans. Indeed, they covet their impulses and see them as the center of their lives. They do not wait to act or to consider their moves, for to wait is to see their impulse wither and die; rather, they live intensely in the here and now, and as gracefully as possible, with little or no planning or preparation. Submergence in their artistry is not preparation for something later, and neither is it artful play, such as Crafters engage in with their tools. Composers are seized by the act of artistic composition, as if caught up in a whirlwind. The act is their master, not the reverse, and, in a sense, the doing is elicited by the action itself. ISFPs paint or sculpt, they dance or skate, they write melodies or recipes—or whatever—simply because they must. They climb the mountain because it is there.

Captured as they are by whatever actions are underway, Composers seem oblivious to the fatigue, and even the pain, that accompanies many of their activities. It is not that they are hardened to these difficulties as much as it is that, absorbed and excited, and wholly engaged by an action, they simply do not notice the difficulties. In this the ISFP is similar to other Artisans and different from all the other types.

This ability to lose themselves in action accounts for the spectacular individual works some Composers are capable of, and yet they also have a social side. The ISFP is the kindest of all the types, with only the ESFP as a near competitor. Here is unconditional kindness carried to its most extreme form. In addition, Composers are especially sensitive to the pain and suffering of others, and with a sympathetic impulsivity they give freely to the sufferer. Some have a remarkable way with young children, almost as if there were a bond of mutual sympathy and trust. In some instances a similar bond may be seen between the ISFP and animals, even wild animals. Many Composers have an instinctive longing for the pastoral, the bucolic, the out-of-doors, the wilds, and nature seems to welcome them.

Of course, all ISFPs have not been and need not be artists in the narrow sense of the word. Art, broadly conceived, is any action the next move of which is a free variable, and thus Composers have a lot of leeway in choice of occupation, especially if they don't drop out of school early (though a great number do, since the school offers little that is of interest to them or that challenges their special talents). These ISFPs do quite well in business, particularly in decorative design (from automobiles to book covers) and purchasing (selecting a line of clothing, home furnishings, or gift shop items). With their kindness, they make wonderful nurses, and they can satisfy their love of nature by working in forestry, in landscape design and gardening, and even in veterinary medicine. Composers also make excellent teachers, especially of a school's arts curriculum, subjects such as drawing, music, drama, photography, and so on. Notice that all of these careers allow them a great deal of freedom and spontaneity. It is a sad day indeed when the ISFP chooses work wherein the operations are fixed by rule or iron-clad necessity. To be happy and productive they must choose free, variable actions and be rewarded for doing them.

These friendly and soft-spoken Artisans tend to seek a safe anchorage in their home and family. While they enjoy their personal freedom as much as any Artisan, and will roam when the opportunity presents itself, they seem to value the stability and patience of a dutiful spouse (most often an SJ Guardian of some sort) to help keep them from wandering off too far and for too long. Conflict in such marriages is almost inevitable, but Composers will put up with a lot more interpersonal tension than the other Artisans, hanging in there to keep the family intact—then will leave when the children are grown and go off to paint in the mountains. With their children, as with their mates, Composers are great friends and play-mates, though they can be hard to get to know, and their reserve can be a barrier to close relations.

4

Guardians

If you speak of solid information and sound judgment, Colonel Washington is undoubtedly the greatest man present.

Thus Patrick Henry proclaimed his support for George Washington to be Commander of the Virginia militia, but such words would ring true throughout Washington's long career in public life.

Washington's first great feat was leading the rag-tag Continental army to victory over the powerful British expeditionary forces in the American colonies. To achieve such a stunning success, he had to hold his tiny army of volunteers together for eight desperate years, always under unbelievably harsh conditions. Further, he had to avoid engaging the British in open battle, or if he did engage them, to do so only on his own terms. Fortunately for his country, General Washington's abilities were not those of a tactical commander, such as Andy Jackson, or of a strategic commander, such as Dwight Eisenhower. Washington was instead a brilliant quartermaster with highly developed logistical skills, and what concerned him was equipping and sheltering his soldiers, and as far as possible keeping them out of harm's way. He knew full well that he was out-numbered, out-provisioned, out-gunned, and very much out-generaled. And he knew that, despite his prodigious efforts to supply his troops, his men would have to fight in rags, and on empty stomachs and bare feet. So his task was to conserve his meager forces and resources, letting the British wear themselves out chasing after him. In this way he managed to make the Revolutionary War a guerrilla war, a war of harassment and retreat, that was too wearisome and expensive for British taste.

Freeing the colonies from the British was not Washington's only achievement. He also saw it as his duty to oversee the United States of America's ascent into democracy. And so, for eight more difficult and discouraging years as the first President of the United States, Washington struggled with internecine disputes within his cabinet and among the states. It would appear that he and he alone kept the new nation from regressing into monarchy or dictatorship, as had all previously liberated regions in Europe and Asia.

In the mid 1970s I referred to Myers's SJs as "Epimetheans," after

Epimetheus, the Greek god of duty. During the eighties, with a powerful nudge from my editor, Stephen Montgomery, it became clear that the Greek goddess Demeter was a far better choice. Demeter was worshipped in autumn, and her duty was to protect the harvest and to insure the careful provisioning of home and family as the year turned toward the long months of winter. Even Demeter's name suggests the logistical intelligence of the "Guardians" (as I now call them) in both its essential forms: first, Administering, or measuring stores and meting out portions, keeping track of quantities, seeing to it that everything's in its proper place, and that everyone's doing what they're supposed to be doing; and second, Conserving, or carefully husbanding goods and services, meeting the needs of others and keeping them from want or harm.

Of late I have come to think of the Guardian as well represented by the Beaver. The only other animal that comes close to the beaver as totem for the Guardian temperament is the squirrel. Although the squirrel is diligent about storing nuts and other edibles for a time when food is scarce, the beaver is an indefatigable worker for the good of the whole woodland community. First the beaver dams up a stream, creating a pond in which to build a safe house for protecting its family and for storing bark to eat during the winter months. But the beaver also stands guard over the pond, ever on the lookout for lurking predators, and, detecting one, spanks the water with its broad tail to warn its family and neighbors of the impending danger. What better totemic symbol of the Guardian temperament?

Looking back, I must say that most of my friends have been and still are Guardians. At school all through the twelve grades such was the case. And this was true even during flight training in World War II, for I was invariably drawn to the Guardians rather than the Artisans, who were too reckless for my taste. In my own fighter squadron my buddy and wingman was a Guardian. And when working for public schools after the war my friends and tennis partners were invariably Guardian administrators. Though diametrically opposite in temperament from me, I admire Guardians for their logistical capabilities (my short suit) and for their abiding social interest and constant dependability. I like them and appreciate them for what they are, the pillars of society.

Plato's Guardians

The word 'Guardian' is the English equivalent of the Greek word *'pistike,'* which means "those with trustworthy convictions." In Plato's *Republic* the social function of Guardians was to keep watch over the activities as well as the attitudes of the people in their circle. Centered in the world of visible and tangible things, Plato's Guardians were known for relying on common sense and for holding morally correct beliefs, and they were alert to both the needs and the perils of others.

Plato's pupil, Aristotle, said that some men find happiness not in "sensuous living" (*hêdonê*), or in "ethical musing" (*ethikê*), or in "theoretical dialogue" (*dialogikê*), but in "a life of money-making," in "a life of gain," or in the acquisition and control of "property" (*propráietari*). So in Aristotle's view the social role of Plato's Guardians is that of the Proprietary.

Galen called these Guardians the "Melancholics" because their temperament was dominated by black bile or gall, causing them to expect unfavorable outcomes, and making them glum, doleful, and solemn. Galen's interests, however, lay on the dark side of temperament, on the four negative extremes, such that he regarded the somber Melancholics as different from, but no worse than, the over-optimistic Sanguines (Artisans), the irascible Cholerics (Idealists), or the taciturn Phlegmatics (Rationals).

Paracelsus patterned this sort of person on the Gnome, one of a fabled race of dwarflike creatures who live in underground caves and hollows, where they look after treasures. Tales of Gnomes such as Santa Claus and his helpers, together with tales of the Niebelungs, the Hobbits of the J.R.R. Tolkien tales, and Snow White's Seven Dwarves tell much of the character of Gnomes. Also, the Leprechaun in Irish folklore is an elfin creature who can reveal hidden treasure to someone who catches him. Besides being treasurers, or keepers of whatever is of most value, Gnomes are thought to be well-versed in pithy or "gnomic" old sayings such as adages, aphorisms, maxims, morals, precepts, proverbs, and truisms, and feel it helpful to offer them to those who seek their advice.

Adickes's name for Plato's Guardian was the "Traditional," identifying those who believe in and take part in the time-honored practices of their social groups. Adickes thought of his Traditionals, like his Innovatives (the Artisans), as "heteronomous" or "other-centered" beings, but whose heteronomy took the form of careful observance of tradition, custom, ceremony, and ritual at home and in the community.

Spränger considered the Guardian as the "Economic" type, and thus very similar to Aristotle's Proprietary, economics pertaining as it does to the production, development, and management of material wealth. It might be said that in Spränger's view the Economic type tries to find security in money and property, and so has what I like to call a "Security Seeking Personality."

Kretschmer was first to take a careful look at the dark side of character, and he named the Guardians "Depressives," even on occasion using Galen's term 'Melancholics.' Thus he echoed Galen in seeing them as somber, doleful, and solemn, but Kretschmer was also suggesting much more, that the kind of irrational behavior that befalls some Guardians is a matter of temperament rather than a matter of choice. If Guardians are forced by untoward circumstances to become downcast for no apparent reason, it is because they are beset by strong negative feelings that overwhelm them and render them immobile and helpless.

Like Kretschmer, Fromm examined both sides of character, negative as well as positive. He called the Guardians the "Hoarding" type, considering hoarding a bad thing to do, but on the positive side he praised them for their steadfastness and for being "careful," "cautious," "composed," "economical," "imperturbable," "loyal," "methodical," "orderly," "patient," "practical," and "reserved."

Last, we come to Myers's contribution to the study of the Guardian character. As mentioned earlier, she named them the "Sensory Judging" types—"SJs"—and said of them that they are "conservative," "consistent," "dependable," "detailed," "factual," "hard-working," "painstaking," "patient," "persevering," "routinized," "sensible," "stable," "thorough," "undistractable," and "unimpulsive." This is a very clear-cut pattern of action and attitude, quite different from the SPs, and as will be shown, starkly different from NFs and NTs. Though apparently unaware of the contributions of her predecessors Myers was clearly able to identify the more salient traits that characterize Plato's Guardians.

The Concrete Cooperators

These different views of Plato's Guardians, no matter what they're called, all have something in common, namely they all suggest that this type is concrete in thought and speech and cooperative in implementing goals. Thus, in beginning our consideration of the habits of action and attitude of the SJ Guardians, let's look at their quadrant in a matrix of character. As shown, the foundation of the SJ character, setting them apart unmistakably from the other personalities, is their unique combination of concrete word usage with cooperative tool usage—and so I call them the "Concrete Cooperators."

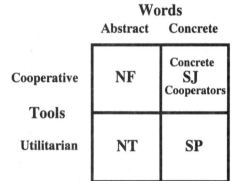

| | Words | |
	Abstract	Concrete
Cooperative	NF	Concrete SJ Cooperators
Tools		
Utilitarian	NT	SP

Concrete Word Usage

Like their Artisan cousins, Guardians talk for the most part about the concrete particulars they observe in their material or social surroundings. They might listen politely to conversation on theoretical or fanciful topics, but they tend not to respond in kind and will shift to more concrete things to talk about, more solid and sensible topics, such as goods and services, food and clothing, credits and debits, prices and wages, gains and losses, transportation and recreation, weather and shelter, accidents and disasters, rich and poor, famous and infamous, radio, TV, and the movies. Of course they can and will discuss abstractions, but lacking much interest in them, they are inclined to shift the conversation away from the abstract to the concrete.

Guardian speech is coherent in the associative sense, which means they move from one topic to another associatively rather than deductively or inductively, as do Rationals and Idealists. When Guardians are reminded of something, however distant from or unrelated to the topic at hand, they mention it. And often this reminds others of something else, who then mention that. And so the conversation goes from topic to topic, by contiguity rather than implication, like a row of dominoes, each toppling the next. Such conversations are interesting to all who participate, since each is speaking of what is pertinent to his or her own life, but no single topic is pursued at length, and issues, if surfaced, tend not to get settled. SJs are very good at this sort of small talk, something their opposites, the NTs, are very poor at—which puts the SJs firmly in the social driver's seat and the NTs in the trailer.

On topics that interest them Guardians are able to store an enormous fund of facts, which they will call up and, again, freely associate in conversation. They can remember people's names, birthdays, the names of their friends' parents and children, how those children are doing at school, who their relatives' friends are, who's gotten what job, who's recently been born or has died (when, and of what), the date, time, and location of family, social, or civic events, and so on, one bit of information easily calling forth another.

This is concrete information, concerning specific persons, products, times, and places, and lending itself to comparative value (this better than that) and amount (too much, not enough). It is the storage, retrieval, and effortless association of such data that makes Guardians the most comfortable at conversation of all the types.

Besides being associative and comparative, Guardian speech is predominantly orthodox. SJs are ever wary of putting on airs or getting fancy in what they say. So they tend to use a rather conventional vocabulary and phrasing, often throwing in old sayings, proverbs, and adages (particularly about value and amount), such as "a penny saved is a penny earned," "a stitch in time saves nine," "one bad apple spoils the barrel," or "it's either feast or famine." Guardians also use words and sentences common to the area they call home. Harry Truman, for instance, grew up in a rural setting, and always considered himself a hometown boy. Not surprisingly he was well-known for his folksy comments. When in 1945 Franklin Roosevelt died in office, and Truman suddenly found himself President of the United States, he told newsmen that he felt like "a load of hay" had fallen on him. History has shown that the feisty Truman was up to the job, indeed thrived under its enormous responsibilities. And he expressed his satisfaction in true Guardian style when he admitted that being President "is an all day and nearly all night job," but that "just between you and me and the gatepost, I like it."

At the same time, Guardian speech is often laced with admonition. SJs are inclined to warn others of possible danger, whether of hurting themselves or others—"be careful, you'll hurt yourself." They are also inclined to caution others about the danger of committing moral transgression—"It wouldn't be right to do that." And when their warnings are ignored they are the most likely of all to chide or reprove the transgressor, for they are reluctant to let others get away with much.

Guardians usually avoid showy hand gestures when they speak. But when they do get animated out come the hands: the index finger wags in warning, or the fist rises in front of them—not the square, menacing fist of the SPs, but a fist with the thumb atop the curled index finger, as if holding the reins and driving a team of horses. And perhaps most familiar of all, SJs will bring one or both hands swiftly down in a chopping motion, to emphasize their statements or to cut off further discussion, something Truman himself did when he summed up the responsibility of the Presidency: "The buck stops here."

Cooperative Tool Usage

Civilization is a cluster of cities, and cities are clusters of tools. Streets, sidewalks, buildings, and conveyances are all tools. And the millions of instruments, implements, and machines in those buildings, on those streets, and in those conveyances are also tools. Now, wherever there are tools there must be rules that govern their use. Our inclination can be either to cooperate with these rules or to go our own way, and SJs are very much on the side of cooperation. For example, SJs believe we should park on the right side of the street even if the left side is empty, stop at red lights when there is no other traffic, signal when turning even if there's no one to signal to, and on and on. Cooperation, compliance, conformity, obedience: these attitudes toward the rules loom larger in the consciousness of Guardians than any other temperament.

Indeed, Guardians can regard the Artisans' utilitarian style—do whatever it takes to get the job done—as somehow anti-social and irresponsible. No one is permitted to ignore the rules merely to have fun or just to speed things up. Ignoring the rules might work for a while, but that way is the road to ruin. Cooperation is the safer way, and this requires giving up one's selfish concerns and working with others—mutual conformity to mutual agreements long held—else there will surely be chaos. Let us all cooperate with one another in pursuit of common goals, says the Guardian, for in the long run discipline and teamwork get us where we want to go.

Guardians work hard to make and enforce the laws that govern action, insisting that only by establishing and obeying rules and regulations can we hope to maintain civil order, and thus safeguard our homes, communities, and businesses. The other types, though they may be grateful that somebody is keeping order, are not vitally interested in either rule making or rule enforcing, and so are quite willing to leave this task to the ever-vigilant Guardians. In Myersian terms, the SPs, NTs, and even the NFs, are content to let the SJs run the show in this area. It is fortunate indeed that most

Guardians seek out the responsibility of command, and it should come as no surprise that nearly half of the Presidents of the United States have been Guardians, and in all probability most high ranking officers in the American military and CEOs of American corporations have Guardian personalities.

But even when not in the White House, the Pentagon, or the board room, Guardians become members of university rules committees and community review boards, of government regulatory agencies and public watchdog groups, of state licensing departments and panels on industry standards. SJs also take pride in serving on grand juries and disciplinary bodies, not to mention seeking careers as police officers and customs officers, as bailiffs, prosecutors, and as judges. And Guardians come well-equipped for all of these activities. Artisans might be known for having highly discriminating senses, but some Guardian senses are just as acute when it comes to observing the rules. SJs know what the rules say, where the lines are drawn, and with a cocked ear and a sharp eye they are able to detect the smallest hint of non-compliance, the slightest degree of deviation, violation, or transgression.

The Guardians' grasp of regulation is exceeded only by their faith in regulation as the cornerstone of society. SJs have confidence that legal authority is the only proper means of sanctioning action or solving problems, and indeed, the numerous laws, bylaws, codes, ordinances, statutes, and charters found in every community or institution exist for the Guardian as the best hope of maintaining civil order.

Moreover, Guardians believe in officially registered ownership of real property. The SJ does not agree with the SP that possession is nine tenths of the law. On the contrary, law for the SJ is the only trustworthy basis of possession. Illegal possession—even excessive indebtedness—is high on the SJ's list of evils, while rightful ownership is something to be deeply respected. In fact, we move much closer to understanding the Guardians if we can see the strongly regulatory basis for their outlook on doing and not-doing, on having and not-having.

Such confidence in the rule of law seems to find a natural home in Guardians, readily absorbed into their very bones, as Supreme Court Justice William Brennan admits:

Q: You seem to possess an abiding faith that the most difficult problems are susceptible to legal resolution.
A: I certainly believe so. We must never give up trying, because how are we going to have an ordered society unless the problems are redressable somehow by law?
Q: Where do you think that faith of yours in the law comes from?
A: I can only suggest, I don't know if by osmosis, but I surely came away from law school with that....It is what is so magnificent about law.

The Logistical Intellect

Logistics is the procurement, distribution, service, and replacement of material goods. Logistics is vital to the success of any institution—a business, a household, a school, an army—and Guardians can be enormously creative in seeing to it that the right personnel have the right supplies in the right place at the right time to get the job done. Even though SJs can develop skills in the other three spheres of activity, tactics, strategy, and diplomacy, it is much easier and enjoyable for them to practice and thus to develop their logistical skills.

While Artisans have an eye for artistic variation, Guardians care about being reliable, particularly in the maintenance and continuity of materiel. In other words, SJs are less interested in fitting things together in new ways than in holding things together as they are. Although new products and procedures might not be immoral or illegal, they must be viewed with a measure of suspicion, for they introduce change, and change for the Guardian is unsettling. The SJ knows as well as others that change is inevitable, necessary, and even, on occasion, desirable; but it should be resisted when it is at the expense of old standby products and time-tested ways of the institutions that have served us well. Better that change occur through slow evolution than by sudden revolution.

When Harry Truman became President, for example, he had no intention of following in the Artisan Franklin D. Roosevelt's footsteps. Truman quickly stepped back from many of FDR's quick-fix, budget-busting New Deal social programs and proposed a more fiscally responsible plan he called the "Fair Deal." "I want to keep my feet on the ground," Truman said; "I don't want any experiments; the American people have been through a lot of experiments and they want a rest from experiments."

Truman was certainly no ordinary Guardian, but the talents he showed as President (as well as in his earlier jobs as mail clerk, railroad timekeeper, and storekeeper) show clearly the Guardian's abiding interest in working with materiel, both in administering and conserving, regulating and supporting.

Interest, Practice, Skill

Skills are acquired by practice. No practice, no skill; much practice, much skill. Any skill will wither on the vine and gradually fade away in the degree that it is starved of practice, and the same skill will increase precisely in the degree that it is given exercise in practice. The neural cell is no different from the muscle cell in this. Use it or Lose it is Nature's inviolable law.

In addition, there is a feedback relation between interest and ability. We improve in doing things we're interested in doing, and have greater interest in things we do well. Interest reinforces skill, skill reinforces interest, and neither seems to be the starting point. So the Guardians' lifelong interest in logistical action fuels their daily exercise of logistical skills, and as logistical skill increases so then does interest in it, precisely and exclusively measured by the amount of practice.

Now, in a sense every individual has not one but four IQs, and it is virtually impossible for one person to develop all four of his or her capabilities equally. The kind of operation practiced most develops most, while that practiced least develops least. Nothing preventing, Guardians instinctively practice logistical operations far more and far earlier than tactical, diplomatic, and particularly strategic operations, and therefore end up with logistical intelligence outstripping the others by a wide margin. In other words, while SJs practice logistics early in life, they don't get around to exercising their sense of strategy until it becomes necessary to do so, if ever. Of course, circumstances can sometimes move Guardians to engage in those activities that are not so natural to them, and with lots of practice (especially as children) they can develop the other abilities, becoming quite the diplomat with other people, learning to spot immediate tactical advantage, and even showing a good deal of skill in their short suit of long-range strategic planning, such as shown by General Omar Bradley in World War II.

Note that in the graph below the Guardians tend to do better at logistics than at diplomacy and tactics, and that their strategic capabilities lag far behind. Logistics comes easy, strategy not so easy.

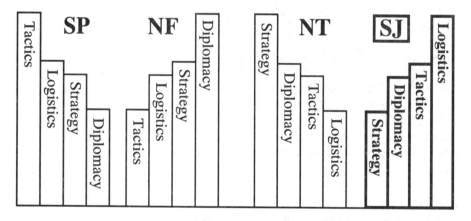

Something else to note is that the SJ Guardian IQ profile is the exact opposite of the NT Rational profile. Where the SJ is long, the NT is short, and where the SJ is short the NT is long. All the same, both can be nearly equal in their tactical and diplomatic abilities, because SJs share cooperative implementation with the diplomatic NFs and concrete communication with the tactical SPs, just as NTs share abstract communication with NFs and utilitarian implementation with SPs. Thus both SJs and NTs tend to develop their tactical and diplomatic intelligence from time to time as nearly equal second and third suits; and even though they are diametric opposites in how they use tools and words, they are not likely to outdo one another in these two middle kinds of intellectual development.

Logistical Role Variants

While all the Guardians have logistical intelligence in common, they differ among themselves a good deal in the kinds of logistical roles they are inclined to practice. Broadly speaking, Guardians are interested in taking up the role of what I call the "Administrator" or the "Conservator," and these differentiate into four logistical role variants, the "Supervisor" (ESTJ), the "Inspector" (ISTJ), the "Provider" (ESFJ), and the "Protector" (ISFJ), all Guardians through and through, but quite distinct in their guardianship. Consider the following chart which shows the Guardians' logistical roles and role variants opposite their most often practiced intelligent operations:

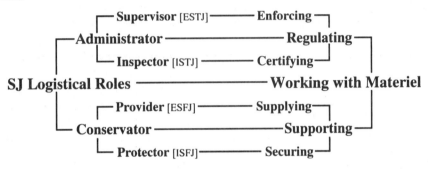

Logistical Administrators

Tough-minded Guardians are particularly interested in the role of Administrator, that is, they are given to regulating those procedures and products in their charge in the light of a standard of performance. These Administrators are the directive Guardians, which means that their first instinct is to take charge and tell others what to do. Several terms may be used to depict the Administrator's function: captain, commander, conductor, director, executive, governor, and superintendent.

Administrators run a tight ship in two basic ways: by acting either as the expressive Supervisor or the reserved Inspector.

Supervisors enforce standard operating procedures, keeping one eye on their people's performance, and the other on the rules and regulations that govern their activities, making sure that they behave in keeping with agreed upon procedures and standards of conduct—or else face the agreed upon consequences. These expressive Supervisors let you know how you're doing; their business is to mind others' business, overseeing what they do, surveilling the premises, controlling work areas, directing operations, refereeing disputes, all to ensure compliance with the rules and regulations.

Inspectors, in contrast, often work behind the scenes, taking a close look at products and accounts, putting the farmer's crops, the manufacturer's goods, the company's books, the importer's shipments, and so on, under a magnifying glass so that each and every unit is properly inventoried and certified, with no deviation from the legal standard left undetected. There are several ways of speaking of the Inspector's seclusive role: appraiser, assessor, auditor, checker, examiner, evaluator, judge, measurer, surveyor, tester, and weigher—all keeping a watchful eye out for irregularities.

Logistical Conservators

The friendly Guardians are prone to choose the part of the Conservator, that person whose job it is to support institutions by insuring the supply and security of those persons and properties they are responsible for. In their support role, Conservators tend to be more informative than directive, giving information—reports, accounts, records and so on—first, and giving orders only as a last resort. As in the case of the Administrator, there are many words that define the Conservator's function: amass, bank, budget, collect, deposit, garner, gather, hold, husband, keep, reserve, save, stock, store, and warehouse.

As Conservators, Guardians look after their responsibilities by working either as the expressive Provider or the reserved Protector.

Providers work to furnish others with the necessities of life, to serve others, to see to their welfare, to make sure they feel well-provisioned and a part of the group. This outgoing, public role can be acted out in the form of banker, benefactor, caterer, equipper, distributor, financier, furnisher, host or hostess, outfitter, patron, sponsor, subsidizer, and, in general, supplier of someone in need with whatever is needed.

Protectors, in contrast, take on the task of shielding others from the dirt and the dangers of the world. This seclusive, private role also has many forms: attendant, custodian, caretaker, insurer, fortifier, ombudsman, preserver, shelterer, shepherd, steward, underwriter, warder, and in general, anyone who sees to the physical safety and security of those in need of care.

Comparing the Logistical Role Variants

Every Guardian plays these four roles well, but no Guardian plays them all equally well. Indeed, what distinguishes Guardians from one another is the structure of their intellect, that is, their profile of logistical roles. Some Administrators are better as Supervisors of personnel and procedures, others as Inspectors of products and accounts, even though supervising and inspecting are two sides of the same coin, with Supervisors often inspecting their people, and Inspectors often supervising operations. Similarly, some Conservators are better as Providers of goods and services, others as Protectors against loss and injury, even though Providers must often protect their supplies and Protectors must often provide protection. To help visualize the differences among Guardians in their likely development of logistical skills, consider the following chart:

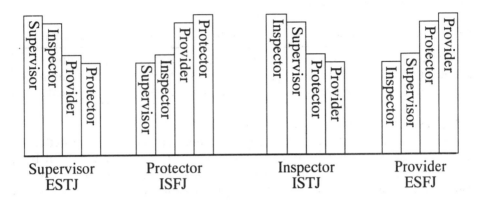

Supervisor ESTJ	Protector ISFJ	Inspector ISTJ	Provider ESFJ

Note that Supervisors (ESTJs) are the mirror image of Protectors (ISFJs), as are Providers (ESFJs) of Inspectors (ISTJs). Thus the Supervisors are usually eager to see to it that people do what they are supposed to, or else be called to task, while they are less inclined to safeguard the people they supervise. The reverse holds for the Protectors, who leave nothing to chance in insuring the safety of their charges, while they find it more difficult to let them know when they step out of line. Just so, the Providers are the most skilled in supplying their people with what they need to fare well, though not as skilled in taking care to inspect their products. And last, the Inspectors are quite willing and able to check up on the quality and quantity of the work done by their charges, but less so to provide for the wants and needs of those whose products they inspect. All the same, though each of the Guardians is less skilled in some logistical roles than in others, they still practice their short suit more, and therefore develop it more, than any of the tactical, diplomatic, and strategic roles of the other types.

A more detailed portrait of each of the four Guardian role variants may be found at the end of this chapter, beginning on page 104.

The Interests of Guardians

Everyone has interests, but not everyone has the same interests. Moreover, our interests go hand in hand with our abilities. Thus we are interested in doing what we do well, and tend to do well in what we are interested in doing. As for Guardians, their interests are diametrically opposite from those of Rationals and quite different from those of Artisans and Idealists. At school the Guardians typically seek out courses that have some application in the world of commerce, and study arts & crafts, humanities, and sciences only as required to. They are far more interested in morality—right and wrong—than in building morale or in acquiring new techniques, and many have an aversion to technology. They work best with materiel, rather than with equipment, personnel, or complex systems. In considering their unique educational, preoccupational, and vocational interests, it might be helpful to study the following chart:

Interests	Guardians	Artisans	Idealists	Rationals
Education	**Commerce**	Artcrafts	Humanities	Sciences
Preoccupation	**Morality**	Techniques	Morale	Technology
Vocation	**Materiel**	Equipment	Personnel	Systems

Educational Interest in Commerce

The world of commerce is the place where society comes together to evaluate and to exchange goods and services, and is thus the natural field of education for Guardians. They will study other subjects, of course, particularly the Applied Sciences, English, History, and Education, but their eye is ever on the practical advantages of learning business skills. When his Artisan son questions why he has to read the classics in high school, Sinclair Lewis's Guardian businessman George Babbitt tries to explain:

> It's because they're required for college...and that's all there is to it! Personally, I don't see why....Be a good deal better if you took Business English and learned how to write an ad, or letters that would pull.

Other types study commerce, too: Artisans, in order to find out how to play the game of wheel-and-deal; Rationals to learn about economics and human engineering, and to understand financial markets as complex systems. (Idealists, it must be said, find little of personal value in learning about commerce.) Guardians, however, regard companies and corporations as indispensable social institutions that allow them to earn their keep and to provide for their families. And so Guardians fill the ranks of Business Schools and of college Business Departments, where they take accounting and administration, and of Law Schools, where they tend to specialize in business, tax, and insurance law.

Preoccupied with Morality

Guardians, even as children, feel responsible for the morality of their group, whether it be their family, their classmates, or their circle of friends. And they are never able to shake off that responsibility, even if they sometimes want to. In this they resemble the Idealists, who early on assume the responsibility for the morale of their companions. But morale and morality, though related, are two different things. Morality is concerned with people doing what they're supposed to and not doing what they're not supposed to, while morale is concerned with how people feel about themselves, and how they get along with others. Thus, both SJs and NFs are interested in helping or bettering others, but while the NFs nurture good feelings, the SJs guard right and wrong. Perhaps it is because of their preoccupation with morality that Guardians so often study the right and wrong of business practices and seek occupation as administrators and conservators.

Vocational Interest in Materiel

Guardians are interested in occupations that have to do with procedures for managing materiel, that is, for gathering, storing, recording, measuring, and distributing equipment and supplies. In jobs of this nature SJs are incomparable, for no other area of work is so well suited to standard operations and by-the-book procedures. Of course, SJs come up with new ideas, too, but their creativity comes to the fore most easily in the areas of arranging and scheduling. Listen to Antonio Panizzi, Keeper of Printed Books for the British Museum, describe in 1848 his idea of a card catalogue,

> [in which] the titles be entered under some 'headings' alphabetically arranged. Now, inasmuch as...it would be impossible to arrange them in the requisite order, if they cannot be easily shifted, each title is therefore written on separate 'slips' of paper...which are frequently changed from one place to another as required. It is self-evident that if these 'slips'...be not uniform, both is size and substance, their arrangement will cause mechanical difficulties.

Alphabetical arrangement, requisite order, uniform size and substance: these notions are near and dear to Guardians, and perhaps this is why they find such satisfaction in office work and clerical jobs—keeping records, checking inventory, attending to correspondence, filing, accounting—with the brightest becoming executives, administrators, plant or office managers, CPAs, bankers, brokers, insurance underwriters, and so on. Indeed, many of the giants of the business world—particularly in commodities, finance, and retail sales—have been SJs, from John D. Rockefeller to J. Paul Getty, from J.P. Morgan to E.F. Hutton, from J.C. Penney to F.W. Woolworth.

But the word 'materiel' has a more down-to-earth meaning as well, and, as you might expect of Demeter's children, agriculture is second nature to the SJs, particularly the tasks of planting, tending, harvesting, and warehousing, all skills which Chaucer noted nearly six hundred years ago in his Canterbury pilgrim the Reeve (an estate steward):

> He kept his bins and garners very trim;
> No auditor could gain a point on him.
> And he could judge by watching drought and rain
> The yield he might expect from seed and grain.

Commercial food production, packing, and distribution are also natural vocations for Guardians, and men such as H.J. Heinz and Charles W. Post made fortunes bringing processed foods to the tables of American families.

The Orientation of Guardians

We are born into a social field and we live out our lives in that field, never, for long, stepping outside of it into social isolation. Of course we can be disoriented now and then, perhaps because of surprise, danger, or shock. But we soon reorient ourselves and return to our ordinary social frame of reference. After all, we are the most social of all the animals, with our sociability ending in great and complicated societies. Whatever we think or feel, say or do, occurs, indeed must occur, in our own and no other's social context. Each act and attitude is shaped and governed by a prevailing outlook or perspective determined by our social matrix. We are oriented always from a certain angle, a slant, a standpoint, something Adickes spoke of as a built-in point-of-view—our *"Weltanschauung,"* or "worldview."

But different personalities have different orientations, viewing time and place as well as past, present, and future, differently. Consider the following chart in making these comparisons:

Orientation	Guardians	Artisans	Idealists	Rationals
Present	**Dutiful**	Practical	Altruistic	Pragmatic
Future	**Pessimistic**	Optimistic	Credulous	Skeptical
Past	**Stoical**	Cynical	Mystical	Relativistic
Place	**Gateways**	Here	Pathways	Intersections
Time	**Yesterday**	Now	Tomorrow	Intervals

Here it is claimed that Guardians are dutiful about the present, pessimistic about the future, stoical about the past, that their preferred place is at the gates of social interaction and their preferred time is yesterday. How different are the other temperaments in the way they view these things. So let us look closely at these five dimensions of orientation so that we will not be surprised or disappointed when our Guardian friends prove, for example, to be less optimistic, or less mystical, or less skeptical than we are.

Dutiful in Looking Around

While Artisans have a practical outlook, Guardians have a dutiful outlook, particularly in the sense of hard work and saving. Both of these outlooks are moral. One is not right and the other wrong; they are both differing views of the Good. For SPs, if it does not have a quick payoff, don't do it; but for SJs, a penny saved is a penny earned, and if there's a job to be done, they must do it, feeling obligated to shoulder the responsibility of working hard and accumulating assets so that family members will fare well and prosper.

This dutiful perspective can be seen in the SJs' conduct even when they are small children. By the age of five Guardians have already adopted a surprisingly adult work ethic, and as they grow up they take on their school and family duties with little complaint: they help with family meals (preparing the food, setting the table, washing the dishes), they do their homework, get the yard work done, and even find odd jobs (paper routes, baby-sitting) to earn a little extra money. And both hard work and saving become more and more important as the SJ gets older. Clipping coupons, making ends meet, saving for a rainy day—these are all actions which come naturally to Guardians. And no one ever accused an SJ of not giving his or her all to family, career, church, and social organization—and usually all at the same time! Even when they have retired SJs work harder and spend less than the other types. Artisans might believe you can't take it with you, but Guardians save money by cooking and canning, vegetable gardening, shopping at sales, and making their own repairs on the house and car. The truth is that from this save-and-work ethic SJs can never retire, because, like the tireless beaver, it is in their temperament to keep at it all their lives.

Aesop's "The Ant and the Grasshopper" gives us a splendid analogy for the contrasting styles of Guardian and Artisan. In the fable, Ant is dutifully transporting large crumbs of bread from site to storage while Grasshopper reclines on a blade of grass near Ant's path, playing the fiddle, chewing tobacco, and singing "The World Owes Me a Living." Ant, without losing stride, scolds Grasshopper for not preparing for the upcoming winter months: "Join me," he urges, "and we will fill the store-house, thus ensuring that none will suffer cold or hunger." Grasshopper replies, "Ant, if you keep up this feverish pace, you won't make it to winter. Join me on my blade of grass, and we will enjoy together the warm summer, the food that abounds, and celebrate the world's debt to us in song." Each, of course, ignores the other's warning and goes his own way. When it turns out to be a long, cold, hungry winter, Grasshopper must knock at Ant's door and stand there frostbitten and starving. Ant, snug in his storehouse of goodies, can't help but say "I told you so," then shakes his head and lets Grasshopper in.

Pessimistic in Looking Ahead

Because so many of their efforts are holding actions, trying to maintain the status quo in fast-paced, ever-changing situations, Guardians have learned to expect the worst. To be sure, even the most cursory glance at thorough-going SJs will detect a streak of pessimism coloring their attitude, in complete contrast with the SPs' things-are-looking-up optimism. Certainly the Boy Scouts' motto, "Be Prepared," must have been coined by a strong Guardian. Above all else, Guardians are prepared, and even though many of their preparations are for things to go wrong, we must not conclude that they are gloomily forecasting calamity and disaster. Rather, we might see them as being realistic about setbacks and shortages.

Although Guardians do not readily confess that they are pessimistic, if pressed they will admit it. Of course they'd much rather be optimistic, like their Artisan cousins, but they cannot easily shake off their worries about all the possible things that can, and often do, go wrong. After all, the Murphys of this world—surely SJs—are the makers of the laws of pessimism. Remember Murphy's Law, which says "whatever can go wrong will." There are many variants of this basic law, such as "everything costs more and takes longer," and Olsen's addendum, "Murphy's Law is optimistic."

Stoical in Looking Back

It is one thing to expect things to go wrong, but quite another to explain away errors, failures, losses, and setbacks when they happen. In their times of trouble, Guardians tend not to blame their bad luck (as do Artisans), or to blame themselves (as do Rationals). Rather, SJs believe with the Stoics that pain and suffering are unavoidable in this world, are indeed part of some predetermined plan, and therefore that men and women must endure their hardships bravely and patiently. Ill and nearing death, Prince Albert comforted Queen Victoria and resigned himself to his fate:

> Not for the first time he explained to Queen Victoria quite calmly that he...was happy in his lot but if he were attacked by a severe illness he would let go without a struggle..., [a 'melancholy' attitude which] Victoria generally interpreted as Albert's saintly acceptance of God's will.

The Place is at the Gateways

Guardians naturally assume the role of society's gate-keeper, standing guard at the door and keeping a watchful eye on the coming and going of the people under their jurisdiction. Those without proper credentials (outsiders) cannot be allowed through, those who ignore boundaries (trespassers) must be caught and reprimanded, and those who think they have the right just to barge in (gate-crashers) need to be stopped and expelled—"shown the door," as SJs tend to say.

When the four heroes in *The Wizard of Oz* finally reach the Emerald City, they find it surrounded by a great green wall, broken only by a huge, emerald-studded gate manned by the Guardian of the Gates. The Guardian asks them, "What do you wish in the Emerald City?" and cautions them that their business with the Wizard had better not be frivolous: "He is powerful and terrible, and if you come on an idle or foolish errand...he might be angry and destroy you all in an instant." The four assure him of the seriousness of their quest, and the Guardian gives them permission to enter through an inner gate, but only after they have put on green spectacles to protect their eyes from the emerald brilliance of the City. The spectacles, says the Guardian, "are all locked on, for Oz so ordered it when the City was built, and I have the only key that will unlock them." In just this way, caring about protocol, caution, seriousness, and protection, Guardians man the gates and keep the keys of all our social institutions.

The Time is Yesterday

Eric Adickes, the German philosopher who defined the worldviews of the four types of character, saw the Guardians as keepers of tradition, of custom, of continuity with the past. This means that SJs do not usually focus on the now, as do the opportunistic SPs. Nor on tomorrow, as do the romantic NFs. And certainly not on timeless intervals, as do the scientific NTs. Rather, SJs are more inclined to turn their thoughts to yesterday, to look fondly upon the good old days when people earned their living, when products were solidly built (they don't make 'em like they used to), and when the schools kept discipline and gave plenty of homework in the three Rs. To the Guardians, the new, the improvised, and the innovative seem almost an affront to time-honored traditions, and are certainly unsettling—or, as Tevye the milkman says in *Fiddler on the Roof*, "Without our traditions our lives would be as shaky as a...fiddler on the roof!"

This reverence for the past perhaps explains why, more than any of the other types, SJs are creatures of habit, following faithfully the same routines in their daily lives. SJs like to get up the same time every morning, they wash and dress according to the same routine, they drive the same way to work, they eat at the same restaurants at the same times, they shop at the same stores, buy the same brands, and even like to be served by the same salespersons. Guardians say, "the old ways are the best ways," and "you can't teach an old dog new tricks."

Guardians often come to focus their traditionalism on the family. SJs prize family possessions, the longer possessed the better, and they take great satisfaction in looking after the family property, the heirlooms and collections and photograph albums—the treasures of family history—regardless of their value in monetary terms. And it is the SJ who will take seriously the tracing and updating of the family tree, keeping track of births and deaths, weddings and baptisms, knowing that all such family observances become more important with each passing year.

But even in the community at large, Guardians have a great and lasting respect for age. They hate to see old buildings torn down, even old trees cut down—as though age, by itself, confers importance, a certain rank in the social hierarchy. In a sense, SJs are their society's or their family's historian, for it is the historian who honors the past, who values the lessons of history, and who passes on this traditional knowledge.

The Self-Image of Guardians

Our self-image is composed of qualities we attribute to ourselves, ways in which we see ourselves and would like to be seen by others. Three aspects of this image are particularly important in determining our sense of well-being: self-esteem, self-respect, and self-confidence. Thus the self-image is a triangular affair, with the three bases of self-regard bound together in mutual support or mutual decline. For example, when our self-esteem diminishes, I believe this undermines our self-respect and self-confidence. In the same way, as we gain self-respect, it is easier for us to keep up our self-confidence and self-esteem.

Different types of character, however, base their self-image on entirely different attributes. Since having a good opinion of ourselves is a major key to our happiness, and often to our success, we would do well to pause for a moment to compare the four types on this all-important aspect of personality:

Self-Image	Guardians	Rationals	Idealists	Artisans
Self-Esteem	**Dependable**	Ingenious	Empathic	Artistic
Self-Respect	**Beneficent**	Autonomous	Benevolent	Audacious
Self-Confidence	**Respectable**	Resolute	Authentic	Adaptable

Thus to feel good about themselves Guardians must see themselves, and be seen by others, as dependable, beneficent, and respectable, while other attributes, like authenticity and autonomy, are likely to contribute little to their sense of well-being. This triangular relationship between dependability, beneficence, and respectability is shown in the figure at the side. Note how dependability reinforces beneficence, which reinforces respectability, and so on.

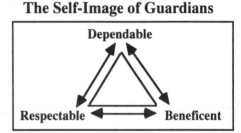

The Self-Image of Guardians

Whether or not they are mutually reinforcing, the paramount importance of these three attributes in undergirding our sense of well-being makes it advisable to look carefully at each of them.

Self-Esteem in Dependability

Guardian self-esteem is greatest when they present themselves as dependable, trustworthy, or accountable in shouldering their responsibilities. "No matter what," says the SJ, "you can count on me to fulfill my obligations and to honor my contracts." Picture the traditional Guardian male: the loyal company man at work, performing his duties conscientiously, even working late to finish the job; and the faithful family man at home, washing the car, mowing the lawn, going to the kids' games or recitals, remembering his wedding anniversary. Then there is the traditional Guardian female: working to keep the house clean, shopping, preparing meals, dressing (and ferrying) the children, volunteering her time at school and church, and finding that special gift for her husband's birthday.

Unfortunately, the Guardian's tireless sense of dependability can take its toll. The problem is that SJs seem almost incapable of refusing added responsibility. If there is a job to be done, a duty to fulfill, Guardians feel somehow obligated to see that the task is undertaken, and brought to conclusion, even if they are already overburdened, and even if others are contributing far less than they. The Guardian worries, "If I don't do it, who will?" and reluctantly agrees to shoulder the extra load—anything to keep from appearing irresponsible or shiftless. And thus a vicious circle is set up, with others coming to count on, and even to take advantage of, the SJ's reliability. "Jane will do it," becomes people's attitude, with little awareness or appreciation of the demands this may make on Jane, who only too often is exhausted, sad, and perhaps even ill. Thus E.M. Forster describes Henry Wilcox, the Guardian banker in *Howards End*. Henry is not exactly "ill," Forster says, just "Eternally tired. He has worked hard all his life."

Guardians suffer when not appreciated for their efforts, but even worse they often fail to appreciate themselves and to find satisfaction in their own hard work. SJs seem burdened and obligated by their very nature—no matter how hard they work—and they spend much of their lives doing a thousand thankless jobs, apparently trying to discharge the feeling that somehow they haven't done enough. Much like the beaver, who labors to stock his lodge with food for the winter, Guardians take on additional duties almost as if trying to stock their self-esteem against some future obligation.

Self-Respect in Beneficence

While self-esteem does not come easily to Guardians, they can develop a healthy self-respect based on their beneficence, which means doing good deeds. (This is quite different from benevolence or good will, which is an attitude displayed by Idealists.) SJs are natural Good-Samaritans, ever on the lookout for ways to help their fellow man, especially when it comes to matters of food, clothing, shelter, and transportation. SJs do a great part of community and church volunteer work, lending a hand with the Scouts or the Red Cross, candy-striping at hospitals, and helping the needy by collecting and distributing food, blankets, toys, and the like. And Guardians serve tirelessly in their own homes. At the Thanksgiving or Holiday dinner, the SJ hosts (and even the SJ guests) will be found in the kitchen both before and after the meal, seeing to the cooking and the cleanup, worrying about the time, or if there's enough food, and insisting that everyone go on and enjoy themselves. At the same time, it is the Guardian host who may also feel a bit put upon if a few guests don't at least offer to help so that they can be shooed away. Of course, the SJ accepts all at the banquet despite the ingratitude of other character types, many of whom are quite happy to be the so-called "members of the wedding" and eat their fill at the SJ's expense.

The care of others, particularly the young and old, the impaired and infirm, and those in positions of authority, is another concern of the Guardians, and they fill the ranks of the traditional service occupations: teaching, accounting, secretarial work, clerking in banks, retail sales, civil service, housekeeping, barbering and hair dressing, dentistry, pharmacy, general medical practice, and nursing. SJs also make devoted public servants, seeing their role in government or the military in almost sacred terms of self-sacrifice and service to others. Once, when reading a document to his staff, George Washington begged indulgence for his aging eyesight: "Gentleman, you will permit me to put on my spectacles, for I have not only grown grey, but almost blind in the service of my countrymen." And in a speech to mark his appointment as Chairman of the Joint Chiefs of Staff, General Colin Powell, in my view a Guardian, described a painting hung in the Pentagon of a soldier and his family kneeling in prayer on the eve of war. Under the painting is an inscription from the Prophet Isaiah answering the question, "Who will do the work of the Lord?" with the simple statement, "Send me." Powell spoke of this inscription as "the essence of what we are supposed to be doing in this building—that's serving....That's the ultimate statement of selfless service: Send me."

Although service to others comes quite naturally to them, Guardians do not do it freely and joyously; rather, they look upon their service as obligatory—to do otherwise is to be shiftless and selfish. In a sense, then, SJ self-respect is built on fulfilling their obligation to serve, and in turn the greatest blow to their self-respect is to become dependent on the charity or the service of others. The SJ must be the giver, not the receiver, the care taker, not the cared for. Witness the Guardian who goes to a party, but in order to have a good time helps the host serve the refreshments—and then insists on cleaning up afterwards. And though SJs make fine, caring physicians and nurses, they are often miserable patients. When debilitated or ailing, SJs often seem grouchy and embarrassed to be receiving care, almost as if they feel derelict in their duties.

One twist on this pattern is worth mentioning. When on vacation, insofar as they can vacation (many never take the time), Guardians thoroughly enjoy being catered to and indulged. To take a short rest from their duties, to forget their responsibilities for a little while, to let themselves be served and entertained, this is the best kind of recreation for these nose-to-the-grindstone people. Even on vacation, however, SJs can feel a sense of obligation—an obligation to enjoy themselves!—and they will schedule their time to see the sights, to take the tours, to visit the historical buildings or ruins, as if it's their duty to pack into their trip (and to record in snapshots) as many must-sees as possible.

Self-Confidence in Respectability

Self-confidence can be a problem for Guardians. More than others, Guardians are innately modest, unassuming, even self-effacing—and putting themselves forward comes perilously close to showing off, a kind of behavior which they find truly repugnant. But if having confidence in themselves is difficult for SJs, being respected by others is a great comfort, and public recognition is indeed the foundation of their self-confidence. Such recognition usually comes in the form of physical tokens of respect such as plaques, certificates, awards, and diplomas. The Guardian's office or den may be conspicuous for its large display of such formal honors, side by side with photographs of awards ceremonies, autographed pictures of political leaders, and photographs of spouse, children, and grandchildren. SJs take very seriously all of these public and personal honors, since being highly respected in their business, in their community, or by their family proves they have put in long years conscientiously doing their part.

Guardians will even take on extra burdens if they are sufficiently honored. Having successfully conducted the War of Independence, and having presided over the fierce intellectual battles of the Constitutional Convention with great dignity, George Washington was entreated by his fellow-delegates to become the first President of the United States. It was not his wish to become President. He had served long enough, he felt, and wished to retire to his home at Mount Vernon. But he could not resist this last call to duty, which can be summed up in the words of one Maryland official: "We cannot, sir, do without you." Washington never thought of himself as worthy of such a grand position, but to be honored by others, to be chosen for a position of prestige and high standing, and then to accept the honor humbly—this is a scenario which fills the SJ with legitimate self-confidence and lifelong satisfaction.

The Values of Guardians

Different people value different things, and it is in this, the domain of values, that the four types of personality stand apart most noticeably. The temperaments differ in their preferred mood, in what they put their trust in, in what they yearn for, in what they seek, in what they prize, and in what they aspire to. These contrasts in values are usually what people see first in others, when they begin to recognize the four temperament patterns, and are indeed much more easily discernible than differences in other domains, such as the self-image, or the forms of intelligence. Let's look at the following chart:

Value	Guardians	Artisans	Idealists	Rationals
Being	**Concerned**	Excited	Enthusiastic	Calm
Trusting	**Authority**	Impulse	Intuition	Reason
Yearning	**Belonging**	Impact	Romance	Achievement
Seeking	**Security**	Stimulation	Identity	Knowledge
Prizing	**Gratitude**	Generosity	Recognition	Deference
Aspiring	**Executive**	Virtuoso	Sage	Wizard

I believe that Guardians are often concerned about some serious matter, trust authority, yearn to belong to groups, seek security, prize expressions of gratitude, and sooner or later aspire to be an executive. These values are radically different from those of the other temperaments. Therefore it will serve us well if we study these six kinds of value in the case of Guardians lest we are surprised and disappointed to find them, for instance, less excitable, less intuitive, or less reasonable than the rest of us.

Being Concerned

The prevailing mood of Guardians is one of concern. They are concerned about their homes, their jobs, their families, their neighborhoods. They are concerned about their duties and responsibilities, their health, their finances, about how they dress, and whether they're on time. SJs are concerned about big things, like crime and punishment, school standards, public morality; and they are concerned about little things, like doing the dishes, aphids on the roses, their gas mileage. Of course, others concern themselves with many of these matters, too, but not as extensively or as seriously as the Guardians. Of all the types, Guardians can truly be said to be the "concerned citizens."

Such thoroughgoing concern about anything and everything makes Guardians vulnerable to being down in the dumps, which is very likely what prompted Galen to name them the "Melancholics." To put it simply, SJs tend to worry too much, especially about their loved ones, but also about the direction of society in general. To many SJs, society seems to be decaying, morals and manners aren't what they used to be, no one shows respect anymore—what's the world coming to? These grave concerns can furrow the brow of even the happiest SJs, and worry those around them, as Oscar Wilde shows us in his comedy with the perfect Guardian title, *The Importance of Being Earnest.*

> CECILY: Dear Uncle Jack is so very serious! Sometimes he is so serious that I think he cannot be quite well.
> MISS PRISM: (*Drawing herself up.*) Your guardian enjoys the best of health, and his gravity of demeanor is especially to be commended in one so comparatively young. I know of no one who has a higher sense of duty and responsibility.

This is not to say that Guardians don't lighten up and have just as good a time as others. SJs can have a great sense of humor, lots of friends, and will usually cultivate a full and satisfying social life. But even when giving a party Guardians can find things to worry about. Bilbo Baggins, Tolkien's hospitable little hobbit, enjoys having friends over for tea, but frets about invitations, service, and supplies:

> He liked visitors, but he liked to know them before they arrived, and he preferred to ask them himself. He had a horrible thought that the cakes

might run short, and then he...found himself scuttling off to the cellar to fill a pint beer-mug, and to the pantry to fetch two beautiful round seed-cakes which he had baked that afternoon for his after-supper morsel. As the host, he knew his duty and stuck to it however painful.

Trusting Authority

Guardians trust authority. They believe in a hierarchical structure of authority—rule from the top down. They believe there should be subordination and superordination, that the actions of members of communities, schools, churches, and corporations, but also of families, should be governed by those in the highest positions. SJs tend to take the word of authorities in matters of education and medicine—their unquestioned assumption is "the doctor knows best." Moreover, SJs have an abiding trust in the heads of church and state, and popes and pontiffs, presidents and prime ministers, and royalty of all types seem to capture their trust and their loyalty. And many SJs believe that an even higher authority keeps an eye on us: "The propitious smiles of Heaven can never be expected on a nation that disregards the eternal rules of order and right which heaven itself has ordained." So said George Washington, the father of his country.

The Guardian's belief in authority makes its appearance early in life. If we watch a newly convened kindergarten class, we can easily observe about half of the five-year-olds earnestly and tensely looking to their teachers to tell them what they are "s'posed to do." The rest of the children (mostly SPs) are more like puppies, tussling, sniffing, and chewing the happy hours away, while a smattering of NFs and NTs will seem self-conscious and somewhat lost in the shuffle. By the way, in elementary and secondary schools usually two out of three, and more often, three out of four of the teachers are Guardians. This occupational choice makes sense for many SJs, since the traditional school is committed not only to supplying students with certain basic clerical skills and a core body of factual information, but also to handing down to the next generation a sense of order and a respect for authority.

Yearning for Belonging

Perhaps hoping in some degree to fulfill their search for security, Guardians are prone to join a number of social and civic groups. Maintaining their membership status in such groups is fundamental to the SJ character; it is not too much to say that Guardians actually yearn to belong, needing each and every day to confirm that they are a member-in-good-standing. To this end, Guardians, far more than others, create and foster the social arm of the institutions they serve: the church auxiliary, the PTA, the community service club, the lodge, the municipal or political organization, the professional association. George Babbitt, Sinclair Lewis's finely observed Guardian businessman, belongs not only to the Presbyterian Church, and the Chamber of Commerce, but he is a member of the Brotherly and

Protective Order of Elks, vice-president of the Boosters' Club, and serves on a committee of the State Association of Real Estate Boards. Lewis tells us that Babbitt's various memberships "made him feel loyal and important...a Prominent Citizen," well-respected in his profession and his community.

Seeking Security

While the Artisan is the Sensation Seeking Personality, the Idealist the Identity Seeking Personality, and the Rational the Knowledge Seeking Personality, it is safe to say that Guardians have little interest in any of these other pursuits. The SJs' concerns are more pressing than sensations, identity, and knowledge, for they are more aware than the other types of the dangers of living. What, after all, is a guardian but one who stands guard, prepared for the worst, a warden of safety and security?

Guardians know better than the rest of us what dangers lurk nearby, ready to pounce. Property can be lost or stolen; health can fail; relationships can fall apart. The world can go to hell in a handbasket. Perhaps this is why they put such trust in institutions. Institutions are bastions of security in a chaotic world, and SJs devote themselves to establishing them, tending them, and perpetuating them. Observe how one Texas social worker defends public institutions, and expresses himself in a Guardian's oft-used terms of "guilt and innocence," "good and bad," and "accountability":

> It is important for people to be connected to institutions....If you say I'm conservative because I think the family's important, I plead guilty. If you say I'm conservative because I think the church is important, I plead guilty. If you say I'm conservative because I think communities are important, I plead guilty. If you say I'm conservative because I think the public schools can be made to work, then I plead guilty....We can't rely on people by themselves to be good. They have to participate through institutions...that hold people accountable and teach them certain values.

Guardians seem drawn to the role of social protector, standing watch against the insecurities of life, searching for ways to defend—both themselves and others—against loss, defeat, and disappointment, but also against what many of them regard as the irresponsibility of human nature. Let us then think of the Guardian as the Security Seeking Personality, and be glad that such a one rightly has grave concerns about matters of safety in a dangerous, unstable world. "Better safe than sorry" SJs are wont to say, and rightly so.

Prizing Gratitude

More than other types, Guardians feel appreciated in the degree that others are grateful for what they, the Guardians, have done for them. It is galling to them when others take their services for granted and express no gratitude, but they can never say that they're galled. In truth, no one deserves gratitude as much as Guardians. Their guardianship is conscientious and unstinting, their attention to duty unflagging. Yet of all the types the Guardians are least able to ask others to express gratitude. Perhaps this is because they shift from the position of the child to the position of the parent far sooner than the other types do, and imagine that parental responsibility far outweighs parental entitlement to gratitude.

Their attention to duty has a natural consequence: they help others, often doing the many thankless jobs, cleaning up, washing, record-keeping, and all the other routine and burdensome—but usually crucial—tasks associated with meeting logistical necessity. Imagine what happens to the glorious two-week family vacation if nobody remembers to check the car's gas and oil. These are important tasks, but by their very nature they are almost invisible to others. The result is that Guardians may not be (are almost certain not to be) thanked for what they have done. In fact, these jobs may be noticed only when they are not done. Finally the Guardian is likely to protest resentfully that he or she has worked long and hard, and his or her efforts have not even been noticed—"After all I've done, this is the thanks I get." And well might they protest, for those they help do owe thanks that is all too seldom given.

Aspiring to be an Executive

Many a Guardian's loftiest aspiration is to become a distinguished head of an important and well-regarded institution. To run the show, to be in charge of things, to direct operations, to hold the reins of power—in a word, to be an "executive"—appeals strongly to the Guardians' feeling for the rightful exercise of authority. Perhaps this is why royalty, where it still exists, seems to have a special place in the heart of most SJs, particularly someone of royalty who has the common touch, as did Lady Diana Spencer, fondly known as "Princess Di," the ill-fated "people's Princess." However, whether the institution is a royal family or something less exalted, such as a business, a school, a church, a military unit, a local community, or a democratic nation, Guardians dream of becoming its Director, its Chief Executive Officer, its Chairman of the Board, its Commanding Officer, its Supervisor, its Commissioner, its Regent—or its President. Indeed, nearly half of the forty-one Presidents of the United States have been Guardians, their attitude toward the office summed up in the words of Jimmy Carter: "The President of the United States is the steward of the nation's destiny." Interestingly, William Howard Taft coveted his appointment to the Supreme Court even more than his time in the White House. Though elected to the Presidency, he was not truly content until he became Chief Justice of the Supreme Court—presiding over the nation's legal hierarchy and thus achieving, for a Guardian, the most honored executive status of all.

The Social Roles Guardians Play

There are two kinds of social roles, those that are allotted to us by virtue of our position in our social milieu, and those that we reach out and take for ourselves. It is impossible not to play a role in all of our social transactions. We perforce play offspring to our parents, siblings to our brothers and sisters, and relatives to our extended family members. On the other hand we willingly play mate to our spouse, parents to our offspring, superior to our subordinate, subordinate to our superior, friend to friend, and so on. Allotted or embraced, we have no choice but to enact our social roles, since to interact with others can never be role-free.

Three of our social roles are of special importance in the context of the study of personality: mating, parenting, and leading. In enacting these three roles the different kinds of personality differ significantly in the effects they have on mates, offspring, and followers. Let us consider a chart which shows the four ways that the mating, parenting, and leading roles are played:

Social Roles	Guardians	Artisans	Idealists	Rationals
Mating	**Helpmate**	Playmate	Soulmate	Mindmate
Parenting	**Socializer**	Liberator	Harmonizer	Individuator
Leading	**Stabilizer**	Negotiator	Catalyst	Visionary

Note the striking difference between playing the Helpmate role in the case of the Guardians, and the Playmate, Soulmate, and Mindmate roles in the cases of the other three temperaments. These different mating roles will require careful study and so a chapter on this topic is provided in Chapter 7.

Separate chapters (Chapters 8 and 9) are also required for defining and describing the noticeable differences in the parenting and leadership roles of the four temperaments. The Guardian Socializer parent plays a far different part in the family than the Artisan Liberator, the Idealist Harmonizer, or the Rational Individuator, just as the Guardian Stabilizer leader performs a vastly different function in a business operation than the Artisan Negotiator, the Idealist Catalyst, or the Rational Visionary. Still, a few remarks on each of the Guardian's social roles can give outlines of how they are played.

The Helpmate

In their spousal role, Guardians regard themselves as Helpmates, ready to roll up their sleeves and work side-by-side with their spouses to build a comfortable, stable family life. In addition, SJs are extremely loyal to their mates and feel obliged to stand by them in times of trouble and help them straighten up and fly right. As a result, Guardians more easily than any other temperament can be hooked into becoming the rescuer of troubled mates. Remember that SJ self-respect rests on doing good deeds, and so, to be good mates, they must help their spouses, and want to help their spouses. Other types, of course, wish to be helpful to their mates, but they do not pursue this objective with the seriousness of Guardians.

The Socializer Parent

In the parental role, Guardians are more often than not set upon seeing to it that their children are civilized, enculturated, fully in support of and in step with the community—in a word, "socialized." A Guardian's children are to be increasingly helpful and productive in the home, at school, at church, at scout meetings, and other social gatherings, and certainly at gatherings of the extended family. It is not too much to say that the SJ parent's highest value for his or her children is that they fit in smoothly and helpfully with the community, and are in all ways conducive to its welfare. Guardian parents are far more concerned with this project than they are with the concerns of other types, that is, with encouraging their children's venturesomeness, nurturing their positive self-image, or strengthening their independence.

The Stabilizer Leader

The soundest basis of leadership in the Guardian view is carefully considered administration of what is to be done, how it is to be done, and who is to do it. This means that there ought to be schedules, regulations, and standard operating procedures that employees know about and are ready, willing, and able to follow. If no such routines exist, then it is up to the SJ leader to establish them and disseminate them, and make sure that the mavericks and nonconformists (who are itching to set aside protocol and go off on their own) conform to the leader's regimen. Even when some individualist does better with his own unique style of operating, the Guardian leader has cause to question this show of initiative, regarding it as possibly destabilizing and disruptive of the normal flow of work, besides being upsetting to some members of the staff. Rules and regulations are there for the good of all, and are to be observed, lest there be chaos and discontent. In the Guardian view, the leader who fails to stabilize an enterprise by not standardizing operations is liable to be met with misdirected efforts and diminished returns.

Matrix of Guardian Traits

The matrix on the next page gathers together and highlights the terms I have used to define and describe the Guardian personality. The traits of the other three types are listed in parallel columns, so that all four temperaments can be compared and contrasted at a glance. Those who study this matrix, and occasionally consult it as they read on, will have a better chance of grasping the complete configuration of the Proprietary Guardian Personality, and of appreciating its uniqueness and radical difference from the Hedonic Artisans, the Ethical Idealists, and the Dialectical Rationals.

The Traits of Temperament and Character

Communication Implementation Character	┌─ Concrete ─┐ Utilitarian Artisan	Cooperative Guardian	┌─ Abstract ─┐ Cooperative Idealist	Utilitarian Rational
Language	**Harmonic**	**Associative**	**Inductive**	**Deductive**
Referential	Indicative	Imperative	Interpretive	Categorical
Syntactical	Descriptive	Comparative	Metaphoric	Subjunctive
Rhetorical	Heterodox	Orthodox	Hyperbolic	Technical
Intellect	**Tactical**	**Logistical**	**Diplomatic**	**Strategic**
Directive Role	Operator	Administrator	Mentor	Coordinator
• Expressive Role	• Promoter	• Supervisor	• Teacher	• Fieldmarshal
• Reserved Role	• Crafter	• Inspector	• Counselor	• Mastermind
Informative Role	Entertainer	Conservator	Advocate	Engineer
• Expressive Role	• Performer	• Provider	• Champion	• Inventor
• Reserved Role	• Composer	• Protector	• Healer	• Architect
Interest				
Education	Artcraft	**Commerce**	Humanities	Sciences
Preoccupation	Technique	**Morality**	Morale	Technology
Vocation	Equipment	**Materiel**	Personnel	Systems
Orientation				
Present	Practical	**Dutiful**	Altruistic	Pragmatic
Future	Optimistic	**Pessimistic**	Credulous	Skeptical
Past	Cynical	**Stoical**	Mystical	Relativistic
Place	Here	**Gateways**	Pathways	Intersections
Time	Now	**Yesterday**	Tomorrow	Intervals
Self-Image				
Self-Esteem	Artistic	**Dependable**	Empathic	Ingenious
Self-Respect	Audacious	**Beneficent**	Benevolent	Autonomous
Self-Confidence	Adaptable	**Respectable**	Authentic	Resolute
Value				
Being	Excited	**Concerned**	Enthusiastic	Calm
Trusting	Impulse	**Authority**	Intuition	Reason
Yearning	Impact	**Belonging**	Romance	Achievement
Seeking	Stimulation	**Security**	Identity	Knowledge
Prizing	Generosity	**Gratitude**	Recognition	Deference
Aspiring	Virtuoso	**Executive**	Sage	Wizard
Social Role				
Mating	Playmate	**Helpmate**	Soulmate	Mindmate
Parenting	Liberator	**Socializer**	Harmonizer	Individuator
Leading	Negotiator	**Stabilizer**	Catalyst	Visionary

Guardian Role Variants

These "Concrete Cooperators," as I like to call them—Plato's Guardians, Aristotle's Proprietaries, Galen's Melancholics, Myers's SJs—have a tightly configured personality, so that each trait of character entails the other traits. This means that Mother Nature does not permit Guardians, any more than other types, to pick and choose their traits. If their environment enables them to develop a given trait it can only be one that is predetermined by their temperament.

While it is useful to think of each of the four temperaments as a single, unified configuration of attitudes and actions, individual members of each temperament clearly differ from one another. Thus, all the Guardians seem to have a great capacity for logistical reliability, but some (the tough-minded SJs) are drawn to the directive role of Administrator of policies and procedures, while others (the friendly SJs) prefer the informative role of Conservator of people and property. These two divisions can be further broken down to reflect an expressive or a reserved social attitude, with the Administrators tending to play the role variants of Supervisor or Inspector, and the Conservators playing Provider or Protector.

The Supervisor [ESTJ]

Supervising is making sure that others do as they should do, and don't do as they shouldn't do, and some Guardians—the ESTJs—naturally gravitate to this role in their relations with others. These Supervisors are eager to enforce the rules and procedures, and they can be serious about seeing to it that others toe the mark—or else face the consequences. They do not hesitate to give their stamp of approval, nor do they withhold their directions or demands for improvement. Like seasoned, stalwart umpires, Supervisors will set their jaw and make the call on anyone who steps up to bat. They even feel obligated to do so, and they're sometimes surprised when others don't seem grateful for their judgments.

As a variant of Plato's Guardians and Aristotle's Proprietaries, the ESTJs are little different from the other SJs in most respects. Like all the Guardians they are concrete in communicating and cooperative in using tools. They are interested in learning about commerce, are preoccupied with morality, and work well with materiel. In orientation, they tend to be dutiful, pessimistic, and stoical as they guard the gateways and look to yesterday. They base their self-image on being seen as dependable, beneficent, and respectable. Often concerned about things, they trust authority, yearn for belonging, seek security, prize gratitude, and aspire to executive position. Intellectually, they are prone to practice logistics far more than tactics, diplomacy, and especially strategy. Further, with their tough-minded nature Supervisors tend to take on the Administrator's directive role more readily than the soft-hearted Conservator's informative role. And with their outgoing expressiveness they seem to find it more rewarding to act the role of Supervisor than Inspector. To visualize ESTJ intellectual development consider the following graph that depicts the most probable profile of their logistical roles:

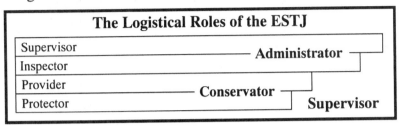

Supervisors abound, comprising at least ten percent of the population. Highly materialistic and concrete, ESTJs believe the table of particulars and the manual of standard operating procedures are what count, not speculation and experimentation, and certainly not fantasy. They keep their feet firmly on the ground and make sure that those under their supervision do the same, whether employee, subordinate, offspring, or spouse for that matter. If others wish to fool around and daydream, fine, as long as they do it on their own time—which means after the job is done. But if they fritter away their time while on duty, they should not be surprised when the Supervisor calls them on the carpet. The top sergeant will not put up with such nonsense.

Sociable and civic-minded, Supervisors are usually pillars of their community. They are generous with their time and energy, and very often belong to a variety of service clubs, lodges, and associations, supporting them through steady attendance, but also taking a vocal leadership role. Indeed, membership groups of all kinds strongly attract ESTJs, perhaps because membership satisfies in some degree their need to maintain the stability of social institutions. Like all the Guardians, Supervisors worry a good deal about society falling apart, morality decaying, standards being undermined, traditions being lost, and so on, and they do all they can to preserve and to extend the institutions that embody social order. These Guardians are so in tune with the established, time-honored institutions and ways of behaving within those institutions that they have a hard time understanding those who might wish to abandon or radically change them.

Supervisors are cooperative with their superiors and carry out orders without fail and to the letter. And they expect the same cooperation—even obedience—from their subordinates or dependents. Rank, they are wont to say, has its obligations, but it also has its privileges. ESTJs are comfortable issuing orders. Telling others what to do is a matter of duty, so demands, commands, requests, and directions come easily to them. At the same time, they may not always be responsive to points of view and emotions of others and have a tendency to jump to conclusions too quickly. They may not always be willing to listen patiently to opposing views, and are particularly vulnerable to this tendency when in positions of authority. They may need to make special effort to remain open to input from others who are dependent on them—their children, spouses, and employees.

Supervisors enjoy and are good at scheduling orderly procedures and in detailing rules and regulations. In their view things are to be done correctly and established procedures observed. ESTJs put their trust in authority, and believe it fitting and proper that government agencies grant licenses and permits only to those passing the scrutiny of sanctioned officials—who are usually Guardians of some sort. ESTJs are comfortable evaluating others and tend to judge how a person is doing in terms of his or her compliance with rules and procedures. They may, at times, be abrupt with those who do not follow the rules correctly, or who do not pay sufficient attention to those details that will get the job done right.

This type finds success in many occupations which require a high degree of dedication and discipline: corporate law, politics, police work, military service, and most especially business. The world of business is the ESTJs' natural habitat. They follow routines well, are neat and orderly, are punctual themselves and expect others to be so. They are loyal to their institutions, are unbelievably hard working in their jobs, and the bright ones frequently rise to positions of responsibility in their company or firm. And yet, no matter how successful they become, Supervisors are always looking for ways of improving themselves, taking night classes, attending seminars, reading professional journals, listening to instructional tapes, and so on.

Such earnestness and industriousness show up quite early in the Supervisors. They are dependable and dutiful almost from infancy, and they usually respect their parents whether or not their parents have earned it. If, for example, they are punished by a parent, they do not hold it against that parent, and are likely, in retrospect at least, to say they deserved it. And in school ESTJs are usually model students, conscientiously following directions, doing all their homework, doing it thoroughly, and on time. Above all else, they wish to do what they are supposed to do, and they rarely question the teacher's assignments, method of instruction, standards, or authority. School, particularly the first twelve grades, was made for them.

Supervisors approach human relations through traditions and rituals, wanting to promote cooperation and contentment in their relationships through well-worked out routines and procedures. Social gatherings and ceremonies have great meaning for them, and they enjoy opportunities to see friends, colleagues, and relatives at functions such as holiday gatherings, weddings, and awards dinners. In social situations, ESTJs are relatively easy to get to know. They tend not to confuse people by sending double messages or putting on airs, and they are dependable and accountable.

At home these tough and outspoken Supervisors insist that each member has an assigned position in a hierarchy—in so many ways, they want a place for everything and everything in its place. Thus, elders are due both privileges and respect, and older siblings have higher status than the younger. The ESTJ tends to take control of the family and to define roles and duties. Spouse and children have certain jobs to do, and it is not enough just to do them; they are to want to do them, and for the right reasons.

As mates and parents Supervisors are faithful and conscientious. They make sure to remember birthdays and anniversaries, and to mark such occasions with appropriate ceremonies and gifts. They worry about their children and take a firm hand in their upbringing—seeing to it that their children become well-mannered, hard working, productive members of society. Supervisors are especially watchful over their children, some perhaps even over-watchful. Individualism and rebelliousness worry them, and the older their children are the more closely the ESTJ supervises them, rarely missing a chance to point out the dangers they face in straying from the norm.

The Inspector [ISTJ]

Inspecting is the act of looking carefully and thoroughly at the products and accounts of an institution—the company's ledger, the farmer's produce, the manufacturer's merchandise, the family's budget—and ISTJs take on this role with quiet dedication. These Inspectors are earnest and attentive in their inspecting; to be certified as right and proper, all must go under their scrutiny, so that no irregularities or discrepancies are let go by. Most often reporting to higher authorities, Inspectors tend to work behind the scenes, only rarely having to confront others with their findings. Indeed, Inspectors make their examinations without flourish or fanfare, and, therefore, the dedication they bring to their work can go unnoticed and unappreciated.

As a variant of Plato's Guardians and Aristotle's Proprietaries, the ISTJs are little different from the other SJs in most respects. Like all the Guardians they are concrete in communicating and cooperative in implementing goals. They are interested in learning about commerce, are preoccupied with morality, and work well with materiel. In orientation, they tend to be dutiful, pessimistic, and stoical as they guard the gateways and look to yesterday. They base their self-image on being seen as dependable, beneficent, and respectable. Often concerned about things, they trust authority, yearn for belonging, seek security, prize gratitude, and aspire to executive position. Intellectually, they are prone to practice logistics far more than tactics, diplomacy, and especially strategy. Further, with their tough-minded nature they tend to choose the directive Administrator's role over the soft-hearted Conservator's informative role. And because of their natural reserve and softspokenness they seem to enjoy the role of Inspector more than that of Supervisor. To visualize ISTJ intellectual development consider the following graph depicting the most probable profile of their logistical roles:

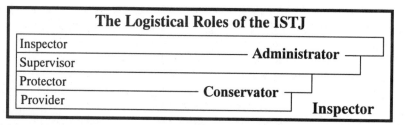

There are a great many Inspectors—they make up perhaps as much as ten percent of the general population. They are characterized by decisiveness in practical affairs, are the guardians of institutions, and if only one adjective could be selected, 'superdependable' (a term used by Myers) would best describe them. Whether at home or at work, ISTJs are nothing if not reliable, particularly when it comes to inspecting the people and things in their jurisdiction—quietly seeing to it that uniform quality of product is maintained, and that those around them uphold certain standards of attitude and conduct.

These hard-nosed and silent Guardians have a distaste for and distrust of fanciness in speech, dress, and place. Their words tend to be simple and down home, not showy or high-flown; their clothes are often homespun and conservative rather than of the latest fashion; and their home and work environments are usually neat, orderly, and plain, rather than up-to-date or luxurious. In their choice of personal property (cars, furnishings, jewelry, and so on) price and durability are of primary concern, comfort or appearance given small consideration. Classics, antiques, and heirlooms are especially valued, having achieved a certain time-honored status—Inspectors prefer the old-fashioned to the newfangled every time. Even on vacation, ISTJs are no-nonsense types who tend not to be attracted by exotic foods, beverages, or locales.

While not outgoing like the ESTJs, ISTJs are likely to be involved in community service organizations that transmit traditional values to the young, such as Sunday School, Little League, or Boy and Girl Scouting. They understand and appreciate the contributions these institutions make in preserving the national heritage. Along with all the Guardians, the Inspectors find value in ceremonies and rituals—weddings, birthdays, and anniversaries, for example—although they tend to be shy if the occasion becomes too large or too public. At work, they are apt to see the company picnic or holiday office party as a necessary nuisance, but are likely to enjoy these events once they arrive and loosen up a bit. More to the male Inspector's liking is the men-only party, where he can drop his guard and use a bit of off-color language. The yearly hunting or fishing trip is often a cherished male ritual for an ISTJ.

As Administrators they are patient with their work and with procedures within an institution, although not always patient with the individual goals and unauthorized behavior of some people in that institution. These Inspectors are comfortable when people know their duties, follow the guidelines, and operate within the rules—rules are there to be followed, they say, not gotten around for personal reasons. For their part, ISTJs will see to it that goods are inspected and schedules are kept, that resources will be up to standard and delivered when and where they are supposed to be. And they would prefer that everyone's attitudes and actions be this law-abiding. They can be adamant about the need for rule-compliance in the workplace, and do not hesitate to report irregularities to the proper authorities. Because of this they are often misjudged as having ice in their veins, for people fail to see their good intentions and their vulnerability to criticism.

Their interest in thoroughness, detail, legality, standard procedures, and orderly flow of materiel leads this type to a number of occupations. Inspectors can handle difficult, detailed forms and columns of figures, and thus they make excellent bank examiners, auditors, accountants, or tax attorneys. Investments in securities are likely to interest this type, particularly investments in municipal bonds and blue-chip securities. Inspectors are not likely to take chances either with their own or others' money, and the thought of a bankrupt nation, state, institution, or family gives them more than a little uneasiness. The idea of dishonoring a contract also bothers an ISTJ—their word is their bond—and they naturally communicate a message of trustworthiness and stability, which can make them successful in business. With their inspector's eye, ISTJs make good librarians, dentists, optometrists, legal secretaries, and law researchers. High school teachers of business, home economics, physical education, civics, and history tend to be Inspectors, as do quartermaster officers in the military.

As a husband or wife, Inspectors are a source of strength. Just as they honor business contracts, so do they honor the marriage contract. Loyal and faithful mates, they take responsibilities to children and spouse seriously, giving lifelong commitment to them. In family matters, as in all other, "duty" is a word the Inspector understands. The male ISTJ's concept of masculinity is patriarchal, and he sees himself as the head of the household and breadwinner of the family. He can accept a working wife—as long as she does not shirk her responsibilities to the children. The female ISTJ makes a steady, dependable partner, but with a commitment to respectability that may not always allow her to express her sensuality.

In their parenting role, Inspectors are firm and consistent in handling their children; they make the rules of the family clear and expect them to be followed. A rebellious, nonconformist child may have a difficult time with an ISTJ parent, and vice versa. Inspectors care about passing along their work ethic to their children, and will often require them to help with household chores and projects. They patiently teach their children basic home maintenance skills, cooking, gardening, carpentry—time-consuming activities which sometimes leave them little opportunity to play with their children. The Inspector child is apt to be obedient and a source of pleasure to parents and teachers.

The Provider [ESFJ]

Providing is the act of furnishing others with the necessities of life, and the ESFJs seem eager to serve others, making sure they feel well-supplied with provisions and a part of the group. These Providers take it upon themselves to arrange for the physical health and welfare of those in need, but they are also the most sociable of all the Guardians, and thus are the great nurturers of established institutions such as schools, churches, social clubs, and civic groups. Wherever they go, Providers take up the role of social contributor, happily giving their time and energy to make sure that the needs of others are met, that traditions are supported and developed, and that social functions are a success.

As a variant of Plato's Guardians and Aristotle's Proprietaries, the ESFJs are little different from the other SJs in most respects. Like all the Guardians they are concrete in communicating and cooperative in implementing their goals. They are interested in learning about commerce, are preoccupied with morality, and work well with materiel. In orientation, they tend to be dutiful, pessimistic, and stoical as they guard the gateways and look to yesterday. They base their self-image on being seen as dependable, beneficent, and respectable. Often seriously concerned about things, they trust authority, yearn for belonging, seek security, prize gratitude, and aspire to executive position. Intellectually, they are prone to practice logistics far more than tactics, diplomacy, and especially strategy. Further, with their friendly or soft-hearted nature, they tend to take up the Conservator's informative role more readily than the tough-minded Administrator's directive role. And because they are so expressive and personable they seem happier taking the part of Provider than that of Protector. To visualize ESFJ intellectual development consider the following graph depicting the most probable profile of their logistical roles:

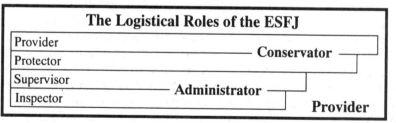

Providers are very likely more than ten percent of the population. This is very fortunate for all of us, because cooperation and social facilitation is a key to their nature. Natural proprietors, ESFJs are skilled in maintaining teamwork among their helpers, and are also tireless in their attention to the details of arranging goods and services. They make excellent chairpersons in charge of banquets, rummage sales, charity balls, and the like. They are without peer as masters of ceremonies, able to approach others with ease and confidence, and seemingly aware of what everyone's been doing. And they are outstanding hosts or hostesses, able to remember people's names, usually after one introduction, and always concerned about the needs of their guests, wanting to insure that all are involved and provided for.

These expressive Conservators are personable and talkative, and may become restless when isolated from people. Even among strangers (on an airplane, in line at the grocery store, in a doctor's waiting room), they will strike up a conversation and chat pleasantly about any concrete topic that comes to mind. Like all the Guardians, they follow a sort of free association, bouncing from subject to subject, from weather to sports to food to prices, and so on. In addition, ESFJs show a delightful fascination with gossip, not only concerning celebrities, but also their friends and neighbors. If we wish to know what's been going on in the local community, school, or church, they're happy to fill us in on all the details.

Providers tend to have observable things on their mind rather than imaginary things. They are likely to be aware of and to enjoy discussing events and problems in people's lives; but when conversations turn to philosophic or scientific abstractions, they may become restive. Wondering about abstract issues such as in anthropology, epistemology, psychology, sociology, theology, or whatever, does not excite their interest, as it does the Idealist's or the Rational's. On the contrary, ESFJs tend to listen to acknowledged authorities on abstract matters, and often rely on officially sanctioned views as the source of their opinions and attitudes.

Social traditions matter to the Providers, and their conversations often drift to nostalgic recounting of past experiences in the good old days. At the same time, however, ESFJs can cause others undue tension by expressing anticipations of gloom and doom, exhibiting a bent toward the pessimistic that can be contagious. They need to control their fears that the worst is sure to happen.

Providers are highly sensitive and are not at all reluctant to express their emotional reactions. They are quick to like and dislike, tending to put on a pedestal whatever or whomever they admire, and to come down hard on those people and issues they don't care for. Ever conscious of appearances, they take very seriously the opinions of others regarding their own acceptability. They can be crushed by personal criticism, and will function effectively only when appreciated both for themselves and for the abundant service they give to others. ESFJs need to be needed, and may spend much energy making sure that they deserve to be. If treated unkindly, they can become downhearted, and are prone to take the blame for whatever might be wrong in their institution or their relationships.

In their choice of careers, Providers may lean toward service occupations. They have such pleasant, outgoing personalities that they are far and away the best sales reps, not only regularly winning sales contests, but earning seniority in any sales group within an organization. Observation of ESFJs at work in a sales transaction will demonstrate how this type personalizes the sale. They are visibly—and honestly—concerned with their customer's welfare, and thus the customer is not simply buying the product, but is buying personally from the Provider. This same characteristic causes them to be good in many people-to-people jobs, as teachers, clergy, coaches, and so on. ESFJs seldom become a source of irritation to their superiors, for they are duty and service-oriented and respect and obey the rules and regulations. Conscientious and orderly, they are loyal to their employers, and make invaluable personal secretaries and office receptionists.

These Providers take their role as family provider seriously, in both a material and a moral sense. They provide a sound and safe home, good food, nice clothes, and a store of possessions. But they are also conscientious about home responsibilities, are orderly about the house, and prefer that other family members be the same. In addition, they have a strong set of values with clear shoulds and shouldn'ts, which they expect their family to abide by. Providers want family decisions settled quickly and with little fuss, and they want family living regularly scheduled and correctly executed. They do not rebel against routine operations, are devoted to the traditional values of home and hearth, and are the most sympathetic of all the types.

Providers make loyal and loving mates, willing to stand by their husband or wife through good times and bad, going beyond the call of duty to maintain the marriage and the appearance of happiness, even when the road is rocky. They enjoy socializing and entertaining, and observe all the rituals connected with serving wholesome food and beverages. They thrive on traditional festivities, and seem able to express the right feeling for a given social occasion. They are fond-hearted, sentimental, and usually observe with flourish birthdays and anniversaries, making them joyous occasions.

Providers are fiercely devoted to their children, and will sacrifice to see that they get everything they need for their physical well-being. At times, ESFJs get their own sense of success as a parent wrapped up in their children's successes and failures. They can see their children as an extension of the family, with whatever their kids do reflecting on them as parents. If their children are polite and productive, Providers glow with pride; but if their kids are rowdy or unappreciative, the Provider parent may be embarrassed and become critical toward them, trying to instill in them a sense of social decorum and gratitude. As children, Providers usually respect and revere their own parents, and in school are responsive and obedient pupils.

The Protector [ISFJ]

The primary desire of the Protector is to be of service and to minister to others. But here "service" means not so much furnishing others with the necessities of life (the Provider's concern), as guarding others against life's pitfalls and perils, that is, seeing to their security. These ISFJs derive a great deal of satisfaction from caring for others, and they offer their comfort gently and helpfully, quietly seeing to it that caretaking is scheduled to protect the health and welfare of those in need.

As a variant of Plato's Guardians and Aristotle's Proprietaries, the ESFJs are little different from the other SJs in most respects. Like all the Guardians they are concrete in communicating and cooperative in implementing their goals. They are interested in learning about commerce, are preoccupied with morality, and work well with materiel. In orientation, they tend to be dutiful, pessimistic, and stoical as they guard the gateways and look to yesterday. They base their self-image on being seen as dependable, beneficent, and respectable. Often seriously concerned about things, they trust authority, yearn for belonging, seek security, prize gratitude, and aspire to executive position. Intellectually, they are prone to practice logistics far more than tactics, diplomacy, and especially strategy. Further, being friendly or fond-hearted in nature, they tend to take up the Conservator's roles of Protector and Provider more comfortably than the tough-minded Administrator's roles of Supervisor and Inspector. And owing to their sense of quiet reserve they seem more comfortable acting as a Protector than a Provider. To visualize ISFJ intellectual development consider the following graph depicting the most probable profile of their logistical roles:

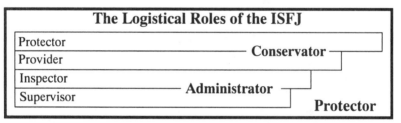

There is a large proportion of Protectors in the population, perhaps as much as ten percent. And a good thing, because they are vigilant in their protecting, and seem fulfilled in the degree they can insure the safekeeping of those in their family, their circle of friends, or their place of business. Also, they enjoy assisting the downtrodden and can handle disability and neediness in others better than any other type. ISFJs go about their task of caretaking modestly, unassumingly, and because of this their efforts are sometimes not fully appreciated. They are not as open and talkative as the ESFJs, except with close friends and relatives. With these, however, they can chat tirelessly, and for as long as it takes to cover in minute detail everything concrete in their lives. But their shyness with strangers is often misjudged as stiffness, even coldness, when in truth these Guardians are warm-hearted and sympathetic, giving happily of themselves to those in need—although, curiously, their interest may wane when the recipient is no longer in trouble.

Their reserve ought really to be seen as an expression, not of coldness, but of their sincerity and seriousness of purpose. Like all the Guardians, Protectors have a strongly held work ethic, which tells them that work is good, and that play must be earned—if indulged in at all. The least hedonic of all types, ISFJs are willing to work long, long hours doing all the thankless jobs the other types seem content to ignore. Thoroughness and frugality are also virtues for them. When they undertake a task, they will complete it if at all humanly possible. They also know the value of a dollar and abhor the squandering or misuse of resources. These reserved Conservators are quite content to work alone; indeed, they may experience some discomfort when placed in positions of authority, and may try to do everything themselves rather than direct others to do their jobs.

For all these reasons, Protectors are frequently overworked, just as they are frequently misunderstood and undervalued. Their contributions, and also their economies, are often taken for granted, and they rarely get the gratitude they deserve. This can cause them to harbor feelings of resentment, with their bottled up emotion gnawing inwardly, causing them much undeserved suffering.

Protectors are keenly aware of status given by birth, titles, offices, and credentials. They are impressed by visiting royalty, they admire high-ranking politicians, they honor judges, the police, and the military, and they tend to be devoted and loyal to their superiors. Not that they think of themselves as superior. On the contrary, they are humble to the core, and find the putting on of airs offensive. For the ISFJ, people should behave according to their place in the social order, and they may be annoyed by others who act above their station. They believe in the safety of a traditional social hierarchy, and do everything they can to uphold custom and convention.

The same holds true at work. Protectors are dependable and are seldom happy working in situations where established ways of doing things are not respected. To them, regulations are tried and true, and they rarely question the effectiveness of going by the book. ISFJs often seem to feel personally responsible for seeing to it that people in an institution or business abide by rules, carry out routines, and behave as they are supposed to behave. If others, including their bosses, violate or ignore these standard operating procedures, Protectors are distressed and embarrassed, although they usually will not display these reactions. More likely, such irritation is turned inward and may be experienced as fatigue and as chronic stomach disorders.

With their extraordinary sense of safety and responsibility, and with their unusual talent for executing routines, Protectors do well as curators, private secretaries, librarians, middle-management personnel, and especially as general medical practitioners. To be sure, the hospital is a natural haven for them; it is home to the family doctor, rescuer of life and limb, and to the registered nurse, or licensed practical nurse, the true angels of mercy. The insurance industry is also congenial to these Conservators. To save, to put something aside against an unpredictable future, to prepare for emergencies—these are important actions to ISFJs, who as insurance agents want to see their clients in good hands, sheltered and protected.

Speculation and innovation do not intrigue Protectors, who would rather leave such risky matters to others, while remaining themselves safely anchored and down-to-earth. For their part, ISFJs value tradition, both cultural and familial. They carry with them a sense of history, a sense of continuity with past events and relationships. They seem to have an innate regard for the past, for whatever is long-established and deeply rooted. They are honored to care for collections of rare old things, books, paintings, china, and so on, seeing to it that they are safely shelved and regularly dusted. But they are also the keepers of simple family things, old photograph albums, timeworn furniture, old tools and wedding dresses. Of all the types, ISFJs are most likely to care about tracing family trees.

Protectors are devoted to mate and family, and are usually excellent homemakers. The ISFJ female often displays a flair for making the interior of the home attractive in a traditional manner, and often gives herself full-time to the duties of housewife. She provides attractive, nourishing meals, sees to the shopping, does the laundry, mends the clothes, and follows a daily routine for keeping the house clean and tidy, with rooms straightened up, dishes done, and beds made. The ISFJ male takes on all the other duties of keeping up the home: he usually handles the finances, cares for the yard (and often tends a vegetable garden), maintains the car, and is usually handy when it comes to minor repairs in masonry, carpentry, painting, plumbing, electrical work, and the like.

In their parenting role, these friendly and soft-spoken Protectors expect their children to conform to the rules of society, feeling a personal responsibility to see to it that these standards are not only adhered to but honored. Such parents worry a great deal, and may try too hard to protect their children from the dirt and dangers of life. Protector mothers in particular need to learn how to encourage their children's independence and to cut the apron strings. Occasionally an ISFJ mother may be able to find humor in the wayward son, but she still raises her daughters to respect traditions and to do the Right Thing at the Right Time—and always for the Right Reason.

5

Idealists

Generations to come will scarce believe that such a one as this ever in flesh and blood walked upon this earth.

With these glowing words Albert Einstein eulogized one of the most remarkable men of the twentieth century, Mohandas K. Gandhi. Not only did Gandhi almost single-handedly free India and its then five hundred million people from their long subjection to the British Empire, but he did so without raising an army, without firing a gun or taking a hostage, and without ever holding a political office. How could one slight, soft-spoken man accomplish such an incredible feat? The answer must wait upon an examination of the Idealist character.

Like George Washington one hundred and fifty years before him, Gandhi knew he could never defeat British colonial power in armed confrontation, but, at the same time, he had no interest in waging a Washington-style logistical war. It was not in Gandhi's nature to undertake military operations in any form. Gandhi's interests were in ethical matters and his talents in diplomacy, so he instinctively sought to oppose the British colonial government on humane, moral, even spiritual grounds. Gandhi believed that an entrenched political and economic system could only be overthrown by acting in accord with noble principle. And so, over a period of years he developed a highly principled course of action, a form of non-violent passive resistance which he called "satyagraha." Armed only in this manner, Gandhi courageously stood his ground even in the face of frequent incarcerations and sometimes brutal assaults, finally bringing the British to their knees through an exercise of moral authority that journalist William Shirer referred to as "soul force."

Gandhi's objective was political freedom for India, and yet, for all his social activism, he never lost sight of a higher goal for himself and his people. He was an Idealist, and it was his idealism that led him to seek divine truth and justice, human dignity and integrity, and true knowledge of God. Gandhi wrote in his *Autobiography*:

All that appears and happens about and around us is uncertain, transient. But there is a Supreme Being hidden therein as a Certainty, and one would be blessed if one could catch a glimpse of that Certainty and hitch one's wagon to it. The quest for that Truth is the *summum bonum* of life.

Rare indeed is the man or woman with such confidence in a Certainty beyond earthly certainty, in a Truth behind the worldly illusion of truth. Truth, Integrity, Justice, Virtue: so ardently devoted are the Gandhis of this world to these ideals that we need not hesitate to call them the Idealists.

In the mid 1970s I wrote that Apollo was the guiding deity of these Idealists (Myers's NFs). For the Greeks, Golden Apollo was the god of light, sometimes referred to as the sun-god, but more often portrayed as the god of light in the symbolic sense of the word—the god of truth or insight, of spiritual illumination or personal enlightenment. He was also the seer and the revealer, whose oracle at Delphi was the hallowed and feared voice of prophecy throughout the ancient world. And he was the healer, particularly the psychic healer, whose lyrical music purified his followers and taught them how to find inner wholeness. While some fascination with the primitive and the profane seemed to lurk just beneath his shining surface, Apollo was for the Greeks the most ideal of all the gods, a radiant figure of beauty and poetry in whom little of the savage remained.

In the 1980s I began to think of the Dolphin as an appropriate totem animal for the Idealists, because they are one of the most cooperative of all animals. Not only do they communicate in a complex sonic language, they also live in close-knit family groups, playing and hunting together, and helping family members who are ill or in trouble, holding them up near the surface with their backs or flippers so they can breathe. Even more, dolphins seem genuinely interested in relating with human beings. In captivity these friendly creatures get along well with their trainers and handlers, and they cooperate freely with researchers. And in the wild dolphins will follow ships for many miles, racing and diving around the keels, and are believed to offer a kind of mysterious guidance of ships into port, as in Scott O'Dell's children's novel, *Island of the Blue Dolphins*:

> Dolphins are animals of good omen. It made me happy to have them swimming around the canoe....I was very lonely before they appeared, but now I felt I had friends with me....
> The blue dolphins left me shortly before dusk. They left as quickly as they had come, going on into the west, but for a long time I could see the sun shining on them. After night fell I could still see them in my thoughts and it was because of this that I kept on paddling when I wanted to lie down and sleep.
> More than anything, it was the blue dolphins that took me back home.

In retrospect, I don't remember coming across any of these people during World War II. The war years, for me at least, were filled with deadly dull days punctuated by terrifying hours. Everyone seemed so very concrete in what they talked about and either very utilitarian or very by-the-book in what they did. The people around me seemed to be Artisans and Guardians, just as they were in high school. Indeed, the first Idealist I ever met was a classmate of mine in Junior College, and she was the girl I married after the war. At the time I did not know what to say to most girls, but I could chat for hours with her. It was a revelation. By nature a nerd, I had thought that there was some secret that other boys were on to, some special technique that one must know about and use in talking to girls; but with my new classmate no technique was required—we just talked about what we were interested in, and totally without effort or forethought. My guess is that it was our mutual interest in things abstract, aside from our interest in each other, that made all the difference and made our daily conversations delightful. With her I could be myself; with others I could not. This wonderful companionship has lasted for over half a century.

During my years managing the work of school counselors I saw to it that most of them were Idealists. They were beautifully fitted for that kind of work and were able to learn quickly and apply effectively the many methods of corrective intervention I had managed to collect. And during my years training graduate students in the technology of corrective counseling, the vast majority of them were Idealists. They flocked to the counseling department, and rightly so. Teaching them to intervene effectively into the lives of troubled children and their parents and teachers was enormously gratifying because they were so ready, willing, and able to learn these skills—and they learned them far better than other types. At the very heart of corrective counseling is diplomatic intelligence, something Idealists are well endowed with, as I will discuss below.

I don't think there are enough of these caring people, for they are affirmed and coveted by most of us for their enthusiasm and for their often expressed appreciation of the rest of us, whatever our temperament.

Plato's Idealists

Plato was the quintessential Idealist, the inventor of a philosophy in which ideas are even more real than earth and its inhabitants. Plato's word for an idealist like himself was '*noetic*' which, roughly translated, means "intuitive thought," that is, pure thinking done without recourse to either logical or empirical investigation. Plato saw these inspiring Idealists, and no others, as the philosopher-kings of his ideal republic, destined to serve a philosophic function in society, their job no less than to divine moral principles and the full meaning of life.

Aristotle said that happiness is "the highest realizable good" and that some men, those of "superior refinement and active disposition," identify happiness not as the "sensual pleasure" (*hêdonê*) of the Artisans, nor as the "proprietorship" (*propráietari*) of the Guardians, nor even as the "logical inquiry" (*dialogikê*) of the Rationals, but as the "study of ethics" (*ethiké*), which leads to an understanding of the Good Life and thus to happiness. So Plato's Idealists, in Aristotle's view, become the Ethical Idealists.

Centuries later Galen named this type the "Cholerics." The word 'choleric' is Greek for yellow bile, one of the four humors or body fluids that were thought at the time to determine one's predisposition to act in certain ways. Those with a choleric temperament are thus bilious, that is, easily annoyed and quick to show their displeasure, unable, in other words, to put their feelings on hold. Note that Galen was more interested in the negative side of temperament, the irascible Cholerics being seen as different from but no worse than the taciturn Phlegmatics, the over-optimistic Sanguines, and the doleful Melancholics.

During the Renaissance the Viennese physician Paracelsus chose as the Idealists' guiding spirit the Nymphs, those rarefied, often invisible beings who watch over the different realms of nature, the forests, mountains, lakes, rivers, and the sea, and who are thought to have the power of prophecy and enlightenment. Thus water Nymphs (or Naiads) are believed to give profound insight to those who drink from their brooks and streams, and wood Nymphs can inspire great poetry, as did the "light-winged Dryad of the trees" in Keats's "Ode to a Nightingale." Nymphs are also passionately devoted to others, and their affairs are affairs of the heart. The little Mermaid in the harbor at Copenhagen symbolizes undying love, as she waits eternally for her lost sailor.

Adickes called these Idealists the "Dogmatics." They, like his Agnostics, are autonomous beings, and thus are focused on the self, but autonomy in the Dogmatics takes the form of certitude regarding what they consider important social issues. In other words, Dogmatics are inclined to embrace some humane doctrine and cling to it tenaciously, certain as they are of its immense value to mankind. Thus, by "dogmatism" Adickes did not mean bigotry or narrow-mindedness; rather, he meant a devotedness to an ideal way of life, and an intention to invite others to join in that way of living. Note that 'dogma,' 'doctrine,' and 'doctor' have the same root ('dek,' to "teach" or "cause to accept"); thus a doctor or dogmatist is one who embraces a doctrine strongly, offering it to others for their benefit.

Spränger thought of the Idealists as the "Religious" types, in the sense of having a creed of personal ethics, a frame of moral orientation. Thus religion for Spränger was a cause, a principle, an activity pursued with conscientious devotion, not an object of piety. The religious types seek the meaning of life and the meaning of Self, refusing to believe that they are insignificant or that life is meaningless. Thus Idealists in Spränger's view have what can be called an "Identity Seeking Personality."

Kretschmer was first to take a careful look at the dark side of character, and he named the Idealists "Hyperesthetic," which roughly translated means "oversensitive." In this way he echoed Galen and Paracelsus in seeing Idealists not only as tempestuous but also as passionate. And yet Kretschmer was saying much more, namely that the kind of irrational conduct that befalls some Idealists is a matter of temperament rather than a matter of choice. If Idealists are forced by difficult circumstances to become estranged from themselves and others, they do so as if beset by negative feelings that overwhelm them and numb their will.

Like Kretschmer, Fromm examined both sides of personality, the negative as well as positive character traits. When he termed the Idealists "Receptive" he considered being a passive recipient of goods and services as bad. But he also praised this type for their responsiveness and other desirable traits, describing them as "accepting," "adaptable," "adjusted," "charming," "devoted," "idealistic," "modest," "optimistic," "polite," "responsive," "sensitive," "sentimental," "tender," and "trusting."

Myers's contribution to the study of the Idealist personality is quite remarkable, no doubt because she was herself an Idealist, and so understood them better than most and approved of them heartily. As indicated earlier she named them the "Intuitive Feeling" types—"NFs"—and said that they are "creative," "enthusiastic," "humane," "imaginative," "insightful," "religious," "subjective," and "sympathetic." Though apparently unaware of the contributions of her predecessors, Myers by herself was clearly able to identify the more salient traits that characterize Plato's Idealists.

The Abstract Cooperators

These different views of Plato's Idealists, whatever they are called, all have something in common: they all imply that this temperament is abstract in communicating and cooperative in implementing goals. As we begin our study of the NF Idealist traits of character, then, let us get our bearings by looking at the underlying basis of their personality in the matrix of temperament. As shown at the side, the foundation of the Idealist temperament is their unique combination of abstract word usage with cooperative tool usage, and so they can be called the "Abstract Cooperators."

	Words	
	Abstract	Concrete
Cooperative	Abstract **NF** Cooperators	**SJ**
Tools		
Utilitarian	**NT**	**SP**

Abstract Word Usage

Abstract words refer to things that cannot be observed but only imagined, while concrete words refer to things that can be observed and therefore need not be imagined. Idealists talk little of what they observe—"of shoes and ships and sealing wax, of cabbages and kings." They talk instead of what can only be seen with the mind's eye: love and hate, heaven and hell, comedy and tragedy, heart and soul, tales and legends, eras and epochs, beliefs, fantasies, possibilities, symbols, selves, and yes, temperament, character, and personality. "Exultation is the going of an inland soul to sea, past the houses—past the headlands—into deep Eternity," wrote the Idealist poet Emily Dickinson, and only an NF would dare to speak of an emotion—exultation—in this poetic way, or to measure the journey to so great an abstraction as Eternity. All of us, of course, can observe what is before us as well as imagine what is not. But this does not mean that we do both equally. Very early in life we begin to exercise one focus of thought and language—observation or imagination—more than the other, and we continue to do so throughout life. Idealists opt for imagination.

Idealists are naturally inductive in their thought and speech, which is to say that they move quickly from part to whole, from a few particulars to sweeping generalizations, from the smallest sign of something to its entirety. With their focus on unseen potentials, on the not visible and the not yet, Idealists show an extraordinary sensitivity to hints of things, mere suggestions, inklings, intimations, symbols. To be sure, such inductive inferences, requiring what is called the "intuitive leap," can be astonishing to others, especially in cases of mind reading and extra-sensory perception. At the very least, Idealists are the best suited of all the types to read between the lines, or to have a sixth sense about people, and they do indeed follow their hunches, heed their feelings, and insist they "just know" what people are really up to, or what they really mean. Even with complicated issues, NFs need hear only the first words of an explanation to feel they understand the subject fully, jumping from telling details to larger meanings. When William Blake imagined in *Auguries of Innocence* that one can "See a World in a Grain of Sand, And a Heaven in a Wild Flower, Hold Infinity in the palm of your hand, And Eternity in an hour," he was surely describing the Idealist's inductive style.

Wanting to uncover meaning and significance in the world, and trying to understand what they believe is the real nature of things, Idealist thought and speech tends to be interpretive, which means they frequently comment how one thing is really something else. Not tied to observable objects like the SPs and SJs, and not disciplined by the deductive logic of the NTs, NFs spontaneously transform one thing into another, erasing distinctions, combining categories, and joining opposites. Margaret Schlegel, the Idealist heroine in E.M. Forster's *Howards End,* tries passionately to connect "the seen to the unseen" in her life, a joining she imagines as the

> building of the rainbow bridge that should connect the prose in us with the passion. Without it we are meaningless fragments, half monks, half beasts, unconnected arches that have never joined into a man. With it love is born, and alights on the highest curve, glowing against the grey, sober against the fire.

This zeal to connect disparate ideas is why Idealist communication is often laced with metaphors, ascribing features to people and things that belong to other people and things—animate or inanimate, visible or invisible. NFs have no trouble saying this person is a devil, that one an angel. It isn't that the first person acts like a devil, he is one; and the other person doesn't simply have the attributes of an angel, she is one. And the sun smiles at us, a corporation is grasping, a train roars, and love is a rose. In just this way Gandhi described his search for what he called "Absolute Truth": "The little fleeting glimpses...I have been able to have of Truth can hardly convey an idea of the indescribable lustre of Truth, a million times more intense than that of the sun we daily see with our eyes."

Beyond the vivid metaphor, Gandhi also shows the Idealists' charming habit of overstatement, quite the opposite of the Rationals' penchant for understatement. Idealist expression is rich in hyperbole and exaggeration, and at the same time short on gradation. NFs do not say they are "somewhat" interested in an idea, or dissatisfied "in some degree" with a person's behavior; they are "totally" fascinated or "completely" disgusted, "perfectly" delighted or "absolutely" appalled. This is just how Eleanor Roosevelt in her *Autobiography* described herself as a young woman: "I had painfully high ideals and a tremendous sense of duty entirely unrelieved by any sense of humor or any appreciation of the weaknesses of human nature. Things were either right or wrong to me."

While they tend to ignore degrees of gradation, Idealists are highly sensitive to the nuances of communication that qualify messages, the body language, facial expressions, and voice inflections which, quite often, the other character types are not even aware of. And NFs are so sensitive to the subtleties of spoken language, finding implications and insinuations in the slightest remark, that they seem to have invested language with super-natural powers, what might be called "word magic." Word magic refers to the ancient idea that words have the ability to make things happen—saying makes it so—and it has been the basis for many books on self-improvement, *The Magic of Believing*, for example, or *The Power of Positive Thinking*. Our speech, the NF reminds us, produces results in the world, so we must be careful, very careful, about what we say. One consequence of this hypersensitivity is that now and then NFs make mistakes in attributing meanings to communications that are not intended by the senders.

Idealists can become so caught up with their insights, interpretations, and metaphors that it is almost impossible for them to keep their hands still. But unlike the SP's paw, the SJ's cleaver, or the NT's claw, NFs extend their open hands to others, as if offering their counsel freely, or accepting another's words as a gift. They will also row their hands like oars or wings in front of them, as if trying to help the flow of words and ideas between themselves and others. Or they will bring their hands together in various ways, with their palms crossed and fingers wrapped, with their palms meeting and fingers extended vertically, or with their fingers inter-locked—all as if trying to hold together two halves of a message.

Cooperative Tool Usage

Bear in mind that civilization is a cluster of cities, and that cities are clusters of tools—streets, sidewalks, buildings, conveyances: all are tools.

And the countless instruments, implements, and machines in those buildings, on those streets, and in those conveyances are also tools. Now, for all the millions of tools that enable us to do our work and live together in harmony, Idealists would have a consensus on how they are to be used. This is a slightly different shade of cooperation than that which characterizes the Guardians, who are more interested in compliance than consensus. Thus Idealists observe the many laws that govern our conduct—building codes, tax laws, rules of the road, and many more—not simply because they are laws, but because they represent a common assent of their community, a unity of purpose or like-mindedness that NFs hold dear. Accord, concurrence, agreement, accommodation: this side of cooperation is what looms large in the consciousness of Idealists.

Acting in concert with others for the good of the group—cooperation—is considerably more important to Idealists than the functional utility of their chosen tools and operations. In the Idealist's view, people's instruments and actions need to be acceptable to others, even if they prove less effective than some other disapproved instruments or actions. NFs, like SJs, regard the Artisans' and Rationals' utilitarian style—get the job done any which way—as counterproductive if not unethical and offensive. Conventional uses of tools should not be lightly set aside for the sake of increased utility without due regard for people's feelings about working together in harmony.

Indeed, NFs can be quite suspicious of utilitarian actions which go after results too coldly or single-mindedly; they worry that the warm human touch will be lost, that good feelings will be sacrificed, and that unity will dissolve in a quest for expediency. For their part, Idealists dream of perfect interpersonal relationships, mutually supportive interactions lifted high above the fray of competition and contention. Fighting in any form is inordinately painful to NFs and they will do whatever is necessary to avoid it or prevent it. Sustaining amicable relationships through conciliation, pacification, facilitation is much more their style.

This is not to say that Idealists are indifferent to acquiring and using better ways and means of pursuing their goals. Surely they are not at all resistant to the utility of tools, but these must undergo scrutiny lest there be some adverse consequence that undermines morale or makes for discontent among their companions. In any enterprise the NFs' first consideration is always to foster caring human relationships—this seems to them necessary if they are to accomplish their ends. Their ideal is to help the people in their circle get along with each other, even care about each other, and thus work with each other for the good of all.

The Diplomatic Intellect

Diplomacy is the ability to deal with people in a skillful, tactful manner, only here 'tact' is not the concrete term I have used to describe the tactile Artisans, but is a metaphor for the interpersonal touch or sensitivity in which Idealists seem to be both interested and particularly talented. This sensitive way with people shows up so early in NFs that it is tempting to assume they are born with it—born to use their personal empathy and interpersonal skills to improve relations between people. Indeed, while SPs usually become more tactical, SJs more logistical, and NTs more strategic as they grow and mature, NFs become more diplomatic in working with people or personnel—working in both ways, using their eye for possibilities to develop human potentials, and using their verbal fluency to mediate interpersonal conflicts. With their instinct for seeking common ground, with their ability to interpret each side's communications in a positive way, with their gift for putting themselves in another's place, and with their metaphorical language easily and fluidly turning one thing into another, Idealists are well-equipped for the difficult task of influencing people's attitudes and actions, not only inspiring them to grow, but also settling differences among them, smoothing difficulties—ever looking to enlighten the people around them and to forge unity among them.

Gandhi's earliest success as a lawyer revealed just this kind of diplomatic intelligence. Having finally persuaded two Indian businessmen to settle a bitter dispute out of court, Gandhi beamed inwardly:

> My joy was boundless. I had learnt the true practice of law...to find out the better side of human nature and to enter men's hearts. I realized that the true function of a lawyer was to unite parties riven asunder.

Needless to say, Gandhi's is a striking, and uniquely Idealist, view of the practice of law.

The Idealist's eye is always focused on inclusion, not exclusion, on what gifts people can offer each other, not what walls divide them. In just this all-embracing spirit did Eleanor Roosevelt welcome to the United States a group of refugees from Hitler's Europe:

> We Americans are well aware that this is not a one-sided relationship. We are offering you a home and a haven, to be sure. However, you...are bringing us your skills, your talents, and your cultures. We are grateful to you for broadening our scope and enriching our country which consists of newcomers just like you.

Perhaps Idealists are given to diplomacy because they are so deeply disturbed by division and discrimination. Conflicts and controversies unsettle them, disputes and debates set them on edge, even the Rational's insistence on clear-cut definitions and discrete categories can seem antagonistic to them. Idealists consider all such differentiations (religious, ethnic, political, logical, and so on) to be artificial impositions onto the common experience of humanity, and they prefer to focus on what they call those "shared experiences" and "universal truths" that project similar talents and potentials into everyone, and that minimize differences. Only rarely do NFs entertain the idea that their global belief that "down deep, everyone's alike" might itself be an artificial imposition onto the experience of other types.

Interest, Practice, Skill

Any skill is acquired by practice, increasing precisely in the degree it is exercised, and diminishing in the degree it is neglected. Neural cells are like muscle cells; if they aren't used they lie dormant and even degenerate.

In addition, there is a feedback relation between interest and ability. We improve in doing things we're interested in doing, and have greater interest in things we do well. Interest reinforces skill, skill reinforces interest, and neither seems to be the starting point. So the Idealists' lifelong interest in diplomatic action fuels their daily exercise of diplomatic skills, and as diplomatic skill increases so then does interest in it, precisely and exclusively measured by the amount of practice.

Now, in a sense every individual has not one but four IQs, and it is virtually impossible for one person to develop all four of his or her capabilities equally. The kind of operation practiced most develops most, while that practiced least develops least. In normal development the Idealists instinctively practice diplomatic actions far more and far earlier than the others, and therefore end up more highly skilled in diplomacy than in logistics and strategy, and much more than in tactics. Of course, circumstances can sometimes induce Idealists to develop those operations that do not come easily to them, and with lots of practice they can even show a good deal of talent in their short suit, tactics. For example, as adults NFs often try their hand at tactical activities such as gourmet cooking, ceramics, sculpting, painting, or playing a musical instrument, and given enough practice they can come to be quite skilled in these hobbies.

Note in the chart below that the NFs' diplomatic skills develop far beyond their tactical skills. Also, note that their strategic and logistical skills can be almost equally developed, depending of course on circumstances equalizing the amount of practice they are given.

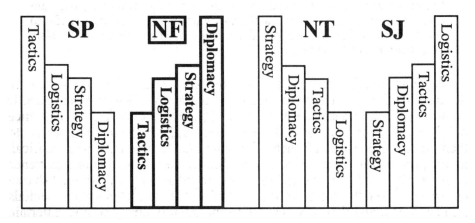

The reason for this potential equality in their second and third suits is that NFs share abstractness of thought and speech with NTs, the strategists, and they share cooperativeness in implementing their goals with the SJs, the logisticals, and so have some interest and aptitude for long-range planning and for managing supplies and services. SPs, by the way, have the same potential as NFs for developing their logistical and strategic skills, but for the opposite reasons: SPs share concrete communication with SJs and utilitarian implementation with NTs. Thus, the NFs and SPs usually end up mirror images of each other in their IQ profile, just as happens in the case of NTs and SJs.

Diplomatic Role Variants

While Idealists all share diplomatic intelligence, they differ significantly among themselves in the sorts of diplomatic roles they feel drawn to practice. In broad terms, Idealists are interested in following the path of what I call the "Mentor" or the "Advocate," and these lead to four diplomatic role variants, the "Teacher" (ENFJ), the "Counselor" (INFJ), the "Champion" (ENFP), and the "Healer" (INFP), all Idealists in essence, but quite unique in their diplomacy. Consider this chart of the NF diplomatic roles and role variants, mirrored by their most skilled intelligent operations:

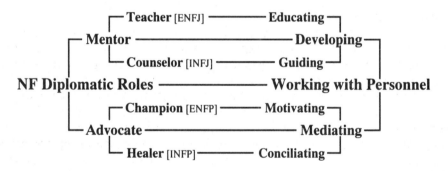

Diplomatic Mentors

Taking the role of Mentor is deeply satisfying to some Idealists, particularly the scheduling Idealists, those who prefer a clear agenda or program, and who are comfortable directing others to act or to think in certain ways. Mentoring is the act of developing the mind or mentality of others, and Mentors are so enthusiastic and charismatic—in a word, so inspiring—that without seeming to do so they can help others to grow, kindling in them a passion for learning and guiding them in the search for their true nature. There are other less benign kinds of mental influence, of course, brainwashing and mind-control, for instance, but fortunately Mentors are diplomatic in their directiveness, which means they are ethical and benevolent with others, sensitive to their needs, and wanting the best for them.

Mentors work to develop human potential in two different but related ways, depending on whether they are inclined to be the outgoing, expressive Teacher or the reserved Counselor.

Teachers are naturally able to take control of almost any group of learners with extraordinary confidence and creativity, as classroom teachers, certainly, but also as journalists, clergy, lecturers, therapists, personnel consultants—in any situation where the quest for learning takes place. These expressive Mentors see themselves less as instructors (installing mental structure) than as educators or facilitators, dreaming up imaginative learning experiences that call forth each learner's potentials, always with the intention of broadening, edifying, enlightening, illuminating, improving, and refining the attitudes and actions of pupils or students.

Counselors tend to be more private in their style of facilitating personal growth, but they still work enthusiastically with their clients, guiding them along the pathways that their nature allows them to follow. These quiet Mentors have profound insight into the emotional needs of others, a keen intuition about their buried feelings, and they can affect their clients in unconscious ways, encouraging and enabling them to get in touch with themselves. Counselors advise, appeal, prescribe, recommend, shepherd, suggest, urge—all with the intention of helping others discover those things that enhance their well-being.

Diplomatic Advocates

The probing Idealists, those who prefer open-ended experience, and who tend to give information rather than issue directives, take the role of Advocate. To the Idealists, advocating is literally "giving voice" to views and positions, beliefs and causes—ideas that people often can't put into words for themselves—in order to nurture rapport and understanding between people. Advocates act on behalf of others, in support of others, serving as their client's activist, adherent, ambassador, enthusiast, exponent, proponent, supporter—whenever speaking up and standing up for others can help resolve differences and bring about justice. As with mentoring, there are other less honorable kinds of advocating, for example, propagandizing and proselytizing, which emphasize one side against the other. But the NF's diplomatic advocating is most often done with the hope of mediating disputes and bringing people together.

Advocates work to bring harmony to others in two complementary ways, either as the expressive Champion or the reserved Healer.

Champions are eager to go everywhere and to experience, first hand, all the meaningful things happening in their world. Once these outgoing Advocates have explored issues and events, they are filled with ardent conviction and enthusiastically champion—adopt, embrace, espouse, fight for, and go to bat for—the truth of a cause or an ideal they have come to believe in, all in an effort to motivate (to encourage, even to inspire) others to settle their conflicts and to act justly and wisely.

Healers are deeply committed to personal conciliation, that is, to preserving or restoring, as the case may be, the wholeness and health of those near and dear to them. Healers are spiritual go-betweens, acting as a bridge between conflicting factions, with the hope of assisting others to find health through inner peace. In this way healing is a matter of acceptance, accommodation, reconciliation, forgiveness, resolution, reunification—all in the interest of mending relationships between people or making whole a divided self. Healers are deeply reserved in nature, and are thus more comfortable working out of the limelight; indeed, they need to retreat periodically to private places to contemplate the mysteries of life, and to regain their own threatened wholeness. But when their ethical view of events thrusts them into public roles, they can be quite effective as leaders, filled as they tend to be with an exalted sense of mission.

Comparing the Diplomatic Role Variants

Every Idealist plays these four roles well, but no one Idealist plays them all equally well. What distinguishes Idealists from one another is the structure of their intellect, that is, their profile of diplomatic roles. Some Mentors are better as Teachers of groups, others as Counselors of individuals, even though teaching and counseling often develop side-by-side in the same person, with Teachers counseling students in and out of class, and Counselors holding group sessions or teaching seminars. In the same way, some Advocates are better as Champions of causes, others as Healers of conflicts, even though Champions want to bring healing to warring factions and Healers are forever championing ideals. Consider the following chart of the four NF role variant profiles:

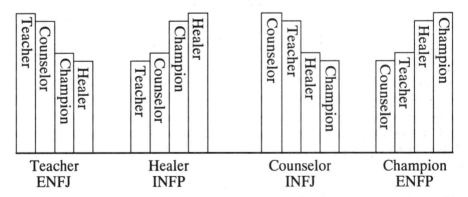

Teacher	Healer	Counselor	Champion
ENFJ	INFP	INFJ	ENFP

Notice that the Teachers (ENFJs) are the exact opposite of the Healers (INFPs) in likely diplomatic development, just as the Counselors (INFJs) are exactly opposite of the Champions (ENFPs). Thus Teachers are usually able to help even resistant students learn what they need to do or know, while they are less inclined to heal people in their times of conflict. The reverse holds for Healers, who are likely to leave no stone unturned in making others whole, while being rather hesitant to take on a group of learners, especially if resistant to learning. It is also the case that Counselors are eager to guide those in need of it for long periods of time and with untiring effort, but less eager to serve as a champion for someone with a burning cause. Lastly, Champions, with their contagious enthusiasm, are likely to be the best of all at fighting for causes, though not the best at giving counsel. However, even with their long and short suits, Idealists will tend to practice, and thus will develop, any one of these four diplomatic skills well above those strategic, logistical, or tactical skills developed by the other temperaments.

Detailed portraits of the four Idealist role variants can be found at the end of this chapter, beginning on page 149.

The Interests of Idealists

All of us have interests, but we certainly don't have the same interests, mainly because our interests are reciprocal with our abilities. Thus we are interested in doing what we do well, and tend to do well in what we are interested in doing. The interests of Idealists are diametrically opposite of those of Artisans and quite different from those of Rationals and Guardians. These differences are best seen when charted:

Interests	Idealists	Artisans	Guardians	Rationals
Educational	**Humanities**	Artcrafts	Commerce	Sciences
Preoccupational	**Morale**	Techniques	Morality	Technology
Vocational	**Personnel**	Equipment	Materiel	Systems

At school the Idealists are typically drawn to courses in the humanities and not to commerce or science. Some will dabble in the arts and crafts, seeing it as a romantic thing to do, but they rarely stick with that sort of thing long enough to become more than enthusiastic amateurs. Preoccupied from early on in morale building, they have little interest in acquiring new techniques or in developing a watchdogging morality, and, far from being preoccupied with learning about new technology, they are often averse to it. At work, given their diplomatic skills, they are best off doing personnel work rather than working with tools, materiel, or systems. Let us then consider the Idealists' interests in the humanities, morale, and personnel.

Educational Interest in the Humanities

Most Idealists show little interest in buying and selling, nor do many pursue careers in the physical sciences. Some will try their hand at the fine arts (usually without much patience), but they find their true niche in the studying and teaching of the humanities, or, more generally, in professions which involve transmitting ideas through words. NFs prefer working with words, and need and want to be directly or indirectly in communication with people. Those who work at it come to speak and write fluently, often with poetic flair, and often make excellent students and teachers of literature. The fictional narrative in any of its forms—stories, poems, legends, myths—is their delight and their strength, and not only are themes and characters meaningful to Idealists, but stylistic details and symbolic motifs loom for them with amazing significance. NFs are so easily moved by literature, and interpret it with such intuitive ease, that they can inspire their teachers, and their own students, with their insight and enthusiasm.

But Humanities is not confined to the study of literature. Idealists heavily populate the social sciences, particularly the fields of mental healing and personal or religious counseling—professions directed toward human metamorphosis, or the unfolding of the mind and heart toward greater self-understanding and spiritual peace. NFs find great satisfaction in the mental health services, where they tend to take the most humanistic of approaches, those advocating growth models of counseling and psychotherapy rather than the more confronting or controlling models. The human potential movement, with its encounter groups—so popular in the 1960s—was chiefly the creation of NFs like Carl Rogers and Abraham Maslow, and in its time served to focus interest in the Idealist's pursuit of personal growth and self-actualization. NF ministers, priests, and rabbis also tend to take on the role of group or individual counselor, the spiritual guide who helps the members of a congregation learn how to become more loving and more reverent human beings. The movement after World War II called "religious existentialism," stressing a new humanistic or being-centered theology, was certainly the work of Idealists, developing from Sören Kierkegaard through Martin Buber, Karl Barth, Reinhold Niebuhr, and Paul Tillich.

Preoccupied with Morale

Morale has to do with the state of one's spirits, and Idealists, from the time they are children, seem preoccupied with how those around them, their loved ones, their classmates, or their circle of friends, are feeling about themselves. Thus NFs are concerned with others' feelings of worth, or with their self-image—their self-esteem, self-respect, and self-confidence. And they want to do everything they can to keep people feeling good about themselves, to lift their spirits, to brighten their mood, to boost their morale. Many Guardians have a similar interest in helping others, but they are more preoccupied with morality, people's sense of right and wrong, than with nurturing a positive self-image. Both NFs and SJs are guardians of the Good ('morale' is the French feminine of 'moral'), but one cares for happiness and the other righteousness. Perhaps it is because of their preoccupation with morale that Idealists are drawn to the studies of the humanities and seek out occupations in mentoring and advocating.

Vocational Interest in Personnel

In the workplace Idealists have one very special talent: they are drawn to and can do wonders in recruiting, training, deploying, advancing, and counseling personnel. With their insight into people, their interest in human potential, and their glow of enthusiasm, NFs shine when they take on the job of finding quality employees, of guiding them into the right positions, and of helping them develop over the course of their careers.

Not only in business, but at school as well, individual development is the Idealists' domain, which is to say they are naturally good at influencing the growth and maturation of others. Teaching, counseling, interviewing, and tutoring come easily to Idealists, and are highly intuitive pursuits for them. Even without much formal training, NFs seem able, in Faber and Mazlish's phrase, to "talk so others will listen and listen so others will talk," and this with young and old and with male and female. Indeed, the Idealist sees education not so much as a process of training and certifying, but more as an invitation to a personal relationship, as one UCLA writing teacher explains:

> Education has often functioned as a gatekeeper...the intent is to evaluate people and keep them out or let them in. The way I view education is really very different from that. It's an invitation. It is an attempt to bring people into a kind of conversation, into a set of ideas, into ways of thinking, talking, writing, and reading that are new to them. If you see education as an attempt to bring people in, then you automatically see it as a relationship. And if the relationship works right, it is a kind of romance.

Forming personal relationships, especially relationships which help others fulfill themselves, is of prime importance to Idealists, and they instinctively communicate caring for others and a willingness to become involved. Teaching is this sort of personal, in some sense romantic, occupation for NFs, and so is counseling, where they can be uncanny at divining the nature of others' distress, at soothing those of low self-esteem, and at helping uncover their latent potential. And when championing causes and healing divisions NFs naturally empathize with others, becoming personally engaged and finding themselves seeing through another's eyes.

But close involvement with others can be troubling. No doubt because of their compassionate identification with others, Idealists are often turned to for moral support, and they seem to have little natural buffer against becoming caught up in others' troubles. Idealists become involved so instinctively that they can easily become weighted down with too many troubled relationships. Idealist counselors, in particular, have to learn to disconnect themselves from their clients to some extent, or risk being emotionally overwhelmed.

The Orientation of Idealists

We are born into a social field and we live out our lives in that field, never, for long, stepping outside of it into some no-man's-land disconnected from social reality. Of course we can be disoriented for short periods of time, owing to a surprise, a danger, or a shock. But we soon reorient ourselves and return to our ordinary waking social frame of reference. Indeed, we are the most social of all the animals, with our choice of social membership groups creating our life-long framework, and with our sociability ending in massive and complex societies. Whatever we think or feel, say or do, occurs, must occur, in the iron crucible of social relationships. Each act and attitude is shaped and governed by a prevailing outlook, perspective, or point of view determined by our social matrix. We are oriented always from a certain angle, slant, or standpoint, something Adickes spoke of as a built-in vantage point or viewpoint—what he called our *"Weltanschauung,"* or "worldview."

But different personalities have different perspectives, viewing time and place as well as past, present, and future, differently. Consider the following chart in making these comparisons:

Orientation	Idealists	Artisans	Guardians	Rationals
Present	**Altruistic**	Practical	Dutiful	Pragmatic
Future	**Credulous**	Optimistic	Pessimistic	Skeptical
Past	**Mystical**	Cynical	Stoical	Relativistic
Place	**Pathways**	Here	Gateways	Intersections
Time	**Tomorrow**	Now	Yesterday	Intervals

Here it is claimed that Idealists are altruistic about the present, credulous about the future, mystical about the past, their natural place is on the pathways to understanding and their natural time is tomorrow. How different the other temperaments in the way they view these things. So let us look closely at these five dimensions of orientation so that we will not be surprised when our Idealist friends, in their devotion to altruism, for instance, prove to be less practical, or less stoical, or less skeptical than we are.

Altruistic in Looking Around

All of us have a point of view, a way of construing what we see around us—our perspective on the here and now. Our temperament dictates what sort of perspective we develop and hold to. The Artisan perspective is practical, the Guardian dutiful, the Rational pragmatic, all so different from the altruistic perspective of the Idealist. Altruism is the belief that it's bad to be self-serving and good to be other-serving, or put another way, that our greatest happiness comes in selflessly giving to others, even when this involves self-sacrifice. This is by far the most metaphysical of the four worldviews, and the ever-skeptical Rationals will sometimes doubt the Idealists' motives, reasoning that if the payoff for altruism is self-satisfaction, then, paradoxically, Idealists are being selfish when giving to others, and altruism is only the illusion that one is acting selflessly. Idealists, however, are quite comfortable with paradoxes, and quite sincere in reaching for this goal of sacrificing for others, as Mark Twain, a notoriously skeptical Rational, came to appreciate about Joan of Arc, the altruistic Maid of Orléans whose life fascinated him:

> What could have put those strange ideas in her head?...Grieving and brooding over the woes of France had weakened that strong mind, and filled it with fantastic phantoms—yes, that must be it.
> But I watched her, and tested her, and it was not so. Her eye was clear and sane, her ways were natural, her speech direct and to the point. No, there was nothing the matter with her mind; it was still the soundest in the village and the best. She went on thinking for others, planning for others, sacrificing herself for others, just as always before. She went on ministering to her sick and to her poor, and still stood ready to give the wayfarer her bed and content herself with the floor. There was a secret somewhere, but madness was not the key to it.

Few Idealists are as saintly in their altruism as Joan of Arc, of course, but even ordinary NFs often dedicate their lives to helping others. Idealists see potential good in everyone, and they will gladly give of themselves to cultivate that potential, to help others grow and develop. This is why teaching and the ministry attract NFs, but also why missionary work can call to them, as does community volunteer work and the Peace Corps.

But altruism also serves another, more coveted purpose for Idealists: self-actualization. To put others first is the best way for NFs to rid themselves of selfishness or egocentricity, which they see as the great stumbling block to self-actualization. Thus, NFs believe that as they let go of selfishness they get a clearer and clearer picture of who they really are—a glimpse of their true nature, unfettered by worldly fears and desires. And the clearer the picture becomes, the closer they come to the spiritual essence they believe is inside them. As Gandhi explains it:

> If I found myself entirely absorbed in the service of the community, the reason behind it was my desire for self-actualization. I had made the religion of service my own, as I felt that god could be realized only through service.

Credulous in Looking Ahead

Idealists are credulous. They believe in things easily and without reserve—exactly the opposite of their skeptical cousins the Rationals. NFs are really quite innocent in their credulism. They see good everywhere, and in everyone, as if believing that goodness is real and permanent in the world, and thus they are quick to join causes and to go on missions, especially if they believe personally in the leaders of the movement. After pledging themselves to some individual or group, NFs are the most loyal of all the types, and will often use their enthusiasm to win followers and to advance the cause. NFs may even exhibit an unusually passionate devotion to a cause, or to a cult, though more to the persons involved than to the principles espoused. And in extreme cases they can lose their perspective and come to have what Pierre Janet called a "fixed idea" about their beliefs, clinging to them rigidly, unmoved and unmovable by any appeal to reason or experience.

However, while Idealists can get caught up in a movement, they do not stay involved for very long if it fails to have deep, lasting significance, with some hope of bettering the conditions of people in the world. For example, when the Flower Power movement of the 1960s was centered in San Francisco's Haight-Ashbury district, it was chiefly populated by SPs, but it was joined by many NFs who watched the SPs living in the moment, spontaneously, and who wanted to experience this freedom themselves. But they could neither be unconscious of self nor give up their concern for the future, so the movement held them only for a brief time and they left, disenchanted. As fast as the NFs moved into the communes, they moved out to search elsewhere for self-actualization and ways to express their unique identities. So, while Idealists are apt to be passionate in pursuit of their beliefs, they can also appear to be intellectual and emotional butterflies, flitting from idea to idea, from person to person, or from cause to cause, dilettantes in their pursuit of meaning and authenticity.

Mystical in Looking Back

Unlike the Rationals, who tend to rationalize their misfortunes and setbacks, seeing them as neutral events relative to one's individual point-of-view, Idealists are more metaphysical in their explanations, and will usually take one of two enigmatic attitudes when trying to come to terms with life's difficulties.

Some Idealists believe that accidents are mystifying and inexplicable—that bad things simply happen, and cannot be accounted for by any rational means. These NFs are content to live with a mysterious sense of causation, bravely accepting that the whys and wherefores cannot be known or communicated, even though such an attitude can make them appear at best naive, and at worst in denial, as if hiding their head in the sand.

Other Idealists attribute the cause of unhappy events to some power above themselves, not so much to the influence of bad Luck or Divine will (as do, respectively, the SPs and SJs), but to more esoteric, mystical causes. The dogma of the traditional religions concerning the source of evil—Original Sin in Christianity, the Angel of Death in Judaism, or Karma in Hinduism and Buddhism—satisfy many Idealists. But they will also search for causes in occult religions and cabalistic writings, and in various arcane, metaphysical systems, theosophy, astrology, Swedenborgianism, anthro-posophy, transcendentalism, spiritualism, and the like. In *Memories, Dreams, Reflections,* Carl Jung remembers that even as a teenager he was fascinated by this question of causation—"What were the reasons for suffering, im-perfection, and evil?" he asked—and dissatisfied both by Christian teaching and Western rationalism, he sought for answers in the occult world of myth, Eastern religion, and parapsychology:

> If such [parapsychological] phenomena occur at all, the rationalistic picture of the universe is invalid, because incomplete. Then the possibility of an other-valued reality behind the phenomenal world becomes an inescapable problem, and we must face the fact that our world, with its time, space, and causality, relates to another order of things lying behind or beneath it, in which neither 'here and there' nor 'earlier and later' are of importance.

The Place is the Pathway

If Artisans like to be in the middle of the action, Guardians at the gateways of exit and entrance, and Rationals at the crossroads mapping coordinates, then Idealists are most comfortable on the pathways that lead them on the search for the meaning of existence, that take them on the journey to some higher stage of personal development. The notion of the spiritual odyssey, the crusade, the pilgrimage, or the quest, is deeply satis-fying to Idealists, and is perhaps their favorite metaphor for their experience of life. In *Man of La Mancha,* Don Quixote sings of his glorious quest "to follow that star" of ideal honor and virtue, "no matter how hopeless, no matter how far." And in Robert Pirsig's *Zen and the Art of Motorcycle Maintenance: an Inquiry into Values,* a young philosopher imagines his spirit of inquiry roaming through the "high country of the mind" in pursuit of an elusive wisdom:

> Many trails through these high ranges have been made and forgotten since the beginning of time....Even within a single civilization old trails are constantly closed and new ones open up....Phaedrus wandered through this high country, aimlessly at first, following every path, every trail where someone had been before, seeing occasionally with small hindsights that he was apparently making some progress, but seeing nothing ahead of him that told him which way to go.

The Time is Tomorrow

The Idealist is future-oriented and focused on what might be, rather than what is. To the NF, whatever is is never quite sufficient—indeed, it is unendurable to think that the here-and-now, the SP place and time, is all there is in life. Listen as early women's suffrage advocate Susan B. Anthony imagines the future of American women, and really of all humanity:

The woman of the future will far surpass her of the present, even as the man of the future will surpass him of today. The ages are progressive, and I look for a far higher manhood and womanhood than we have now....I look for the day...when women all over this country will have equal property rights, equal business rights, and equal political rights; when the only criterion of excellence or position shall be the ability, honor, and character of the individual.

The Idealists' interest in the future also has a mystical aspect to it. The NFs' fantasies, as well as their favorite stories, are often excursions into the world of oracular powers, prophetic sensibilia, omens, fortune telling, Tarot cards, and the like, all of which help the NFs to create in their imaginations a magical world, a world of signs and portents, and a world pregnant with possibilities. Idealists believe that life is rich with potentials waiting to be realized, filled with meanings calling out to be understood. The Idealist is drawn to exploring these potentials and uncovering those meanings, to divining the true nature and significance of things.

The Self-Image of Idealists

All of us have a concept of ourselves made of things we believe, or want to believe, about ourselves. As in the case of the other kinds of personality, three aspects of our self-concept are of special importance in determining how well we regard ourselves—self-esteem, self-respect, and self-confidence. I believe that these three bases of self-regard are mutually reinforcing. For example, when our self-esteem increases, this tends to bolster both our self-respect and our self-confidence. Likewise, as we gain self-respect, it becomes easier for us to gain in self-confidence and self-esteem. And this reciprocity can work the other way: a loss of self-confidence can undermine respect for and pride in ourselves.

Different types of personality, naturally, base their self-image on quite different things. Having a good opinion of ourselves makes for our happiness, and often our success, so it is well that we pause for a moment to compare the four types on this all-important aspect of personality.

The chart below shows that most Idealists see themselves, and wish to be seen by others, as empathic, benevolent, and authentic, with other attributes, such as artistic gracefulness and audacity, important to Artisans, contributing almost nothing to the Idealists' positive sense of themselves:

Self-Image	Idealists	Guardians	Rationals	Artisans
Self-Esteem	**Empathic**	Dependable	Ingenious	Artistic
Self-Respect	**Benevolent**	Beneficent	Autonomous	Audacious
Self-Confidence	**Authentic**	Respectable	Resolute	Adaptable

As illustrated by the figure at the side, I think there is a triangular relationship between empathy, benevolence, and authenticity, each undergirding or undermining, as the case may be, the others. But even if the three attributes are not interdependent, they still deserve close scrutiny, considering that they are

The Self-Image of Idealists

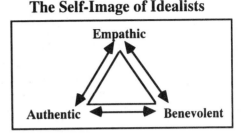

the bases of the Idealist's self-image. Let us then take a close look at empathy, benevolence, and authenticity.

Self-Esteem in Empathy

Idealist self-esteem is greatest when they see themselves and are seen by others as empathic in bonding with people in their circle. Idealists feel a kind of natural sympathy for mankind, but they base their self-esteem on the empathy they feel with those people closest to them. To the NFs, even introverted NFs, life is nothing without sensitive personal ties, without shared experiences and intimate attachments, without rapport so close that consciousness itself seems to be shared. NFs, after all, cannot not be personal, and the health of their relationships is beyond everything else the measure of their self-worth—enhanced when their relationships are deeply connected and vital, and diminished when they are distanced or troubled. Idealist journalist and author Elie Wiesel remembers just how vital in his personal development were empathic friendships:

> As a child I needed friendship more than tenderness to progress, reflect, dream, share, and breathe. The slightest dispute with a friend gave me a sleepless night as I lay wondering whether I would ever again know the excitement of a nighttime walk, of discussions about happiness, humanity's future, and the meaning of life. Disappointment in this domain caused me greater pain than a failure in school.

Idealists can become absorbed in drawing close to a single person, or they can become deeply involved with a group (their family, friends, the class they're teaching, a church congregation, and so on). But they are simply not interested, not for very long at least, in things other than empathic human relationships.

That religion of the 1960s, called the "encounter group movement," was mainly motivated and populated by NFs seeking greater empathy in their relationships, trying to capture an elusive intimacy. Many of them joined T-groups, sensitivity groups, Gestalt groups, marathons (nude and otherwise), Transcendental Meditation groups, Primal Scream groups, and of course EST—all in an effort to find a way to live more freely and lovingly. They explored verbal and nonverbal dimensions of communication, hoping to become more fully aware of their emotions, and to learn how to relate more closely and sensitively with others. In many of these groups they found, for a time at least, the sense of communion they sought, describing the experience as a kind of high of spiritual bonding—or what Terry O'Bannion and April O'Connel referred to as a "Shared Journey":

> At the exact moment when I encounter someone I feel as if I am some place I have never been before. It's hard to describe. Like you and this other person are out in space with each other and looking down on the earth.

Sadly, however, many Idealists report that after such an initial encounter is over the glorious empathy usually fades away in the routine of daily living.

Self-Respect in Benevolence

Idealists base their self-respect on their ability to maintain an attitude of benevolence or goodwill toward other people—toward all of existence, for that matter. NFs are without question filled with good intentions and kind feelings; they have a fierce aversion to animosity of any sort, and they will suppress their own feelings of enmity and hostility as best they can. Perhaps this is because Idealists have a powerful and ever-present conscience which hurts them deeply whenever they harbor feelings of malice, cruelty, revenge, or other mean-spirited intentions.

In truth, any evidence of cruelty in the world stabs Idealists to the heart and they cry out against it. E.M. Forster's character Mrs. Moore in *A Passage to India* simply cannot accept the smug superiority and callous prejudice of the British in India. Mrs. Moore fervently believes the British should base their colonial administration on the principle of everlasting kindliness—"Good will and more good will and more good will"—and she insists to her son that "The English are out here to be pleasant....India is part of the earth. And God has put us on the earth to be pleasant to each other...to love our neighbors and to show it." To the Idealists, the Guardians' good deeds and the Rationals' sense of autonomy are admirable as well, and worthy of cultivation, while the Artisans' audacity seems superficial. But without question benevolence is the greatest virtue, and malevolence the greatest evil.

Self-Confidence in Authenticity

Idealist self-confidence rests on their authenticity, their genuineness as a person, or put another way, the self-image they present to the world allows for no façade, no mask, no pretense. To be authentic is to have integrity, inner unity, to ring true, and, driven by a Gandhi-like desire for Absolute Truth, Idealists insist on an ever higher standard of authenticity for themselves. On the other hand, if NFs somehow undercut their authenticity by being phony or false or insincere, they can be taken over by fear and self-doubt. In his brilliant book, *The Divided Self*, psychotherapist R.D. Laing describes the anxiety NFs can feel when they have lost their authenticity, or when they find themselves being what Laing calls "like everyone else, being someone other than oneself, playing a part." In one client's case, Laing writes,

> As his feeling of what properly belonged to his 'true' self contracted more and more, this self began to feel more and more vulnerable and he came to be more and more frightened that other people could penetrate through his sham personality.

In extreme cases (and since Idealists believe the Self is something one finds), this loss of self-confidence can become a truly debilitating fear of the losing of Self entirely—or as Laing puts it,

> The 'inner' secret self hates the characteristics of the false self. It also fears it, because the assumption of an alien identity is always experienced as a threat to one's own. The self fears being engulfed by the spread of the identification.

Few Idealists become this lost in inauthenticity, of course, but many live with some vague feelings of uncertainty about their genuineness, some secret doubt about their wholeness.

The problem for Idealists is that this ardent wish to be genuine at all times and everywhere actually separates them from the authenticity they demand of themselves, and forces them, to a certain extent, into the very role-playing they want to avoid. NFs report over and over that they are subject to an inner voice which urges them to "Be real, Be authentic"—always in the NF is that voice reminding them about being whole, unified, and true. But with this other voice in their head, Idealists are inevitably caught in a dual role. Instead of the whole-hearted, authentic person they want to be, they are at once director and actor: they are on stage, and, at the same time, they are watching themselves being on stage, and prompting themselves with lines. The irony of this wanting to be authentically themselves is that it often leaves Idealists feeling divided and false, standing to one side and telling themselves to be themselves.

Authenticity is also difficult for Idealists because of their spontaneous and uninvited self-consciousness. From very early in life, NFs (more than SPs, SJs, or NTs) seem to feel others' eyes upon them, and to grant those around them the right to pass judgment on them, which is to say that they are highly aware of themselves as objects of moral scrutiny. While Rationals typically reserve to themselves the right to judge their own actions, Idealists are very sensitive to how they are seen by others, and care a great deal about meeting others' expectations. So here again NFs are caught in a dilemma: confident of their integrity, yet at the same time devoted to pleasing others, they must walk on a razor's edge, with authenticity on one side, and moral approval on the other. Learning to reconcile these two often conflicting facets of their self-image is an important and sometimes arduous task for many NFs.

The Values of Idealists

Arthur Schopenhauer, in *The World as Will and Idea* (1814), said that our will dominates our intellect. William James, in *The Principles of Psychology* (1890), and Leon Festinger, in *A Theory of Cognitive Dissonance* (1957), followed suit, thus advising us that our values dominate our thoughts. Now this may or may not be true of Artisans, Guardians, and Rationals, but it is certainly true of Idealists. Let me put it this way: Idealists are more prone to wishful thinking or value judgment than the other types, and they make no bones about it. Indeed, they are glad to let their heart rule their head, telling all of us that this is the wise thing to do, for the heart, they believe, is the soul of humanity.

How different they are from the other temperaments. How different especially from their opposites, the Artisans. Where Artisans value <u>ex</u>citement (from without) Idealists value <u>en</u>thusiasm (from within); where Artisans value their impulses, Idealists value their intuition; where Artisans value impact on others, Idealists value romance with others. And so it goes, Idealists valuing identity over stimulation, recognition over generosity, and the sage over the virtuoso.

Generally speaking, we can differ in our preferred being, in what we put our trust in, in what we yearn for, in what we seek, in what we prize, and in what we aspire to. It is perhaps in this, the domain of values, that the four types of personality display discernible patterns most clearly, far more clearly, certainly, than in domains such as the self-image or the forms of intelligence.

We are wise to pay attention to how the Idealists' values differ from ours lest we be caught off guard in our natural assumption that they value what we do, and so question why they seem less calm or less authoritarian than we, or less reasonable or less impulsive than expected. To make these comparisons let us study the following chart:

Value	Idealists	Artisans	Guardians	Rationals
Being	**Enthusiastic**	Excited	Concerned	Calm
Trusting	**Intuition**	Impulse	Authority	Reason
Yearning	**Romance**	Impact	Belonging	Achievement
Seeking	**Identity**	Stimulation	Security	Knowledge
Prizing	**Recognition**	Generosity	Gratitude	Deference
Aspiring	**Sage**	Virtuoso	Executive	Wizard

Being Enthusiastic

Idealists are highly emotional people, in the sense that their emotions are both easily aroused and quickly discharged. Fortunately, NFs tend to be positive types, and so their emotional intensity is usually expressed as unbounded enthusiasm. Particularly when discussing ideas, or sharing personal insights, their display of enthusiasm can be both delightful and contagious, often making them inspiring figures in their groups. But this sort of exuberance also has a darker side. NFs, young or old, male or female, cannot shake off their intuitive understanding that existence is bittersweet, with defeat the other side of triumph—that, in the midst of happiness, sadness but awaits its turn.

Moreover, when frustrated in their idealism, or when treated unjustly, NFs can become quickly irritated—Galen, remember, called them "Cholerics"—and they will respond furiously, the fire of their enthusiasm suddenly flaring out in anger. Edith Wharton was well-known for her moods of light and dark. Not only did her friend and fellow-novelist Henry James tease her about her "ravaging, burning and destroying energy," but her biographer R.W.B. Lewis notes the contradictions in her character:

> Externally, she was a creature of gaiety, given to bursts of enthusiasm, to harmless vanities and constant physical activity. She also experienced chills of embarrassment and self-doubt. But all the time her inner life was burgeoning; beautiful objects made her senses race, and great poetry set her aglow. Almost by the same token, she was overcome at times by the mysterious and dreadful sadness of life. She took nothing calmly.

Trusting Intuition

While Rationals trust their reasoning powers, Idealists trust their intuitive powers, their feelings or first impressions about people, not needing to wait for a rationale, or even wanting one, for what they believe. The Rational's logic is acceptable for some conclusions—so is the Guardian's authority, by the way—but to be really sure, Idealists wait for their intuition to show them the way.

Perhaps Idealists trust their intuition about people so unreservedly because of their extraordinary ability to identify with others, to put themselves in the other's place. As the saying goes, NFs will "crawl into another's skin," or they will "walk a mile in someone else's shoes," which means they will unconsciously take into themselves another's desires and emotions—or what they believe these to be. Such identification can be so close that Idealists will even find themselves beginning to talk or laugh or gesture like the other person. This mimicry is unconscious and usually unwanted by Idealists, but their ability to introject does give them the belief (rightly or wrongly) that they have accurate insight into others, that they know what's going on inside the other person's head and heart. NFs have to be particularly careful in this regard, because as much as they introject the traits of others, they also tend to project their own attitudes onto those around them, investing others with their own idealistic view of life.

Yearning for Romance
The most important thing to remember about Idealists is this: one and all, they are incurable romantics. Each type has an abiding hunger, some restless longing that needs to be satisfied each and every day. Artisans hunger for social impact, Guardians for belonging, Rationals for achievement. Idealists are not without these other yearnings, but they have much less hold on them than their hunger for romance. Romance—in the sense of idealized love—is not something which NFs can take or leave; it is vital to their growth and happiness, a nourishment they cannot live without, just as its opposite, the uninspiring, commonplace relationship, is flat and stale and lifeless.

In all areas of life, Idealists are concerned not so much with practical realities as with meaningful possibilities, with romantic ideals. But particularly in their love relationships, NFs have a keen appetite for romance—if any type can be said to be "in love with love," it is the NF. And yet, while they fall in love easily, Idealists have little interest in shallow or insignificant relationships. On the contrary, they want their relationships to be deep and meaningful, full of beauty, poetry, and sensitivity.

If their love life lacks this romance, Idealists have been known to romanticize their relationships, infusing them with a glow of perfection that can rarely be sustained in the harsher light of reality. All too often the NF falls into this pattern of romantic projection, accompanied by a considerable investment of effort and emotion, ending in a painful disillusionment. Such disparity between what is and what might have been is the theme of countless novels and plays. Leo Tolstoy, an Idealist himself, describes in *Anna Karenina* a moment he had experienced in his own marriage:

> Levin had been married three months. He was happy, but not in the way he had expected. At every step he was disappointed in his former dreams....Levin was happy, but having embarked on married life, he saw at every step that it was not at all what he had imagined. At every step he experienced what a man experiences when, after admiring the smooth, happy motion of a boat on a lake, he finds himself sitting in it himself.

This kind of sobering reality check confronts Idealists sooner or later in all of their romantic relationships, and how they deal with it—whether they choose to develop what they have, or move on to other dreams—determines to a great extent the course of their personal lives.

Seeking Identity
Idealists devote much of their time to pursuing their own identity, their personal meaning, what they signify—their true Self. It is not, mind you,

that they are self-centered, self-serving, or selfish; they focus on the Self of others as surely as on their own. But whether their own or another's, NFs are centered on the Self, concentrated on it, committed to it. And the Self upon which they focus is not the self that the other types think of when they use the word. To the SPs, SJs, and NTs, the word 'self' (when they bother to think about it) simply indicates their separateness from other people, or, at most, their individual actions or point of view. To the Idealists, however, Self has a capital "S" and is a special part of the person—a kind of personal essence or core of being, the vital seed of their nature, not unlike the Soul or Spirit of religious thought. NFs are passionate about finding this true Self, about becoming who they are, or self-actualized. Thus Gandhi wrote that "What I want to achieve—what I have been striving and pining to achieve these thirty years,—is self-realization." To be sure, NFs are so intent on self-realization that they may be called the "Identity Seeking Personality," the type of person so often written about by humanistic psychologists. For instance, Carl Rogers, in his book, *On Becoming a Person*, describes the Idealist's search for Self with remarkable insight:

> Becoming a Person means that the individual moves toward *being*, know-ingly and acceptingly, the process which he inwardly and actually *is*. He moves away from being what he is not, from being a façade. He is not trying to be more than he is, with the attendant feelings of insecurity or bombastic defensiveness. He is not trying to be less than he is, with the attendant feelings of guilt or self-depreciation. He is increasingly listening to the deepest recesses of his psychological and emotional being, and finds himself increasingly willing to be, with greater accuracy and depth, that self which he most truly is.

Idealists often dedicate their lives to this kind of self-realization—seeking to become realized, trying to get in touch with the person they were meant to be, and to have an identity which is truly theirs. "How can I become the person I really am?" they ask. And so, like Hermann Hesse's character Siddhartha, they wander, sometimes intellectually, sometimes spiritually, sometimes physically, looking to actualize all their inborn possibilities, and so become completely themselves, even though the paths in search of identity are never clearly marked. As Siddhartha wonders,

> But where was this Self, this innermost? It was not flesh and bone; it was not thought or consciousness. That was what the wise men taught. Where, then, was it? To press towards the Self—was there another way that was worth seeking? Nobody showed the way, nobody knew it—neither his father, nor the teachers and wise men, nor the holy songs....They knew a tremendous number of things—but was it worthwhile knowing all these things if they did not know the one important thing, the only important thing?

Idealists regard this search for identity as the most important enterprise in their lives, and with their gift for language they can be powerful advocates for it being a necessary pilgrimage for all people. Very often the other types, the SJs, NTs, and SPs, are troubled by the thought that they ought to be pursuing this goal, even if the search for Self does not beckon them. The reluctance of over ninety percent of humanity to join the search for self-actualization is a great source of mystification to the Idealists.

But even more mystifying is the paradox coiled at the very center of this search, namely, that the search for Self is fundamentally incompatible with the achievement of finding the Self. For many NFs the search for Self is a quest which becomes very much an end in itself, and which can come to dominate their lives. Thus, the Idealists' truest Self comes to be the Self in search of itself, or, in other words, their purpose in life becomes to have a purpose in life. But how can one achieve a goal when that goal is to have a goal? Intent on becoming themselves, Idealists can never truly be themselves, since the very act of reaching for the Self immediately puts it out of reach. In their enthusiasm for self-discovery, then, Idealists can become trapped in paradox: they are themselves only if they are searching for themselves, and they would cease being themselves if they ever found themselves.

Late in his life Siddhartha tries to explain this contradiction between seeking and finding to his friend Govinda, a Buddhist monk who has spent his life searching for himself. It might be, Siddhartha tells him, that

'you seek too much, that as a result of your seeking you cannot find.'
'How is that?' asked Govinda.
'When someone is seeking,' said Siddhartha, 'it happens quite easily...that he is unable to find anything, unable to absorb anything, because he is only thinking of the thing he is seeking, because he has a goal, because he is obsessed with his goal. Seeking means: to have a goal; but finding means: to be free, to be receptive, to have no goal.'

The seeking impedes the finding; the search for identity is its own obstacle. Some Idealists no doubt reach Siddhartha's perspective and find their true Self, which means that they finally give up struggling to become some perfected idea of themselves, and simply accept themselves as they are, somewhat short of ideal. But for many NFs, the search for identity only winds them more deeply in the complexities of inner division and self-contradiction: the more they seek their ideal Self, the more frustrated they are in their search.

Prizing Recognition

The way to the Idealists' heart is to show them that we know their inner person, the Being behind the social role that must be played, behind the public mask that must be worn. In other words, to make them feel appreciated we must encounter them, "meet them at their view of the world," as they put it. This is not an easy thing to do, and so it happens only rarely, and they, more than others, go through life feeling misunderstood, unknown, mistaken for the roles they are forced to play by social reality. You see, Idealists believe that each of us is a unique and special person. So it makes sense that they would feel prized by having their person known by another, if only on rare occasions. Idealists idealize themselves, and, as mentioned above, continue searching for their true self or real self. They are devoted to bringing the true self more and more into being, so that recognition by someone they care about is very important to them and very gratifying when it comes.

Aspiring to be a Sage

The Sage is the most revered role model for the Idealists—that man or woman who strives to overcome worldly, temporal concerns, and who aspires to the philosophic view of life. Plato, perhaps the greatest of all Idealist philosophers, characterized the sage by saying that the "true lover of wisdom" is on a metaphysical journey,

> is always striving after being—that is his nature; he will not rest in...appearance only, but will go on—the keen edge will not be blunted, nor the force of his desire abate until he have attained the knowledge of the true nature of every essence by a sympathetic and kindred power in the soul, and by that power drawing near and mingling and becoming incorporate with very being, [he will] live and grow truly, and then, and not till then, will he cease from his travail.

To transcend the material world (and thus gain insight into the essence of things), to transcend the senses (and thus gain knowledge of the soul), to transcend the ego (and thus feel united with all creation), to transcend even time (and thus feel the force of past lives and prophecies): these are the lofty goals of the sage, and in their heart of hearts all Idealists honor this quest.

The Social Roles Idealists Play

It is impossible not to play a role in all of our social transactions, and in essence there are two kinds of social roles, those that are allotted to us by virtue of our position in our social milieu, and those that we reach out and take for ourselves. We perforce play offspring to our parents, siblings to our brothers and sisters, and relatives to our extended family members. On the other hand we choose to play mate to our spouse, parents to our children, superior to our subordinate, subordinate to our superior, friend to friend, an so on. Allotted or embraced, we have no choice but to enact our roles, since interacting with others can never be role-free.

Three of our social roles are of special interest in the context of the study of personality: mating, parenting, and leading. In these three roles the different temperaments differ in very important ways, important, that is, in the effects these ways of relating to others have on mates, offspring, and followers.

Let us consider a chart which compares how the different ways mating, parenting, and leading roles are played:

Social Roles	Idealists	Artisans	Guardians	Rationals
Mating	**Soulmate**	Playmate	Helpmate	Mindmate
Parenting	**Harmonizer**	Liberator	Socializer	Individuator
Leading	**Catalyst**	Negotiator	Stabilizer	Visionary

Note the striking difference between playing the Soulmate role in the case of the Idealists, and the Playmate, Helpmate, and Mindmate role in the case of the other three types of personality. These different mating roles will require lengthy and complex study, and so a chapter (Chapter 7) on this topic is provided later in this book.

A separate chapter is also required for defining and describing the enormous differences in the parent-child relationship, and so Chapter 8 presents portraits of the four kinds of children, and then distinguishes the Idealist Harmonizer parent from the Artisan Liberator parent, the Guardian Socializer parent, and the Rational Individuator parent. Likewise, a chapter (Chapter 9) is provided to differentiate leadership styles, contrasting the Idealist's Catalyst role with the Artisan's Negotiator role, the Guardian's Stabilizer role, and the Rational's Visionary role. Even so, a few remarks on each of the Idealist's social roles can at least give outlines of how they are played.

The Soulmate

What Idealists wish for in their spouse is a Soulmate, a spouse who knows their feelings without being told of them, and who spontaneously expresses words of endearment, words that acknowledge their mate's unique identity. Idealists want the marital relationship to be, as they put it, "deep and meaningful." Other types will settle for much less than this. Guardians, for instance, would be Helpmates though they may not ask their Idealist spouse to be the same. Artisans, on the other hand, prefer to be Playmates, and wonder what the Idealist means by a deep and meaningful relationship. And Rationals, wishing to share their consciousness with their mates, are more for being Mindmates than Soulmates. More about this soulful relationship in Chapter 7. Here, suffice it to say that Idealists are asking their spouses for something most of them do not understand and do not know how to give.

The Harmonizer Parent

Idealist parents are mainly concerned with their children's self-image, so in order to know how their children see themselves, and how they would be seen by others, Idealist parents make every effort to increase the strength of their harmony with their children, wanting to keep themselves closely bonded or *en rapport* with them, even into adult life—harmony the means, a positive self-image the end. Here it is well to recall the constituents of the self-image. First, there is self-esteem, then self-respect, then self-confidence. Idealist parents encourage their children to grow in all three respects. The concerns of Guardian and Rational parents—civility and individuality—take a back seat in the case of Idealist parents. Not that they are indifferent to these concerns, only that they see them as subordinate and dependent upon the growth of a healthy, positive self-image. As for the venturesomeness encouraged by Artisan parents, Idealists have little time for it and little concern if it does not emerge, and so tend to leave it to circumstance.

The Catalyst Leader

The Idealists' style of leadership is quite unlike that of other types, for they are the Catalysts, acting as facilitators, motivators, or energizers with their unique capability of bringing their subordinates together in cooperative actions and of maintaining high morale in them. Since Idealists cannot not be personal in their relationships, it follows that when they are in positions of leadership they are compelled to lead in a personal way. To Idealists, every subordinate is a person whom they must know and must keep track of. In a way, this disinclination and perhaps inability to be impersonal as they direct operations can complicate matters, particularly if there are many individuals to relate to in managing an enterprise. Catalytic leadership is hard to define and even harder to explain, something that must be left to Chapter 9. Here, note that with the good feelings of their subordinates as their major concern, Idealist leadership is starkly different from that of other temperaments.

Matrix of Idealist Traits

The matrix on the next page brings together and highlights the terms I have used in this chapter to define and describe the personality of Plato's Idealists. To aid in comparing and contrasting all four temperaments, I have listed the traits beside those of the other personalities.

Those who take time to study this matrix, and refer back to it occasionally, will have a better chance of comprehending the whole configuration of the Ethical Idealist Personality, as well as getting a feel for its uniqueness and radical difference from the other three temperaments, the Hedonic Artisans, the Proprietary Guardians, and the Dialectical Rationals.

The Traits of Temperament and Character

Communication	┌─ Concrete ─┐		┌─Abstract─┐	
Implementation	Utilitarian	Cooperative	Cooperative	Utilitarian
Character	Artisan	Guardian	Idealist	Rational
Language	**Harmonic**	**Associative**	**Inductive**	**Deductive**
Referential	Indicative	Imperative	Interpretive	Categorical
Syntactical	Descriptive	Comparative	Metaphoric	Subjunctive
Rhetorical	Heterodox	Orthodox	Hyperbolic	Technical
Intellect	**Tactical**	**Logistical**	**Diplomatic**	**Strategic**
Directive Role	Operator	Administrator	Mentor	Coordinator
• Expressive Role	• Promoter	• Supervisor	• Teacher	• Fieldmarshal
• Reserved Role	• Crafter	• Inspector	• Counselor	• Mastermind
Informative Role	Entertainer	Conservator	Advocate	Engineer
• Expressive Role	• Performer	• Provider	• Champion	• Inventor
• Reserved Role	• Composer	• Protector	• Healer	• Architect
Interest				
Education	Artcraft	Commerce	Humanities	Sciences
Preoccupation	Technique	Morality	Morale	Technology
Vocation	Equipment	Materiel	Personnel	Systems
Orientation				
Present	Practical	Dutiful	Altruistic	Pragmatic
Future	Optimistic	Pessimistic	Credulous	Skeptical
Past	Cynical	Stoical	Mystical	Relativistic
Place	Here	Gateways	Pathways	Intersections
Time	Now	Yesterday	Tomorrow	Intervals
Self-Image				
Self-Esteem	Artistic	Dependable	Empathic	Ingenious
Self-Respect	Audacious	Beneficent	Benevolent	Autonomous
Self-Confidence	Adaptable	Respectable	Authentic	Resolute
Value				
Being	Excited	Concerned	Enthusiastic	Calm
Trusting	Impulse	Authority	Intuition	Reason
Yearning	Impact	Belonging	Romance	Achievement
Seeking	Stimulation	Security	Identity	Knowledge
Prizing	Generosity	Gratitude	Recognition	Deference
Aspiring	Virtuoso	Executive	Sage	Wizard
Social Role				
Mating	Playmate	Helpmate	Soulmate	Mindmate
Parenting	Liberator	Socializer	Harmonizer	Individuator
Leading	Negotiator	Stabilizer	Catalyst	Visionary

Idealist Role Variants

These "Abstract Cooperators" as I like to call them—Plato's Idealists Aristotle's Ethicals, Galen's Cholerics, and Myers's NFs—have, like the other types, a tightly configured personality, so that each trait of character entails the other traits. Mother Nature will not permit Idealists, any more than other types, to pick and choose the traits that make up their character. If their environment enables them to develop a given trait it can only be one that is predetermined by their temperament.

While it is useful to think of each of the four temperaments as a single, unified configuration of attitudes and actions, individual members of each temperament clearly differ from one another. Thus, all the Idealists seem to have a great capacity for diplomatic empathy, but some (the scheduling NFs) are drawn to the directive role of Mentor of human development, while others (the probing NFs) prefer the informative role of Advocate of harmonious interaction. These two divisions can be further broken down to reflect an expressive or a reserved social attitude, with the Mentors tending to play the role variants of Teacher or Counselor, and the Advocates playing Champion or Healer.

The Teacher [ENFJ]

Learning has to be beckoned forth, led out of its hiding place, or, as suggested by the word 'education,' it has to be educed by an individual with educative skills. More than any of the other Idealists ENFJs are natural teachers, with the uncanny ability to influence those around them, and without seeming to do so. Even as children these Teachers may attract a neighborhood gang of children ready to listen to them and to follow them in play. And adult Teachers are wonderful leaders of group learning experiences, more capable than any other type of calling forth each learner's potentials.

As a variant of Plato's Idealists and Aristotle's Ethicists, the ENFJs are little different from other NFs in most respects. Like all the Idealists they are abstract in communicating and cooperative in implementing goals. They want to learn about the humanities, are preoccupied with morale, and work well with personnel. In orientation they are altruistic, credulous, mystical, situated on pathways, and with their eye on tomorrow. They base their self-image on being seen as empathic, benevolent, and authentic. Often enthusiastic, they trust intuition, yearn for romance, seek identity, prize recognition, and aspire to the wisdom of the sage. Intellectually, they are prone to practice diplomacy far more than strategy, logistics, and especially tactics. Further, with their scheduling nature, they tend to choose the directive Mentor's role over the probing Advocate's informative role. And because of their expressiveness they prefer the part of Teacher over that of Counselor. To help visualize ENFJ intellectual development, consider the following bar graph depicting the most probable profile of their diplomatic roles:

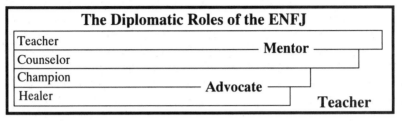

Teachers expect the very best of those around them, and their enthusiasm inspires action in others and the desire to live up to their expectations. ENFJs (around two percent of the population) have the delightful characteristic of taking for granted that people will meet their expectations, never doubting that people will obey their implicit commands. And, more often than not, people do, because this type has extraordinary charisma.

These outgoing Mentors arrange work and social engagements ahead of time and tend to be absolutely reliable in honoring these commitments. But they are also comfortable in complex situations which require the juggling of much data with little pre-planning. An experienced ENFJ group leader can dream up, effortlessly, and almost endlessly, activities for their groups to engage in, and stimulating roles for members to play. In some Teachers, inspired by the responsiveness of their students or followers, this can amount to a kind of genius which other types find hard to emulate. Such ability to preside without planning reminds us somewhat of an ESFJ Provider Guardian, but the latter acts more as a master of ceremonies than as a leader of groups. ESFJs are natural hosts and hostesses, making sure that each guest is well looked after, or that the right things are expressed on traditional social occasions. In much the same way, ENFJs value harmonious relations, can handle people with charm and concern, and are usually popular wherever they are. But they are not so much social as educational leaders, interested primarily in the growth and development of individuals.

Teachers consider people their highest priority, and they naturally communicate caring, concern, and a willingness to become involved with others. As a result, people often turn to them for nurture and support, which they usually manage to deliver, showing sincere interest in the problems of those around them, employees, colleagues, students, and so on. But they can also become over-involved in these problems, and find themselves unable to turn away from such demands even when they become unreasonable. At times, indeed, the personal needs of others can overwhelm ENFJs, and they may find themselves over-extended emotionally, feeling responsible for the feelings of others to an extent which can place a burden on their families. Or, if forced to let go of other relationships through sheer unavailability of time or energy, they experience a guilt all out of proportion to the realities of their commitments.

Teachers have a highly developed ability to empathize by introjection, that is, taking into themselves the characteristics, emotions, and beliefs of others—even to the point of unconsciously mimicking others. But this unusual ability to relate to others with empathy can also pose a danger for them, because they can easily over-identify with others and pick up their burdens as if they were their own, actually putting at risk their own identity.

ENFJs are also vulnerable to idealizing their personal relationships, raising them to a plane which seldom can sustain the realities of human nature. Because of this tendency to project their own ideals into their relationships, they may unwittingly overpower their friends and loved ones, who doubt that they can live up to such an exalted conception of themselves, unaware that Teachers are their boosters, not their critics.

A wide range of occupations offer Teachers success, even though their longing for the ideal often carries over to their careers and can cause them some restlessness. Good with language, they contribute to an unusual level when dealing with people, particularly face-to-face. The media and the ministry are populated with talented ENFJs, and they make excellent therapists, educators, and primary care physicians. They should avoid occupations that do not make use of their interpersonal talents (accounting, law practice, the military); otherwise, almost any activity where sustained personal contact is involved suits their diplomatic skills.

Teachers take communication for granted and believe that they are instinctively understood and that their communications are naturally accepted. Just as they themselves are accepting of others, so do they assume that others are the same with them. When they find that their position or beliefs were not comprehended or accepted, they are surprised, puzzled, and sometimes hurt. Fortunately, this does not happen with high frequency, since ENFJs have a remarkable fluency with language, especially when communicating in speech, face to face. They are influential, therefore, in groups, having no hesitation about speaking out, no matter how large or small the group may be.

Outgoing, and perhaps the most expressive of all the types, ENFJs do not hesitate to communicate their feelings. Their negative feelings can be blurted out, like steam from a boiling teakettle with a rattling lid, and their positive feelings can be voiced with dramatic and even histrionic flourish. Teachers can, with practice, become spell-binding orators.

These ENFJs would do well to follow their hunches, for their intuition tends to be well developed. On the other hand, their use of logic in decision-making may not be so sound, and checking with a Rational might be at times advisable for them. In the framework of personal and interpersonal insight, however, they are unparalleled. Without a doubt, they know what is going on inside themselves, and they can read other people with remarkable accuracy. Seldom are they wrong about another's intentions.

Teachers place a high value on mutual cooperation in their closest relationships, and thus make excellent companions and mates. They are tireless in their efforts to promote harmony with their loved one, giving generously of their time and energy to make sure their mate is happy. Indeed, ENFJs feel personally responsible when home life does not go smoothly. Unfortunately, this dedication often exists side by side with their dream of the perfect relationship—a characteristic of all Idealists, but one which is particularly strong in the Teachers. Their longing for an ideal mate can even cause them some restlessness, at times bringing on a vague dissatisfaction with the mate they already have.

As parents, Teachers are deeply devoted to their children, yet tend not to be domineering. On the contrary, they are supremely affectionate and nurturing, so much so that they can be taken advantage of by a particularly demanding child.

The Counselor [INFJ]

Counseling is the side of mentoring that focuses on helping people to realize their human potential, and INFJs have an unusually strong desire to contribute to the welfare of others and genuinely enjoy guiding their companions toward greater personal fulfillment. INFJs are scarce, little more than one percent of the population, which is too bad, considering their usefulness in the social order. Although these Counselors tend to be private, sensitive people, and thus are not usually visible leaders, they work intensely with those close to them, quietly exerting their influence behind the scenes with their families, friends, and colleagues. These seclusive and friendly people are complicated themselves, and so can understand and deal with complex ethical issues and with deeply troubled individuals.

As a variant of Plato's Idealists and Aristotle's Ethicists, the INFJs are little different from other NFs in most respects. Like all the Idealists they are abstract in communicating and cooperative in implementing goals. They want to learn about the humanities, are preoccupied with morale, and work well with personnel. In orientation they are altruistic, credulous, mystical, situated on pathways, and with their eye on tomorrow. They base their self-image on being seen as empathic, benevolent, and authentic. Often enthusiastic, they trust intuition, yearn for romance, seek identity, prize recognition, and aspire to the wisdom of the sage. Intellectually, they are prone to practice diplomacy far more than strategy, logistics, and especially tactics. Further, having a scheduling nature they tend to choose the directive Mentor's role over the probing Advocate's informative role. And because they are quiet and reserved they seem more comfortable acting as a private Counselor than as a classroom Teacher. To visualize INFJ intellectual development consider the following graph depicting the most probable profile of their diplomatic roles:

The Diplomatic Roles of the INFJ		
Counselor	Mentor	
Teacher		
Healer	Advocate	
Champion		Counselor

Counselors can be hard to get to know. They have an unusually rich inner life, but they are reserved and tend not to share their reactions except with those they trust. With their loved ones, certainly, they are not reluctant to express their feelings, their face lighting up with the positive emotions, but darkening like a thunderhead with the negative. Because of their strong ability to take into themselves the feelings of others, Counselors can be hurt rather easily by those around them, which, perhaps, is one reason why they tend to be private people, quietly withdrawing from human contact. At the same time, friends who have known them for years may find sides emerging which come as a surprise. Not that Counselors are inconsistent; they value their integrity a great deal, but they have mysterious, intricately woven personalities which sometimes puzzle even them.

This type of Idealist has strong empathic abilities and can become aware of another's emotions or intentions—good or evil—even before that person is conscious of them. Such mind-reading can take the form of feeling the hidden distress or illnesses of others to an extent which is difficult for other types to comprehend. Even INFJs can seldom tell how they came to penetrate others' feelings so keenly. Furthermore, the Counselor is most likely of all the types to demonstrate an ability to understand psychic phenomena. What is known as "ESP" may well be exceptional intuitive ability—in both its forms, projection and introjection. Such super-normal intuition is found frequently in INFJs, and can extend to people, things, and often events, taking the form of visions, episodes of foreknowledge, premonitions, auditory and visual images of things to come, as well as uncanny communications with certain individuals at a distance.

Because of their vivid imaginations Counselors are often seen as the most poetic, even mystical, of all the types. They use an unusual degree of imagery in their language, the kind of imagery found in complex and often aesthetic writing such as novels, plays, and poems. To be sure, they often select liberal arts as a college major, and they may be attracted to creative writing as a profession. In all their communications they are masters of the metaphor, and will naturally describe a thing in terms of something else. Their great talent for metaphorical language—both written and verbal—is usually directed toward communicating with people in a personalized way. INFJ writers comment that they write with a particular person in mind, whereas writing to a faceless audience leaves them uninspired.

In school INFJs are usually good students, high-achievers who exhibit an unostentatious creativity. They enjoy problem-solving, take their work seriously, and enjoy academic activity, but they can also exhibit qualities of perfectionism and put more into a task than perhaps is justified by the nature of the task.

Counselors thrive in occupations which involve interacting with people, nurturing their personal development, especially on a one-to-one basis. As with all NFs, teaching and the ministry hold attraction, although INFJs must develop an expressive attitude in both professions, which for them requires a great deal of energy. More suited to them is the general practice of medicine, or therapeutic counseling. Counselors make outstanding individual therapists who have a unique ability to get in touch with their patients' inner lives, though they are also the most vulnerable of all the types to the eruption of their own repressed thoughts and feelings. As therapeutic counselors, INFJs may choose clinical psychology or psychiatric medicine, or may choose to teach or to write in these fields. Whatever their choice, they generally are successful in therapeutic counseling because their personal warmth, their enthusiasm, their insight, their devotion, their originality, and their interpretive skills can all be brought into play.

Although they have a capacity for working at jobs which require solitude and close attention, Counselors also do well when in contact with groups of people, providing, of course, that the personal interactions are not superficial. They are highly sensitive in their handling of others and tend to work effectively in an organizational structure. They enjoy helping people with their problems, and can understand and use human systems creatively and benevolently. They value staff harmony and want an organization to run smoothly and pleasantly, making every effort themselves to contribute to that end. As employees or employers, INFJs are concerned with people's feelings and are able to act as a barometer of the feelings of individuals and groups within the organization. They listen well and are adept at consulting and cooperating with others. They enjoy pleasing others and they find conflict disagreeable and destructive. INFJs respond to praise and use approval as a means of motivating others, just as they themselves are motivated by approval. If they are subject to hostile working conditions or to constant criticism, they tend to lose confidence, become unhappy and immobilized, and can eventually become physically ill.

These soft-spoken Mentors also want harmony in their homes and find interpersonal conflict, overt or covert, extremely destructive to their happiness. Their friendship circle is likely to be small, deep, and long-standing. As mates, they are devoted to their spouses, but may not always be open to sexual approaches. They tend to be physically affectionate, but wish to choose when—which is when they are in the mood—and such a hot and cold style may be quite confusing to their mate. Often an INFJ's expressions of affection will be subtle, taking a romantic, even poetic turn.

Counselors are devoted parents. A female INFJ can bond with her children in a kind of mental symbiosis, sometimes so strong an identification be unhealthy for both mother and child. More often, however, Counselors tend to be good friends with their children, exceptionally loving, while firm in discipline. They are typically concerned about the comfort, physical health, and emotional well-being of both mates and children.

The Champion [ENFP]

In the view of the Champions nothing occurs that is without significance, without profound meaning. And they don't want to miss any of it. ENFPs must experience all the events that affect people's lives, and then they are eager to relate the stories they've uncovered, hoping to disclose some truth about people and issues, and to motivate others with their powerful convictions. This strong drive to speak out on social events can make these Champions tireless in conversing with others, like fountains that bubble and splash, spilling over their own words to get it all out. Their enthusiasm is boundless and is often contagious, making them the most vivacious of all the types, and also inspiring others to join their cause.

As a variant of Plato's Idealists and Aristotle's Ethicists, the ENFPs are little different from other NFs in most respects. Like all the Idealists they are abstract in communicating and cooperative in implementing goals. They want to learn about the humanities, are preoccupied with morale, and work well with personnel. In orientation they are altruistic, credulous, mystical, situated on pathways, and with their eye on tomorrow. They base their self-image on being seen as empathic, benevolent, and authentic. Often inspired, they trust their intuition, yearn for romance, seek identity, prize recognition, and aspire to be a sage. Intellectually, they are prone to practice diplomacy far more than strategy, logistics, and especially tactics. Further, having a probing or exploring nature they tend to prefer the Advocate's informative role over the more schedule-minded Mentor's directive role. And because of their irrepressible expressiveness they are more eager to be a Champion of causes than a Healer of troubled souls. To visualize ENFP intellectual development consider the following bar graph depicting the most probable profile of their diplomatic roles:

The Diplomatic Roles of the ENFP	
Champion	
Healer	Advocate
Teacher	
Counselor	Mentor
	Champion

Like the other NF role variants, ENFPs are rather rare, say two or three percent of the population, but even more than the others they consider intense emotional experiences as being vital to a full life. Champions have a wide range and variety of emotions, and a great passion for novelty, and so can become bored rather quickly with both situations and people, and resist repeating experiences. Also, they can never quite shake the feeling that a part of themselves is split off, uninvolved in their experience. Thus, while they strive for emotional intensity, Champions often see themselves in some danger of losing touch with their real feelings.

These expressive Advocates are fiercely independent, repudiating any kind of subordination, either in themselves or in others in relation to them. Unfortunately, Champions constantly find themselves surrounded by others who look toward them for wisdom, inspiration, courage, and leadership, a dependency which, at times, weighs rather heavily on them. In the same vein, ENFPs strive toward a kind of spontaneous personal authenticity, and this intention always to be themselves is usually communicated non-verbally to others, who find it quite attractive. All too often, however, they fall short in their efforts to be authentic, and they tend to heap coals of fire on themselves for the slightest self-conscious role-playing.

In their probing way, Champions exercise a continuous scanning of the social environment, and no suspicious motive is likely to escape their attention. Far more than the other NFs, ENFPs are the keen and penetrating observers of the people around them, and are capable of intense concentration on another individual. Their attention is never passive or casual, never wandering, but always directed. In fact, seeing life as an exciting drama, pregnant with possibilities for both good and evil, Champions tend to be hypersensitive and hyperalert, always ready for emergencies, and because of this they may suffer from muscle tension.

At the same time, ENFPs have outstanding intuitive powers and often find themselves trying to read what is going on inside of others, interpreting events in terms of another's hidden motives, and giving special meaning to words or actions. While this interpretation can be accurate, it can also be negative, sometimes inaccurately negative, and may introduce an unnecessarily toxic element into the relationship. For instance, Champions tend to attribute more power to authority figures than is there, and to give over to these figures an ability to see through them—a power of insight which is usually not there. In this way they can make serious mistakes in judgment, mistakes which derive from their tendency to project their own attributes onto others, and to focus on data which confirm their own biases.

Despite the occasional misinterpretation, Champions are good with people and make extensive use of their interpersonal powers. They usually have a wide range of personal and telephone contacts, expending energy in maintaining both career and personal relationships. They are warm and have fun with people, and are unusually skilled in handling people. They are likeable and at ease with colleagues, and others enjoy their presence. Their public role tends to be well developed, as is their capacity for the spontaneous and the dramatic. They are characteristically positive in their outlook, and are surprised when people or events do not turn out as anticipated. Often their confidence in the innate goodness of life and human nature is a self-fulling prophecy.

Champions have a remarkable latitude in career choices and succeed in many fields. As workers, they are warmly enthusiastic, high-spirited, imaginative, and can do almost anything that interests them. They have a strong sense of the possible and can solve most problems, particularly those dealing with people. They enjoy the process of creating something, an idea or a project, but are not as interested in the more monotonous follow-through. Once people or projects become routine, ENFPs are likely to lose interest—what might be is always more fascinating than what is. Champions are outstanding in getting people together, and are good at initiating meetings and conferences, although not as talented at providing for the logistical or operational details of these events. They are good at inventing new ways of doing things, and their projects tend to become quickly personalized into a cause. They are imaginative themselves, but can have difficulty picking up on ideas and projects initiated by others. If they are to lend their energy and interest to a project, they must make it their own.

People-to-people work is essential for Champions. They make excellent teachers, ministers, and in general are attracted to the communicative arts, making talented journalists, orators, novelists, screen writers, and playwrights. In institutional settings they can be gadflies, challenging obsolete procedures and policies. Sometimes they get impatient with their superiors; and they will occasionally side with detractors of their organization, who find in them a sympathetic ear and a natural rescuer. In occupational choice, ENFPs quickly become restless if the choice involves painstaking detail and follow-through over a period of time. Variety in day-to-day operations and interactions best suits their talents, since they need quite a bit of freedom in which to exercise their creativity.

As mates, ENFPs tend to be appealing, gentle, sympathetic, but nonconformist. Since they often seek new outlets for their inspirations, their mates can expect surprises. They can swing from extravagance to frugality, and their home may contain expensive luxuries, while necessities may be missing. They are largely disinterested in such things as domestic maintenance, savings accounts, life insurance, and even ready cash.

In their parenting role, Champions are devoted although somewhat unpredictable in handling their children, shifting from a role of friend-in-need to stern authority figure. While they voice strong opinions about discipline, they may not be willing to enforce their dramatic pronouncements, fearing to lose rapport with their children, and thus leaving it to their mate to follow through. ENFPs can be creative parents, providing their children with all sorts of intriguing experiences. On the other hand they have little patience with whining or demanding children, and can be quite short with such behavior.

The Healer [INFP]

To the INFP healing means mending those divisions that plague one's private life and one's relationships. It means treating oneself and relating to others in a conciliatory manner, helping to restore lost unity, integrity, or what INFPs call "oneness." These Healers present a tranquil and noticeably pleasant face to the world, but while to all appearances they might seem gentle and easy-going, on the inside they are anything but serene, having a capacity for caring not usually found in other types. Healers care deeply—passionately—about a few special persons or a favorite cause, and their fervent aim is to bring peace to the world and wholeness to themselves and their loved ones.

As a variant of Plato's Idealists and Aristotle's Ethicists, the INFPs are little different from other NFs in most respects. Like all the Idealists they are abstract in communicating and cooperative in implementing goals. They want to learn about the humanities, are preoccupied with morale, and work well with personnel. In orientation they are altruistic, credulous, mystical, situated on pathways, and with their eye on tomorrow. They base their self-image on being seen as empathic, benevolent, and authentic. Often enthusiastic, they trust intuition, yearn for romance, seek identity, prize recognition, and aspire to the wisdom of the sage. Intellectually, they are prone to practice diplomacy far more than strategy, logistics, and especially tactics. Further, with their probing or exploring nature they lean more toward the Advocate's informative role than the scheduling Mentor's directive role. And because of their seclusiveness and reserve they seem to care more to be a Healer of conflicts than a people's Champion. To visualize INFP intellectual development consider the following bar graph depicting the most probable profile of their diplomatic roles:

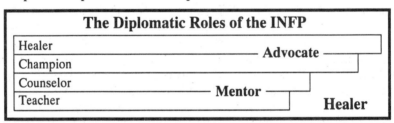

Healers have a profound sense of idealism derived from a strong personal morality, and they conceive of the world as an ethical, honorable place. Indeed, to understand Healers, we must understand their idealism as almost boundless and selfless, inspiring them to make extraordinary sacrifices for someone or something they believe in. They are the Shaman, Medicine Man, or Witch Doctor of the tribe, the Prince or Princess in fairy tales, the True Knight or Defender of the Faith, like Don Quixote or Joan of Arc. Isolated by their seclusiveness and infrequency (around one percent of the general population), their idealism leaves them feeling even more isolated from the rest of humanity.

It may be that Healers seek unity within themselves, and between themselves and others, because of a feeling of alienation which comes from their often unhappy childhood. INFPs live a fantasy-filled childhood, which, sadly, is discouraged or even punished by many parents. With parents who require them to be sociable and industrious in concrete ways, and also with down-to-earth siblings who conform to these parental expectations, Healers come to see themselves as ugly ducklings. Other types may shrug off parental expectations that do not fit them, but not the INFPs. Wishing to please their parents and siblings, but not knowing quite how to do it, they try to hide their differences, believing they are bad to be so fanciful, so unlike their more solid brothers and sisters. They wonder, some of them for the rest of their lives, whether they are OK. They are quite OK, just different from the others—swans reared in a family of ducks.

Even so, Healers find it difficult to believe in themselves and to trust themselves. Deeply committed to the positive and the good, yet taught to believe there is evil in them, they can come to develop a certain fascination with the problem of good and evil, sacred and profane. They are drawn toward purity, but can become engrossed with sin, continuously on the lookout for the wickedness that lurks within them. Then, when they believe they have yielded to an impure temptation, they may be given to acts of self-sacrifice in atonement. Others seldom detect this inner turmoil, however, for the struggle between good and evil is within the INFP, who does not feel compelled to make the issue public.

In evaluating things and making decisions, Healers prefer to follow their intuition rather than logic. They respond to the beautiful versus the ugly, the good versus the bad, and the moral versus the immoral. Impressions are gained in a fluid, global, diffused way. Metaphors come naturally to them but may be strained. They have a gift for interpreting symbols, as well as creating them, and thus often write in lyric, poetic fashion. They show a tendency to take deliberate liberties with logic, believing as they do (and unlike the Rationals) that logic is something optional. They may also, at times, assume an unwarranted familiarity with a certain subject matter, believing in their impressionistic way that they "know all about that," though they've never really mastered the details. They have difficulty thinking in conditional "if-then" terms; they tend to see things as either black or white, and can be impatient with contingency.

At work, Healers are adaptable, welcome new ideas and new information, are well aware of people and their feelings, and relate well to most others, albeit with some reserve. They dislike telephone interruptions and work well alone. They are patient with complicated situations, but impatient with routine details. They can make errors of fact, but seldom of feeling. The INFPs' career choices should tend toward the ministry, missionary work, social work, library research, tutoring, child counseling, college teaching in the humanities—and away from business. They seem capable of applying themselves scholastically to gain the necessary training for professional work, and often do better in college than in high school. They have a natural interest in scholarly activities and demonstrate, as do the other NFs, a remarkable facility with language. Often they hear a calling to go forth into the world to help others, and they seem ready to make the personal sacrifices involved in responding to that call, even if it means asking their loved ones to do likewise.

In their mating role, Healers have a deep commitment to their vows. They are loyal to their mates and, while they might dream of greener pastures, if they stray into those pastures they soon locate the nettles. They like to live in harmony and they go to great lengths to avoid interpersonal conflict. They are sensitive to the feelings of their mates and enjoy pleasing them, although they may have difficulty in expressing interest and affection openly or directly. INFPs cling to their dreams, and often find it difficult to reconcile a romantic, idealized concept of conjugal life with the realities of everyday living with another person. Even at the best of times, they seem fearful of too much marital bliss, afraid that current happiness may have to be paid for with later sacrifices. The devil is sure to get his due if one experiences too freely of happiness, or, for that matter, of success, or beauty, or wealth, or knowledge. This almost preconscious conviction that pleasure must be paid for with pain can cause a sense of uneasiness in INFPs when they marry; they may feel they must be ever-vigilant against invasion, and can therefore have trouble relaxing in the happiness of mating.

These reserved and soft-spoken Advocates are fierce protectors of home and family—their home is indeed their castle. As parents, they are devoted to the welfare of their children, treating them with great sympathy, and adaptability. In the routines of daily living, INFPs tend to be flexible, even compliant with their mate's ideas of discipline, and thus are easy to live with. They will often give their children a voice in family decisions—until their value system is violated. Then they dig in their heels and will not budge from their ideals. Life with a Healer parent will go harmoniously along for long periods, until an ideal is stepped on. Then they will resist and insist.

6
Rationals

To me it suffices to wonder at these secrets and to attempt humbly to grasp with my mind a mere image of the lofty structure of all that there is.

This is how Albert Einstein concluded his essay, *My Credo*, a statement summing up his philosophy of life, and expressing the essence of his fascination with science. Einstein's insatiable curiosity about the secrets of the natural world, coupled with his prodigious (and reportedly rather arrogant) ability to comprehend the structure of "all that there is," enabled him to change fundamentally the way in which, not just physicists, but all educated people look at the universe. From 1905 to 1925, Einstein not only conceived the theory of relativity, but he made indispensable contributions to new understandings of thermodynamics, the nature of light, atomic structure, and quantum physics, and created in the process nothing less than the first new model of the universe since Isaac Newton's, over two centuries earlier.

A truly astonishing achievement for any human being, but particularly for someone who was considered a slow-learner as a child, who dropped out of (and was then expelled from) his secondary school, who graduated from a mere technical college with a teaching diploma, and who, of all his classmates, was passed over for a teaching position and post-doctorate appointment. Rejected by academia, Einstein went his own way and took a job at the Swiss Patent Office, where he evaluated the plans of would-be inventors, correcting errors of design, and deciding (he could do this almost instantaneously) if an invention would work. In his youth, Einstein had enjoyed building models and playing with mechanical devices, and so his work at the Patent Office taxed him very little, and left him free in his spare time, and on his own, to do the theoretical work that would change the face of physics for the rest of the century.

Professorships at leading universities soon came his way, and as his fame grew so did the legend of his eccentric character. Shy and reserved as a child, with a calm detachment from all personal ties, Einstein grew into an thoroughly self-contained young man. Though popular with his colleagues and students, he remained remote, enjoying the company of other brilliant friends, but letting none get close to him. And then in his later years he became the very icon of the absent-minded professor, the abstracted, fuzzy-haired scientific genius all but unaware of his social context. Stories about his forgetfulness are legion, but one is delightfully succinct: on his way to an important meeting, Einstein telephoned his wife and asked, "Where am I and where am I meant to be?"

One thing he never forgot, however, throughout his long and celebrated life: what he called "the never-ending task of Reason."

In the mid 1970s, while writing *Please Understand Me,* I chose the Greek god Prometheus to represent these Rationals (Myers's NTs), naming them the "Prometheans." Myth has it that Zeus commissioned Prometheus to fashion a creature to live on earth with the animals. The animals had already been given many different means of survival, weapons and defenses such as fangs, claws, and horns, fur, feathers, and shells, not to mention powers such as strength, swiftness, and flight. Very few protections and powers were left to give human beings, so Prometheus decided to provide his creation with gifts outdoing those of the animals. First he shaped Man differently, upright like the gods; then he went to heaven and stole fire from the wheel of the sun, giving this precious knowledge to mankind as its means of surviving among the animals, even of triumphing over them. This gift of fire, however, cost Prometheus dearly. Zeus, CEO of the Greek Pantheon, was so enraged that mortal humanity had been given divine knowledge that he condemned Prometheus to live forever chained to a barren rock, with, in some stories, a vulture eating daily at his liver ('liver' symbolizing life-sustaining). But Prometheus suffered this agony with dignity and serenity, for his was the noble cause of imparting to mankind knowledge of light and energy (symbolized by fire) in defiance of authority. Prometheus, the god of pre-learning ('pro' = pre + 'metheus' = learning), secured for humanity the powers of science and technology, thereby rescuing human beings from helplessness and ignorance, even though he had to rob heaven to do so.

In the 1980s I chose the Owl as the Rational's totem animal. Owls are among the most efficient winged predators, rarely missing their prey owing to their keenness of sight, swiftness, and timing. With their ability to see in the dark, and with their oversized talons, owls surpass even the hawk and the eagle in their ability to spot and to seize their prey. And this is very much the nature of Rationals, particularly in abstract matters: to penetrate the dark recesses of nature with their keen insight, and to grasp ideas with their sharp intellects. It is no wonder that, of all the animals, it is the professorial owl that best serves as the symbol of Rational pragmatics.

Looking back, I remember meeting only two Rationals during the war years. The first was another cadet like me. We were buddies during preflight and primary flight training. After that, only one other, an engineer sent along with my squadron to oversee our use of a giant rocket. Then in graduate school after the war I met two students and one professor in the psychology department who were Rationals, the rest of the students and professors seemingly quite different from us. Strangely, I found the professors and students in the philosophy department more given to reason than those in the psychology department. Finally, in the thirty years I worked for schools in corrective counseling I met so few Rationals that I kept lowering my estimate of their numbers. My guess now, as I've said elsewhere, is that they're no more than five or six percent of the population. In any case that ought to be enough of these strategic pragmatists to keep science and technology advancing at a steady pace.

Plato's Rationals

Plato's word for men like Einstein was *'dianoetic'* which roughly translated means "dialectical thought"—coordinate thought, parallel reasoning, ratiocination—hence he considered this type as the "Rationals." Plato regarded the Rationals as serving a particular function in society: to study nature and figure out ways to tame it, that is, to make the natural order confluent with the social order. Not, mind you, to violate Nature, but to civilize it.

A generation after Plato, his student Aristotle defined logic for the Western world. Aristotle said that the "Dialectical" types (Plato's Rationals) try their best to be accurate, to get things straight, to sort things out, in order to avoid errors in reasoning. Logic, he said, tells us how to avoid such errors. One way is to realize that whatever we can identify is unique, has an identity, no matter how hard it is to distinguish it from other things. For example, though two peas in the same pod may seem identical, they really aren't, and careful scrutiny will reveal their difference. This is Aristotle's Law of Identity. The other cornerstone of Aristotelian logic is that things that are identifiable in a given context are either one thing or another, and so can't be both. For example, there is no such thing as half man and half beast, such as a Centaur, even though we can imagine such a creature. This is Aristotle's Law of Contradiction. These two rules of logic are called "truisms," meaning that they are obvious even though unprovable. But provable or not, to violate them is to talk nonsense, something that Aristotle's Dialecticals are careful to avoid doing.

Galen named the Rationals the "Phlegmatics." The word 'phlegmatic' has come to mean disinterested, bland, distant, seemingly detached from social involvement. And indeed these Rationals, concerned as they are with logical investigation, seem detached and distant from others, who conclude that this type has no interest in social reality. This conclusion is correct in the sense that when the Rationals are concentrating on some complex problem they do detach themselves from their social context and remain distant until they solve the problem. At that moment they are not interested in others, but that does not mean they do not care about others. They are just as caring as any other type when they are focused on those they care about.

Plato's Rationals are not only logical and contemplative, they are also usually absorbed in some enquiry, some investigation into complexity, some experimental probing into the nature of things. Perhaps this was why Paracelsus chose the mythical Sylphs to be their tutelary spirit. Sylphs were believed to live high above the ground, in forest canopies, and on mountain tops; they were cerebral spirits (much like the owl, who might have given rise to them), with their enlarged eyes which gave them penetrating sight, their oversized forebrain which gave them powerful reasoning, their sensitive antennae which gave them vivid imagination, and their gossamer wings which gave them access to places otherwise impossible to explore. Thus it was Paracelsus who first emphasized the insatiable curiosity and restless research of the Rationals.

Adickes spoke of Plato's Rationals as "Agnostics," for these people have their doubts about everything complicated. Despite all their rigorous logic, their studied contemplation, and particularly their probing empiricism, this type maintains a hint of uncertainty. With certitude so hard to come by, Rationals think it best to speak only of the possible and the probable. So it was Adickes who first touched upon one of the more puzzling features of the Rational character, their doubting nature.

In his intricately reasoned treatise on what he called different "forms of living" (translated as "types of men"), Spränger saw the Rationals, as did Plato, Aristotle, and Adickes, as rational, logical, and skeptical. But he focused even more closely on their penchant for theory building, calling them the "Theoretic" type. For the Rationals, to be sure, theory building is heady wine, one of the most fulfilling operations that tests and measures the mettle of their intellect.

Kretschmer, the first investigator to look carefully at the dark side of character, called the Rationals the "Anesthetics" which roughly translated means "unfeeling." In thus speaking of them he was echoing Galen, who had said that they are distant and detached, but Kretschmer was saying more than this. He believed that if and when life's problems get the better of them, Rationals, like the other three types, have no choice in which kind of absurd behaviors to use in their self-defense, their temperament alone deciding the matter.

Like Kretschmer, Fromm examined both sides of personality, presenting negative as well as positive traits of character. Fromm considered the Rationals to be "Marketers," thinking of marketing (or pragmatic transacting) as a negative trait, while he lauded them for their efficiency and other desirable traits. Thus in his view Rationals are not only "efficient," they are also "adaptable," "curious," "experimental," "farseeing," "flexible," "generous," "intelligent," "open-minded," "purposeful," "sociable," "tolerant," "undogmatic," "witty," and "youthful." It would appear that Fromm, probably a Rational himself, thought better of them than the other types.

Myers contributed to the study of the Rational personality by naming them the "Intuitive Thinking" types—"NTs"—and saying of them that they are "abstract," "analytical," "competent," "complex," "curious," "efficient," "exacting," "impersonal," "intellectual," "independent," "inventive," "logical," "scientific," "theoretical," "research-oriented," and "systematic." Though apparently unaware of the contributions of her predecessors, she was clearly able on her own to identify the more salient traits that characterize Plato's Rationals.

The Abstract Utilitarians

Plato's Rationals, Aristotle's Dialecticals, Myers's NTs, whatever their name, have something very important in common with the Idealists and Artisans, and little in common with the Guardians. With the Idealists they share a predominantly abstract manner of communicating their messages, and with the Artisans a predominantly utilitarian manner of implementing their goals. Of necessity we communicate messages with words, and implement goals with tools, and thus these two dimensions, word usage and tool usage, constitute the underlying basis of personality development. As shown in the matrix at the side, the base of NT personality is their unique combination of abstract word usage with utilitarian tool usage. It is for

	Words	
	Abstract	**Concrete**
Cooperative	NF	SJ
Tools **Utilitarian**	**Abstract** **NT** **Utilitarians**	SP

this reason that I think of Plato's Rationals as the "Abstract Utilitarians." Since these two dimensions are the bases of personality development, it is well that we examine them in some detail.

Abstract Word Usage

Abstract words refer to imaginable things, concrete words to observable things. Rationals talk little of what is observable and much of what is imaginable. They are inclined to speak more of what can be seen only with the mind's eye, conceptual things rather than perceptual things, ideas rather than objects. All of us, of course, can observe what is before us as well as imagine what is not. But this does not mean that we do both equally. Very early in life we begin to exercise one focus of language—observables or imaginables—more than the other, and we continue to do so throughout life. Like the NFs, the NTs choose the imaginative, conceptual, or inferential things to speak of over the observational, perceptual, or experiential.

In conversation Rationals try to avoid the irrelevant, the trivial, and the redundant. They will not waste words, and while they understand that some redundancy is necessary they still are reluctant to state the obvious, or to repeat themselves on a point, limiting their explanations and definitions because they assume that what is obvious to them is obvious to others.

NTs assume that if they did state the obvious their listeners or readers would surely be bored, if not offended. Their tacit assumption is that what is obvious to them is obvious to others, and the overly terse and compact style of speech that results is hard for others to follow. Because of this Rationals sometimes lose their audience and wonder why.

The basis of coherence in Rational thought and speech is deductive inference. This basis has much in common with the inductive inference of the Idealists, little in common with the harmonic thought and speech of the Artisans, and nothing in common with the associative thought and speech of the Guardians. Although inferential, induction requires the so-called "intuitive leap," a leap only dubiously taken by NTs, even when it is necessary to get on with their current speculation. On the other hand, associative thought and speech requires topic hopping, something NTs will only occasionally and reluctantly do, and only as an excursion before returning to the unfinished topic. And harmonic thought and speech requires selecting and arranging words for the way they sound, a skill not usually acquired by Rationals, though some (like Shakespeare) can become masters of it when they take it as their province.

While we cannot observe deductive thought (going from general to specific, whole to part), we can observe the language that makes it possible. Defining words to limit their usage is a deductive process, so too is arranging words in logical order to control coherence, and so too is choosing words to control shades of meaning. Thus, the coherence, reference, arrangement, and choice of words tend to be done deductively by Rationals.

Rationals are unusually exacting about definitions. Our words can have distinct reference only if we are careful in defining them, and so NTs make distinctions, lots of them, most of the time. Indeed, they're sometimes called "nitpickers" and "hairsplitters" by other types. NFs are even affronted by NT hairsplitting, bent as they are on erasing the NTs' finely drawn distinctions. But Rationals don't mind being teased with such names because they assume that their distinctions enable them to control arguments and, it might be added, enterprises. The way Rationals see it, whoever controls categories, controls useful operations. They leave control of other things to others.

Many Rationals are dictionary readers, even specialty dictionaries—anthropology, aphorisms, etymology, law, medicine, philosophy, psychology, slang. Some spend a good deal of time with their dictionaries, and so are aware of definitions and word families, of roots and derivations, of denotations and connotations, things the other types are content to gloss over.

While their word arsenal grows through the years, Rationals also tend to enjoy playing with words, finding pleasure in puns and paradoxes. They are delighted by comments such as Einstein's reference to mathematics: "The laws of mathematics, as far as they refer to reality, are not certain, and as far as they are certain, do not refer to reality." And the more puckish of them are tickled by Disraeli's retort to Gladstone. Gladstone:

"You will either die on the gallows or from syphilis." Disraeli, in instant repartee: "Depending on whether I embrace your morals or your wife."

Rationals are careful in subjoining one word to another to avoid errors of sequence or of category. An obvious sequence error would be to join the word 'meow' to the word 'dog' such as in saying that "The dog's meow is worse than its bite." Everyone minds such obvious errors, but the NT, far more than others, is mindful of unnoticed errors of category that result in subtle contradiction. For example, the expression 'disorder leads to chaos' presumes that chaos differs from disorder, when in fact the words are synonymous. Chaos cannot follow disorder because it *is* disorder.

Errors of category are just as scrupulously avoided by Rationals. For example it's a mistake to say that "there were weeds among the plants" because weeds are plants, the latter being the category that weeds belong to. NTs frequently note such trivial errors of category in others' speech, but they rarely comment on them. However, let the error occasion contradiction in an argument being made, and NTs are compelled by their very nature to point out the error.

Many Rationals are obsessed with speculative enquiry, so their speech tends to be laced with assumptions and presuppositions, probabilities and possibilities, postulates and premises, hypotheses and theorems. In such speech data plays only a supportive and secondary role, as does the merely factual. It is this feature of their language—their disinterest in dative and factual information—that sets NTs farther away from their concrete cousins, the SPs, and their concrete opposites, the SJs. Hegel, the most arrogant of the German philosophers, is credited with (and condemned by some for) saying "if the facts do not comport with my theory, so much the worse for the facts." Facts, say the NTs, cannot speak for themselves, but must be spoken for by those conversant with and observant of the canons of logic.

Above all else Rationals want to be coherent in their arguments, and so they try to make certain that each phrase and clause advances the argument, introducing nothing that doesn't logically belong, and leaving out nothing that is logically required. This style produces carefully crafted communications, NTs tending to qualify their statements with modifiers such as 'likely,' 'probably,' 'usually,' 'occasionally,' and 'in some degree.' Note how concerned the great anthropologist James Frazer is with the accuracy of his statements in *The Golden Bough*, and how he qualifies almost everything he says, as if he cannot allow himself to overstate his case:

Now that the theory, which necessarily presented itself to me at first in outline, has been worked out in detail, I cannot but feel that in some places I may have pushed it too far. If this should prove to have been the case, I will readily acknowledge and retract my error as soon as it is brought home to me. Meantime my essay may serve its purpose as a first attempt to solve a difficult problem, and to bring a variety of scattered facts into some sort of order and system.

Rationals can also become highly technical in their vocabulary. Not only will they use an extensive, erudite vocabulary (the speech of William F. Buckley, Jr., is a good example), but NTs in emerging scientific or technological fields will often develop their own high-tech terminology to talk about their theories and inventions—thus the computerese of the 1980s, with its esoteric vocabulary of 'RAM,' 'ROM,' 'bits,' 'bytes,' and so on.

The opposite of high-tech speech is small talk, a way of communicating in which Rationals are notoriously disinterested. In Shaw's play *Pygmalion*, Professor Higgins' mother has learned not to let her famous NT son meet her high society friends:

> Mrs. Higgins: ...I'm serious, Henry. You offend all my friends: they stop coming whenever they meet you.
> Higgins: Nonsense! I know I have no small talk; but people don't mind.
> Mrs. Higgins: Oh! Don't they? Small talk indeed! What about your large talk?...Henry: you are the life of the Royal Society [of Science]; but really you're rather trying on more commonplace occasions.

Rationals prefer to appear unemotional when they communicate (and they can seem rather stiff), trying to minimize body-language, facial expression, and other non-verbal qualifiers as much as possible. But when they become animated their characteristic hand gestures express their need for precision and control. NTs will make one or both hands into claws or talons, as if to seize the idea they are discussing. They will also bend their fingers and grasp the space in front of them, turning and shaping their ideas in the air. They will use their fingers like a calculator, ticking off point after point, and they will take small objects at hand (salt and pepper shakers, pens and paper weights) and arrange them on a table or desk to help map out their ideas. But perhaps the most telling gesture of all is the apposition of the thumb against the finger tips, as if the NT is bringing an idea or an argument to the finest possible point and is savoring the precision.

Utilitarian Tool Usage

Rationals are utilitarian in going after what they want, which means that they consider the usefulness of their tools as more important than their social acceptability—whether they should be used, are moral, are legal, are legitimate. Not that Rationals prefer to be immoral, illegal, or illegitimate in their tool usage. They do not refuse to cooperate with their social groups, but like their utilitarian cousins, the Artisans, they see pleasing others and obeying rules as secondary considerations, coming only after they have determined how well their intended means will work in achieving their ends. However, it must be emphasized that the Artisan's concrete utility is different from the Rational's abstract utility. Where SPs are interested in effective operations, NTs are interested in efficient operations. If a given operation promises to be too costly for the results it gets, that is, inefficient though effective, the NT will look for operations that are likely to take less effort to get the same result.

If not socially or politically correct, neither are Rationals at all snobbish in their utilitarianism. Indeed, they will listen to anybody who has something useful to offer regarding their choice of ways and means, but they will also disregard anyone who does not. Status, prestige, authority, degree, licence, credential, badge of office, reputation, manners—all of these marks of social approval mean nothing to the NTs when the issue is the utility of goal-directed action. They will heed the demons if their ideas are fruitful, and ignore the saints if theirs are not. Niccolò Machiavelli acquired his knowledge of statecraft by studying many effective means of taking and holding power: "With the utmost diligence I have long pondered and scrutinized the actions of the great," he wrote in *The Prince*, and by "the great" he meant any successful ruler, from the trusted Moses to the treacherous Cesare Borgia. The design of efficient action toward well-defined goals is no place for incompetents, even nice ones.

Rationals are wont to think of themselves as the prime movers who must pit their utilitarian ways and means against custom and tradition, in an endless struggle to bring efficiency and goal-directedness to enterprise, an attitude regarded by many as arrogant. But if this be arrogance, then at least it is not vanity, and without question it has driven Rationals to engineer the technology upon which civilization is based.

The Strategic Intellect

Strategy has to do with identifying the ways and means necessary and sufficient to achieve a well-defined goal. But not just any goal is of interest to Rationals; invariably the goal that Rationals set for themselves is increasing the efficiency of systems.

Some Rationals concern themselves mainly with social systems, like families and companies, while others are concerned with organic systems, like plants and animals, and still others with mechanical systems, like computers and aircraft and automobiles. But no matter what system they're working with, NTs want to increase the efficient operation of that system. Other sorts of objectives are of considerably less interest and so are given little effort. The way Rationals reach their objective of maximizing efficiency in systems is by analyzing systems in search of inefficiency, which is to say, they look for error in the order or in the organization of systems. Indeed, perhaps the most important thing to understand about the strategic intellect is that it is activated by errors found in complex systems. In other words, Rationals are ever on the lookout for systemic problems and are bent on solving them. They're problem solvers, one and all.

The concept of systems was understood and used by only a handful of behavioral and physical scientists during the first half of the 20th century. Then at mid-century Norbert Wiener wrote his seminal work on what he called "cybernetics," meaning by that term network ('netics') governance ('cyber'), that is, network control. He made his concept of cybernetics intelligible to those not conversant with systems theory by borrowing the term 'feedback' from radio technology and using it as a metaphor for circular processes in systems. Magorah Maruyama would later say that feedback in systems is a matter of "mutually causal processes," thus distinguishing sharply between linear and circular causality. Causality, in the view of systems theorists, is always relative to the conditions surrounding an event, as the "necessary and sufficient conditions for the occurrence of an event." Rationals, never really having much use for the notion of linear causality, now embraced circular causality with enthusiasm and undertook the construction and reconstruction of complex systems with renewed vigor.

Order and Organization

Unity in systems is a two sided matter. On the one hand there is the unity of order, while on the other hand there is the unity of organization. Order and organization are different from each other: order is concerned with what follows what, organization with what is simultaneous with what. Those Rationals interested primarily in order I call the "Coordinators," and those primarily interested in organization I call the "Engineers." Before we consider what the Coordinators and Engineers do, let us study for a moment the distinction between their different objectives, the one in search of disorder in systems, the other in search of disorganization in systems.

Order, first of all, has two forms, one having to do with above-and below, and the other with before-and-after. Some things are of higher order than others. For example, a colonel in the army has higher rank than a major, a major higher than a captain, a captain higher than a lieutenant, and so on down the ranks to the buck private. Lower ranks are said to be subordinate to higher ranks, being as they are of lower order. This kind of order is hierarchical and is usually referred to as "rank order."

The other kind of order can be called "serial order." For instance, certain technical procedures require a series of actions that must follow in a very specific order. Take firing a single action revolver. First load it, then cock the hammer, then pull the trigger. Reversing this order will not do. Of course the kind of series that interests Rationals is a bit more complex than firing a gun. The preparations for the invasion of Europe in World War II is an example of extreme complexity involving hundreds of planners over a period of years, any error in the sequencing of operations fraught with peril and inviting disaster.

Organization, on the other hand, has to do with either devising (and revising) or configuring (and reconfiguring) complex systems that are composed of parts, not ranks or steps. Where the ranks or steps of an ordinal system are separate from each other, the parts of an organizational system are connected organically to each other, such that what happens anywhere in the system reverberates throughout the system. Thus organizations, of whatever kind, are said to be integrated, every part being present to every other part of that system.

Now, Coordinators do the work of what might be called "arranging." Arranging is the act of determining the various levels of rank (in other words, hierarchy, layers, echelons) or the consecutive steps (sequence, series, succession) that are required to achieve long range objectives. Hierarchical arrangement enables the mobilizing of field forces in conducting campaigns. Serial arrangement, in contrast, enables the entailing of contingencies in a plan of action.

For their part, Engineers do the work of constructing. Constructing is the act of determining what the parts of a system are supposed to do (its mechanism) or what parts of a system are required for it to work (its configuration). Mechanical constructing involves building functional, working prototypes, while configurational constructing involves making detailed two-dimensional blueprints and three-dimensional models. Both kinds of construction are undertaken to determine what structures are necessary and sufficient for the system to do its work most efficiently.

To summarize: Arrangement works to reduce disorder in systems, the two forms of it being the mobilizing of campaign forces and the entailing of contingency plans. Construction, in contrast, works to reduce disorganization in systems, the two forms of it being the devising of prototypes and the designing of models. To help visualize the relationship between these many concepts of strategic operations, consider the following diagram:

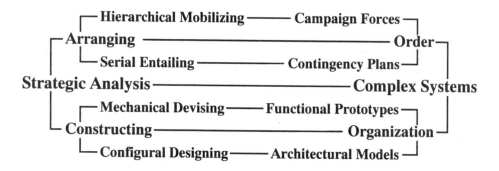

Interest, Practice, Skill

Any skill is acquired by practice, increasing precisely in the degree it is exercised, and diminishing in the degree it is neglected. Neural cells are like muscle cells; if they aren't used they lie dormant and even degenerate.

Moreover, there is reciprocity between interest and skill, which means that we practice and so improve in doing things we're interested in, and are interested in things we practice and improve in. Interest reinforces skill, skill reinforces interest, in a feedback relationship. So the Rationals' lifelong interest in strategic operations—both arranging and constructing—fuels their daily exercise of such operations, and as strategic skills increase so then does interest in them, precisely and exclusively measured by the amount of practice.

Now, in a sense every individual has not one but four IQs, and it is simply not possible for one person to develop all four of his or her capabilities equally. The kind of operation practiced most develops most, while that practiced least develops least. Unless stunted by unfavorable circumstances, Rationals instinctively practice strategic actions far more and far earlier than the others, and therefore end up more highly skilled in strategy than in tactics and diplomacy, and much more than in logistics. Consider the following graph:

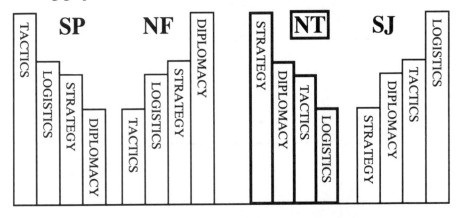

Notice in the graph above that logistics in the case of the NT profile falls far short of strategy. Note also that diplomatic and tactical skills lag behind strategic skills but outdo logistical skills, owing to the middling amount of practice usually given them as second and third suits. Another glance at the bar graph will suggest that, although NTs and SJs are opposites in the way they tend to use words and tools, they are likely to be equal in the extent they develop their diplomatic and tactical skills. Why? Rationals, like Idealists, are abstract in word usage and do considerable introspection, so it is not difficult for them to identify with others and to talk in a diplomatic way. As for tactics, Rationals share with Artisans a utilitarian way of selecting and using tools, so they, given enough practice, can get very good at making the right moves when in the field of action. On their side, Guardians share cooperative implementation with Idealists and concrete communication with Artisans, so they can match with Rationals in both diplomacy and tactics.

Strategic Role Variants

Rationals all have strategic intelligence in common, but they differ sharply among themselves in the kinds of strategic operations they choose to practice. The two sides of strategy explained above mark the first division, with one side having to do with the order in which things are to be done, that is, coordinating operations, and the other side having to do with the organization of things, or engineering operations. Thus Rationals naturally set their minds to mastering the roles of Coordinator or Engineer, and these enable them to play four strategic role variants, what I call the "Fieldmarshal" (ENTJ), the "Mastermind" (INTJ), the "Inventor" (ENTP), and the "Architect" (INTP)—all Rational to the core, but decidedly singular in their rationality. Let us examine the strategic roles that Rationals are temperamentally inclined to take.

The diagram below indicates the symmetry between the strategic roles and role variants, and systemic work. Those Rationals who develop their strategic intelligence to a high degree tend to gravitate to work with systems and to be preoccupied with the technology involved in such work. Note on the right side that work with systems involves both arranging and constructing; that arrangement is concerned with either mobilizing forces or entailing contingencies; and that construction is concerned with either devising prototypes or designing models.

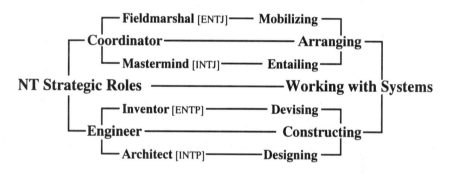

Strategic Coordinators

Those Rationals who are quick to judge and to make schedules are eager to take the part of Coordinator. Coordinators determine who is to do what at a given time and place, and this role requires a directive character. Coordinators steadily increase in directiveness as they mature, such that they easily and comfortably command others and expect to be obeyed. Indeed, Coordinators are surprised by any resistance to their directives, because it is so clear to them that others do not know what to do, presumably because their goal is unclear or absent, and because they apparently have no strategy in mind by which to proceed. So, in the view of the Coordinator, most people are operating blindly and going around in circles, plainly in need of direction.

Fieldmarshals arrange a well-ordered hierarchy that makes possible the chain of command and the mobilizing of forces. In their campaigns these expressive, energetic Coordinators commandeer whatever human capabilities and material resources are available and use them to execute a complex strategy, such as was done by Napoleon in his twenty years of campaigning in Europe, by Grant at Vicksburg and Chatanooga, by Sherman in his "scorched earth" march from Atlanta to Savannah, by Eisenhower at the beachheads of the Normandy invasion and the conquest of Germany, and by MacArthur in his Pacific island hopping, his reconstruction of Japan, and his Inchon landing. I hasten to add that although military campaigns are the most publicized, they are by no means the most common form of mobilized operation. Any kind of undertaking, whether commercial, educational, political, or military—whatever—can be arranged hierarchically, indeed must be if success is to be achieved, and the more efficient the hierarchy, the greater the success.

Masterminds arrange things in coherent and comprehensive sequential order, that is, they coordinate operations by making efficient schedules, with each item entailing the next, as a necessary precursor or consequence. Moreover, Masterminds make contingency plans for keeping their schedules on track. If plan A is in jeopardy or is aborted, switch to plan B. If that doesn't work, then plan C. Often working behind the scenes, these quiet, reserved Coordinators are able to anticipate nearly everything that can go awry and generate alternatives that are likely to avoid the fate that might befall the first operation. And so it goes, the Mastermind ending with a flow chart of alternate ways and means to reach clearly defined objectives.

Strategic Engineers

Engineers structure the form and function of the instruments to be employed in pursuing objectives, and is the domain of the probing Rationals, those who prefer to keep their options open and to follow an idea where it leads them. Concentrated as they are on determining the ways and means of operation, Engineers tend to have an informative rather than a directive character, which is to say that they are usually eager to provide information and reports regarding what they are currently engineering, but not at all eager to tell others what to do.

Inventors develop their skill in devising prototypes more than their skill in designing models. To these outgoing Engineers, functionality is the objective, as in the case of Nikola Tesla, the gifted inventor of the split-phase electric motor, the giant coil, alternating current, the radio, the inert gas light bulb, and countless other ingenious devices. Inventors must make sure their prototypes don't just make sense on paper, but work in the real world, or else face the consequences. Consider the international airport at Denver, Colorado, completed in early 1994. Doubtless the construction of the airport was coordinated well enough, but the devising of the automated baggage transport apparatus was flawed, delaying the opening of the airport for nearly a year. Whoever engineered it apparently was insufficiently skilled for the level of complexity involved.

Architects make structural plans, models, blueprints. To these reserved Engineers, often working alone at their desks, drafting tables, and computers, the coherence of their designs is what counts, the elegance of their configurations, be they plans for a building, an experiment, a curriculum, or a weapon of war. Howard Hughes, for example, designed a wonderfully versatile fighter aircraft in the late thirties. He offered his design to the United States, then to Britain and other European nations, all of which turned him down. But Japan bought the plans, and when the plane came to be built and used in the Pacific theater, it turned out to be the marvelous Zero, for which the allied fighters, the Curtiss P40, Brewster Buffalo, and Grumman Wildcat, were no match. And Hughes's racer, and much later, his giant seaplane, the "Spruce Goose," were like the Zero ingeniously designed, at least in the eyes of aviators.

Comparing the Strategic Role Variants

Every Rational plays these four roles well, but not equally well. Rationals differ from one another in the structure of their intellect, that is, their profile of strategic roles. Some Coordinators are better as Fieldmarshals, getting campaigns on track and moving, others as Masterminds, formulating a plan of operations; and even though campaigning is not contingency planning, these coordinating operations are interdependent, and so can never be found far apart. Similarly, some Engineers are better as Inventors of functional prototypes, others as Architects of structural designs, even though the two skills are often side-by-side, with Inventors drawing plans and Architects building working models of their designs. Consider the following chart of the four strategic role variant profiles:

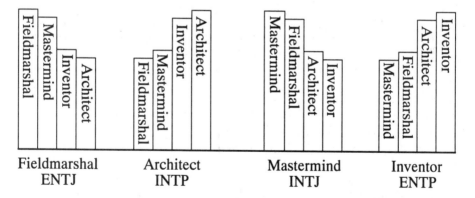

| Fieldmarshal | Architect | Mastermind | Inventor |
| ENTJ | INTP | INTJ | ENTP |

Note that in the most likely development of their strategic capabilities the Fieldmarshals (ENTJs) are the mirror image of the Architects (INTPs), as are the Masterminds (INTJs) of the Inventors (ENTPs). Thus Fieldmarshals are usually better able to mobilize forces to achieve a goal than to make structural configurations. The reverse holds for the Architects, who are better at designing efficient models than marshalling efficient campaigns. Just so, the Masterminds are better able to do the exacting research required to make contingency plans than to engage in technological invention. And last, the Inventors are the best of all in devising ingenious prototypes, though not the best at detailing a strategic plan. Still, even with their long and short suits, Rationals will tend to practice, and thus will develop, any one of these four strategic operations well above those tactical, logistical, or diplomatic operations developed by the other temperaments. (Portraits of the four variants of the Rational type can be found at the end of this chapter, beginning on page 196.)

The Interests of Rationals

Everybody has interests, but not everybody has the same interests. Moreover, our interests are reciprocal with our abilities, so that we are interested in doing what we do well, and tend to do well in what we are interested in doing. The interests of Rationals are diametrically opposite of those of Guardians and quite different from those of Artisans and Idealists. It may help to juxtapose the interests of all four types so that comparisons can be easily made:

Interests	Rationals	Artisans	Guardians	Idealists
Education	Sciences	Artcrafts	Commerce	Humanities
Preoccupation	Technology	Techniques	Morality	Morale
Vocation	Systems	Equipment	Materiel	Personnel

At school Rationals typically choose courses in the sciences (and mathematics) and avoid the humanities and commerce. Some will try arts and crafts owing to their utilitarian way with tools, but they only rarely stay with a given art or craft long enough to develop saleable skills in it. While preoccupied with technology from an early age, NTs are rarely interested in morality, and only slightly interested in morale building. On the other hand, they will work hard in adding new techniques to their collection, but they are not as consumed by this as they are by mastering technology. In career choice, it is best that they work with systems and not materiel, tools, or personnel. We will understand the Rationals better if we look carefully at their interests in science, technology, and systems.

Educational Interest in the Sciences

It is hard to get Rationals in school to study information that does not pertain to one of the sciences, and even harder to get them to practice clerical or maintenance operations. Long ago Rationals were the tribal sorcerers, attempting to bend nature to their will; later, in medieval times, they were the alchemists seeking the philosopher's stone. Today, the largely clerical curriculum in most elementary and secondary schools is boring to NTs, simply because the curriculum is wrong for them. What arouses their inherent curiosity is the work of science—logical investigation, critical experimentation, mathematical description—and it can engage and absorb them in lifelong study. Rationals do not have the function-lust of the Artisans so much as a lust to discover natural law, that is, an indomitable drive to find in nature what Francis Bacon thought of as

> those laws and determinations of absolute actuality, which govern and constitute any simple nature....Of a given nature to discover the [fixed law]...is the work and aim of Human Knowledge...and the investigation, discovery, and explanation of it is the foundation as well of knowledge as of operation.

The Rationals' desire to know how nature works never really ends for them. Even when in their nineties, if fortunate enough to reach them, NTs are still studying their books, still observing the world's patterns, still designing their experiments, still learning what there is to learn about whatever sciences captured their attention and interest in youth.

Preoccupied with Technology

Rationals are preoccupied with technology, and continue to be preoccupied with it all their lives. Technology is related to technique, something that Artisans are preoccupied with—to be sure, both words stem from the IndoEuropean root 'tekt,' with some of its more important derivatives being 'architect,' 'technical,' 'tectonics,' and 'text' (as in 'context,' 'pretext,' 'textile,' and 'texture'). All of these terms have something to do with build, structure, fabric, form, configuration, and the like. In the word 'technology,' however, the suffix, 'logy' modifies the stem 'techno' so as to make it an abstract word meaning "the logic of building." Compare this with the Artisan's 'technique' which means "skill in building." The abstract logic and the concrete skill are thus fundamentally different, indeed, so different that Rationals and Artisans usually end up going down totally different paths in life.

Two widely different pioneers in electricity, Nikola Tesla and Thomas Edison, were both Rationals, and both preoccupied with technology all their lives, although Tesla was more interested in prototyping and Edison in product development. Then there was Abraham Lincoln, one of our eight Rational Presidents, who constantly tinkered with mechanical objects, (including his son's toys, which he occasionally wrecked in the process), and who had an invention registered in the U. S. Patent Office. Then, when the Civil War erupted, Lincoln gathered information on how to conduct military campaigns, and he took special pleasure in trying out new weapons in the course of examining the latest technology of warfare. Another of our Rational Presidents, Thomas Jefferson, was more preoccupied than most others of his time with the technological aspects of 18th century science—astronomy, botany, optics, zoology, and more—keeping up with them to his dying day.

Vocational Interest in Systems

Rationals are intrigued by machines and by organisms, the two kinds of systemic entities. Organisms are the province of anthropologists, biologists, ethologists, psychologists, and sociologists; machines, the province of engineers of any kind. Organismic systems are self-regulating and self-developing, while mechanical systems are regulated by servo-mechanisms developed by engineers. Of course, any organism, whether plant or animal, is infinitely more complex than any machine. Even a sub-system, the mammalian eye for instance, is vastly more complex than the most modern airport, a giant machine itself with countless sub-assemblies. But whatever the level of complexity, it is complexity itself that intrigues NTs and therefore beckons them to take up systems-work, whether organismic or mechanical. Indeed, if some Rationals do systems-work in an organismic domain as their vocation, biology for example, those same Rationals will sooner or later get into mechanical systems as an avocation. And the reverse holds true, with many physicists in their later years getting into anthropology, biology, or psychology, Schrödinger, for example, writing *What is Life?* or Capra *The Tao of Physics.*

The Orientation of Rationals

We are born into a social field and live out our lives in that field. Our periods of disorientation, owing to shock, danger, or surprise, are usually short-lived, after which we quickly reorient ourselves and come back to our ordinary waking social frame of reference. After all, we humans are the most social of all the animals, our intense sociability ending in massive and complex societies, and it is our choice of social membership groups that creates our life-long frame of reference. Whatever we think or feel, say or do, occurs, indeed must occur, in the iron crucible of social reality. Each act and attitude is shaped and governed by a prevailing outlook, perspective, or point of view determined by our social matrix. We are oriented always from a certain angle, a standpoint, something Adickes spoke of as our built-in *"Weltanschauung"* or "worldview."

But different personalities have different perspectives, viewing time and place as well as past, present, and future, differently. Consider the following chart in making these comparisons:

Orientation	Rationals	Artisans	Guardians	Idealists
Present	**Pragmatic**	Practical	Dutiful	Altruistic
Future	**Skeptical**	Optimistic	Pessimistic	Credulous
Past	**Relativistic**	Cynical	Stoical	Mystical
Place	**Intersections**	Here	Gateways	Pathways
Time	**Intervals**	Now	Yesterday	Tomorrow

Here it is claimed that Rationals are pragmatic about the present, skeptical about the future, relativistic about the past, their preferred place is at the intersections of interaction, and their preferred time is the interval. How different from the other temperaments in the way they view these things. So let us look closely at these five dimensions of orientation so that we will not be surprised when our Rationals friends prove, in their insistent pragmatism, to be less practical, for example, or less altruistic, or less dutiful than we are.

Pragmatic in Looking Around

All of the different types of personality have a different way of viewing the world around them. For Artisans, the prevailing perspective is practical, which means that they look for effective actions in the here and now. Guardians are dutiful in perspective, requiring themselves to keep an eye on the current needs and responsibilities of others. And Idealists are altruistic in this matter, always concerned with giving of themselves to those they care about.

The perspective of the Rationals is like none of these. The Rationals instead construe their immediate surroundings from a pragmatic perspective. Pragmatism consists in having one eye on what John Dewey called "the relationship between means and ends," and the other eye on what William James called "the practical consequences" of achieving one's ends. Now, one of the most important things to know about the Rationals is that they are pragmatic to the core, and so must look to the efficiency of their means and must anticipate the practical consequences of their intended actions before they act. Thus they go for what might be called "mini-max" solutions, those that bring about maximum results for minimum effort. Minimum effort, not because they are lazy—this they could never be—but because wasted effort bothers them so much. To NTs, the other types, the SPs, SJs, and NFs, seem relatively unclear about ends, and all but incapable of coming up with effective means, so they feel it incumbent upon themselves to select if available, or to devise if not, the most efficient tools, materials, and actions possible to make sure that the goal is reached. Efficiency is always the issue with Rationals. They are efficiency-mongers at all times, everywhere they go, no matter what they do, no matter with whom they interact.

Rationals regard social custom neither respectfully nor sentimentally, but, again, pragmatically, as something useful for deciphering the lessons of history, and thus for avoiding errors. (NTs heed the warning that "Those who are ignorant of the lessons of history are doomed to repeat them," and they have a horror of repeating an error.) All too often, however, Rationals find that the actions of others are based on mere prejudice or convention, both of which they brush aside, unless some use can be found for them. Even when they take part in the customary or the conventional, Rationals tend to do so somewhat halfheartedly, and never seem to learn to do such things as a matter of habit. Since NTs are naturally disinterested in tradition and custom, it should be no surprise that they readily abandon the customary for the workable.

Unfortunately, other types, especially Guardians and Idealists, believe that everyone should observe—and respect—social conventions, and so are likely to believe that Rationals are uncaring, and this can lead to interpersonal problems. Rationals, though seemingly indifferent to convention in their single-minded pursuit of pragmatic ways and means, are just as caring as others, but are reluctant to communicate such feelings.

Skeptical in Looking Ahead

In their anticipation of things to come Artisans are optimistic, expecting to get the breaks, Guardians are pessimistic, expecting pitfalls, and Idealists are credulous, expecting the best of people. Rationals are strikingly different in their anticipations: they are skeptical, and thus expect all human endeavors, even their own, to be shot through with error. To an NT, nothing can be assumed to be correct; all is uncertain and vulnerable to mistakes—all evidence of the senses, all procedures and products, means and ends, observations and inferences—and thus all must be doubted. That's what skepticism is, an attitude of doubt about whether appearances or beliefs are to be trusted. René Descartes, that quintessential seventeenth century Rational mathematician and philosopher, began his *Meditations concerning First Philosophy* by arguing for the rational necessity of Universal Doubt:

> Since reason already convinces me that I should abstain from the belief in things which are not entirely certain and indubitable no less carefully than from the belief in those which appear to me to be manifestly false, it will be enough to make me reject them all if I can find in each some ground for doubt.

One must doubt, says the Rational, for error ever lurks in what appears true just as much as what appears false. Best therefore to take a long and careful look at any proposed method or objective, otherwise those inevitable errors of order or organization are likely to go undetected. The only thing that cannot be doubted is the act of rational doubt, and this first principle Descartes expressed in his famous formula: "I think, therefore I am. Of nothing else can I be certain."

If not born skeptical, Rationals soon become so, having their doubts about almost everything proposed either to them or by them. If looking for solutions is the engine of research and development, looking for errors in coordinating or engineering is its brake. Too often what appears to be the way to go ends up in a box canyon with no way out except back to the entry. Not that one can or should put a solution to all possible tests before a prototype is built. That of course is impossible. But the new solution will be flawed in many ways, that's for sure, no matter how careful its creator.

Rationals know this, and that's why they consider their skepticism as a useful and even necessary attitude.

Relativistic in Looking Back

The different temperaments have different ways of looking back, of reflecting on past events, of coming to terms with things that have transpired, especially those things that did not turn out well. Guardians are usually fatalistic about their troubles, Idealists mystical, Artisans cynical. But Rationals, while at times they might use any of these other ways of rationalizing the past, are far more often relativistic in their hindsight. To Rationals, events aren't of themselves good or bad, favorable or unfavorable. It's all in the way one looks at things, they say—all is relative to one's frame of reference. Reality, like truth and beauty, is in the eye of the beholder, or so the Rational phenomenologists Husserl, Sartre, and Merleau-Ponty tell us in their poetic manner. And bear in mind that Einstein, on presenting his theory of relativity, saw the real as subjective—"Reality," he said, "is a joint phenomenon of the observer and the observed."

Such a relativistic way of dealing with setbacks also gives Rationals a solipsistic view of the world. Rationals believe that others, even those who care about us, cannot really share our consciousness, cannot know our minds, cannot feel our desires and emotions, much as they might wish to. Each of us is alone in an envelope of consciousness, marooned, as it were, on the earth as its sole inhabitant. There is no way to contact directly some independent reality, what Kant called the "thing-in-itself." All is subjective; we live in our mind's eye and can only imagine the world about us. All is relative to our point-of-view; we make up our world and only then find it outside of us. "Physical concepts," Einstein reminds us, "are free creations of the human mind and are not, however it may seem, uniquely determined by the external world."

The Place is the Intersection

Rationals do not view places as simply positioned in space. With their eye always on relations between things, Rationals structure space as if making a map or plotting a graph—as a two-dimensional network, with an "x" and a "y" axis—and they define a place as the junction of these two independent coordinates, the point at which these two lines cross each other. "I'll meet you at the corner of First and Main" is a common enough expression, indicating the spot at which two dimensions intersect, and to a Rational it is this intersection which defines the "place." Nor do they confine themselves to two dimensions, often adding a third, specifying "on the fifth floor," and to finish defining the event, they might add the fourth dimension (time): "at four P.M." Or look at any global model of the earth and you will see lines of latitude and longitude, and some modern maps add lines of altitude. It is in terms of such axes or crossing lines that the Rationals look at spaces and places.

Now consider the matrix, or more recently, the spread sheet of the computer, with its row and column factors, and with the intersection of rows and columns—cells—resulting in a systematic array of combinations. Such coordinate tables speak powerfully to Rationals, since they enable them to stay on target and to produce accurate distinctions. With such an orientation the Rational has little time and no interest in other spatial orientations, such as the Artisan's centers, the Guardian's gateways, and the Idealists' pathways. It is this attitude about spaces and places that is probably more puzzling to other kinds of character than any other of the Rational's strange ways of construing reality.

The Time is the Interval

The other types tend to view time as a line or a stream running from yesterday (the focus of the Guardians), through the now (the focus of the Artisans), and into tomorrow (the focus of the Idealists). But not so the Rationals. For them time exists not as a continuous line, but as an interval, a segment confined to and defined by an event. Only events possess time, all else is timeless. For example, Dagny Taggart, Ayn Rand's Rational heroine in *Atlas Shrugged*, is aware of time only in relation to the task at hand—in this case, getting her small airplane aloft:

> Then she climbed aboard—and the next span of her consciousness was not separate moments and movements, but the sweep of a single motion and a single unit of time, a progression forming one entity, like the notes of a piece of music: from the touch of her hand on the starter—to the blast of the motor's sound that broke off, like a mountain rockslide, all contact with the time behind her—to the circling fall of a blade...—to the start for the runway—to the brief pause—then to the forward thrust—to the long, perilous run...that gathers power by spending it on a harder and harder and ever-accelerating effort...—to the moment, unnoticed, when the earth drops off...in the simple, natural act of rising.

In a sense, the focus of Rationals is outside of time as it is ordinarily understood, and it is in this sense that they can be considered atemporal. Rationals instinctively, if not deliberately, heed Einstein's dictum that events do not happen in time, rather that time is of events: "Every reference-body (coordinate system) has its own particular time; unless we are told the reference-body to which the statement of time refers, there is no meaning in a statement of the time of an event."

The Gestalt psychologists describe time similarly when they speak of "temporal configurations," in which the parts or movements of a whole are "contemporaneous." Thus a melody is composed of notes all of which belong to the same time, even though the last note comes well after the first note. The melody is not complete until the last note is sounded. Thus time for Rationals, like time for Gestaltists, is not fixed and flowing, but relative and contingent, since it is created by events rather than being a medium in which events occur.

This concept that events are not mere points on a time-line, but create their own period of time, unfolding across their own temporal interval, might be difficult to understand, but it does explain why Rationals tend to lose track of clock time, and can be oblivious to schedules, timetables, calendars, even changes from day to night, absorbed as they are in the unique time interval of whatever event they are considering.

The Self-Image of Rationals

All of us have a concept of ourselves composed of things we believe about ourselves. Three aspects of our self-image, or "self-concept" as it is sometimes called, are of special importance in determining how well we regard ourselves: self-esteem, self-respect, and self-confidence. For all the types, including the Rationals, I think the self-image is a triangular matter, the three bases of self-regard affecting each other. Thus when our self-esteem increases, this increment tends to bolster our self-respect as well as our self-confidence. Likewise, as we gain in self-respect, it becomes less difficult for us to maintain our self-confidence and self-esteem.

But different types of personality base their self-image on different things. Since having a good opinion of ourselves is one of the keys to our happiness, and often to our success, it is well that we pause for a moment to compare the four character types on this vital aspect of personality:

Self-Image	Rationals	Artisans	Guardians	Idealists
Self-Esteem	**Ingenious**	Artistic	Dependable	Empathic
Self-Respect	**Autonomous**	Audacious	Beneficent	Benevolent
Self-Confidence	**Resolute**	Adaptable	Respectable	Authentic

Note that Rationals, to feel good about themselves, must look upon themselves, and be seen by others, as ingenious, autonomous, and resolute, while feeling or appearing, say, dependable and beneficent, attributes so important to Guardians, contributes little to their sense of well-being.

If ingenuity, autonomy, and resolve are mutually reinforcing, then the self-image of the Rationals is triangular, with the three bases interdependent, as suggested by the figure at the side. But even if they are not interdependent, they still deserve individual attention, so that we can understand how Rationals are alike in

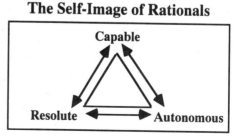

The Self-Image of Rationals

this regard and how they are so different from others in how they view themselves.

Self-Esteem in Ingenuity

Rationals pride themselves on their ingenuity in accomplishing the many and varied tasks they set their minds to. Indeed, so important is ingenuity to the Rationals' self-esteem that artistry, dependability, and empathy, so important to the other character types, pale into insignificance for them. It doesn't matter whether the task be to design a machine or an experiment, to develop a theory or a long-range plan, to build a computer or a business. The degree of inventiveness which they bring to these tasks is the measure of their ingenuity and therefore the measure of their pride in themselves. Rationals aren't comfortable bragging on themselves, but listen as one of the engineers of the national information highway lets his NT pride show for a moment when he speaks of ingenuity:

> You want to be the first to do something. You want to create something. You want to innovate something....I often think of Edison inventing the light bulb. That's what I want to do. I want to drive over the bridge coming out of New York there and look down on that sea of lights that is New Jersey and say, 'Hey, I did that!'

And yet Rationals do not confine their ingenuity to business or professional matters; they apply it to almost anything they set out to master. For example, Rationals play not so much to have fun but to exercise their ingenuity in acquiring game skills. Fun for NTs means figuring out how to get better at some skill, not merely exercising the skills they already have, and so for the Rational the field of play is invariably a laboratory for increasing their proficiency. In tennis or golf, for example, each game or round must be the occasion for pondering the physics of the most effective swing, and for trying out new strokes that seem to fit the paradigm.

Thus it is impossible for Rationals to play with the thoughtless abandon of Artisans. For the Artisans, playing is a free, impulsive activity, engaged in for the fun of it, with improved game skills coming as a result of the doing. Rationals are just the opposite, in that they mightily tax themselves with improving their skills during play, which makes improvement come rather slowly and with great difficulty. In this sense the Artisans are the Rationals' mirror image. Both can become absorbed in practicing their sport or game, but if the SP's practice is absorbing because it is free, unconscious doing, the NT's doing is absorbing, and less effective, because it is deliberate, conscious practice. If the Artisan is naturally impulsive and effortless in action, the Rational is naturally thoughtful and purposeful in action. If the Artisan cannot be induced to try, the Rational cannot be induced not to try.

Although it is too much to say Rationals are grim in their recreational activities, they can be quite unhappy with themselves when they fail to eliminate errors. When an NT plays sports, or even cards and board games, there must be continuous improvement, with no backsliding. On the golf course or the tennis court, at the bridge table or the chess board, others may shrug off mistakes, but not Rationals. In other words, just as ingenuity is the NTs' pride, so lack of it is their shame, and when they see themselves as slow or second-rate in any activity they are merciless in their self-condemnation, calling themselves "klutz," "idiot," "numbskull," "turkey," and other pejoratives. Such self-recriminations are not mere critiques of their performance, but are also likely to be scathing self-denunciations, with each term indicating the unforgivable crime of stupidity.

Rationals are easily the most self-critical of all the temperaments regarding their abilities, rooting out and condemning their errors quite ruthlessly. But others beware. NTs allow no one else to criticize them without warrant—and even with warrant, the critic is advised to be cautious and accurate. Just as NTs hold themselves to be precise, so they require those who remark on their errors to be precise as well, at the risk of learning the precise value they put upon such criticisms. And when unjustly or inaccurately criticized, Rationals burn with resentment and have even been known to fantasize about revenge, efficiently and poetically executed.

Self-Respect in Autonomy

While ingenuity is the basis of Rational self-esteem, autonomy is the basis of their self-respect. As much as possible, at times even regardless of the consequences, Rationals desire to live according to their own laws, to see the world by their own lights, and they respect themselves in the degree that they act independently, free of all coercion. Individualists all, NTs resist any effort to impose arbitrary rules on them. Indeed, they prefer to ignore any law, regulation, or convention that does not make sense to them, though they are willing to obey those that do. Little wonder that the Declaration of Independence, the United States Constitution, and the Bill of Rights were largely the work of Rationals such as Thomas Jefferson, Benjamin Franklin, and James Madison.

Rationals want to govern themselves, and also to think for themselves. From an early age Rationals will not accept anyone else's ideas without first scrutinizing them for error. It doesn't matter whether the person is a widely accepted authority or not; the fact that a so-called "expert" proclaims something leaves the Rational indifferent. Title, reputation, and credentials do not matter. Ideas must stand on their own merits, and NTs simply do not trust anyone else to have done the necessary research and applied the rules of logic adequately. "I understand that Einstein said so," comments the Rational, "but even the best of us can err." This natural lack of respect for established authorities tends to make the Rationals seem irreverent, some might say arrogant.

Instinctively taking autonomy to be the greatest virtue, Rationals regard dependence on others as the greatest vice. Whether or not they agree entirely with Ayn Rand's political and economic theories, Rationals are hard pressed, after careful consideration, not to join in her contempt for interpersonal dependency: "All that which proceeds from man's independent ego is good," she wrote in *The Fountainhead*, "All that which proceeds from man's dependence upon men is evil." Self-respecting Rationals want to be self-directed and self-determined, and their own occasional lapse into dependency is their only source of guilt.

Self-Confidence in Resolution

Rationals are self-confident in so far as they sense in themselves a strength of will or an unwavering resolution. NTs believe they can overcome any obstacle, dominate any field, conquer any enemy—even themselves—with the power of their resolve. In Charlotte Brontë's *Jane Eyre*, Rochester must will himself to live with the secret of Thornfield Hall:

> He ground his teeth and was silent: he arrested his step and struck his boot against the hard ground. Some hated thought seemed to have him in its grip, and...to hold a quivering conflict...under his ebony brow. Wild was the wrestle which should be paramount; but another feeling rose and triumphed: something hard...self-willed and resolute: it settled his passion and petrified his countenance; he went on:— 'During the moment I was silent, Miss Eyre, I was arranging a point with my destiny.'

Once Rationals resolve to do something they have in a sense made a contract with themselves, a contract they dare not go back on. Indeed, their worst fear is that their determination might weaken, their will power might falter, and that they will fail in their resolve. Why is this? Why are NTs so fearful of their will power weakening? It is because they can never take will power for granted, however strong it has proved itself in the past. They know, perhaps better than others, that they are not in charge of their will, but that their will is in charge of them. Einstein was fond of quoting Schopenhauer's words: "Man can do what he wants, but he cannot will what he wills." Rationals know, for instance, that they cannot will themselves to control involuntary functions, such as speech, sexual desire, digestion, warding off infection, and so on. After all, the involuntary is by definition not subject to the will, but must occur spontaneously.

And yet, even though they know some things must happen of themselves, Rationals can dread this loss of control. This is why so many NTs turn out to develop unreasonable fears, especially of germs and other forms of filth, something they have no control over. The Rationals Mark Twain, Nikola Tesla, Howard Hughes, and Buckminster Fuller each developed disease phobias, some of them incapacitating, as in the case of Hughes. And speech is a special problem for the Rationals, who are the most likely of all the types to develop gestural tics when they try to take control of their speech. Though it tends to impair their performance, strength of resolve is of such extreme importance to Rationals that, under stress, they have no choice but to invoke their will and try harder.

The Values of Rationals

The different kinds of personality differ in what they value. Thus they can differ in their preferred mood, in what they put their trust in, in what they long for, in what they continuously seek, in what they prize most, and in what they aspire to. It is in the domain of values that Rationals separate themselves most clearly from the other types, and particularly from the Guardians. Where Guardians value being concerned, Rationals value being calm; where Guardians trust authority, Rationals trust reason; where Guardians yearn for belonging, Rationals yearn for achievement; where Guardians seek security, Rationals seek knowledge. And the contrast extends to what they prize and what they aspire to, Guardians gratitude and executive power, Rationals deference and wizardry. But NTs are also very different in their values from SPs and NFs, as shown in the following chart:

Value	Rationals	Artisans	Guardians	Idealists
Being	**Calm**	Excited	Concerned	Enthusiastic
Trusting	**Reason**	Impulse	Authority	Intuition
Yearning	**Achievement**	Impact	Belonging	Romance
Seeking	**Knowledge**	Stimulation	Security	Identity
Prizing	**Deference**	Generosity	Gratitude	Recognition
Aspiring	**Wizard**	Virtuoso	Executive	Sage

These differences in values are so extreme that it will serve us to study all six Rational values in some detail, lest we are surprised to find them, say, less generous, less authoritarian, or less enthusiastic than we are.

Being Calm
The preferred mood of Rationals, as Galen suggested, is one of calm. This is particularly true in stressful situations, when things around them are in turmoil, as C.S. Forester's Horatio Hornblower discovers in a moment of crisis, after having set fire to the enemy ship which held him captive:

> A side pane fell in as they watched, and a rush of flame came through the opening. That store of paint, Hornblower calculated—he was calmer now, with a calm that would astonish him later, when he came to look back on it—must be immediately under the cabin, and blazing fiercely.

Artisans like to be excited, Guardians are likely to get concerned about their responsibilities, and Idealists give their enthusiasm free rein, Rationals prefer to remain calm, cool, and collected. And if they cannot avoid these emotional states, they will try hard to avoid letting their concern, excitement, or enthusiasm show. SPs, SJs, and NFs are puzzled more by this seeming unflappability in trying circumstances than by any other trait of the NT character. Indeed, because they are reluctant to express emotions or desires, NTs are often criticized for being unfeeling and cold. However, what is taken for indifference is not indifference at all, but the thoughtful, absorbed concentration of the contemplative investigator. Just as effective investigators carefully hold their feelings in check and gauge their actions so that they do not disturb their inquiry or contaminate their results, so Rationals are prone to examine and control themselves in the same deliberate manner, being careful to avoid reading their own desires, emotions, and expectations into their observations.

But make no mistake, although they hold back on any intemperate displays, Rationals are not the cold and distant persons they are often made out to be. For one thing they can get quite intense and pressured about matters under their control (and few things will they admit they cannot control), becoming as tight as a bowstring when they think they might be able to solve a problem if they put their mind to it. For another, being closet romantics, their feelings are just as varied and strong as those of other character types, though again, and more than others, Rationals tend to hold them tightly in check.

Trusting Reason

The only thing Rationals trust unconditionally is reason—all else they trust only under certain conditions. Thus they trust their intuition only now and then, their impulses even less often, and they completely distrust titular authority. Of all these only reason, NTs say, is universal and timeless, and only its laws beyond dispute. Thus Rationals take it for granted that "if men would but reason together," even the most difficult of problems might be solved. When the Rational Thomas Jefferson wrote the charter for the University of Virginia, he insisted that here education "will be based upon the illimitable freedom of the human mind, for here we are not afraid to follow truth wherever it may lead, nor tolerate error so long as reason is left free to combat it."

Jefferson's vision was of a free competition of ideas, unfettered by convention or tradition, an inquiry limited only by the scope of the human mind and the laws of reason. In this he was a typical Rational. More than the other temperaments, NTs listen carefully to new ideas as long as they make sense—as long as they are logical. But they have little or no patience for ideas that don't make sense, and they will not be swayed by any argument that fails to meet their criterion of logical coherence.

Yearning for Achievement

One of the most important things to remember about Rationals, if they are to be understood, is that they yearn for achievement. Some might suppose that these seemingly calm and contemplative types have no strong desires. But beneath the calm exterior is a gnawing hunger to achieve whatever goals they set for themselves. While NTs prefer to acquire know-how, and would like to be ingenious, they must achieve, and their longing is never fully satisfied.

Because their hunger for achievement presses them constantly, Rationals live through their work. For them, work is work and play is work. Condemning an NT to idleness would be the worst sort of punishment. However, Rationals work not so much for the pleasure of action (like the Artisans), nor for the security a job provides (like the Guardians), nor for the joy of helping others (like the Idealists). Rationals work with a single-minded desire to achieve their objectives; indeed, once involved in a project, they tend to be reluctant, if not unable, to limit their commitment of time and energy. Unfortunately, at this point they can be unreasonably demanding of both themselves and others, setting their standards too high and becoming quite tense under stress. No wonder that NTs frequently achieve notable success in their chosen field.

Achievement eats at NTs in this way because it demands of them ever greater knowledge and skill, a challenge they eagerly accept, as Sinclair Lewis explains in *Arrowsmith*, his novel about a gifted young scientist:

> There was no strength,...no knowledge, that Arrowsmith did not covet, when consciousness of it has pierced through the layers of his absorption. If he was but little greedy for possessions, he was hungry for every skill.

Thus, and because of their persistence, Rationals tend over their lifetimes to collect a large repertoire of skilled actions, few of which they employ very extensively. In this they are quite unlike the Artisans, who also become skillful. For the SPs, skills are opportunities for action and have no meaning if they are not used, while for the NTs skills are competencies to be sharpened through practice, then held in reserve until actually needed.

Rationals demand so much achievement from themselves that they often have trouble measuring up to their own standards. NTs typically believe that what they do is not good enough, and are frequently haunted by a sense of teetering on the edge of failure. This time their achievement will not be adequate. This time their skill will not be great enough. This time, in all probability, failure is at hand.

Making matters worse, Rationals tend to ratchet up their standards of achievement, setting the bar at the level of their greatest success, so that anything less than their best is judged as mediocre. The hard-won triumph becomes the new standard of what is merely acceptable, and ordinary achievements are now viewed as falling short of the mark. NTs never give themselves a break from this escalating level of achievement, and so constant self-doubt and a niggling sense of impending failure are their lot.

Seeking Knowledge

While Artisans go in search of stimulation, Guardians security, and Idealists identity, Rationals are on the lookout for knowledge. Some of them are so relentless in their search, that (like their benefactor, Prometheus) they would steal knowledge even from the gods. Francis Bacon declared at the beginning of the 17th century that knowledge is power, and advised that nature be "put to the rack," so that her secrets could be extracted by scientific experimentation. In doing so he established the Rational method of scientific investigation which has prevailed in the West for 400 years.

The Rationals' search for knowledge has two objectives: they must know *how to* as well as know *about*. To know about is to comprehend the necessary and sufficient conditions under which events occur. To know how to is to comprehend the operational capabilities and limits of technologies—the possibilities and constraints of their tools, be they cutters, carbines, or computers. By knowing about and knowing how to, Rationals increase their capability to predict and to control events.

Knowledge for Rationals is never merely speculative. When NTs ask "why?" they are really asking "how?" or even "how to?" To ask why the sky is blue, why water is wet, why a lever has power, is not to ask for the meaning or significance of these things (something that greatly concerns their abstract cousins, the Idealists). The Rationals' questions are about why things take the form they do, about how things work—and thus about definition and description of structure and function. As his biographer James Gleick notes, Nobel prize winning physicist Richard Feynman had no use for what he called the philosopher's "soft" questions:

> Feynman's reinvention of quantum mechanics did not so much explain how the world was, or why it was that way, as tell how to confront the world. It was not knowledge of or knowledge about. It was knowledge how to....There were other kinds of scientific knowledge, but pragmatic knowledge was Feynman's specialty. For him knowledge did not describe; it acted and accomplished.

Such a quest for pragmatic knowledge arises early for Rationals, as soon as they have the language for inquiring, and seems fueled by an insatiable curiosity. But since they are likely to pose their question as a "why?" they will often be unsatisfied with the answer they receive, for they are actually interested in "how?" not "why?" And since they can be insistent in their questioning, they often dismay their parents and teachers, who don't understand what they are really asking. Further, NTs want to be given a rationale in the answers they receive, something most parents and teachers have difficulty giving them.

As Rationals grow up, their pursuit of knowledge leads them to grapple with an ever-widening range of complex problems. Whether the problem is one of engineering machines or of coordinating operations, Rationals consider problems of central importance, and they will persist in their search for models and maps, for paradigms and algorithms, with which to construe and attack these problems. Problem-solving for the Rationals is a twenty-four hour occupation, and if they don't have a problem to work on they will actually set one for themselves as a way of exercising their skills. They are especially drawn to problems that tax their knowledge base, since practice with such problems adds to their knowledge and naturally expands their repertoire of useful models. And the more extreme the Rational style, the more exacting and stringent the demand they place on themselves for acquiring knowledge.

Another way of looking at this is that, in contrast to the social and moral shoulds and oughts of the Guardians and Idealists, the Rationals have a good many should-knows itemized in massive lists inside their heads. And though they can concentrate fully on one thing at a time, they are inclined to accumulate more and more useful knowledge, rarely deleting or forgetting any, and to work continually on solutions to the many problems that intrigue them. Having won a Nobel prize in 1972 for his work on immunology, biologist Gerald Edelman was not at all content to cease his inquiries:

> About three years after Edelman won the prize he essentially left the field to pursue even bigger questions—the biggest ones imaginable, concerning the essential mysteries of biology....'I have a small romantic streak and a very definite belief that's coupled to it, which is that the asking of the question is the important thing....So if you said to me, "Well, now, you're the czar of immunology." Horrors!...None of that really interests me. What interests me is dark areas.'

So intent are Rationals in their pursuit of knowledge, that they might be thought of as the "Knowledge-Seeking Personality." Of all the traits of character that set the Rationals apart—and at the same time group them together—it is their life-long search for knowledge.

Prizing Deference
What is pleasing to one sort of person may not be nearly as pleasing to another. Artisans are quite pleased by generous treatment, Guardians by gratitude, Idealists by being recognized as their unique selves. Certainly Rationals are not indifferent to generosity, gratitude, or recognition, but they are much more pleased when asked by an admirer to comment on something the NT has produced, especially if the request is for an exposition of their rationale. NTs regard such deference as being given not so much to themselves personally as to their productions. After all, when they make something or do something it is usually after long and sometimes obsessive analysis. So even if they are not especially brilliant, it is to be expected that their productions have been carefully devised, with pros and cons considered, and errors of inclusion and exclusion rooted out.

But Rationals cannot ask for deference, any more than Guardians can ask for appreciation, or Idealists for recognition. It must come to them spontaneously, out of interest in their work. And, of course, if in their view they haven't achieved anything they regard as worth noting, then they have no desire to be consulted in the matter. But if they have done something rather well, they are pleased when someone defers to them for definition and explanation of their production, and they can be disappointed if none comes their way, or worse, if someone else is asked to expound on what they've accomplished.

Their problem is that their accomplishment is often so highly technical—designing a computer chip for instance—that most people are only vaguely aware of how difficult it was to make, and so have little or no reason to acknowledge and give credit to its maker. So the vast majority of Rationals who manage to achieve something great are unsung heroes to the public, and therefore heroes only to their family or their colleagues—and perhaps in their own eyes.

Aspiring to be a Wizard

Because Rationals value the strategic intellect so highly, they tend to take as their idol the technological wizard, especially the scientific genius. After all, a wizard is the ultimate scientist, with what seems an almost magical power over nature, and in single-minded pursuit of the four aims of science: the prediction and control of events, and the understanding and explanation of their contexts. Scratch a Rational, find a scientist; but glimpse the figure the Rationals would aspire to become, and behold a wizard. Listen as Merlin, King Arthur's wizard in Lerner and Loewe's *Camelot*, teaches young Arthur what he considers the most important lesson of all:

> *Merlin:* There's only one thing for all of it. Learn! Learn why the world wags and what wags it.
> *Arthur:* How could I learn if I couldn't think?...
> *Merlin:* Yes...thinking, boy, is something you should definitely get into the habit of making use of as often as possible.

But listen also to Jonas Salk as he explains his view of the magic of biological science:

> When I discovered there was more to learning than the books we were exposed to, and then when I became interested in bringing science into medicine, I recognized that there was a logic to the magic. Life is magic; the way nature works seems to be quite magical....I started to try to understand how that system works. I began to tease out the logic of the magic that I was so impressed by.

The Social Roles Rationals Play

It is impossible not to play a role in all of our social transactions, and there are two kinds of social roles, those that are allotted to us by virtue of our position in our social milieu, and those that we reach out and take for ourselves. We perforce play offspring to our parents, siblings to our brothers and sisters, and relatives to our extended family members. On the other hand we choose to play mate to our spouse, parent to our offspring, superior to our subordinate, subordinate to our superior, friend to friend, and so on. Allotted or embraced, we have no choice but to enact our roles, since to interact with others can never be role-free.

Three of our roles—mating, parenting, leading—are of special interest in the context of the study of personality. In these three roles the different kinds of personality differ significantly in the effects their roles have on mates, offspring, and followers. Consider the following chart which compares how differently the mating, parenting, and leading roles are played:

Social Roles	Rationals	Artisans	Guardians	Idealists
Mating	**Mindmate**	Playmate	Helpmate	Soulmate
Parenting	**Individuator**	Liberator	Socializer	Harmonizer
Leading	**Visionary**	Negotiator	Stabilizer	Catalyst

Note the striking difference between playing the Rational's Mindmate role and the Guardian's Helpmate role, the Idealist's Soulmate role, and the Artisan's Playmate role. These different roles will require lengthy and complex study and so a chapter (Chapter 7) on mating is provided later in this book. Separate chapters (Chapters 8 and 9) are also furnished on the NT's parenting and leadership roles, to distinguish the NT Individuator parent from the SP Liberator, the SJ Socializer, and the NF Harmonizer, as well as to differentiate the NT Visionary leader from the SP Negotiator, the SJ Stabilizer, and the NF Catalyst. Even so, a few remarks can at least give an outline of how Rationals play their social roles.

The Mindmate

Sharing with their spouses what they have on their minds is of primary importance to Rationals. They are prone to initiate discussions with their mates on a wide variety of topics and to pursue them until the issue is clear, whether or not there is agreement. The issues they pursue with their mates are almost invariably abstract rather than concrete—issues such as theories of politics and economics, questions in ethics and religion, epistemology and linguistics, and, of course, breakthroughs in science and technology, although the latter are usually too technical for much sharing, if, that is, the Rational is a scientist or technologist and the mate is not.

This desire for intellectual sharing puts limits on the kind of mate that Rationals are apt to choose. The desire will not be fulfilled in the event they are mated with either Guardians or Artisans, neither of whom are willing to pursue abstract topics either recurrently or for more than a few minutes. So, if the desire for cognitive sharing is the Rational's primary criterion for choosing a mate, he or she is prudent to choose another Rational or an Idealist. On the other hand, if for some reason the Mindmate role is set aside, the Rationals have just as much leeway as other types in finding their mate, though choosing the more friendly types, Conservator Guardians (ESFJs and ISFJs) and Improvisor Artisans (ESFPs and ISFPs), will probably entail less marital conflict.

Rationals usually approach mate selection as a difficult and even threatening problem, one requiring careful empirical study and calm but rigorous introspection. After all, they say to themselves, there is no room for error in this choice since mating is for life. Those who do err in this are likely, owing to their rather stringent code of ethics, to honor the contract they made and do their best to minimize the underlying conflict of values. Even in marriage NTs are pragmatic.

The Individuator Parent

Rational parents are usually more concerned about the growth of individuality in their children than the other types. It is vitally important to them that each and every child in the family becomes progressively more self-directed and self-reliant in handling the challenges of life. Other concerns, such as the Idealist's self-esteem and the Artisan's venturesomeness, important though they may be, are thought to follow along naturally in the wake of their children developing a firm sense of their individuality and autonomy. And civility of conduct, so important to Guardian parents, is all but ignored by Rational parents in their determination to encourage their children's individuation.

The Visionary Leader

Rational leaders usually have a vision of how an organization will look and how it will fare in the long haul, their long suit in intelligence being strategic planning. They look far ahead and all around, their plans leaving nothing important to chance. And owing to their early and long pursuit of coherent and comprehensive speech, they are often able to convey their vision of things to come to their followers, such that their followers heartily join them in the enterprise they have envisioned.

Matrix of Rational Traits

The matrix that follows arranges and highlights the terms used in this chapter to define the personality of the Rationals. These terms are placed beside those used to define the other three personalities, thus enabling us to compare the Rational traits to those of others.

There can be considerable payoff for those who take time to study this matrix, and refer back to it from time to time, the payoff being that of getting a grip on the whole configuration of the Platonic-Aristotelian Dialectical Rational Personality and getting a feel of its uniqueness and radical difference from the others.

The Traits of Temperament and Character

Communication Implementation Character	┌─ Concrete ─┐		┌─Abstract─┐	
	Utilitarian **Artisan**	Cooperative **Guardian**	Cooperative **Idealist**	Utilitarian **Rational**
Language Referential Syntactical Rhetorical	**Harmonic** Indicative Descriptive Heterodox	**Associative** Imperative Comparative Orthodox	**Inductive** Interpretive Metaphoric Hyperbolic	**Deductive** Categorical Subjunctive Technical
Intellect Directive Role • Expressive Role • Reserved Role Informative Role • Expressive Role • Reserved Role	**Tactical** Operator • Promoter • Crafter Entertainer • Performer • Composer	**Logistical** Administrator • Supervisor • Inspector Conserving • Provider • Protector	**Diplomatic** Mentor • Teacher • Counselor Advocating • Champion • Healer	**Strategic** Coordinator • Fieldmarshal • Mastermind Engineer • Inventor • Architect
Interest Education Preoccupation Vocation	Artcraft Technique Equipment	Commerce Morality Materiel	Humanities Morale Personnel	**Sciences** **Technology** **Systems**
Orientation Present Future Past Place Time	Practical Optimistic Cynical Centers Now	Dutiful Pessimistic Stoical Gateways Yesterday	Altruistic Credulous Mystical Pathways Tomorrow	**Pragmatic** **Skeptical** **Relativistic** **Intersections** **Intervals**
Self-Image Self-Esteem Self-Respect Self-Confidence	Artistic Audacious Adaptable	Dependable Beneficent Respectable	Empathic Benevolent Authentic	**Ingenious** **Autonomous** **Resolute**
Value Being Trusting Yearning Seeking Prizing Aspiring	Excited Impulse Impact Stimulation Generosity Virtuoso	Concerned Authority Belonging Security Gratitude Executive	Enthusiastic Intuition Romance Identity Recognition Sage	**Calm** **Reason** **Achievement** **Knowledge** **Deference** **Wizard**
Social Role Mating Parenting Leading	Playmate Liberator Negotiator	Helpmate Socializer Stabilizer	Soulmate Harmonizer Catalyst	**Mindmate** **Individuator** **Visionary**

Rational Role Variants

These "Abstract Utilitarians," as I like to call them—Plato's Rationals, Aristotle's Dialecticals, Galen's Phlegmatics, and Myers's NTs—have a tightly configured personality, so that each trait of character entails the other traits. This means that Mother Nature does not permit Rationals, any more than other types, to pick and choose their traits of character. If their environment enables them to develop a given trait it can only be one that is predetermined by their temperament.

While it is useful to think of each of the four temperaments as a single, unified configuration of attitudes and actions, individual members of each temperament clearly differ from one another. Thus, all the Rationals seem to have a natural gift for strategic ingenuity, but some (the scheduling NTs) are drawn to the directive role of Coordinator of efficient campaigns and contingency plans, while others (the probing NTs) prefer the informative role of Engineer of efficient prototypes and models. These two divisions can be further broken down to reflect an expressive or a reserved social attitude, with the Coordinators tending to play the role variants of Field-marshal or Mastermind, and the Engineers playing Inventor or Architect.

The Fieldmarshal [ENTJ]
Myers had a special name for the ENTJs. She called them "the leaders of leaders," in a word, "superleaders." This no doubt because she could see how efficient the ENTJs are in marshalling task forces in the field in preparation for launching major enterprises. Marshalling forces is the coordinating of personnel and materiel in the service of a clearly defined objective, something ENTJs seem especially cut out for. Best then to call them the "Fieldmarshals."

Another word that is useful in defining this kind of coordinating activity is 'mobilizing.' Personnel and materiel can be mobilized as well as marshalled, the only difference being that mobilizing connotes moving effective forces toward a goal, while marshalling connotes binding effective forces to a goal. Either way, the basic, driving force of these Fieldmarshals is to command forces that promise to be effective in achieving the objectives that they are able to visualize.

It was no accident that World War II saw three of these ENTJs in command of our armed forces—George Marshall, Dwight Eisenhower, and Douglas MacArthur—each a genius in strategic mobilizing and marshalling of personnel and materiel toward world-wide aims. Marshall, chairman of the Joint Chiefs of Staff at the outbreak of war, was already at the top, and he knew full well which commanders to pick to run the campaigns in the eastern and western theaters—Eisenhower, a mere colonel at the time, but a brilliant student of warfare who had worked for Marshall as his best campaign planner; and General MacArthur, languishing with little to do in the Philippines. No, it was no accident, because Marshall had long experience with both of these men, and he fully appreciated the high strategic intelligence of each.

As a variant of Plato's Rationals and Aristotle's Dialecticals, the ENTJs are little different from the other NTs in most respects. Like all the Rationals, they are abstract in their communication and utilitarian in how they implement their goals. They choose to study science, are preoccupied with technology, and work well with systems. Their point of view is pragmatic, skeptical, relativistic, focused on spatial intersections and intervals of time. They base their self-image on being ingenious, autonomous, and resolute. They would if possible be calm, they trust reason, are hungry for achievement, seek knowledge, prize deference, and aspire to be wizards of science and technology. Intellectually, they are prone to practice strategy far more than diplomacy, tactics, and especially logistics. Further, having a decisive or scheduling nature, they tend to choose the Coordinator's directive role over the probing, exploring Engineer's informative role. And because they are so forceful in their expressiveness they find greater satisfaction in the role variant of Fieldmarshal than Mastermind. To visualize ENTJ intellectual development consider the following graph that depicts the most probable profile of their strategic roles:

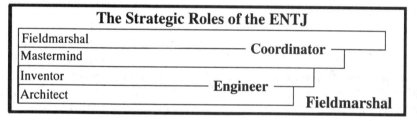

Although Fieldmarshals are just as rare as the other Rationals, something less than two percent of the total population, they seem to have influence beyond their numbers. Such individuals, male or female, of whatever age, are bound to lead others, and from early on they can be observed taking command of groups, so forceful is their climb to the top. In some cases, Fieldmarshals simply find themselves in charge of groups, and are mystified as to how this happened. But the reason is that they have a strong natural urge to bring order and efficiency wherever they are—to harness people and resources and to lead them toward their goals with minimum waste of effort and maximum progress. Every operation needed for achieving the objective shall be executed, and all unnecessary operations are quietly and permanently eliminated from the planned sequence of events.

Take building a house, for example. Put a Fieldmarshal in charge of the job and he or she will coordinate all the steps in the operation, hiring a cement contractor to pour the foundation, but also hiring a plumber to set the water pipes and connect the sewer lines before pouring the slab. Then come the framer, electrician, roofer, drywaller, painter, and cabinet maker, with the ENTJ requiring that the construction follows a logical order so that there is minimum waste of manpower and material resources.

In just the same way, Fieldmarshals cannot not build organizations, and cannot not push to implement their goals. More than all other types ENTJs are from an early age bent on the exacting and untiring practice of their budding coordinating skills, which enable them to be good at systematizing, arranging priorities, generalizing, summarizing, compiling evidence, and at demonstrating their ideas. When in charge of an organization, whether in the military, business, education, or government, ENTJs desire and have the ability to visualize where the organization is going, and they seem unusually able to communicate that vision to others.

These decisive and outspoken Rationals will usually rise to positions of responsibility in the workplace and enjoy being in charge. They are so single-minded and easily caught up in some project or campaign that they can easily block out other areas of life for the sake of their work. Superb executives, they mobilize their forces into smooth-functioning systems, planning in advance, keeping both short-term and long-range objectives well in mind. For the ENTJ, there must always be a reason for doing anything, and people's feelings usually are not sufficient reason. More than any other type they are skilled at reducing bureaucracy in any of its forms, and they are willing to dismiss employees who cannot get with the program and increase their efficiency. Although Fieldmarshals are tolerant of some established procedures, they can and will abandon any procedure when it can be shown to be ineffective in accomplishing its goal. Fieldmarshals are the supreme pragmatists, always aware of the relationship of means to ends. Any procedure the objective of which is no longer pursued is instantly eliminated and its users reassigned to more productive actions. Parkinson's law has little chance of survival where an ENTJ is in charge.

Fieldmarshals take full command at home, leaving little doubt about who makes the decisions. Male or female, they expect a great deal of their mates, who, if not to be steamrolled, need to possess a strong personality of their own, a well-developed autonomy, many and varied interests, and a healthy self-esteem. A career-woman, however, may not be appealing to an ENTJ male, who is apt to view his home and family as a part of his professional background, as a resource, and thus adjunct to his own career development. He might expect his mate to be active in civic and community affairs, to be socially sophisticated, and to continue her education. The ENTJ female, on the other hand, may find it difficult to select a mate who is not overwhelmed by the force of her will.

Also in their parenting role, Fieldmarshals are thoroughly in command, and their children will know what is expected of them—and will be expected to obey. When they don't, the ENTJ parent is not apt to make a scene; rather, there is more likely to be a low-key clarification about who is in charge, what is expected, and what the inevitable consequences of disobedience will be. Few children are not in awe of this sort of command. While both mating and parenting are highly important to the Fieldmarshals, these roles must sometimes take a back seat to their strong career drive, and to the enormous amount of time they spend on the job.

The Mastermind [INTJ]

All NTs are good at planning operations, but Mastermind INTJs are head and shoulders above all the rest in contingency planning or what is called "entailment management." A contingency plan has if-thens in it, put there to deal with foreseeable operational errors and shortages of personnel and materiel. All sorts of contingencies are bound to arise when any complex project is undertaken, from planning a family vacation in Europe to preparing for the invasion of Europe, as in World War II. Such operations involve many, many steps, each of which must be coordinated to follow one another in a necessary progression, and each of which can be subject to unforeseen problems. Masterminds are able to grasp how each step necessitates or entails the next, and to prepare alternatives for difficulties that are likely to arise. INTJs never set the course of their current project without a Plan A firmly in mind, but they are always prepared to switch to Plan B—or C or D if they are called for.

As a variant of Plato's Rationals and Aristotle's Dialecticals, the INTJs are little different from the other NTs in most respects. Like all the Rationals, they are abstract in their communication and utilitarian in how they implement their goals. They choose to study science, are preoccupied with technology, and work well with systems. Their point of view is pragmatic, skeptical, relativistic, focused on spatial intersections and intervals of time. They base their self-image on being ingenious, autonomous, and resolute. They would if possible be calm, they trust reason, are hungry for achievement, seek knowledge, prize deference, and aspire to be wizards of science and technology. Intellectually, they are prone to practice strategy far more than diplomacy, tactics, and especially logistics. Further, with their schedule-minded nature, they tend to choose the Coordinator's directive role over the probing Engineer's informative role. And because they are reserved around others they seem more comfortable in the role variant of Mastermind than Fieldmarshal. To visualize INTJ skills development consider the following graph depicting the most probable profile of their strategic roles:

The Strategic Roles of the INTJ		
Mastermind		
Fieldmarshal	Coordinator	
Architect		
Inventor	Engineer	
		Mastermind

Masterminds are rare, comprising no more than, say, one percent of the population, and they are rarely encountered outside their office, factory, or laboratory. Although they are highly capable leaders, INTJs are not at all eager to take command, preferring to stay in the background until others demonstrate their inability to lead. Once in charge, however, they are thoroughgoing pragmatists, seeing reality as nothing more than a chess board for working out and refining their strategies. When planning, the Mastermind is completely open-minded and will entertain any idea holding promise of utility. Fruitful theories are quickly applied, all else discarded.

To the INTJ, order is never arbitrary, set in concrete, but can be improved. Thus authority based on degrees, credentials, title, or celebrity does not impress them, nor do slogans or catchwords. They will adopt ideas only if they are useful, which is to say if they work efficiently toward accomplishing well-defined goals. Only ideas that make sense to them are adopted; those that don't, aren't, no matter who the author is.

Masterminds tend to be much more self-confident than other Rationals, having usually developed a very strong will. Decisions come easily to them; indeed, they can hardly rest until they have things settled and decided. They have a drive to completion, always with an eye to long-term consequences. Ideas seem to carry their own force for them, although they subject every idea to the test of usefulness. Difficulties are highly stimulating to INTJs, who love responding to a problem that requires a creative solution. These traits of character lead them to occupations where theoretical models can be translated into actuality. They build data and human systems wherever they work, if given the slightest opportunity. They can be outstanding in scientific research and as executives in businesses.

These seclusive Coordinators usually rise to positions of responsibility, for they work long and hard and are steady in their pursuit of goals, sparing neither their own time and effort nor that of their colleagues and employees. They tend, ordinarily, to verbalize the positive and to eschew comments of a negative nature; they are more interested in moving an organization forward than dwelling on mistakes of the past. However, they can become single-minded at times, which can be a weakness in their careers, for by focusing so tightly on their own pursuits they can ignore the points of view and wishes of others.

Masterminds are certain that both internal and external consistency are indispensable in the well-run organization, and if they encounter problems of overlapping functions, duplication of effort, inefficient paper flow, and waste of human and material resources, they are quick to realign operations to the forgotten goal. Remember, their imperative is always cost-effectiveness.

INTJs are the highest achievers in school of all the types. And on the job, because of their tendency to drive others as hard as they drive themselves, they often seem demanding and difficult to satisfy. Their fellow workers often feel as if a Mastermind can see right through them, and often believe that they find them wanting. This tendency of people to feel transparent, and even incompetent, in their presence often results in working relationships which have some psychological distance. Colleagues may describe INTJs as unemotional and, at times, cold and dispassionate, when in truth they are merely taking the goals of an institution seriously, and continually striving to achieve those goals. Fortunately, indifference or criticism from their fellow workers does not particularly bother Masterminds, if they believe that they are right. All in all, they make dedicated, loyal employees whose loyalties are directed toward the system, rather than toward individuals within the system. As the people in an institution come and go, these NTs have little difficulty getting on with their jobs—unlike the NFs, who have their loyalties involved more with persons than projects.

Masterminds want harmony and order in their home and in their marriage, but not at the cost of having a submissive mate. The most independent of all the types, INTJs want their mates to be independent as well, able to stand up to the sometimes formidable strength of their personality. Courtship is a special problem for Masterminds, since they regard the selection of a proper mate as a rational process, a matter of finding someone who correlates highly with their mental list of physical and intellectual requirements. They know quickly—usually on the first or second date—whether or not a relationship has any future, and they will not waste their time on courtships that seem to hold little promise. In general, Masterminds rely on their head and not their heart to make these choices, and at times, therefore, they will seem cold and calculating. Even in more casual social situations, they may appear cold and may neglect to observe small rituals designed to put others at their ease. For example, INTJs may communicate that time is wasted if used for idle chitchat, and thus people receive a sense of hurry from them which is not always intended. Make no mistake, the emotions of an INTJ are hard to read, and neither a male nor female of this type is apt to be very outgoing or emotionally expressive. On the contrary, they have a strong need for privacy, and they do not enjoy physical contact except with a chosen few. For all that, however, Masterminds are deeply emotional, even romantic types, and once they have decided a person is worthy of them, they make passionate and loyal mates, almost hypersensitive to signals of rejection from their loved one.

With their children, Masterminds are loving and unfailing in their devotion. Their children are a major focus in life, and they loyally support them and tend to allow them to develop in directions of their own choosing. These supremely definite INTJs encourage independence of action and attitude in their offspring. On the other hand, they are fully aware that children need well-defined limits, and they are invariably firm and consistent in setting those limits.

The Inventor [ENTP]

Inventing is the functional side of engineering, that is, the building of prototypes of devices that work to make systems more efficient. It is so natural for ENTPs to practice devising ingenious gadgets and mechanisms that they start doing it even as young children. And these Inventors get such a kick out of it that they really never stop exercising their inventive talent, though in the workplace they will turn their technological ingenuity to many kinds of systems, social as well as physical and mechanical.

As a variant of Plato's Rationals and Aristotle's Dialecticals, the ENTPs are little different from the other NTs in most respects. Like all the Rationals, they are abstract in their communication and utilitarian in how they implement their goals. They choose to study science, are preoccupied with technology, and work well with systems. Their point of view is pragmatic, skeptical, relativistic, focused on spatial intersections and intervals of time. They base their self-image on being ingenious, autonomous, and resolute. They would if possible be calm, they trust reason, are hungry for achievement, seek knowledge, prize deference, and aspire to be wizards of science and technology. Intellectually they are prone to practice strategy far more than diplomacy, tactics, and especially logistics. Further, having a probing or option-minded nature they tend to prefer the Engineer's informative role over the scheduling Coordinator's directive role. And owing to their expressiveness and interest in the world at large they prefer the role variant of Inventor over Architect. To visualize ENTP intellectual development consider the following graph depicting the most probable profile of their strategic roles:

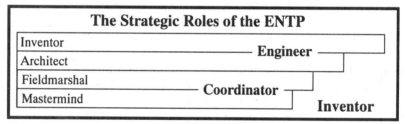

There aren't many Inventors, say about two percent of the population. They are intensely curious and continuously probe for possibilities, especially concerning complex problems, and they find chaos theory intriguing. Such curiosity can be inspiring to others, who find themselves admiring the Inventor's insatiable hunger for know-how. ENTPs are also the most reluctant of all the types to do things in a particular manner just because that is the way things have always been done. They characteristically have an eye out for a better way, always on the lookout for new projects, new activities, new procedures. Inventors are confident in the value of their approaches and display a charming capacity to ignore the standard, the traditional, and the authoritative. As a result of this innovative attitude, they often bring fresh, new approaches to their work and their lives.

Good at functional analysis, Inventors are keen judges of the pragmatics of both social and technological organization, and often become expert at improving relationships between means and ends. Where the INTP Architect sees design as an end in itself, the Inventor sees design as a means to an end, as a way of devising the instrument that works, the prototype that is replicable. To these outgoing Engineers, ideas are valuable when and only when they make possible actions and objects. "It can't be done" is a challenge to an ENTP and elicits a reaction of "I can do it." They are not, however, the movers of mountains as are the INTJ Masterminds. Rather, Inventors have faith in their ability to come up with solutions to problems, and they display an extraordinary talent for rising to the demands of even the most impossible situations. Superficially, they resemble ESTP Promoter Artisans with their talent for improvisation and expedient action. But the focus of the Inventors is on competency and a sense of achievement, rather than on the Promoter's feeling of spontaneity and freedom of action.

Inventors have an entrepreneurial spirit and can cleverly make do with whatever or whoever is at hand, counting on their capability to solve problems as they arise, rather than carefully generating a detailed blueprint in advance. A rough draft is all they need to feel confident and ready to proceed into action. Because of this tendency to depend on their capability and inventiveness, ENTPs may, at times, neglect to prepare themselves adequately for a given task. Even after repeated failures in situations where their capability has met with defeat, they will develop ways of avoiding such situations rather than resorting to more thorough preparation.

ENTPs can succeed in a variety of occupations, as long as the job does not involve too much humdrum routine, at which point they become restless. They are usually outstanding teachers, continuously devising new and intriguing ways to get their students involved in learning. They make good leaders on innovative projects that test their ingenuity. And they are skilled at engineering human relationships and human systems, quickly grasping the politics of institutions and always aiming to understand the people within the system rather than to judge them. Indeed, they are non-directive in their handling of others, and will take charge of activities only when forced to by circumstance.

No matter what their occupation, however, Inventors are seldom conformists in the workplace. If their job becomes dull and repetitive, they tend to lose interest and fail to follow through—often to the discomfort of colleagues. To stave off routine, ENTPs will try to outwit the system and use the rules and regulations within the system to give themselves room to innovate. They may even work against the system just for the joy of holding the upper hand. Inventors have also been known to engage in brinkmanship with their superiors, placing their own careers in jeopardy and behaving as if unaware of the consequences. Thus they may create an unnecessary crisis on the job, just to give them an opportunity to come up with a solution—which, more often than not, they succeed in doing.

Inventors often have a lively circle of friends and are interested in their ideas and activities. They are normally easy-going, seldom critical or nagging. Their good humor and curiosity tend to be contagious, and people seek out their company. ENTPs can be fascinating conversationalists, able to articulate their own complicated ideas and to follow the complex verbalizations of others. They may, however, deliberately employ debate tactics to the disadvantage of their opponents, even when the opponents happen to be close associates and valued friends. Versatile and agile of mind, they respond quickly and adeptly to another's shifting position. Often they are several jumps ahead. Indeed, ENTPs are the most able of all the types to maintain a one-up position with others, while to be taken-in or manipulated by another is humiliating to them, offending their pride in being masters of the art of one-upmanship.

Their home environment also tends to be full of life. They are gregarious, laugh easily and often, and are typically in good humor. Although usually dependable providers of economic necessities, life with ENTPs is at times an adventure, and they can unknowingly navigate the family into dangerous economic waters. Orderliness in the routines of daily living is not apt to inspire them, and they usually solve this problem by letting their mates pick up after them. Inventors like to spar verbally with their loved ones, and if their mates are not intellectually competitive they are likely to find such one-up/one-down transactions somewhat wearying. If the mate is competitive, however, the result might be delightful give-and-take—or, at times, marital conflict.

Inventors tend to have all sorts of hobbies and to be experts in unexpected areas, but they are not apt to share these hobbies with their mate or children in the sense of teaching them. In fact, Inventors may be very inconsistent in the attention they give to their offspring. Usually, it is feast or famine, wonderful warmth and affection when they are with their children, but also benign neglect when they are engrossed in their many outside interests. In particular, Inventors have little time for the everyday tasks of caring for and disciplining their children, and if possible will leave such domestic details to their mate.

The Architect [INTP]

Architectonics is the science of spatial relationships—organization, structure, build, configuration—and Architects from a very early age are preoccupied with spatial relativity and systems design. But INTPs must not be thought of as only interested in configuring three-dimensional spaces such as buildings, bridges, and machines; they are also the architects of curricula, of corporations, and of all kinds of theoretical systems. In other words, INTPs are men and women whose aim is to design systemic structures and to engineer structural models. All of these Architects look upon the world as little more than raw material to be reshaped according to their design, as formless stone that must yield to their coordinate lines of demarcation. Indeed, in their later years (after finding out that most others are faking an understanding of the laws of nature), INTPs are likely to think of themselves as the master organizers who must pit themselves against nature and society in an unending effort to create organization out of the raw materials of nature. Where the Mastermind Rationals are would-be masters of order, the Architect Rationals would-be masters of organization.

As a variant of Plato's Rationals and Aristotle's Dialecticals, the INTPs are little different from the other NTs in most respects. Like all the Rationals, they are abstract in communication and utilitarian in how they implement their goals. They choose to study science, are preoccupied with technology, and work well with systems. Their point of view is pragmatic, skeptical, relativistic, focused on spatial intersections and intervals of time. They base their self-image on being ingenious, autonomous, and resolute. They would if possible be calm, they trust reason, are hungry for achievement, seek knowledge, prize deference, and aspire to be wizards of science and technology. Intellectually, they are prone to practice strategy far more than diplomacy, tactics, and especially logistics. Further, with their probing or exploring nature they tend to opt for the Engineer's informative role rather than the quick-scheduling Coordinator's directive role. And because they are reserved and highly attentive they seem to prefer the role variant of Architect over Inventor. To visualize INTP intellectual development consider the following graph depicting the most probable profile of their strategic roles:

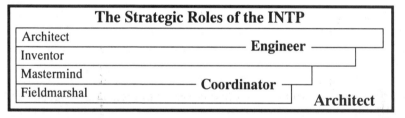

Architects are rare—say one percent of the population—and therefore not to be encountered in ordinary places, or if encountered, not recognized. For this type of Rational, the world exists primarily to be analyzed, understood, and explained. External reality in itself is unimportant, a mere arena for checking out the usefulness of ideas. What is important is that the underlying structures of the universe be uncovered and articulated, and that whatever is stated about the universe be stated correctly, with coherence and without redundancy. Curiosity concerning these fundamental structures is the driving force in INTPs, and they care little whether others understand or accept their ideas. Architects will learn in any manner and degree they can. If knowledge can be gathered from observing someone or taking some action, then such is worthwhile; if not, then not.

Architects prize intelligence in themselves and in others, and seem constantly on the lookout for the technological principles and natural laws upon which the real world is structured. The cognitive scanning of INTPs is not global and diffuse like an NF's; on the contrary, Architects limit their search to only what is relevant to the issue at hand, and thus they seem able to concentrate better than any other type. Architects can also become obsessed with analysis. Once caught up in a thought process, that process seems to have a will of its own, and they persevere until they comprehend the issue in all its complexity. Moreover, once INTPs know something, they remember it. With their grand desire to grasp the laws of unity and diversity, they can be a bit snobbish and may show impatience at times with others less endowed with engineering ability, or less driven. Unfortunately, their pride in their ingenuity can, at times, generate hostility and defensive maneuvers on the part of others.

Architects exhibit the greatest precision in thought and language of all the types. They tend to see distinctions and inconsistencies in thought and language instantaneously, and can detect contradictions in statements no matter when or where the statements were made. Only sentences that are coherent carry weight with them, and thus authority derived from office, credential, or celebrity does not impress them. Like the ENTPs, INTPs are devastating in debate or any form of adversarial discussion, their skill in differential analysis giving them an enormous advantage in discrediting their opponents' arguments and in structuring their own. They regard all discussions as a search for understanding, and believe their function is to eliminate inconsistencies, no matter who is guilty of them. It is difficult for an INTP to listen to nonsense, even in a casual conversation, without pointing out the speaker's error, and this makes communication with them an uncomfortable experience for many.

This type of Rational is the logician, the mathematician, the technologist, the scientist—that person given to any pursuit that requires architectonics, systems analysis, or structural design. Mind you, architecting is not the Artisan's fitting of physical shapes into pleasing forms, but the more abstract process of designing models. For the Architect, the model is the thing, whether a two, three, or four dimensional model.

It is hard for some types to understand these terse, observant Engineers because of their complex and technical speech and their avoidance of redundancy. However, they can be excellent teachers, particularly for advanced students, although here again they rarely enjoy much popularity, for they can be hard taskmasters. They are not good at clerical jobs and are impatient with routine details. They prefer to work quietly, without interruption, and often alone. They are inclined to be shy except when with close friends, and their reserve is difficult to penetrate. For all these reasons, INTPs are often seen as difficult to know, and are seldom perceived at their true level of competency. If an organization is to use their talents effectively, Architects must be given an efficient support staff who can capture their ideas as they emerge and before they lose interest and turn to another idea.

Architects take their mating relationship seriously and are faithful and devoted—albeit preoccupied at times, and somewhat forgetful of appointments, anniversaries, and other common social rituals. They are not likely to welcome much social activity at home, nor will they arrange it, content to leave the scheduling of social interactions to their mate. If left to their own devices, INTPs will retreat into the world of books and emerge only when physical needs become imperative. Architects are, however, even-tempered, compliant, and easy to live with—that is, until one of their principles is violated, in which case their adaptability ceases altogether. They prefer to keep their desires and emotions to themselves, and may seem insensitive to the desires and emotions of others, an insensitivity that can puzzle and frustrate their mates. But if what their mates are feeling is a mystery to them, Architects are keenly aware of what their mates actually say and do, and will often ask their mates to give a rationale for their statements and actions.

Architects are devoted parents; they enjoy children, and are very serious about their upbringing. Each of their children is treated as a rational individual, with rights, privileges, and as much autonomy as that child can handle safely. INTPs encourage their children to take responsibility for their own lives and to chart their own course. They do not visit their own expectations on their children and never attack them physically or verbally. When safe to do so Architects let the natural consequences of their children's actions teach them about reality. When this is unsafe, they somehow contrive to design logical consequences to inform their children's actions.

7

Mating

It is not our purpose to become each other; it is to recognize the other, to learn to see the other and honor him for what he is.
—Hermann Hesse

All sorts of factors enter into how we choose a mate. Where we live plays a large part in determining the people we meet; likewise our age, race, religion, and educational level influence our range of romantic contacts. For some, there are obligations of social class to satisfy, family expectations to consider, or economic circumstances to take into account. And certainly our physique makes us attractive to some and not to others, as well as attracting us to some and not to others.

And yet another factor involved in our choice of mate, at least as powerful if not more, is temperament. Given a number of choices determined by all the other factors—national origin, social background, physical attraction, and so forth—we will select our mate according to temperament.

After all, what do we mean when we say that a person is, or is not, "our type"? For some this might have to do with physical appearance, indicating a preference for a certain height, weight, hair color, or the like. But more often the phrase 'my type' suggests an awareness that we are most attracted to, and get along best with, a particular sort of person. People have long tried to identify some such categories of personality in their dating partners, even looking to questionable astrological signs for clues to character, and devising popular classifications such as the "strong, silent type" or the "girl-next-door," the "gentleman" or the "party girl," just to name a few. Given that people seem to know instinctively that character styles play a significant role in their choice of mates, we might well ask what temperament theory has to tell us, first, about how the temperaments attract each other, and, second, about how the Artisans, Guardians, Idealists, and Rationals get along living with each other.

Attraction

At the outset, it should be emphasized that there are no right or wrong attractions; in individual cases, any temperament can be attracted to any other, and for all sorts of reasons. On the other hand—and this is said cautiously—more than four decades of people-watching (I began observing character styles in 1956) reveal that romantic attractions are not random and indiscriminate, but show clear patterns and frequencies. In other words, persons of certain temperaments tend to be attracted to persons of certain other temperaments, and if they botch up the mating somehow, they are likely to be attracted to, and again marry, another person of the same temperament as their first mate.

But which temperaments are most often attracted to each other? Folk wisdom offers two long-observed but apparently contradictory principles: that "like is attracted to like," and that "opposites attract." On their face, both of these ideas make some sense, and both have their supporters. For "like attracts like," witness the advent of mating bureaus with their computers scanning for similarity of interests as the basis of compatibility—birds of a feather flock together. In contrast, Carl Jung (and Plato, by the way) was convinced that "opposites attract," and not only attract but even fascinate each other. Jung had a mysterious conception of the opposite which he called the "shadow." One casts a shadow, as it were, of all that one is not, or rather, of all that one has not developed, expressed, or lived out in oneself. And so, in being attracted to our opposite, it's as if we are looking for that rejected, abandoned, or unlived half of ourselves. In this view, we are not so much seeking similarity in our mates as complementarity—the idea of contrapletion, or the completion of ourself by our opposite.

Whatever their usefulness, the notions of likes and opposites, or, rather, of similarity and complementarity, become much more useful when the various styles of character are well defined. Thus, in terms of temperament theory, the notion of like attracting like suggests that the excitable, fun-loving SP Artisans should be attracted to other Artisans; that the concerned, responsible SJ Guardians should be attracted to other Guardians; that the enthusiastic, emotional NF Idealists should be attracted to other Idealists; and that the calm, logical NT Rationals should be attracted to other Rationals.

The idea of opposites attract is not so easy to plot out. Indeed, we might ask for some clarification of what is meant by "opposite" in the context of temperament theory. Recall that the four temperaments have been plotted along two axes of orientation: a concrete or abstract way of using words (positively correlated with Myers's S-N scale), and a cooperative or utilitarian way of using tools to implement goals. The matrix at the side summarizes the intersection of these four characteristics.

Words

	Abstract	Concrete
Cooperative	Abstract **NF** Cooperator	Concrete **SJ** Cooperator
Utilitarian	Abstract **NT** Utilitarian	Concrete **SP** Utilitarian

Tools

Now, strictly speaking, two temperaments are opposite when they differ on both orientations, that is, when abstract word usage is set against concrete word usage, and when cooperative tool usage is set against utilitarian tool usage. Thus, as can be seen in the matrix, the SP's diametrical opposite is the NF (Concrete Utilitarian vs. Abstract Cooperator), and the SJ's diametrical opposite is the NT (Concrete Cooperator vs. Abstract Utilitarian). And, in turn, if opposites attract, then the SPs should be attracted to the NFs, and the SJs should be attracted to the NTs, and vice versa.

Certainly instances can be found of both kinds of attractions, "likes" as well as "opposites." For example, Richard Burton and Elizabeth Taylor, two SPs, married each other twice, George and Martha Washington were both SJs, Tolstoy and his wife Sofya were both NFs, while Marie and Pierre Curie were both NTs. On the other hand, Franklin Roosevelt, an SP, married Eleanor Roosevelt, an NF, while Dwight Eisenhower, an NT, married Mamie Doud, an SJ.

But the patterns that emerge from long observation of a large number of marriages tell a different story. By far the most frequent mating appears to be between SP Artisans and SJ Guardians, which is neither exactly a matter of like attracting like nor of opposites attracting. Indeed, the SP-SJ relationship combines similarity with complementarity. Artisans and Guardians share concrete thought and speech, but differ in how they implement their goals, SPs preferring to use tools in a utilitarian way, SJs in a morally cooperative way.

The mating pattern for NT Rationals and NF Idealists is similar, although not quite so clear-cut, owing to the huge numbers of Artisans and Guardians in the population. Rationals and Idealists attract each other most frequently—if given the chance to meet. But since Artisans and Guardians make up roughly eighty-five per cent of potential mates, it is often the case that Idealists and Rationals make their matches with one or the other of these concrete types. And yet, despite the difficulty Rationals and Idealists have in finding each other, the frequency of NT-NF marriages is remarkable, and even more so is the incidence of NT-NF second marriages, after a failed first try with an SP or an SJ. Here again, the NT-NF mating combines similarity with complementarity: The two temperaments share abstract communication, but differ in their style of using tools to achieve their goals, Idealists caring more about interpersonal cooperation, and Rationals insisting on functional utility.

Curiously, the combination of similarity with complementarity does not seem to generate the same power of attraction when worked the other way around—or, in terms of the matrix, when worked horizontally instead of vertically. An SP-NT couple, for instance, shares the same style of using tools (both are utilitarian) but differs in the nature of their communication (Artisans are concrete, Rationals abstract). Similarly, an SJ-NF couple shares a cooperative style of achieving goals, but differs in their style of communicating (Guardians are concrete, Idealists abstract). However, the SP-NT and SJ-NF pairings don't show nearly the same frequency of attraction as the SP-SJ or the NT-NF, and this only underscores how important is the concrete-abstract (S-N) dimension in the make-up of character. It is not too much to say that abstract or concrete communication is the most significant of human differences—the first cut, so to speak—and perhaps it is not surprising that concrete characters and abstract characters are so frequently, and immediately, attracted to someone who, in a sense, speaks the same language.

There are other areas of complementarity, of course, such as differences in expressiveness-reserve, the attraction of which can be observed as the character styles are defined more narrowly. But to sort through all possible combinations of SP-SJ or NT-NF differences is to put too fine a point on what is a readily observable pattern on the level of the four temperaments. Suffice it to say that it is the combination of similarity in thought and speech—concrete or abstract—with complementarity in how tools are used to implement goals—cooperative or utilitarian—which seems to hold the key to explaining human attraction.

Getting Along Together

Attraction is one thing, but living together is something else. At the start of almost all relationships there is a period of harmony, the so-called "honeymoon" period, in which sharing and understanding seem relatively easy to come by. But after the honeymoon is over, when the traits of character of both mates begin to reveal themselves in sharper relief, and the give-and-take of living with another person becomes an everyday reality, the force of temperament comes even more prominently into play. The question we must put to temperament theory is: no matter what the basis of the initial attraction, "likes attract likes," "opposites attract," or a combination of the two, are there certain temperaments which get along better with each other over time, and more easily form stable, satisfying relationships?

Again, individual relationships defy generalizations, and it should be stressed that two well-adjusted people of any two temperaments can find ways of making their marriage work well for them. Forty years of marriage-watching, however, makes it clear to me that there are certain strengths and weaknesses to each of the temperament pairings, strengths and weaknesses which once again have to do with similarity and complementarity. These strengths and weaknesses will be described in more detail in the four portraits that follow, but for now let's look at the larger patterns.

Similarity of thought and speech—abstract or concrete—tends to work for stability in a relationship, up to a certain point, that is. When both mates communicate primarily about what they can observe (S), or about what they can imagine (N), they quickly realize that they are sending and receiving on the same wave-length as their partner. SPs mated with SJs and NTs mated with NFs thus know where each other is coming from or getting at in their messages, and there is pleasure, and strength, in this common bond. But being too exactly alike (SP-SP, NF-NF, etc.) can have its down side, the stability of shared language at times giving way to an irritating predictability, and at other times to an unhealthy duplication, even competition, in the relationship, problems difficult to ignore, and which can grow over time. Remember that familiarity breeds contempt, and if not contempt, then at least boredom, and perhaps rivalry.

On the other hand, complementarity in a couple's style of using tools (cooperation mated with utility) tends to enhance the level of satisfaction in a long-term relationship, at least to a certain extent, by creating not only a feeling of completion or combined resources in the two mates, but also a charming sense of mystery and challenge. In a cooperator's match with a utilitarian, the cooperative partner (Guardian or Idealist) might admire the utilitarian's (Artisan's or Rational's) independence or resourcefulness, while the utilitarian partner might value the cooperator's interpersonal concern or conscientiousness. Each might be intrigued by the other's character, and might even hope to develop the other's neglected side over time. But when the mates are diametrical opposites (SP-NF or SJ-NT), with different styles of implementing their goals, and without the common ground of a similar focus of language, each can feel in the relationship like a stranger in a strange land, and bridging the gulf can present serious, lasting problems.

This is not to suggest that these problems cannot be solved, whether problems of excessive similarity or excessive difference. As has been said, particular couples have a way of working out their relationships no matter what the mix of temperaments. But when speaking of the frequency of long-term compatibility, the combination of similarity and complementarity in the Artisan-Guardian and Rational-Idealist matches seems to give the best chance of successful mating. In essence, the exceptional vitality of these marriages comes from a shared style of communicating messages wedded to an appreciation of, or at least a tolerance for, different ways of using tools to implement goals.

The Pygmalion Project

In 1929 the internationally famous aviator Charles Lindbergh, a concrete, practical joking, restless ISTP Operator Artisan, met and married Anne Morrow, an abstract, soulful, deeply introspective INFP Healer Idealist. Although the early years of the marriage had many "Golden Hours," as Anne termed them, she soon felt strong pressure from her husband to tone down her idealism and her poetic sensitivity, and to become more worldly and adventurous—more like Charles himself. Anne went along with Lucky Lindy as best she could, learning to fly, and accompanying him on expeditions to map airline routes, but in her diary she recorded her private longing to meet with sympathy and understanding and a kind of respect and acceptance of me and how I was trying to live and what I was trying to do, without the unrest of trying to change me, reform me....Why can't one keep that admirable distance when one is married, that respect for another person's solitude, that withdrawal before what they are doing and being? Is it incompatible with a real and powerful love, or is it the result of one's preconceived ideas of marriage, one's preconceived standards?

Anne Morrow Lindbergh's notion of keeping admirable distance in a marriage is an important insight, for all too often—again, after the honeymoon is over—mates who have been in part attracted by each other's differences turn to what they regard as the true, serious business of the marriage, namely, to change their spouse into a person more like themselves. This intention to reform the mate is the Pygmalion Project I mentioned in Chapter 2 (or what Andras Angyal originally called the "Pygmalion theme" in interpersonal transactions). And the Grand Hypothesis of this discussion is that Pygmalion Projects are not only the primary source of ruptured marriages, but a common source of irritation in even the best of marriages.

It is a familiar pattern in our mating behavior. We go to all the bother of finding mates more or less unlike ourselves—in some cases exactly opposite in all important respects—and then we pull out all the stops in our attempt to transform them into our own image. The marriage license seems almost construed as a sculptor's license, giving each spouse the warrant to chisel away in a Pygmalion Project, trying to make the other into the mirror image of the sculptor. And, sadly, our sense of success in the marriage becomes all the greater, the greater the transformation we think we are bringing about.

Not that we want our mates to abandon their own natures completely. We merely want them to take up our task as well as their own, since we all assume that our particular aim in life is the most valuable for everybody. What we fail to realize, however, is that our mates cannot take to heart another aim as their own, not at least without violating their own character. For example, the Artisan, whose basic search in life is for exciting sensations, is simply not very concerned about the Guardian's search for social and economic security, the Idealist's search for personal identity, nor the Rational's search for useful knowledge. And so it is for all the temperaments. They might be able to fake other goals to please their mates—for a while—but they will never adopt another's way as their own. Such differences can be integrated successfully in a marriage, but not in a single person. A leopard cannot change its spots.

Although there is no way we can transform our mates into ourselves, we all seem to want to try, and the attempt does great damage. By chipping away on our spouse we say, in effect, "You are not good enough. I want you other than you are." Here it is only fair to see a little Pygmalion in all of us, an all-too-human desire to control our nearest and dearest, to shape them up according to our wishes. Yet consider the supreme irony were we to succeed in transforming our loved ones. Attracted in the first place by their differences, can we be anything but dissatisfied by changing them into copies of ourselves? In other words, if we win the battle—and it is a battle—to change our mates, do we not actually lose a great deal of satisfaction in our relationships? Or is our desire to control our mates more satisfying than accepting them and loving them as the persons they are?

This does not mean that we should only marry someone exactly like ourselves. Many of the joys of complementarity—the delightful sparks that fly from reconciling different styles—would surely be lost if we only married our exact likenesses. And, indeed, observation shows that types who are exactly alike (two ISTJ Inspector Guardians, say, or two ENTP Inventor Rationals) are highly unlikely to marry each other. No, we seem to prefer opposition on some level in our mates, and Pygmalion Projects happen to be the price we have to pay.

But suppose we could recognize our natural impulse to reform our mates, pause each time the impulse strikes, and hold our tongue—then some interesting phenomena might begin to appear. For example, if we could suspend our efforts toward trying to make our mates change in our direction—to become more adventurous, or more reliable, or more soul-searching, or more rational—then we might, just might, remember to appreciate what attracted us in the first place. Then, and to that extent, could different temperaments live happily ever after...maybe.

The Artisan Playmate

The moment I saw her, I felt as if I'd been struck by a bolt of lightning; she knocked me out. She had an extraordinary combination of dark skin and light blue eyes, with honey-blond hair and a glorious figure. Was I smitten!...While she sang romantic gypsy ballads in a low, sexy voice, she stared straight back into my eyes and her smile was like fire. I just had to meet her.

—Armand Hammer

A number of things attract us to Artisans, their optimism, their spontaneity, their generosity, their physical confidence, and many more. But surely the Artisans' most charming trait, and that quality which most characterizes their style of mating, is the incorrigible sense of fun and excitement they bring to their relationships.

Artisan Courtship

Going out with an Artisan is a little like taking a ride on a roller coaster. Wherever they are, whatever they are doing, no matter who they are with, SPs have a knack for excitement and will try to turn any occasion into a party or a high speed adventure—they are typically the "fast" dates parents often warn their children about. Expressive Artisans are often the life of the party, the center of attraction, teasing and joking with everyone around them; but even the more reserved, private Artisans are full of fun and mischief, and seem to view mating as a game to be played or a wild ride to be taken. Never a dull moment, if an SP can help it.

In dating, as in all other things, Artisans want to be excited in action, and this usually means trying something new or taking some sort of risk—anything out of the ordinary, just to keep things interesting. It also means not getting tied down with one person for too long, but playing the field and experiencing as much freedom and variety as possible. SPs do not often go out with others in a serious search for a life-partner, but are drawn to people impulsively, for the fun of it, and seem happiest when pursuing new relationships, much as they might enjoy travelling to a new part of the world. Such spur-of-the-moment intrigues are exhilarating for SPs, but can also cause them interpersonal problems. Artisans can find themselves quickly involved with another person, only to find the romance growing stale and becoming a burden—the proverbial "tie that binds"—with the SP puzzled as to how to go about getting uninvolved. Confrontation is not likely to be their way of solving this problem; on the contrary, silence and absence are more likely to be the solution of choice.

Certainly a good deal of the Artisans' excitement is sexual. In the first place, Artisans more than the other temperaments seem to care about looking sexy, and will put in more time developing their bodies and keeping in shape, working out at the gym, jogging, doing aerobics, and so on—not just to be fit and healthy, but to turn heads. Also, Artisans are easily the most sexually ambitious of all the types. Adventure in all things, including sex, is likely to appeal to an SP, and whether expressive or reserved, male or female, they have an avid interest in sexual abundance and experimentation. As the bumper sticker says: "So many men...so little time."

Very simply, sex fascinates Artisans: they enjoy talking about sex, they may have an extensive repertoire of sexual stories, and they love to hear about details of sexual activities. At the same time, they are unimpressed with anything abstract, and thus symbolic stimulation (as in love poetry) does not have much power to arouse them. SPs are far more responsive to sensory stimuli, and in their hedonism are apt to spice up their lovemaking with sexy negligee, exotic locales, and erotic films. The slow-moving love story is less likely to have appeal, making SPs impatient to get on with it. Romeo and Juliet or Heloise and Abelard were clearly not Artisans; in fact, to an Artisan such pairs of lovers and their plaintive Idealist style of loving may appear rather boring.

The Artisans' joy of life can be infectious, delighting the other types (at least for a while) with their playfulness and sweeping them along with a rush of excitement. Soulful Idealists can be enchanted by the Artisans' lack of self-consciousness, and by their sheer physical attractiveness, and will often project into the impulsive, unreflective SP their own NF image of the spiritual poet or artist. Rationals, highly theoretical and work-obsessive, can be drawn to the Artisans' delightful sense of play and physical pleasure, and will admire their effortlessness of speech and action. And, most of all, Guardians find in the carefree, sensual Artisans an almost irresistible counterbalance to their own firmly set attitude of concern and responsibility. Indeed, for all the other temperaments, but especially for Guardians, dating an Artisan is a little like taking a wonderful vacation; the freedom and novelty are great fun for a while, and help lift the weight of more serious matters off their shoulders.

On the other hand, the light-hearted, let the good times roll nature of the Artisans often becomes somewhat frustrating and disappointing to the other temperaments. Fun and games are rarely enough to keep Idealists, Rationals, or Guardians well-satisfied for very long in a relationship. The other types eventually want more than a playmate for a partner, and will attempt to steer the SP into deeper waters, the NF into an exploration of self, for example, the SJ into recognition of social responsibilities, or the NT into some comprehensive study, at which point the SP is likely to feel trapped and to become restless. Artisans prefer not to get too serious about things, and will try to keep everyone smiling—to keep the party going—as long as possible.

Furthermore, expressions of emotional commitment are generally a burden to Artisans, and they will often try to sidestep any talk of more permanent relations, such as engagement and marriage, preferring to hang loose and take one day at a time. This is not to say that SPs won't commit to a long-term relationship, but rather that it is difficult for them, and that the effort can put a great deal of strain on the relationship. SPs would prefer not to confront the issue of marriage, and will often remain silent, letting the partner do all the talking; or they will appear to go along with their partner's plans, while in reality they are biding their time, waiting for some painless escape to present itself. However, under more intense pressure, Artisans are capable of tactlessness and even physical force to assert their freedom, though once the scene is over, they may be quite oblivious to any scars they have left on the relationship.

Once an Artisan does agree to a serious relationship, speed is again of the essence. Long, drawn-out courtships are not apt to hold their attention, driven as they are by their need for action, which includes acting on their impulses as they occur. When ready to settle down, SPs may actually appear quite decisive in their choice of mates, but this is apt to be the whim of the moment, rather than the carefully thought through decision that would, for instance, characterize an NT.

While Artisans are extremely alert about concrete reality, their tendency to accept whatever exists at the moment can make it hard for them to recognize true quality or compatibility in a mate. Whoever happens to be there at the right time is likely to be accepted, and in this process the SP might not be able to differentiate between a person who is capable of great loyalty and a person who is just passing through. Always optimistic and risk-loving, Artisans are not usually on the lookout for potential dangers in relationships, and this can lead them, particularly the females, into involvements which might be unwise.

Artisan courtships are often marked by extravagant gifts, by extravagant expressions of affection (SPs often express sexual attraction through expensive gifts), but also by extravagant promises to turn over a new leaf and reform their behavior. Artisans have the chameleon's ability to assume different colors, or different characters, in order to please their mates, and for a time they will do their best to become more like what is expected of them—more responsible for a Guardian, more spiritual for an Idealist, better-read for a Rational. Artisans are quite sincere in their good-intentions, and can be quite convincing in their makeover, although it usually turns out that the promised new behavior doesn't last very long.

When it comes time for the wedding, Artisans don't care much for traditional, formal religious ceremonies, and would just as soon run off and elope, or have a quick wedding in Las Vegas. SPs will endure elaborate church weddings for their mate's sake, and gregarious SPs can even enjoy being the center of attention at a big wedding, replete with beautiful clothes and flowers and photographers—and topped of with a killer wedding party or reception. But SPs are often happier with unorthodox ceremonies, the kind that make a statement about their love of action and adventure: being married by a ship's captain at sea, being married while parachuting, scuba-diving, bungee jumping, and so on. In the same vein, the Artisan's idea of a honeymoon is likely to be exotic, and athletic: two weeks surfing in Hawaii, skiing in Aspen, sailing in the Caribbean, or gambling and seeing shows in Atlantic City.

Artisan Married Life

In married life, as on their honeymoons, Artisans are easy to get along with. They can have a temper, it is true, and may be quick to anger, but the anger is likely to pass as quickly as it arises. More often, SPs have uncritical, happy dispositions, and take their marriages in stride, not looking for a match made in heaven, indeed, willing to put up with a great deal of imperfection. For instance, SPs can accept negative comments about their habits with relative ease, not long bothered by the criticism. Their tolerance for nagging is remarkable—like water off a duck's back—though a carping spouse will usually find the SP spending less and less time at home. And an Artisan is likely to be adaptable and agreeable with whatever is happening in the sexual sphere, though a hopelessly frigid or repetitive sex life can start them looking elsewhere for more stimulation.

Marriage with an Artisan is nothing if not stimulating. They truly do rush in where angels fear to tread—sexually, socially, and, at times, economically. Financial matters, or spending-saving patterns, are a source of conflict in most marriages, but SPs typically present their mates with major money problems. For SPs, money, like sex, is to be used and enjoyed, not saved for a rainy day. They may make a bundle one day, but spend it all the next—here today, gone tomorrow—and their mates must be prepared to accept a life of feast or famine. Generally speaking, Artisans do not tend to attach much priority to saving their resources, either sexually or financially, as might Guardians; rather, time, money, and energy must be used—right away—to explore the chic restaurant, the hottest fashion, the newest tool, the latest model car or motorcycle, regardless of price. New experiences or new gadgets to play with might well fascinate an SP for weeks, until an even newer interest comes along. Artisans mean no harm, mind you. They live so thoroughly in the present that they are sometimes unreliable in meeting the financial obligations of a long-term relationship, but the intention to displease is seldom present.

Artisan impulsiveness extends to people as well, and can lead to some dissatisfaction on the part of their mates. After marriage, SPs may not bother to sort out their personal priorities, responding to each new personal contact with equal energy. They take up with people suddenly, thoughtlessly, and a claim for attention (or for money) from a new-found friend can be given as much attention as a claim from an intimate. The most damaging case is with members of the opposite sex. SPs all too often infuriate their spouses by paying unusual attention to attractive friends, or even strangers; whoever catches their eye seems to delight them for the moment, indiscriminately, and they are unaware of how flirtatious this makes them appear. But Artisans are also known to collect friends of the same sex, cronies and sidekicks, and to spend valuable time and money on them, sometimes to the extent that their spouses feel put in second place.

In essence, Artisans simply can't resist the grand gesture or the act of largess. They love to give gifts, expensive gifts, especially if they have an audience for their exuberant generosity. They will buy a round of drinks for the bar or pick up the check at dinner, even if they're short on money for groceries. In the same way, a mink coat for the wife could well appear on her birthday, even though she might have only a few other clothes in the closet. The fun and excitement involved are what count for the SPs—the pleasure of playing Big Spender—and they will bask in the surprise of the recipients, and delight in the impact on the witnesses. Such generosity can be impressive for the moment, but soon troubles mates of other temperaments.

Married life for Artisans tends to find them satisfying their hunger for action through a number of physical activities. Male SPs spend a lot of time in their garages, working on their cars, making furniture, tinkering with tools of all kinds—and readying their sports equipment. Male SPs are heavily into sports, especially time-consuming sports, needing extensive gear (such as fishing, hunting, off-roading, surfing, sailing, dirt-biking, and the like), so that their wives often come to feel like sports-widows.

Female SPs get involved in sports as well (tennis, golf, skiing), but also use their homes for arts and crafts. Clutter is acceptable to the SP female, and her home tends to be filled with various projects in various stages of completion. She may get excited about gourmet cooking for a time, and then move on to an avid interest in weaving or throwing pots. Color is likely to be abundant and strong. Plants are apt to be set about the rooms in profusion. Drop-in guests are sure to be welcome almost any time, and the female Artisan is not apt, as would the Guardian, to be put off-balance by a less-than-guest-ready home. She is more likely to share cheerfully and freely whatever is there, pushing aside current projects to make room for seating or eating.

Artisan Pairings

Easy-going and fun to be around, Artisans can mate successfully with all the temperaments, particularly if there exists a good degree of sexual compatibility. But each pairing has its strengths and weaknesses.

Artisan-Idealist: Generally, the Artisans' excitement and sensuousness dovetail nicely with the enthusiasm and romanticism of Idealists, and they can be intrigued by the NFs' spirituality and sense of personal ethics, so different from their own hedonism. However, chances are that Artisans will grow puzzled by, and slightly cynical about, the Idealist's moral delicacy, by their need for personal or spiritual enlightenment, as well as by what Artisans sometimes call the NFs' "airy fairy" soulfulness and flights of fantasy.

Artisan-Rational: Artisans can feel right at home with the Rationals' natural pragmatism, irreverence, and love of tools, while they can be impressed by the NTs' theoretical interests, so different from their own practical, tactical grasp of things. On the other hand, it sometimes happens that Artisans grow impatient with a Rational's desire for extensive knowledge. And they can even feel resentful of the NT's calm, detached life of the mind, as if their own SP gift of physical pleasure is somehow inferior when viewed from the NT's abstract heights.

Artisan-Artisan: Artisans have a considerably better time of it mating with other Artisans. Two SPs live primarily in the same world, the world of external, physical reality, speaking the same language of concrete objects, and they also share each other's childlike love of fun and excitement. Two SPs have so many interests and activities in common—travel, sports, parties, shows, clothes, and so on—that they can come together as playmates in a way not possible with persons of other temperament. The only problem is that, with both partners living and playing so hard—going so fast in the same direction—they can quickly exhaust each other and lose interest. This pattern of two Artisans lighting up the sky brightly and then burning out and falling apart is a familiar one.

Artisan-Guardian: The most stable and satisfying marriages for Artisans are with Guardians. Not only do Artisans and Guardians both make their home in the concrete world, but the complementarity of their natures seems to fill a void in each temperament. Here is the adventurous, fun-loving SP, bursting with energy and yearning for the excitement of new experiences, attracted to the concerned and responsible SJ, the Rock of Gibraltar standing watch over the established rules and traditions of society. In many ways, the match seems incongruous and difficult to account for, and yet the frequency with which SPs choose to marry SJs is compelling. Perhaps seeking the stability they lack, perhaps wanting some missing center to their lives, perhaps just needing someone to take care of them—whatever the reason, Artisans choose marriage with Guardians by far over any other temperament.

And just as frequently these SP-SJ marriages do well over time, with Artisans and Guardians often finding a comfortable balance in their opposition: the SJ able to settle the SP down a good deal, and the SP able to loosen up the SJ. Indeed, it often takes the moral weight of Guardian expectations to get Artisans off their motorcycles (surfboards, airplanes, sail-boats) long enough to build careers or to raise families, just as it takes the high jinx of Artisans to bring a smile to Guardian faces and help them bear up under the burdens of life. In many cases, SP-SJ marriages resemble the relationship between a mischievous child and a caretaking parent. SP husbands, in particular, tend to call their SJ wives "Mother," just as SJ wives often refer to their SP husbands as just another of their "boys." The inherent conflicts in such a relationship may even be enjoyable up to a certain point: the Artisan likes to have someone to tease, and the Guardian needs someone to care for. Points of conflict are there, to be sure—between impulse and deliberation, between insubordination and respect for duty, between spending and saving—but as long as these differences are taken in stride, with tolerance and good will on both sides, SP-SJ marriages go along nicely, and the Artisans' Pygmalion Projects remain benign.

Theoretically, this Artisan-Guardian compatibility is even more pronounced in marriages which interweave extra threads of complementarity, namely, the differences of expressiveness or reserve (E-I), and tough-mindedness or friendliness (T-F). Consider the following four pairings as having, on paper at least, all the factors for successful SP-SJ mating.

Promoters and **Protectors** are likely to get along famously. It is great fun for the tough, outgoing Promoters (ESTPs), born gamblers and wheeler-dealers, to see if they can win over the reserved and friendly Protectors (ISFJs) and persuade them to let go of their caution and concern for a little while, and take a few risks.

Crafters and **Providers** can be expected to mate happily. The reserved and tough-minded Crafters (ISTPs), silent, adept with tools and machinery, and hankering for the freedom to adventure, seem to want the care and the kindly anchoring in family or society offered by the expressive and soft-hearted Providers (ESFJs), those given to soothing, doing favors, and hosting. Also, despite their skill with hand tools, Crafters are the least inclined of all the Artisans to try to chisel their mates into their own image.

Performers and **Inspectors** should match up especially well. More than others, the expressive and friendly Performers (ESFPs), entertaining and bursting with energy, yearn for the bright lights, the party, the excitement of putting on a show of some kind, and the reserved and tough-minded Inspectors (ISTJs), the paragons of insurance, preparation, and trustworthiness, usually welcome a little livening up.

Composers and **Supervisors** ought to make a good team. The reserved and friendly Composers (ISFPs), close to nature and absorbed in artistic activity, are the most gentle and sensual of all the types, and the expressive and tough-minded Supervisors (ESTJs), the persons most suited to be in charge of institutions and establishments, like it when someone brings a little pastoral beauty into their hard-nosed, all-business existence.

Whatever the mix of temperaments, however, Artisans generally make charming mates, open-handed, entertaining, physically talented, sexually stimulating, and relatively easy-going with their Pygmalion Projects. Artisans tend to have a live-and-let-live attitude to begin with, and thus their efforts to reform their mates rarely escalate into serious power struggles. For the rest of us, mating with an Artisan requires that we learn to put our hands in our pockets and not project unrealistic expectations onto them. We must not begrudge them their tools (or toys) and their adventures, but provide them with a stable, tolerant home. We must not deny them their grand gestures and their audience, but step back when we can and give them center stage. And we must not demand too much devotion from them, but appreciate them as the exciting, spontaneous, incomparable lovers they are. In short, we must learn to hold our breath and enjoy the fast ride.

The Guardian Helpmate

[Mrs. Ramsay] assured him (as a nurse carrying a light across a dark room assures a fractious child), that it was real; the house was full; the garden blowing. If he put implicit faith in her, nothing could hurt him; however deep he buried himself or climbed high, not for a second should he find himself without her.

—Virginia Woolf

If there is one temperament that best fulfills the traditional, family-oriented mating role, it is the Guardians. Guardians are quite content, even proud, to see themselves (and to be seen) as the Good Wife and the Devoted Husband. Loyal, dependable, hard-working, given to nesting and to nurturing, Guardians provide a solid foundation for all our civilized institutions, including the institution of marriage.

Guardian Courtship

Guardians have these institutions very much in mind when they begin to date. In general, SJs go out with others not so much for the excitement and variety of it (like the SPs), but in order to take part in social activities, to practice social graces, to observe community or family traditions, and ultimately to find a suitable mate. In this comparison with Artisans, it is easy to see Guardians as over-serious, and to wonder, "is it true SPs (like blondes) have more fun?" But we must remember that Guardians want to have fun, too—only this is their fun, the preparation for, and the participation in, social activities.

Nor do social activities need be thought of as boring. Although Guardians have little interest in wild parties or racy entertainment, many love going on dates to popular movies, to church or school dances, to amusement parks, to civic attractions (zoos, gardens, historical monuments), as well as to popular restaurants, hit plays, long-running musicals, and the like, not only to have a good time, but to do their part as active, supportive members of the community. Further, the more extraverted SJs do indeed like to go to parties, not to let loose, mind you, but to interact socially—to help mark special occasions, to keep up with friends and colleagues, and to be a part of social or civic events, such as dinner parties, charity balls, and VIP receptions. And though always reluctant to spend a lot of money, once in a while Guardians love to go to really impressive places, a famous hotel dining room, for example, where they can feel treated like royalty.

On these formal occasions, a female Guardian likes to receive traditional tokens of esteem (flowers, candy) from her escort, but even on the most ordinary dates she expects to be treated with the best of manners, like a lady, with doors opened for her, chair pushed in after her, and help on with her coat. In the same way, the Guardian male always tries to behave like a gentleman, and will attend his date with old-fashioned courtesy, standing when she enters the room, for instance, and walking her to her door at the end of the evening. SJ men are also happy to take responsibility for the proper scheduling of an evening, arriving punctually, making sure of dinner reservations, arranging for tickets in advance, and so on, leaving nothing to chance or to whim. On their side, SJ women also like their dates to be punctual, but they themselves have the habit of fussing over last minute details of dress or makeup, and so often keep their dates waiting downstairs.

With so much of a Guardian's interpersonal energy given over to observing the social etiquette of dating, there is little left for sexual exploration. Of course, SJs have as much curiosity as the next person—they are rarely prudes—and they can be quite affectionate with steady boyfriends or girlfriends. But they are never casual or irresponsible about sex—they do not sleep around—and even with their steadies they are cautious about going too far. SJs tend to regard pre-marital sex in moral terms, as if chastity were Good and sexuality Evil. They also speak of pre-marital sex as a matter of sanitation, referring to a virgin as someone "pure," "clean," or "spotless," and picturing someone sexually active as "dirty," "trashy," or "stained." And, most telling of all, SJs think of pre-marital sex in terms of spending and saving: they are opposed to "free love" and "cheap" sexual experiences, just as they are intent on keeping their "treasure" under lock and key, and on "saving" themselves for marriage. And what Guardian father has not urged his daughter to get the marriage contract signed before giving away the goods—warning, "Why buy the cow when the milk's free?"

Female Guardians, in particular, usually have only limited sexual experience before they marry, even in an age of sexual freedom. For SJs, there is always the unexpressed attitude that "nice girls don't." If they do, it is likely that peer pressure led them into sexual activity because it was the thing to do. Male Guardians have more opportunity, and more social sanction, to sow their wild oats, but they tend not to do so joyously and freely like Artisans, feeling instead a sense of responsibility to their partner, and feeling dishonest, even shabby, if they take advantage of a young woman. Not that Guardians are rigidly straightlaced. When SJ males are in social contact with other males—for example, at conventions, on hunting trips, on the golf course—they can rival the SPs in their command of off-color language and their repertoire of sexual jokes. And female SJs, while often prim and proper in public, can have a surprisingly earthy side in private with close female friends, and can enjoy jokes and sexual gossip with a playful shake of the head and a teasing "aren't you awful." It is with members of the opposite sex that Guardians are alert to be on their best behavior.

The Guardians' caution and conventionality can put other types off at first, but become quite attractive when the other temperaments are ready to settle down and start a family. Idealists, torn about life and identity, can feel safe in the hands of Guardians, calmed by their unambiguous values and knowledge of the world, and they will project a kind of nobility of spirit onto the Guardians' sense of moral earnestness. Rationals, who often dismiss social traditions as being trivial, are generally more critical of Guardians, but can be attracted by their social skills, as well as by their family loyalty and their competence in handling the demands of home and hearth. However, it is the high-flying Artisans who are most attracted to Guardians—that is, when looking to settle down. Under the marriage impulse, SPs are drawn to SJs as to a place of stability and safe harbor where they can rest and recover from their adventures, and they will sometimes place the SJ on a moral pedestal, seeing them as someone more civilized than they, a lady or a gentleman who might be able to straighten them up and make them fly right.

In some cases, naturally, the Guardian style can cause problems for the other temperaments. Idealists, Rationals, and Artisans all in their own way have a strong desire for individuality that can clash with the Guardian's stubborn sense of tradition, compliance, and regulation. SPs press for unfettered action, NFs search for their unique personal identities, and NTs resist any and all constraints on their freedom of thought. This willingness of the other temperaments to strike out on their own and explore new territory both attracts and troubles SJs, and when it troubles them enough to make them dig in their heels, it can be the cause of broken relationships.

Normally, however, Guardians give themselves plenty of time to sort these things out. Although the most marriage-minded of all the temperaments, SJs always try to look before they leap, and so favor long engagements which work to cool the heat of passion, and which allow them to satisfy social obligations. The Idealist notion of the grand passion is likely to mystify a Guardian, who might enjoy the fantasy, but who wants to keep both feet on the ground and go carefully about the business of courtship. And the urging of the Artisan to run off and elope might flatter a Guardian, but also introduces a disturbing element of recklessness into the relationship. SJs like to court in traditional ways, sharing important family and social experiences, verbalizing expressions of love in conventional language, and giving gifts to show their intentions are serious. These gifts are usually not symbolic or emblematic, but have value as objects and are to be kept and treasured. The ritual of transaction—of sealing a bargain—is what's important, not the surprise or audience impression as with an SP.

Once they have a firm commitment to marriage in hand, sex can become a possibility for Guardians, but it is the social side of the wedding plans, and the securing of family, religious, and legal sanction, which really interest them. Asking for Mom and Dad's blessing, reserving the church, obtaining the license, publishing banns, registering for gifts, shopping for clothes: all these necessary, customary preparations for the wedding ceremony—and so many more—give full range to the Guardian's talents for scheduling and accomplishing social rituals.

Guardian Married Life

After the ceremonies have been observed (including the carefully arranged honeymoon), Guardians will turn their attention to what they consider the serious business of living—establishing a home and family, cultivating a circle of friends, making social connections, and getting ahead in their career. The certainty and predictability of married life is much more to their liking than the whirl of dating (courtship is something one does before vows are taken), and at this point SJs are likely to begin neglecting romance, which can prove disappointing to mates of other temperament. SJs are content to live on an even keel, are happy to keep within established routines, and seldom complain of boredom. To be sure, they tend to suppress emotional spontaneity, although when fatigued or under stress they can suddenly flare into grouchiness, or sink into gloom for no apparent reason. For the most part, however, SJs are good-hearted, good-natured adherents of the tried-and-true. They may enjoy eating out at the same restaurant, say, every Friday evening, or they may be willing to visit the same vacation spot year after year, looking forward to the same recreational activities with the same people in the same place.

Clearly, tradition has a strong press for Guardian mates. First of all, they have a diligent sense of family history, and greatly value stories and information about their families. They like to keep in touch with the extended family circle, and they enjoy entertaining relatives, especially with holiday customs such as the Thanksgiving turkey and the Easter ham. In addition, a Guardian mate will likely belong to the traditional civic groups of the community—the Chamber of Commerce, the Lions Club, the League of Women Voters—and probably will be knowledgeable of the status hierarchy and pecking orders in those groups. School and Church-related activities—PTA fund-raisers, Christmas bazaars, Fathers' Club pancake breakfasts—may often occupy the SJs' free time. And they feel good about taking part in the functions of community-based organizations, both charitable and social, from volunteering for the March of Dimes to supporting the home town ball team, whether professional, college, or even high-school.

Family time is apt to be filled by the Guardian mate with domestic activities, straightening up the house, washing the car, sewing, gardening, grocery shopping, and the like. SJs value time as a thing to be used in worthwhile pursuits, not wasted on fantasies. Reading a newspaper usually has more appeal than reading a novel, for example, and taking night school Business courses makes more sense than studying art. Male SJs are punctual and expect their mates to be also; they like to make and keep schedules for themselves and sometimes even for their wives and children. On her side, the female SJ wants social events to proceed in an enjoyable, orderly manner, with no surprises and with everyone having a pleasant but not rollicking good time. Generally, Guardian mates do not mind members of their family (and others) making demands on their time, as long as such demands are for sensible reasons.

Guardians may be possessive about family members, often referring to "their wife," "their husband," or "their children," and material possessions can also be held dear, with "their house" or "their car" claiming much interest and attention. These cherished possessions are to be dutifully serviced and cared for, and never wasted in frivolity. SJs keep up their house and yard faithfully, and they expect their neighbors to do likewise, to show pride of ownership, certainly, but also to maintain property values in the neighborhood. SJs tend to be careful with money and are likely to budget strictly, planning well for the future, sometimes at the cost of much sacrifice in the present. Insurance policies, savings accounts, government bonds, and other conservative investments make sense to Guardians, who understand their safety. Also understood is the value of property, tools, clothes, and the like. Clothing especially should be simple and durable—SJs dress conservatively, appropriately, and they often make their own clothes. Goods of all kinds should be used up, worn out, and then not thrown away, but donated to a charitable agency. "Waste not, want not" is understood and honored as a motto by the Guardians.

As Helpmates, Guardians are ready to roll up their sleeves and work side by side with their spouses to build a comfortable, stable family life. For a female SJ, especially one who is seclusive, home may be a focal point, to the exclusion of all else. Caring for husband and children, preparing meals, and keeping a clean and orderly house may take her time and become her reason for living. When the children leave home, this can occasion a major crisis, with the SJ female highly vulnerable to the effect of the "empty nest syndrome." Retirement can bring about the same trauma for the male SJ, the job or place of business often being to him what the home and family are to the female. Both male and female SJs may worry about loved ones when they are away from home and will tend to make frequent contact by telephone. Guardians sometimes suffer with excessive worry about unlikely calamities happening to their spouses and children.

Guardians are usually conservative about their sexual practices, and are apt to establish their routines early in marriage and to observe them throughout life. The unexpected and unusual are not usually a part of the married SJs' sexual repertoire, making it unlikely for them to experiment very much with sexual approaches or techniques—or partners. Although certainly not blind to the charms of others, SJs prefer sex with their lawfully wedded partner, and, generally speaking, they are more comfortable making love at an accustomed time and in an accustomed place, a regularity which becomes more and more pronounced as the years go by. At bottom, married SJs regard sex as a means of reproduction rather than a form of recreation, and both male and female SJs may reflect the attitude that having children, who will bring joy and comfort, and who will continue the family line, is expected and desirable in a marriage. While this is less true in our so-called sexually liberated age, the view of sex as recreation is still not ordinarily held by most married Guardians.

Guardians, males and females alike, tend to be more serious about their sexual activities than the other temperaments. While Artisans, for instance, might greatly enjoy the playfulness and sensuality of sex, Guardians would be more likely to use sex to forget their troubles, or to ease fatigue, wanting to be comforted both emotionally and physically. And while Idealists and Rationals might consider sex a mutually pleasing activity, Guardians often view intercourse as a service to be delivered by the female, performed dutifully and on request, presumably in return for social and economic security. Because of this, a female SJ is likely to place the sexual needs of her mate over any she might have, perhaps seeing sex as a wifely duty rather than a pleasure, and concerning herself more with her husband's physical comfort and welfare than with her own sexual pleasure. In the same way, the SJ male is apt to express gratitude to his partner for the sexual experience, communicating the message that a favor has been done for him, or that his needs have been served.

Guardian mates may have some difficulty understanding the emotional needs of other types, particularly the Idealists and Rationals, for whom transactions outside the bedroom loom vital as a precursor to sexual response. The notion of getting turned on by books or ideas—philosophy, psychology, literature—does not make much sense to SJs. Sex is sex and philosophy is philosophy. Nor does emotional conflict seem to carry over into the bedroom for SJs. They can be angry with their mates, even scolding them, and then expect them to come to bed with open arms, having separated these criticisms from the sexual relationship. Apparently, Guardians believe that, as long as they care for their mates and take the proper responsibility for their health and welfare, the constructive lessons they offer should not inhibit the other's affection.

Not only in the bedroom, but also in many other areas of married life, Guardians tend to communicate a nurturing attitude as well as a critical attitude. Thus, for the SJ, caring for the mate means having the responsibility both for seeing them safe and well-provided for, and for seeing that they know the Right Thing to do and the Right Way to do it, which means the ways learned from parents and social tradition. SJs have a sure sense of what is Good and Right, and they do not hesitate to impose their values and procedures onto their mates in the form of Pygmalion Projects. This is not to say that all Guardians are devoted Pygmalions, but it does appear that their parental disposition seems naturally turned toward trying to shape up their mates' attitudes and actions. SJs care deeply that their loved ones, of whatever age or temperament, grow up and start behaving responsibly, or sensibly, or respectfully, as the case may be, and, again, they are not shy about communicating their expectations.

Guardian Pairings

Despite their tendency to take a firm hand with their loved ones, Guardians can mate happily with all the temperaments, especially if the mating partner in each case places a high value on home and family. But there are pitfalls.

Guardian-Idealist: Guardians share with Idealists a concern for society and for the morality of behavior, a wish to do right and to help other people; and at the same time they can be impressed by the NFs' spirituality and eye for potentiality, so different from their own down-to-earth, traditional way of life. But there are also areas of likely incompatibility. Guardians can be quite critical of Idealist enthusiasm, their propensity to get carried away with an idea, which the SJ worries might break with tradition and jeopardize a stable home. And they can be badly frustrated when asked by NFs to increase the depth and the meaning of the relationship, with no clue on how to proceed, and with their renewed efforts to stabilize and solidify the marriage only taken as a sign of superficiality.

Guardian-Rational: Guardians are comfortable with the Rationals' skeptical attitude and obsession with their work, which seem very much like their own pessimism and sense of duty; and they often admire the

NTs' ingenuity, which is such a reach from their own reliance on by-the-book routine. However, Guardians can feel blocked out of a Rational's cognitive life, and feel the scorn that many NTs hold for routine and convention. Indeed, of all the temperaments NTs are perhaps the least appreciative of the SJs' interest in everyday household matters, and all too often neglect to thank their Guardian mates for their care and keeping.

Guardian-Guardian: Guardians have similar ups and downs mating with other Guardians. Two SJs can be attracted to each other and get on surprisingly well together. In the first place, Guardians are not particularly troubled by familiarity or predictability in a relationship—being two peas in a pod sounds rather comfortable to them. And then two SJs share so much interest in domestic stability, including a devotion to home and family, an industrious work ethic, conservative attitudes toward parenting, recreation, spending and saving, toward memberships, collecting, civic responsibility, and so on, not to mention an appreciation for each other's carefulness and willingness to do thankless jobs. But this marriage also presents its problems. Two Guardians can step all over each other trying to run the house and do for each other, both insisting that their routine is the right one. And worse, in SJ-SJ marriages the critical attitude of one mate is met with the same critical attitude in the other. Imagine two umpires, each steadfastly trying to call the other's balls and strikes. We can safely guess that this sort of relationship will have its share of conflicts.

Guardian-Artisan: On average, Guardians seem to mate most successfully with Artisans, and while the combination might appear incompatible on the face it—concerned, sober Demeter mated with carefree, sensuous Dionysus—these ant and grasshopper marriages complement each other quite well, with the SP spreading the seed one way or another, and the SJ carefully managing the harvest. For Guardians, the impetuous Artisan is both a child to take care of and, at times, a wonderful diversion from their own shoulder-to-the-wheel existence. For Artisans, on the other hand, the cautious, ever-responsible Guardian is both a fixed center for their footloose way of life and a parental figure they can enjoy surprising and loosening up with their impulsive sense of fun.

Now, in theory, such Guardian-Artisan complementarity should be especially satisfying in marriages which combine differences of expressiveness or reserve (E-I) and tough-mindedness or friendliness (T-F). Consider the following four pairings as probable models of successful SJ-SP mating.

Providers and **Crafters** should mate most happily. The expressive and friendly Provider (ESFJ), giving, caring, and comforting in nature, likes to arrange for rest and sustenance, and the reserved and tough-minded Crafter (ISTP) is a natural born risk-taker who needs someone to be there when the high-speed adventure is over.

Protectors and **Promoters** are apt find their best match with each other. The outgoing, tough-minded Promoters (ESTPs) tend to have high periods during which they are in a whirlwind of euphoric activity, and the seclusive and friendly Protectors (ISFJs) enjoy preparing a quiet place for the high-rolling entrepreneur to crash.

Supervisors and **Composers** might well be mates of choice. Running the establishment, keeping it steady, within the rules, on schedule, that's what's enjoyable and satisfying to the expressive and tough-minded Supervisors (ESTJs). And while they might hope to instill in the impetuous, bohemian Composers some of their own respect for tradition, they might also find in the reserved and friendly ISFP a mate who can help them forget the great responsibilities they manage to accumulate.

Inspectors and **Performers** are likely to be most compatible. Here is the seclusive and tough-minded Inspector (ISTJ), the model of trustworthiness, thoroughness, and legitimacy, wanting to bring some accountability to the Performer, while at the same time enjoying the outgoing and friendly ESFP's vivacity and sparkle. How many times have novelists and playwrights told the story of the "banker and the showgirl"?

However, if the Guardians' greatest chance for happiness comes with Artisan mates, so does their greatest temptation to start up Pygmalion Projects. Guardians take their family responsibilities seriously, just as they take all of their responsibilities seriously, and when married to an impulsive, unruly, devil-may-care Artisan, they see their duty quite clearly. SJs believe in following the rules, in nourishing traditions, and in respecting order, and they regard their efforts to reform their SP mates in the SJ image as a necessary and a worthy, even a loving, attempt to make them over into better human beings. Nor will Guardians give up on their Pygmalion Projects when their Artisan mates get into trouble with excessive drinking, gambling, philandering, and the like. Even in these abusive relationships, SJs are extremely loyal and feel obliged to stand by their SP spouses and help them straighten out. As a result, Guardians more than any other type can be hooked into becoming the rescuer of addictive Artisan spouses.

All told, the Guardians' need to be of service makes them faithful, steady, reliable mates, just as their hunger for membership makes them loyal and hard-working supporters of all the established institutions in their communities. Very simply, Guardians make up the solid, indispensable foundation of our concrete world—they are truly the pillars who hold up society—and we would do well to value their rock-steady support for tradition and order in our more and more fast-paced, unstable existence.

The Idealist Soulmate

You are the call and I am the answer. You are the wish, and I the fulfillment. You are the night, and I the day. What else? It is perfect enough. It is perfectly complete. You and I.

—D.H. Lawrence

Idealists approach mating quite differently from the other three temperaments. In their own ways the other types tend to be realistic about mating, which is to say that Artisans, Guardians, and Rationals assume their mates to be fallible, and they will go along with a good deal of compromise in making their marriages work. Idealists, on the other hand, are singularly idealistic about choosing a mate, and most often take up the romantic task of seeking the perfect mate and the ideal relationship, what they call the "love of their life" or their "one true love," joined with them in a match made in heaven and creating a love timeless and eternal. In other words, NFs are looking for more than life partners in their mates—they want soul partners, persons with whom they can bond in some special spiritual sense, sharing their complex inner lives and communicating intimately about what most concerns them: their feelings and their causes, their romantic fantasies and their ethical dilemmas, their inner division and their search for wholeness. Idealists firmly believe in such deep and meaningful relationships—they will settle for nothing less—and in some cases they try to create them where they don't exist.

Idealist Courtship
    The Idealists' desire that their relationships be deep and meaningful (that is, intense, enduring, and all-important in their lives) is very much in evidence in the way they go about dating. NFs do not usually choose to play the field to any great extent, but prefer to go out with one person at a time and to explore the potential for special closeness in each relationship. Never casual or occasional about dating, NFs typically look past surface relations to more deeply-felt connections, and they lose interest rather quickly with dates which center around social events and physical activities. Idealists can enjoy this skin-deep sort of date for a while, of course, but they usually try to find their own kind of enjoyment as the evening wears on. At parties, for example, NFs will often look for a quiet corner where they can talk with their date (or someone else) on a more personal, intimate level. And at amusement parks or sporting events, Idealists will eventually separate themselves mentally from the rides, the sights, and the action, and begin to observe the people around them, wondering about their personalities and fantasizing about their personal lives.
    Indeed (and this surprises Artisans and Guardians), Idealists would usually rather talk with their dates than do things or go places, although chatting about concrete, literal, or factual things doesn't particularly interest them either. Idealists want to talk about abstract matters—ideas, insights, personal philosophies, spiritual beliefs, dreams, goals, family relationships, altruistic causes, and the like—inwardly-felt topics that break through social surfaces and connect two people heart-to-heart. NFs love to talk about movies or novels that have touched them deeply, but they don't want to describe the plot so much as discuss what the story suggests between the lines, the aesthetic or moral issues involved, and how the characters' lives symbolize their own experience or the wider experience of mankind. And

NFs will talk enthusiastically about art, music, and poetry, particularly about what a work of art signifies to them. The ability to communicate comfortably with their dates in this imaginative, meaningful way most often determines whether or not the Idealist can become serious in a given relationship.

Finding the rare person with whom they can share their inner world is difficult for Idealists, a painful process of trial and error, and often they vow not to date at all for periods of time rather than go through the search. For NFs, dating someone means more than physical fun or social experience; it is an opening of their heart and mind to the other person, in some cases a baring of their soul, and carries with it both a promise and an expectation of deep regard and mutual understanding. And because they are offering so much of themselves to the other, and expecting so much in return, NFs are highly sensitive to rejection, and can be deeply hurt when spurned by another, or when having to break off a relationship themselves. The trauma of breaking up can be so difficult for Idealists that at times they will avoid getting involved with others for fear of things not working out, or, at the other extreme, they will remain in a relationship longer than they should just to put off the soul-hurting scene of rejection.

However, once the special person comes their way (the man or woman of their dreams), Idealists can be carried away with their feelings, and give almost all their attention to pursuing the relationship. For the NF, not just a compatible marriage but an all-consuming, undying passion is in the offing, and so the courtship becomes the center of his or her world. Just as the possible rather than the actual lures NFs in other parts of their lives, so do the possibilities in relationships inspire them, and they see in each new relationship the potential for bringing them the perfect love that will fulfill them completely. Idealists have a flair for dramatizing their courtships, and they spare no effort or flight of imagination to win the heart of their loved one. Often a story book flavor permeates their courtship behavior, and NFs are not afraid of using imaginative language, even poetry and quotations, to give voice to their feelings. NFs can also be romantic when expressing love through gifts, though they are likely to present the gift in private, and to select with extraordinary care something with special or even symbolic meaning—a beloved piece of music, a favorite book of fiction or poetry, a treasured picture. In a sense, Idealists go about turning their courtships into works of art, which is not surprising, since one of the arts at which they are most skilled is that of creating the romantic relationship.

Idealist courtships are marked not only by romantic gestures, but also by the idealization of the relationship. In the early stages of a romance, both NF males and females are likely to be blind to flaws in their beloved, and to believe in the illusion that life together will proceed happily ever after (although the details of this happily ever after are rarely explored in depth). Idealists hold dear a compelling though often vague inner-vision of what their ideal mate will be like, and they tend to project this vision of perfection into their all-too-human loved ones. Thus, at the slightest suggestion, NFs will see soulfulness and poetic sensitivity in the people they've fallen in love with—whether or not they are indeed soulful or poetic. At the same time, NFs believe that everyone has the potential for spiritual growth, and in many cases they intend to use their love to develop this latent mystical side of their mates. Needless to say, most human beings cannot live up to such romantic ideals, nor will they often sit still to have their spirituality nurtured in such a way. Many Artisans react with good-natured sarcasm, many Guardians seem impatient with such foolishness, and the Rational view of this attribution of soulfulness is often skeptical at best. Idealists who attempt to make their loved ones live up to their ideals are sooner or later faced with disillusionment in their relationships.

Although many Idealists are reluctant to admit it, such romantic projection—and such disillusionment—are most often a problem in cases where there is a strong sexual attraction. Idealists can be deeply divided about their sexual feelings. On the one hand, they insist that sex must be an expression of love rather than lust. Even the word 'sex' seems a little crude to the Idealist; 'love' puts the relationship on a higher plain. But make no mistake, for all their other-worldliness, NFs are very intimate, warm, even passionate people who are highly responsive to physical beauty and sexual attraction—to Paracelsus, remember, they were Nymphs. Now, the problem for Idealists is that, with their rich fantasy lives, they tend to idealize physical beauty and to project their own poetic nature into the object of their sexual attraction. They also tend to romanticize sex as soulful communion. In other words, NFs tend to fall in love with a dream of beauty and passion, only to be rather painfully disillusioned by the flesh-and-blood imperfections which they eventually encounter in their loved ones. Many NFs are not fully prepared for the moment of truth when they come to see the imperfect reality of their lovers, and some relationships are unable to survive the truth. Fortunately, both male and female Idealists have a capacity for deep affection and caring over and above sexual expression, and out of this capacity can grow lasting, intimate relationships.

Curiously, it appears that female Idealists are able to sustain the romanticism invested in a relationship longer than male Idealists. Generally speaking, once the physical relationship is consummated, NFs of both genders feel deeply bonded with their partner and are certain the relationship will be blessed with eternal bliss. But for the male NF, anticipation can be more attractive than consummation, and the love which he believes will be perfect and undying can come to seem ordinary and inadequate in the harsh light of everyday reality. And so, after the physical side of the relationship has lost its mystery, some male NFs can become disinterested and hunger after another fantasy, feeling compelled (if only in their imaginations) to pursue the dream of a larger-than-life goddess who will satisfy all their desires and be wife, mother, and mistress to them. Idealists, as do the other temperaments, want a certain amount of variety and change in their lives, but the other temperaments will often seek this through adjustment of living routines, travel, new social or recreational activities, new fields of study, and so on. The male Idealist is most vulnerable to seeking variety through searching out a new person to love, and thus a danger he faces is that he will move from relationship to relationship, rather than make the necessary effort to develop the one he has.

The female Idealist does not as often demonstrate this loss of interest; on the contrary, she is likely to increase her dedication after the physical relationship is consummated. She becomes more and more devoted, continuing to romanticize the relationship and to believe in its perfection, to give small transactions profound significance, to dramatize ordinary interactions with her mate, to be willing (like so many NF fictional characters) to die for love. She seldom seems disappointed in the sexual act; orgasmic response on her part can be seen as secondary compared with the more selfless pleasure of giving herself body and soul to her mate, and she can satisfy herself by exploring the emotional intimacy of sexual intercourse. For the male Idealist, restlessness can set in as a result of familiarity, whereas an indispensable part of the female Idealist's mating identity is the image of falling in love once and for a lifetime. The fact that this does not always work out does not seem to negate the possibility of the dream coming true.

However, in the 1960s and 1970s a striking phenomenon occurred, perhaps arising from the female Idealist's ability to imagine a more perfect mating relationship. The group that spearheaded the sexual revolution was largely made up of female Idealists (particularly the ENFP Champions). Thus, it was the female Idealists who said "No!" most loudly to the double sexual (and other) standards in society, and who became most militant in demanding equal rights in the bedroom. Somehow female Idealists decided that selfless devotion to their mates was not enough, and that a better, more satisfactory relationship with men could be actualized. They seemed willing, in ever growing numbers, to take whatever risks were necessary to find that better relationship, either in or out of a legal contract. In fact, more and more the NF females seemed reluctant to tie themselves down to a traditional legal arrangement, putting off the urging of their housemates, asking that both wait until she was sure she was doing the right thing. More and more NF females seemed willing to bear their children outside a legal marriage and to raise them alone. This is not to say that other types were not also involved in this liberation movement, but it was the NFs, along with a small number of NT females, who provided the vanguard of the revolution. Instead of being ready and willing to die for love, these Idealist females seemed to be willing to live for the possibility of finding a more fulfilling way of relating to males.

But, then, most Idealists—sexual revolutionaries or not—regard the social conventions of marriage as less important, and far less sacred, than their personal commitments. Like the Guardians, Idealists are concerned about having moral sanction for their actions, but with a difference. While Guardians tend to put their trust in institutional authority (including church authority), and thus care a great deal about licenses and wedding ceremonies, Idealists are apt to follow their innermost feelings and personal religious convictions, and thus will consider themselves married when they're sure that deep bonding has taken place with their mates, and when private words of devotion have been exchanged. For many NFs the arrangements and formalities of wedding ceremonies can seem a needless burden, when the mating of souls and the personal vows are the important things. Reserved NFs, in particular, are often embarrassed to express their private feelings in public, and can become quite flustered at the altar, the meaningfulness of their vows so overwhelming them emotionally that they seem lost in a blur during the ceremony, and not able to find themselves again until alone with their mates afterwards. This is not to say that Idealists will try to avoid walking down the aisle, but only that they do not always need this sort of external moral authority to sanctify their relationships. If need be, NFs will go along quite happily with the wishes of mates (or parents) for traditional wedding ceremonies, and they will find enormous significance and holiness in the rituals. Some outgoing NFs will even look forward to their weddings, though this is likely because they've taken a hand in creating non-traditional ceremonies, writing their own vows, for instance, and selecting unconventional readings and music for the occasion.

These Idealists, warm, generous, vivacious, soulful, personally conscientious and interpersonally sensitive, are quite attractive to the other temperaments. Artisans feel some kinship with the Idealists' romantic or poetic sense of life as a work of art, and can feel morally uplifted by the ethical dimension that NFs bring to their relationships. Guardians, on the other hand, feel secure with the Idealists' powerful sense of life's moral seriousness, and can feel livened up a bit by the enthusiasm and creativity with which NFs throw themselves into things. However, it is the Rationals who are most attracted to Idealists, for not only do they share the NFs' abstract, introspective cast of mind, and thus have someone interesting to talk with, but they truly admire the NFs' emotional sparkle, their personal warmth, and their insight into people—traits that the phlegmatic NTs often note are poorly developed in themselves.

Idealist Married Life

Whatever the mix of personalities in their marriages, however, both male and female Idealists are likely to be a source of continuing love, support, and understanding to their spouses. In the affective areas Idealists are without equal, bringing to their marriages an extraordinary sensitivity to the moods and feelings of their mates, and an unsurpassed ability to communicate emotionally. Both NF females and males seem to have their antennae always alert to what others are feeling, especially when this involves hurt and conflict, and they characteristically respond to their mates with kindness, tenderness, and unconditional love. They are usually ready to lend sympathy to a mate when the outside world turns hostile, and are reluctant to use that moment to point out the errors of a mate's ways, something which the other three temperaments are more inclined to do.

Indeed, Idealists often are experts in the arts of appreciation, especially in the area of personal qualities, and they are apt to be generous in expressing heartfelt approval of their loved ones. Possessing facility with language, NFs are able to communicate nuances of emotions that might not even be noticed by the other temperaments, and their private conversations are often liberally sprinkled with terms of endearment and with frequent, passionate expressions of love, both verbal and nonverbal—giving hugs and saying "I love you" are often a natural part of their interaction with their mates and children. It is undoubtedly the Idealist who is the most loving, dedicated, affectionate, and appreciative mate, and is unstinting in the expression of these emotions.

Perhaps Idealists are this sensitive to their mates because of their exceptional ability to introject or to empathize—to see the world through another's eyes. Of all the temperaments the NFs are the most empathic, having the ability to take into themselves another's mental state (both thoughts and feelings) so completely that the other feels totally understood and accepted. With their talent for identifying with the other person, for slipping into another's skin, Idealists find that building close, loving relationships is the most natural thing in the world. They are the true masters of the art of intimacy.

And yet such emotional sensitivity (some would say hypersensitivity) can take its toll, and Idealists have been known to become upset when these affective ties begin to bind, as they do when the amount of emotional input from their mates becomes a psychological overload. NFs report that, at times, they find their emotional circuits so overloaded with their own concerns that they cannot deal positively with the emotional experiences of others who are especially close to them, particularly when those experiences are negative or unhappy.

In addition, emotional dependence in a mate can really bother an Idealist, even though their own sensitivity sometimes encourages dependency. If their mates begin to seem weak and clinging—to need more and more attention, more and more expressions of the NFs' unusual appreciation, more and more signals of deep affection—Idealists can become resentful of pressures to deliver what they had seemed to promise their mates: the ideal love, complete understanding, and total acceptance. At this point NFs can turn irritable, insisting unexpectedly that their mates stop hanging on their approval and learn to stand on their own two feet. This shift in attitude is usually abrupt and the loved ones who heretofore believed that they were very special in the eyes of the Idealist now find themselves apparently rejected. The Idealist does not mean to be unkind; he or she is simply disconnecting from a relationship which can no longer be handled.

Such rejection can take subtler forms as well. Idealists pride themselves on being sensitive to others and caring about them, but their sensitivity tends to be reflexive and indiscriminate. It is almost impossible for NFs to be unaware of others' emotional needs, and it is hard for them not to offer their empathy and special understanding to whoever happens to be near. In other words, NFs may be unable not to respond to the emotional demands of others, and when they leave one person, they no longer resonate to that person, but to the person now present. Thus, Idealists will find themselves responding to relative strangers with a degree of warmth and acceptance which may not, for the moment, be available to their own mates. Understandably, this can cause some difficulty for mates who want the NF's empathy to be exercised more exclusively. Their mates may not realize that Idealists cannot help but respond to others' needs, and may be hurt on coming to believe that they are not valued as uniquely as they first thought.

In much the same way, Idealists may have difficulty freeing themselves from the demands of their careers in order to preserve time for their families. Especially if their jobs involve working closely with others in personal development (teaching, counseling, pastoring, and the like), Idealists can become so wrapped up in the problems and progress of their students, clients, or parishioners that they may neglect their mates and their family priorities. Whoever is there and demanding time gets it, even though their loved ones may be waiting elsewhere. Idealists often have to learn how to detach themselves from their personal involvements away from home, to make sure they give their mates and families first importance in their lives.

Those Idealists (male or female) who cannot order their personal priorities are tempted to move from person to person, using their energies to pursue new significant relationships at the expense of deepening those they already have. Still, the large majority of NFs find their greatest satisfaction in developing one special relationship, and they structure much of their lives around their homes and families. NFs are imaginative and creative around the house, their homes usually filled with a great variety of music and art, along with cherished personal items, family photographs, spiritual icons—and everywhere books, not only books of philosophy and poetry, but books on religion and mysticism, personal growth, novels of all kinds, and often children's books. Much like Artisans, Idealists have a flair for artistic hobbies, especially those that enhance the home, such as interior decorating, gourmet cooking, gardening (NFs love flowers), playing a musical instrument (piano, guitar, recorder), and often they become quite accomplished in the activity. Idealists will also develop other life-enhancing enthusiasms, nutrition, yoga, self-hypnosis, along with various other kinds of personal therapies, and will usually try to interest their spouses in their latest passion.

Idealists care a great deal about keeping the romance alive and well in their marriages, and they love to go on dates with their spouses no matter how many years they've been together, enjoying a romantic weekend getaway, a good restaurant, or an evening at the symphony or the theater. And Idealists strive to be authentic sexual partners, capable of sustaining a deep physical intimacy with their mates. Seeing themselves as a lover as well as a spouse is a major part of their personality, although, again, NFs can be caught up in the romanticized expectations of psychological and sexual perfection generated in their own imaginations. Lovemaking, in particular, can be disappointing in the early stages of NF relationships, for they are strangely innocent about sexuality, and more often than not they expect themselves to know intuitively the most loving and tender approach. Idealists quickly find their way, however, making up in enthusiasm what they might lack in technique, and they would not have it any other way. Being a smooth and suave lover, like an Artisan, would make an Idealist feel inauthentic, even deceitful.

Idealists are generally skilled socially, and people usually feel wanted and well-hosted in their homes. Expressive NFs are likely to be socially active, becoming involved (and hoping to involve their spouses) in a variety of cultural and personal development programs, such as great books courses, drama groups, and film societies, and they will also join discussion groups, taking up vital social issues and current trends in education, psychology, religion, literature, and so on. Reserved NFs keep more to themselves and their immediate loved ones, and tend to make cave-like private spaces in their homes, where they read voraciously and contemplate the mysteries of life, although they will actively support the arts and humanities in their communities, attending concerts, plays, poetry readings, and other cultural events. Expressive or reserved, however, NFs are spontaneously thoughtful with their family members, usually remembering birthdays, anniversaries, and such without being prompted, or at most needing only a hint. If, in turn, their own special days are forgotten, Idealists can be deeply hurt, as deeply as they are appreciative when theirs are noticed.

Idealist Pairings

Creating warm, loving relationships is indeed second nature to Idealists, and they weave their interpersonal spell in marriages with all the temperaments. Still, there can be trouble in paradise.

Idealist-Artisan: Idealists thoroughly enjoy their Artisan mates' freedom and spontaneity in the real world, and they admire the ease with which SPs can live artfully in the moment, so different from their own often torn, conscience-stricken experience of life. Also the sensuality and sexual boldness of SP mates can intrigue NFs and fire their romantic imaginations. However, there is one potent seed of dissatisfaction in these NF-SP marriages, namely, the lack of interest that SPs have in talking of their inner lives. When an Idealist speaks of the "true self," of "transcendental meditation," or of "deep consciousness," their Artisan mates do not really understand and cannot offer much enthusiasm or insight on such abstract topics. And, sadly, it is from this seed that Pygmalion Projects grow in these relationships, as the Idealist partners try with all their imaginative might to cultivate a heightened inner-awareness in their Artisan mates.

Idealist-Guardian: With Guardian mates Idealists find a comfortable, reassuring stability and dependability in the home, traits which can help give the somewhat scattered NFs a feeling of solid earth beneath their feet. SJs also have a firmly fixed moral center—a sure sense of Right and Wrong—that Idealists, so often of two minds about moral issues, deeply respect. And Idealists and Guardians are both social cooperators, which defuses a lot of conflict over following, or at least respecting, the rules and laws that govern everyday life. Yet here again Guardians have trouble sharing the rich inner lives of Idealists, and can disappoint their NF mates' deep longing for soulful bonding and romantic sexuality. The Guardian might listen dutifully to the Idealist's flights of imagination, and might try to be more fanciful and passionate in order to please the NF, but sooner or later the SJ feels unappreciated and begin to resist the force of the NF's Pygmalion Project—and the result can be head-on battles.

Idealist-Idealist: Idealists have much less trouble with mates of their own temperament, and Idealists often get along exceptionally well with other Idealists. Two NFs can find deep-felt satisfaction in sharing each other's inner world and exploring each other's personal development, although if the pair are too much alike in their ethical concerns, or pursue the same spiritual goals for too long a time, they can become rather narrowly devoted to the pilgrim's journey and tire themselves out along the way. In addition, two empathic NFs can create a wonderfully intimate bond for a time, but eventually such mutual introjection can also invade each partner's privacy—constantly getting into each other's skin can result in getting on each other's nerves.

Idealist-Rational: The choice of a Rational mate seems to hold the best promise of success for Idealists. The basis of their compatibility is that NFs and NTs both live primarily in the world of abstract concepts—the world of theories and possibilities, of insights and symbols. After dating more down-to-earth, literal-minded Artisans and Guardians, an Idealist's first encounter with a Rational can be a revelation, putting the NF in touch with a new and intriguing type of person, someone eager and able (like the NF) to dream the world, to build castles in the air, and to see far distances with the mind's eye. Also fascinating is the Rational's calmness and autonomy, two characteristics which give the NT a strength of character—a firm grasp of who they are—that the easily ruffled, soul-searching NF greatly admires, and would like to emulate.

These Idealist-Rational relationships do not always remain harmonious, of course. Conflicts of NF emotional expressiveness against NT self-control, of NF intuition against NT logic, and of NF ethical or humanitarian concerns against NT technical pragmatics can prove challenging in even the best Idealist-Rational marriages. Indeed, NFs often come to regard their NT mates' resistance to expressing emotion, their seemingly aloof rationality, and their preference for what works over what's right as barriers to be broken down, or at least chipped at with Pygmalion's chisel. But while sparks might fly—or maybe because of the sparks—Idealists take to Rationals as to no other temperament.

Now, in theory, such Idealist-Rational compatibility should reach its peak when particular couples complement each other in the expressive or reserved social attitude (E-I), and in making schedules or probing for options (J-P). The following four NF-NT pairings suggest how these added complementary factors might make for successful mating.

Teachers and **Architects** have every chance of being well suited. The educator or growth-catalyst inherent in the expressive and scheduling Teacher (ENFJ) wants to bring out the latent talents in his or her loved ones, and what better target than the reserved and probing Architect (INTP)? For beneath the Architect's cool, collected, detached, and doubting exterior lies an engineer of buildings, machines, tools, operations, languages, mathematics, or whatever can be engineered. If, that is, this diamond-in-the rough can be inspired to fulfill his or her potential.

Counselors and **Inventors** are apt to fit extremely well together. The reserved and schedule-minded Counselors (INFJs), with their complex, mysterious, symbolic inner-worlds, tend to become trapped in introspection and tied in ethical knots, and they can be freed up considerably by the outgoing and probing Inventors (ENTPs). Counselors might also find great satisfaction in trying to help the non-conformist, sometimes even reckless Inventors find their soul and significance in the scheme of things.

Champions and **Masterminds** should match up well. Champions (the expressive and probing ENFPs) are much like Healers in their crusader phase, fiercely dedicated to meaning in life and looking into everything of Good and Evil in the world. Only Champions are more outgoing and high-spirited, and more outspoken about their discoveries, not unlike puppies, sniffing around to see what's new and then barking to let everyone know what they've found. Now who would be likely to enjoy this curious, frisky—yet soulful—person? Strangely, perhaps, the well-ordered, strong-willed Masterminds. Often narrowly focused in their concern with planning and directing projects, Masterminds (the highly reserved and well-scheduled INTJs) can find a vital connection to the outside world in the person who knows what's going on.

Healers and **Fieldmarshals** are likely to find great satisfaction marrying each other. Healers (the reserved and probing INFPs) have more problems in mating than any other type, no doubt due to their fervent view of life as either a crusade against Evil or a retreat into religious contemplation—and the same Healer can tack back and forth, now a crusader, now a monastic. In either case, their spouse will be taxed by having to deal with such spiritual intensity, and the expressive and scheduling Fieldmarshal (ENTJ), busily marshalling his or her forces toward distant objectives, seems well equipped to handle this alternating-phase style of life, able, that is, to provide clear direction to a person who might otherwise get lost in meditation or in devotion to a cause.

No matter what kind of persons Idealists marry, however, it is not too much to say that they are the best of all the temperaments at creating successful and fulfilling marriages. Developing harmonious personal relations is the their joy and their area of expertise, and they bring all their finest qualities to the enterprise. Their sensitivity, their spirit of cooperation, their ability to communicate their feelings, their passion for their mates, their desire for deep bonding, their personal warmth and enthusiasm—all these traits work their magic in the NFs' relationships, and more than compensate for their tendency to start up Pygmalion Projects. Indeed, if we can assume that Pygmalion Projects are an inevitable part of any marriage, that at best such intimate coercion can be kept loving and sympathetic, then Idealists offer their mates the possibility of exceptional happiness.

The Rational Mindmate

I wanted my wife to share all my interests, which included mathematical social science....I was a little worried (I am not joking) that she did not know calculus, but she promised to remedy that, a promise she fulfilled only many years later.
                                                              —Herbert A. Simon

Rationals make wonderful mates—they are loyal, uncomplaining, warmly sexual, honest and aboveboard in their communications, and not in the least possessive. But for all the satisfactions they bring to a marriage, establishing romantic relationships with Rationals usually requires more time and energy than with the other temperaments. Even the outgoing Rationals, although apparently easy to get to know, are fairly difficult to get close to, for their personality structure is characteristically complex and, at times, even hidden from view.

Rational Courtship

Rationals do not care to spend much of their time or energy making social connections. Not only do they find the rituals of dating slightly absurd, but they seem to have more difficulty than other temperaments engaging in play, which makes dating usually something of a trial for them. While some NTs will attempt to cover their lack of social skills by clowning around, they tend, on the whole, to be rather serious and cerebral, enjoying discussions on esoteric topics full of technical details (everything you wanted to know about chemical bonding—and more), a pastime which the other temperaments are apt to find dreadfully dull. For most NTs, intellectual development seems to proceed at a faster rate than does social development—they are often the math whizzes and science nerds in high school and college—and they tend to prefer their books and computers to football games and prom dates. But even in young adulthood, Rationals remain somewhat stiff and awkward when it comes to dating, and many show almost no interest in developing social graces or in being popular.

Once in a college or business environment, extraverted Rationals might decide (quite deliberately) to date around for the fun of it, and some might experiment with sexual practices. But when establishing more lasting relationships they are not likely to give in to impulse. Indeed, and as a matter of personal ethics, Rationals usually regard sexual promiscuity with distaste. Even talking about their sexual experiences is uncomfortable for them, and they are not likely to discuss past involvements with a partner or with others, and almost never discuss their current sex life with friends. A few highly private, seriously committed relationships is the usual pattern of an NT's love life, probably because Rationals (like many Idealists) tend to develop intimate relationships rather slowly.

Thus, generally speaking, dating for Rationals is neither entertainment (as it is for Artisans), social participation (as it is for Guardians), nor deep bonding (as it is for Idealists); rather, dating for Rationals is a sometimes difficult search for a person they deem worthy of their personal investment. Wanting always to know what they're doing and where they're going, NTs think through relationships carefully, giving prolonged consideration to their intentions and expectations. Once the matter has been mapped out to their satisfaction—once their coordinates are clear—they are ready to proceed with investing in the relationship, and, in all likelihood, they will develop the relationship as they have conceived it, provided, of course, that a response has been forthcoming from the recipient. If the relationship calls for a short-term involvement, a short-term investment is made, and the NT makes sure the temporary nature of the affair is clearly understood by the other party. Should this not be agreeable, the NT is likely to shrug his or her shoulders and turn away, with only mild regrets. If, on the other hand, the relationship calls for a long-term commitment, a long-term commitment is made, and will be honored even if the relationship does not develop as satisfactorily as anticipated. Nor is the NT likely to verbalize any disappointment or dissatisfaction if such is the case. Once Rationals have made their search and decided on a mate, they are unlikely to have a change of mind.

The Coordinator NTs (ENTJs and INTJs) are more systematic in this search for a mate than the Engineer NTs (ENTPs and INTPs). Coordinators will often have in mind a list of physical and cognitive features they hope to find in their mate, and they will not be slow to discourage someone who does not fit the bill. Engineers, on the other hand, can be rather passive about the search, seeing the whole courtship process as perhaps more trouble than it's worth, and they are likely to settle down with the first person of quality who happens to show an interest in them—just to get the mating problem solved. Both styles can lead to errors: Coordinators can be naive about their requirements and make faulty lists, while Engineers some-times find that short-term solutions can result in long-term regrets. But unless their choice is a complete disaster, Rationals tend to stand by their commitments and make every effort to see their relationships through.

Although the Rational mating style can seem over-controlled at times, it has its attractions for the other temperaments. Artisans admire both the Rationals' penchant for effective action and their refusal to be bound by convention, while at the same time they enjoy trying to jolly the NTs up a bit, getting them to stop being so serious and obsessive about their work. Guardians, in contrast, think highly of the Rationals' seriousness and hard work, and take real pride in helping the lost-in-thought NTs keep their feet on the ground, providing them with an enjoyable, conventional social life. All in all, however, Idealists feel the strongest attraction to Rationals. Not only do Idealists share with Rationals a rare compatibility of mind, a deeply satisfying mutual interest in abstract ideas, but NFs also marvel at the NTs' ability to focus and to concentrate, so different from their own tendency to be scattered, divided, and distracted.

Once Rationals have given themselves to a mate, they feel pledged to the relationship—with or without a marriage license. NTs often have a curious amorality concerning the generally-accepted standards of mating behavior. The rules and formalities of society have little pressure for them, but their own personal standards of conduct certainly do. Society's seal of approval—in the form of a church ceremony or marriage license—means nothing to them, and will be put up with only to please their family or their mate. What matters to the Rational is individual commitment, and this personal contract is worthy all their loyalty. The same goes for their attitude towards pre-marital sex. The sexual ethics of NTs are carefully considered, and strictly adhered to, but may or may not conform to the general mores of sexual behavior current in any given time. In most cases, Rationals are not at all reluctant to explore their sexuality once they have committed to a relationship.

Rational Married Life

Once an investment has been made in a mate, and Rationals are free to pursue their varied interests—both know-abouts and know-hows—they come face to face rather quickly with a major problem in their marriages. It is frequently, and sadly, the case that Rationals are misunderstood on one important point by their spouses, who will accuse them of being cold and unemotional, and of seeming distant and unconcerned with their welfare. NTs, for their part, are amazed that their way of relating and loving can be seen by their mates as aloof or uncaring, for they know what powerful passions surge within them, and how keenly interested they are in their mates. But the false impression—almost a stereotype—of Rational coldness remains the source of much disappointment and conflict in their marriages. What's the cause of this misunderstanding, this discrepancy between appearance and reality? The answer lies in the combined strength of three of the Rationals' core character traits: their abstractness, their need for efficiency, and last but not least, their desire for autonomy.

In the first place, Rationals spend much of their time absorbed in the abstract world of ideas, principles, theories, technologies, hypotheses, research models, system designs, and the like. When they aren't puzzling over a problem from work, they are studying other subjects (the Civil War, astronomy, photography)—ever in the business of acquiring knowledge—and this makes them often seem out of touch with the real world of people and objects, and oblivious to the daily, homely events that comprise much of family life. Making matters worse, NTs have a unique ability to concentrate on whatever problems they are trying to solve—and they are always working on solutions to problems—which can make them seem remote and preoccupied with their work, lost in thought, as if a million miles away even when sitting with their spouse in the living room. This is one of the major complaints of their mates: that NTs seem to direct exclusive attention to the world of theory and technology, at the expense of giving sufficient attention to them. The Rational, it can sometimes seem to his or her mate, "doesn't know I'm alive."

And yet, while Rationals might seem unaware of their mates and the domestic life around them, they are not indifferent or unresponsive, usually showing genuine interest when these people and events are brought to their attention. It's just that NTs don't notice everyday reality—and this includes their spouses—very well on their own. Thus the problem is not that Rationals are cold and inhuman, but that they are by nature both abstract and highly focused, and have to be reminded to get their nose out of their books, their technical journals, their computer files—to get out of their heads—and join the family circle.

But there's the rub, because many husbands and wives feel humiliated having to ask their Rational mates to pay attention to them, or to give time to the family. They want their Rational mates to think of them and care about them of their own volition, without having to be reminded—as a spontaneous expression of love. And so they will wait with growing anger for the NT to offer interest or affection, and when this fails, they will accuse them of thoughtlessness or indifference. This is an all-too-common impasse in Rational marriages.

Along with their abstractness, Rationals have an almost obsessive need to be efficient in whatever they do and say, which means they want, if at all possible, to achieve maximum results with minimum effort in all their endeavors. This constant striving for peak efficiency, for mini-max operations and communications, explains many things about NT behavior: why they put their trust in the precision of logic, for example, or why they are so hard on themselves when they make errors, or why (always on the lookout for mistakes and wasted effort) they often frown and appear to be angry when concentrating.

At the same time, this obsession with efficiency figures into a familiar problem in Rational marriages, namely, that NTs are reluctant to speak of love to their spouses, who are often hurt by the silence. It's not that NTs don't feel love for their mates, but that they have a distaste for stating the obvious or being redundant, and so once they have indicated their feelings by choosing their mate, they are not apt to engage in sentimental love talk. Their spouses might long for more frequently verbalized expressions of affection and concern, but, to the ever-efficient Rationals, repeating what is clearly established is a waste of time and words, and might even raise a doubt about the sincerity of the message, as if the lady or the gentleman "doth protest too much." Once the NT makes a commitment to a mate, the commitment stands until notified. Nothing more need be said. All too often, however, their mates come to believe that this lack of emotional expressiveness is due to a lack of emotion, and, again, Rationals are accused of being cold and unromantic, or, worse, of selfishly regarding their own efficiency as more important than the feelings of their mates.

The third cause of the seeming coldness of Rationals is their principled insistence on individual autonomy, both for themselves and for their spouses. NTs allow no compromise when it comes to their own autonomy. They are the most self-directed and independent-minded of all the temperaments, and they resist (and resent) any and all forces that would coerce them into acting against their will, that would try to make them march to someone else's drum. To Rationals, every man is an island, alone unto himself, and their resistance hardens against social or moral expectations that are meant to control them, those rituals, manners, regulations, codes of conduct—those shoulds and shouldn'ts—that govern most social behavior. And this is just as true if the coercion comes from educational institutions, governmental institutions, business institutions, or from the institution of marriage.

Thus, if Rationals detect in their mates' messages even the slightest pressure to behave in a socially acceptable way, or to have a better attitude—if they sense the subtlest suggestion of social or moral obligation—they will balk and refuse to cooperate, not only on significant matters such as tending the children, or saying "I love you," but also on seemingly trivial things such as cleaning up the kitchen, dressing for a party, or helping bring in the groceries. Their refusal might take some form of silent, passive resistance, or an icy blast, but it is rare for any NT simply to follow orders without some word of protest or gesture of self-assertion. On occasion, they might bite their lip and go along in order to avoid a quarrel, but they allow their autonomy to be abridged only under duress, and with growing annoyance.

Beyond this resistance to interpersonal constraint, Rationals are not at all comfortable with the involuntary impulses (urges, emotions, appetites, desires) that well up from within themselves and seek to take control of them. NTs have just as many of these irrational impulses as the next person, but they are innately mistrustful of them—after all, they might lead to mistakes and inefficiency, both of which are unacceptable to them.

Basing their self-respect on their autonomy, NTs have difficulty allowing themselves to give up control and go with their impulses and emotions and to express them freely and openly. On the contrary, Rationals try to govern their impulses and bend them to their will by consciously evaluating them and analyzing them, which effectively kills them in the process. "Analysis," as Artisan athletes like to say, "is paralysis."

Not surprisingly, the Rationals' tight rein on their impulses also takes its toll on their marriages. Even with their closest loved ones, NTs prefer to restrain and hide their emotions behind an immobile facial stance, with only their eyes transmitting depth of reaction. A public display of emotion or affection is particularly repugnant to most NTs, not out of modesty or respect for decorum, mind you, but because it shows a lack of self-control—a lack of autonomy—and this attitude contributes to the image of the Rational as the cold automaton. NTs are even inclined to keep certain aspects of their personalities, as well as some of their talents, to themselves. Showing off is loathsome to them (it is acting for others, not for themselves), and so their loved ones are often surprised to learn of some skill, or interest, or facet of character in the Rational that had not been apparent previously.

But not only do Rationals live according to their own lights, they expect their mates to do the same. Personal dependence (on alcohol, for example) is repellant to them, but so is interpersonal dependence. Rationals show little sympathy with mates who look to the Rational to give them happiness or wholeness. To NTs, "People who need people," are not, as the song from *Funny Girl* puts it, "the luckiest people in the world" ("a feeling, deep in your soul, says you were half, now you're whole"). Such people are sorely lacking in self-sufficiency, says the NT, and need to become whole in themselves, self-determined and self-possessed, for the Rational to continue loving them.

In all fairness, Rationals are full of loyalty and support for mates, children, or even old friends who happen to be in need of help, but only if there is no sign of dependency or game-playing in the needy person. If those close to them (especially their spouses) try to make a crutch of the NT, or hope to extort sympathy with some overdone complaint, the NT will turn quickly away and refuse even to meet them half way. We are all on our own in life, says the Rational, and no one can make you happy but yourself.

The Rationals' intention to instill their own fierce sense of autonomy in their loved ones is a common basis of NT Pygmalion Projects, and as in all Pygmalion Projects it is meant benevolently, to help the mate become what the NT believes is a better person. Unfortunately, such a shift for yourself way of relating to loved ones strikes many less self-reliant mates as cold and uncaring, when in truth it is the Rationals' way of showing just how much they care.

For the most part, however, Rationals tend not to own the behaviors of their mates as might those of other temperament, and so do not feel they have the right to interfere with them—even for their own good. The errors, or at least the non-logical errors, of their family members are not the NT's errors, and so can be regarded objectively. (The NT's own errors are those which are inexcusable, and unforgivable.) Parenting, therefore, is usually a pleasure for a Rational, who seems to watch the growth of children with joy but as something of a bystander. And in the case of a quarrelsome mate, Rationals will usually not let themselves be hooked into the interpersonal battle, but will quietly step back and observe their mate's curious, overwrought behavior, waiting for the anger to burn itself out. Unfortunately, such benign detachment often only feeds the fire, and Rationals, instead of being valued for their patience and self-control, are once again accused by their mates of being aloof and uncaring.

This characteristic Rational trait—caring without needing to possess—also extends to many material goods. NTs tend to be relatively uninterested in acquiring material wealth beyond what is necessary for reasonable security and comfort, or in acquiring expensive things (cars, jewelry, clothes) just for the status or the pride of ownership. Possession as an end in itself seems not to motivate Rationals; rather, they are content with enjoying the beauty of, say, a vintage car, a classic airplane, or an exquisite art object, taking pleasure in their efficient design and construction, and finding satisfaction in their elegant functioning. While NTs are periodically inspired to acquire the wealth needed to own such expensive toys, this urge seldom lasts long enough to make that fortune. Their attention quickly turns once again to the theoretical, and the momentary interest in becoming wealthy dissipates—only to return from time to time with the same result.

Certain things, however, Rationals find irresistible to own, sometimes to the delight and sometimes to the irritation of their mates. Land is one kind of property that NTs have a powerful need to possess, and this might well have to do with their wanting to assure their personal freedom and autonomy—the idea of a man's home being his castle, secure from bureaucratic trespass. Owning tools is another weakness for NTs, who will think very little of the cost of buying the latest, most efficient design of any tool they happen to find useful, be it power saw, video camera, or computer hardware or software. Rationals love to feel capable, as if they can handle any problem that might arise, and so they surround themselves with the best tools available. And NTs seldom lose interest in owning books—they are some of their most valuable tools. A Rational's home is likely to be well-lined, even strewn, with books: with technical journals and dictionaries, with works of philosophy, history, biography, and the physical and social sciences, but also with books for recreation, works of far-flung imagination (especially historical novels, spy novels, science fiction, and mysteries), as well as books of math puzzles and complex game strategies (chess, bridge, and the like).

For Rationals, sensuality also has much to do with imagination, as it does for Idealists, and both temperaments are capable of appreciating the imaginative nuances of physical intimacy which Artisans and Guardians might find irrelevant or even unfathomable. The messages that both NTs and NFs send through the physical relationship are apt to become more and more complex over time, as their overtures to the sexual encounter become threaded with subtleties and symbolism. Moreover, the degree of sexual satisfaction in an NT's marriage will be correlated with the mental closeness of the relationship, and normally the sexual act is given meaning beyond mere playfulness or release from sexual tension.

At the same time, the Rationals' imaginative way in sexuality can sometimes block the full expression of their physical nature. The female NT, in particular, may have difficulty with sexual responses unless her mate takes the time, makes the effort, and understands the necessity of making his romantic approach through mutual exploration of ideas, arousing her mind as well as her body. Indeed, it is likely that an NT female will be sexually stimulated only by a mate who is as bright as she is, or at least by someone whose quality of mind she greatly admires. Obviously, this places the intelligent female NT in a position of limited choices. Male NTs have a slightly different standard concerning brain power. While they, too, prefer mates who are just as smart as they are (and unintelligent females actually turn them off), their attitude is more apt to be that, given other personal or domestic talents, their mate need not be quite their intellectual equal.

Rationals tend to enjoy arguing about ideas with their mates, taking great pleasure in the lively discussion of economics, politics, history, science (and many other topics), either one-on-one or within a circle of friends. NTs will insist that logic be adhered to in such discussions; to be sure, logic or rationality is the other major area (besides autonomy) in which Rationals are likely to start up Pygmalion Projects with their spouses. Rationals seem to have eternal hope that one day they can prevail upon their mates to share their fascination with science and technology, and that they can shape up their loved ones into being more logical in their thinking and speaking. Isn't this the way everyone should be?

But such discussions are often as witty as they are logical. Contrary to the stereotype of them as always cold and serious, Rationals generally have a well-developed sense of humor, although the amusing and humorous is usually subtle and, more often than not, based on a play on words. NTs especially enjoy humor which is ironical, or which contains an unexpected double meaning, but this is not to say their wit is always abstract and pedantic. Many Rationals, particularly males, get a kick out of off-color jokes and stories, at least when not in mixed company, though it must be said that they are not that good at telling dirty jokes—they often lose their timing and forget the punch lines.

However, just as quick-witted debate can bring Rationals alive, relationships that are fraught with emotional infighting can aggravate and exhaust them. NTs love to spar over ideas and theories, but conflict on a personal level—quarreling and bickering over acceptable social behavior, for instance, or locking horns over matters of family or domestic control (from big things, like raising children, to little things, like taking out the garbage)—is something NTs find destructive, and they will walk away from this kind of interaction, putting whatever psychological distance is needed between themselves and a cross, coercive mate.

For the social graces, similarly, Rationals tend to have little time or interest. Notoriously absorbed in their research, NTs (especially the reserved NTs) may be utterly unaware, unless reminded, of annual social rituals, and this can lead to difficulty when their mate is a type to whom anniversaries, birthdays, holidays, vacations, and such are important. Moreover, most NTs give very little thought to their personal appearance, particularly to how they dress, and if you happen to see someone wearing two different colored socks, or a shirt with the price tag hanging from the sleeve, it is likely to be an NT. This can embarrass some social-minded mates, who will get after their Rationals for being so careless.

But this is more than absentmindedness; again, there are principles of efficiency and autonomy involved. For Rationals, clothing is to be efficient, not fashionable, which means it must be comfortable and functional, and preferably inexpensive. Indeed, to give more than passing regard to color or style or expensive labels is worse than a waste of time, it is going along with the crowd, trying to please others, and is thus a loss of autonomy. Female NTs have pretty much this same attitude about clothing, and also about hair styles, makeup, jewelry, and the like. The female NT, if she attends to these fashion issues at all, tries to keep her appearance unpretentious, wanting to give as little time and attention as possible to outward form, and caring to please only herself and to keep her husband happy.

Rational Pairings

In spite of these misunderstandings, Rationals, both male and female, do indeed greatly please their mates, and make highly successful marriages with all the temperaments. But watch out for thorns.

Rational-Artisan: The Rationals' lack of possessiveness and reluctance to interfere with their mates makes a very nice fit with the Artisans' freedom-loving nature. In the SPs, NTs find mates just as irreverent as they, just as willing to ignore convention, and just as results-oriented. NTs admire SPs their interest in tools and tool skills, and at the same time they find in SPs an aptitude for fun, improvisation, spontaneity—even mischief—which can help NTs get out of their heads and show them how to let go and wing it. Rationals need to learn how to play, and Artisans love to spread their playfulness around. Of course, if pushed too hard SP fun and games can come to seem frivolous to NTs. But, more than this, SPs can also disappoint their NT mates by their general lack of interest in the internal world. NTs enjoy expounding their theories and hypotheses and describing their latest inventions and paradigms to their mates—at times, in fact, these breakfast-table conversations can turn into lengthy, highly detailed lectures. But it is very difficult for NTs to hold an SP's attention on such abstract subjects, and Rationals are quick to note when interest wanes and their mates begin turning the conversation to more concrete, down-to-earth matters.

Rational-Guardian: While Guardians won't usually take the lead on merrymaking, they do offer Rationals one invaluable gift as a mate: a stable, reliable center in the home. Preoccupied as they are in their ivory towers, NTs often lose touch with the everyday workings of family life, and an SJ mate happily steps in to see that things get done and that the details of running the home are taken care of. SJs also see to it that NTs have a social life—not one as varied and exciting as that whipped up by an SP, perhaps, but a full, enjoyable, often family-oriented social life nonetheless. NTs and SJs share a strong sense of loyalty to close friends and family, and SJs make sure their NT mates remember to take part in the social functions and family traditions they might otherwise forget. Rationals need to be reminded to relate to people, and Guardians love to help their mates remember their social obligations. If pushed too far, of course, SJ social reminders can sound to NTs like nagging, and they will grimly protect their autonomy from SJ bossiness. But a more important problem is that Guardians, no matter how intelligent in their concrete logistical roles, have little interest in the Rationals' abstract world of systems analysis and technological design. NTs may not need a great deal of intellectual interaction with their mates, particularly if they are able to discuss their brainstorms with their colleagues at work. A satisfying social life, family life, and sexual life may be enough for them. But Rationals with concrete mates (Guardians or Artisans) sometimes sense they're missing some vital connection.

Rational-Rational: Two Rationals married to each other do not have this problem. Two Rationals are likely to be fascinated by each other's research and discoveries, by their tools and technologies, and when they find the time to come together they have intense discussions, logical, esoteric, critical, and competitive. This competition can get rough at times—NTs will go for the jugular in the heat of argument—but the main trouble in NT-NT marriages is just the opposite: that each tends to stay absorbed in his or her own cognitive world, each forgetting to notice the other, and thus doubling the distance to be overcome in the relationship. Rationals married to other Rationals need to learn how to get away from their work and meet each other on a personal level.

Rational-Idealist: Marriage to an Idealist is probably the best option for a Rational. NTs and NFs share an abiding interest in the abstract, internal world, and so can find with each other a companionship of ideas, a mutual love of insights and concepts, even a similar fluency with abstract language, that bond them securely. At the same time, NFs bring a personal warmth to their relationships which appeals to the analytical, self-controlled

NTs, and helps them put aside their work and take time for a personal life.

Conflicts, of course, are inherent in both of these areas of Rational-Idealist attraction. If sharing ideas with an NT means arguing over definitions, logical categories, and necessary consequences, it is onerous to NFs, who are willing to engage in such debates for only short periods of time, and only if the discussion remains friendly. And conflict between the NT's cool resistance to showing emotion and the NF's desire for emotional expressiveness is an endless problem in their relationships, though one that is usually overshadowed by these two temperaments' rare compatibility.

If theory holds, this compatibility is enhanced in Rational-Idealist marriages when the other factors of personality, the expressive or reserved (E-I) social attitude and the scheduling or probing mindset (J-P), are complementary. Here are four NT-NF pairings that illustrate the paradigm.

Fieldmarshals and **Healers** would seem to fit well together. Whether in the military or not, the outgoing and schedule-minded Fieldmarshals (ENTJs) are natural mobilizers, that is, they're itching to get their hands on several armies so they can mobilize their forces and conduct their campaigns as they should be conducted—with an eye to long-term strategies and their derivative tactics, logistics, and consequences. What in the seclusive and probing Healer (INFP) seems to fit so well with the Fieldmarshal? First note their one point of similarity. In their questing phase, Healers also become leaders of armies (as did Joan of Arc), and launch their campaigns with missionary zeal. In their saintly or monastic phase, however, Healers can offer their imperious Fieldmarshal mates a welcome respite from the wars, perhaps sharing with them their quiet spirituality, their desire for inner-harmony, and their personal sensitivity.

Masterminds and **Champions** should match up best. Wishing to control events, the reserved and scheduling Masterminds (INTJs) are probably more systematic than all other types in choosing a mate. Mate selection must be done in a logical and methodical way, with each candidate required to meet certain criteria, or else be quickly dropped. It may well be that the stereotype impugning the Rational approach to mating has as its target the thorough-going Mastermind. In any event, Masterminds will rarely go wrong with an expressive and probing Champion (ENFP). On the one hand, Masterminds and Champions speak the same language of ideas and fantasies (INTJs, for all their rationality, have a sometimes secret passion for fairy tales and mythical stories). But ENFPs also complement INTJs significantly, bringing to the marriage an enthusiastic and effervescent enjoyment and wonderment about life—the very antithesis of the tightly focused, thoughtful exactitude of the master of contingency planning.

Inventors and **Counselors** are most likely to find great satisfaction together. The inventor, broadly conceived, is bent on replacing whatever tool, operation, or enterprise now existing with a better one. Out to exercise their ingenuity in the world, the outgoing and probing Inventors (ENTPs) are of necessity iconoclastic and tend to get into a bit of trouble with the custodians of the establishment, who usually are not all that pleased to see the tried-and-true device set aside for the better mousetrap. Counselors (INFJs) share this desire to better things, though it is better personal relationships and the development of the self, not better tools and technologies, that inspire their inventiveness. In the seclusive and scheduling Counselor lies the soul of the advisor—the personal guide to a more harmonious life—and the irreverent, sometimes antagonistic ENTP greatly admires the INFJ's ability to help other people find their way.

Architects and **Teachers** are apt share a rare compatibility. The reserved and probing Architects (INTPs), all-too-easily lost in their abstract designs and desire for coherence, can despair of ever finding a mate who will listen to them and appreciate their visions. Fortunately, the expressive and schedule-minded Teachers (ENFJs), brimming with ideas in their own right, are catalysts of the personal growth process in others, able to bring out the best in others with inspiring personal enthusiasm. All the Idealists seem to have this facilitative capability in some degree, but Teachers seem to have it in abundance—and Architects find this combination of intellectual spark and personal sparkle quite irresistible.

Regardless of the particular pairing, however, and even more than the other types, Rationals need to be appreciated for the many qualities they bring to a marriage, and not criticized for the qualities they lack. Because of their single-minded, logical focus and their fiercely independent character, Rationals are easily seen as cold and uncaring, and thus they become the natural targets of Pygmalion Projects to make them more playful, more law-abiding, or more emotionally expressive, that is, to re-shape them into Playmates, Helpmates, or Soulmates. But if their spouses—of whatever temperament—could recognize the Rationals' focus and independence, not to mention their skepticism, efficiency, resolve, composure, logic, yearning for achievement, and thirst for knowledge, as positive traits, indeed, as the qualities that attracted them in the first place, then Rationals could be accepted as the excellent mates they are.

—In Conclusion—

None of the temperaments are immune from the Pygmalion impulse. Do not Artisans urge their mates to lighten up? Do not Guardians work on their mates to be more responsible? Do not Idealists try to inspire their mates to be more soulful? And do not Rationals pressure their mates to be more logical? If it can be assumed that Pygmalion Projects are an inevitable part of any mating, then the task for all of us is to keep our coercion as loving and sympathetic and playful as possible. If we cannot—if our manipulation becomes bullying or nagging or exhorting or intimidating—then we have to expect our mates to defend themselves, and what might be called the "battle of the types" is joined, a conflict much more serious than the "battle of the sexes."

8

Parenting

*Let us beware and beware and beware...of having an ideal for our children.
So doing, we damn them.*

—D.H. Lawrence

The Pygmalion Project, almost unavoidable in mating, is perhaps even more of a temptation in parenting. Most parents believe quite sincerely that their responsibility is to raise their children, to take an active part in guiding them, or perhaps in steering them, on their way to becoming mature adults. Even more than the husband-wife relationship, the parent-child relationship has this serious factor of interpersonal manipulation seemingly built into it, as though part of the job description of Mother or Father. Unfortunately, this hands-on model of parental responsibility—well-intentioned though it may be—all too often ends in struggle and rebellion. The truth is that kids of different temperament will develop in entirely different directions, no matter what the parents do to discourage one direction in favor of another. To manipulate growth is a risky business. In our natural zeal to discourage moral weeds from springing up we risk discouraging mental flowers from growing, our parental herbicides killing the good and the bad indiscriminately.

The root of the problem is that parents tend to assume that their children are pretty much the same as they are—extensions of their own personality who will naturally follow in their footsteps. But the temperament hypothesis suggests that, in many cases, children are fundamentally different from their parents and need to develop in entirely different directions, so that their mature personalities can take their rightful form. Indeed, parents of other temperament who assume that they share their child's experience of life—that they know what their child wants or needs, thinks or feels—are usually quite wrong. Or worse. Acting on this assumption, well-meaning parents are very likely to disconfirm the different messages their children are sending, just as they are likely to attribute their own attitudes to their children, and perhaps even to intrude on the private space of their children with their own agendas. Such parents fail to realize that, from the beginning, their children are very much their own persons—Artisans, Guardians, Idealists, Rationals—and that no amount of disconfirmation, attribution, or

252

intrusion can change their inborn structure.

How then are we to take up the task of parenting? We dare not make it a Pygmalion Project, giving in to our all-too-human desire to shape our loved ones in our own image. If our children were born to be like us—chips off the old block—then they need no shaping; if not, then shaping can only have disappointing results. No, our project ought not be that of Pygmalion, but of Mother Nature, which means we must allow our children to become actually what they are potentially; in other words, we must let nature take its course by giving our children ample room to grow into their true, mature character.

Maturation

A mature individual is one whose latent attitudes and actions have become fully developed and habitual. A mature Artisan, for instance, is recognizably artistic, as Plato believed, hedonic, as Aristotle believed, and sanguine, as Galen believed. And more than that, the mature Artisan is changeable, innovative, aesthetic, uninhibited, exploiting, and probing, as the other contributors to personology, from Paracelsus to Myers, have told us. How different this pattern is from what these contributors said of the mature Guardian, who was described as having common sense, as proprietary, melancholic, industrious, traditional, economical, solemn, cautious, and scheduling. The same holds for the mature Idealist, who was described as philosophic, ethical, choleric, passionate, doctrinaire, religious, sensitive, receptive, and friendly; and for the mature Rational, who was said to be logical, dialectical, phlegmatic, curious, skeptical, theoretical, calm, marketing, and tough-minded. These four mature types are so different in their character that they can hardly be confused with one another.

The first signs of these larger patterns of character are observable quite early in life. Mother Nature will no more allow a child to come into this world temperamentally undifferentiated and formless—a blank slate—than she would allow a snowflake to be asymmetrical. Babies in the crib show incipient dispositions—parents and pediatric nurses call them "active" babies or "fretful" babies, "alert" babies or "calm," babies, and so on. Then by the time they begin to interact socially children are showing unmistakable signs of having distinct traits of character. Perhaps easiest to observe are differences in gregariousness. Some infants and toddlers are outgoing and easy around strangers, while some are shy and reserved, preferring to peek from behind their mother's leg when introduced to people. Also, when children begin pursuing their own goals—exploring the sooty fireplace, for instance—they are observably utilitarian or cooperative in their behavior. Some little ones seem to go straightaway for what they want, with no regard for the constraints that might alter their course or delay their action. And they can be visibly frustrated by having to obey a parent or a teacher's rules, and will test the limits again and again. Other children seem to comply with rules easily, happily, and seem more comfortable when pleasing the adults around them by behaving as their elders wish. In the case of language, however, differences in abstractness or concreteness take more time to become recognizable. At first a child's words are relatively vague and undifferentiated. Later they become more defined, more specific, and more revealing of the child's personality.

Let us remember that maturation in all these facets of character is an evolving, unfolding, branching, differentiating, expanding process. The change progresses from gross to fine, so that personality, like anatomy, takes on more and more distinct form. Infants look somewhat alike at birth, at least to the casual observer, but by the time they reach their late teens their bodies have taken on a much more mature form and so, in many ways, have their characters.

Now, I learned from organismic psychology that we do not mature as a function of time alone, but that maturation is stimulus induced, which is to say that our character growth must be stimulated, aroused, awakened, and beckoned to come forth into the social environment. Indeed, in the absence of stimulation there is no maturation. This means that the task of parents is stimulation. But stimulation of a special kind: stimulation that is both timely and relevant to whatever attitudes and actions are ready to emerge. In psychology this is called "the teachable moment"; in enterprise, "the window of opportunity."

This means that overseeing Mother Nature's project—maturation—requires parents to become child watchers, not child shapers, acting only when they detect a teachable moment or opportunity to encourage the growth of some attitude or action that is consistent with the child's temperament. To do this, however, parents must understand what these latent attitudes and actions are. Only then can they find ways to help them unfold and develop. If parents do not know what end to seek—their child's innate character structure—then they cannot know what means will help stimulate it. Parents must be able to answer the question, "What kind of person is my child, and what can I do to help him or her grow in that direction?"

Basic Differences

In trying to understand children of any age we must bear in mind that they, like their parents, will lean toward becoming either utilitarian or cooperative in how they use the myriad tools of civilization, and either concrete or abstract in how they communicate the continuous messages of civil life. Learning how to utilize effective ways and means takes a good deal of practice, as does learning how to cooperate with others, so practicing either of these requires some neglect of the other. The same holds for practice in communicating: if concrete thought and speech come naturally to a child and are practiced most of the time, abstract thought and speech have to be neglected, and vice versa. Children begin practicing their particular mix of these two dimensions of character as soon as they can use words meaningfully and tools effectively, so that by around the age of four it starts becoming clear that the child is well on his or her way to being either concretely utilitarian (SP Artisan), abstractly utilitarian (NT Rational), concretely cooperative (SJ Guardian), or abstractly cooperative (NF Idealist). To help keep these four combinations of traits clearly in mind, please refer to the matrix at the side.

Words

Abstract   Concrete

	Abstract	Concrete
Cooperative	**NF** Cooperator	**SJ** Cooperator
Utilitarian	**NT** Utilitarian	**SP** Utilitarian

Abstract headers: Abstract / Concrete over each column; left labels Abstract / Concrete within cells.

Tools

Cooperative

Utilitarian

First consider tool use. When bid by parents and teachers to use tools in a conventional way, utilitarian children (Artisans and Rationals) usually wonder—and some of the bolder ones even venture to ask—"why that way?" or "what's the use of doing it that way?" For example, to use their knives and forks in a socially correct manner at dinner means little to SP and NT children, so if they act that way it is to keep out of trouble and not an admission that it makes sense to them. Conventions in eating are, after all, arbitrary, and differ radically in different cultures. The mere fact that a given tool is used in a conventional way is not sufficient reason for the utilitarians to use it that way; indeed, it doesn't bother SP and NT children at all to use tools in unconventional ways, and they don't give a second thought to ignoring traditions if they can get away with it.

On the other hand, that a given tool is to be used in a conventional or traditional way, or simply because such use is looked upon with favor by their elders, is usually sufficient reason for Guardian and Idealist children to conform. Cooperative children are not at all comfortable with questioning authority and testing limits, and they seem to want to know that they are pleasing others with their respect for convention. Little SJs and NFs want to do what's expected of them, and to fit in with the people around them, and so they are inclined to give great power to adults and their rules, and are chary of going their own way and trying out what might be useful changes in how to do things.

Because of their ready cooperation, Guardian and Idealist children soon become sophisticated about rule-governed social transactions—about traditions, customs, procedures, and protocols. Actually, Artisan children also catch on easily to social conventions, if only to sidestep them. While SJ and NF children learn quickly how to obey and enforce the rules, to the delight of their elders, SP children learn quickly how to appear to obey them while they try to get around them, often to the dismay of their elders. In either case, Guardian, Idealist, and Artisan children are increasingly aware of the rules governing social transactions. It is only Rational children who are not very interested in conventions, unless they make sense, in which case they are interested because such usage makes sense and not because it is conventional. This temperament-based disinterest makes catching on to the conventions a slow and sometimes regressive process for little NTs, making their parents wonder at times if maybe they aren't very bright.

The development of word usage looks a lot different than the development of tool usage. Artisan children, their word usage predominately concrete, are very much like Guardian children in this respect, and nothing like their utilitarian counterparts, the Rational children. Also, both SPs and SJs tend to speak primarily to other children rather than to adults, and they talk about toys and tools, and how to play with them and make things with them. On the abstract side, Idealist children are not at all similar to their cooperative cousins, the Guardian children, in the way they talk, but are more like Rational children in showing interest in talking about imaginative things, in hearing and reading stories, and in talking and listening to adults. Stories especially are the NT and NF children's joy—and from very early in their lives—but particularly stories of fantasy and far-flung imagination, stories such as fables, myths, and fairy tales, stories filled with magic and sorcery, and with metaphors and symbols. Rational and Idealist kids can be captured by such fanciful stories even before they have the vocabulary to understand what they are hearing, in some cases before the age of two, and will often ask their parents to repeat them again and again.

The net effect of all of this exposure to make-believe is that the fantasy life and abstract vocabulary of Rational and Idealist children grow faster than that of Artisan and Guardian children. Of course, concrete children want to hear stories too, but they tend to prefer straightforward stories about the familiar and the factual, stories with lots of action and realistic details, adventure stories and animal stories, folk tales and Mother Goose stories—"The Three Little Pigs" is a good example. And yet even these stories don't have quite the pull for little SPs and SJs that any and all stories do for NTs and NFs. In fact, if given the chance, concrete children will rather easily abandon story time for play time or activity time.

In the same way, because Artisan and Guardian youngsters spend their time playing with toys and making things with tools, they acquire a concrete vocabulary and a repertoire of instrumental actions earlier than Idealists and Rationals do. Of course, the relatively few NF and NT children found here and there certainly enjoy toys and handicrafts, but their abstract style of play is markedly different from that of SP and SJs. For example, toys for a concrete child are likely to retain their character—a truck remains a truck, to be used to move dirt, or to deliver things, or to run up and down a road. An NT or NF child, on the other hand, might well turn the truck into a submarine, or a dinosaur, or a flying chariot. And a tricycle becomes an ice cream maker, and large cardboard boxes become architectural spaces, and a wardrobe cabinet becomes a passageway to a secret world (as in C.S. Lewis's *Narnia* stories), and on and on.

Again, what is the task—indeed, the responsibility—of parents? First, they must bring themselves to abandon the perspective that says "my children are, underneath, just like me." And then they must begin to acquaint themselves with the nature of the character differences in as much detail as they can manage. Only by doing so can they hope to facilitate their children's growth rather than impede it.

Let's begin by looking at the four kinds of character in children, starting with the Artisans, and followed by the Guardians, Idealists, and Rationals.

The Artisan Child

I fear Winston [Churchill] thinks me very strict, but I really think he goes out too much & I do object to late parties for him. He is so excitable. But he goes back to school on Monday. Meantime he is affectionate & not seriously naughty...except to use bad language....Entre nous I do not feel very sorry for he certainly is a handful.

—Duchess of Marlborough

Galen called Plato's Artisans the "Sanguines" because of their obvious good cheer and their irrepressible love of excitement. SP children are indeed excitable, able to get excited more quickly and to stay excited longer than other types of children. But just as they are easily wound up, so too are they easily bored, and thus seem ever on the lookout for some sort of risky business or mischief to get into, just to keep things interesting. At any rate, their excitability is apparent from the start and is the temperamental soil from which spring all their mature Artisan character traits.

These children shine in action, and if they have the opportunity they quickly take to the physical, in-the-moment action roles of Operator and Entertainer—roles of the kind requiring skill in what I have called "tactical artistry." The entire range of fine and practical arts, and of competitive games and sports, will grab budding Artisans—they need physical movement and novelty, and they love contests. The other kinds of intelligent roles—logistical, strategic, diplomatic—can wait until the SP child has developed a positive self-image, from which he or she can branch out. And it is fruitless for parents to count on the schools, public or private, to provide models for the tactical roles. Better to take on this task themselves, or find role-models in the community, rather than get after the school to change its curriculum. It won't because it can't.

Improvising artful works and actions, as well as handling people and equipment, are all activities that SP children find compelling, and should be introduced to them as early as possible. In any of these activities, however, Artisan children are likely to give their attention for hours on end, and then to stop and move on to the next thing that interests them. They can spend day after day on a musical instrument, they can spend hours finger painting, they can manipulate their toys over and over—only to lose interest completely in those paints, or toys, or that instrument tomorrow. Those who do not lose interest will practice endlessly on whatever technique they are drawn toward, and can go on to become outstanding in the four tactical role variants, as Promoters, Crafters, Performers, and Composers.

To be proud of themselves even very young Artisans must be graceful in some form of tactical behavior. Parents would do well to see to it that their little SPs have many chances to develop some kind of fluency of physical action, so that they can see themselves, and be seen by others, as artistic in some manner. At the same time, parents need to be careful not to make their SP children show their skills until they are ready. In learning to skate or to surf, to sing or to dance or to play the guitar, whatever, young Artisans will often practice out of the sight of their peers, wanting to avoid their critical scrutiny, and to hide their clumsy actions from others. On the other hand, once they have achieved some mastery of a given action, they are thrilled to show others how well they can perform, their self-esteem rising with their artistry in action.

As for self-respect, SP children regard themselves highly in the degree that they are bold and daring. Young Artisans feel guilty when they are seen as scaredy cats by other children, and so feel compelled to risk themselves to prove their boldness to their peers. Little SPs have to take up every challenge and answer every taunt—to be the first to jump into the pool. SP children are the first to do dangerous tricks on their bikes or skateboards, the first to try on mother's makeup, and as teenagers they are the first to start smoking and drinking in order to show their bravado. The more reckless Artisan teenagers will even play games of chicken with their cars, sometimes with disastrous results. Here the parent of an SP faces a dilemma: too little restraint can lead to injury, too much restraint can lead to timidity and self-contempt. All things considered, boldness in Artisan children is better encouraged than put down, otherwise they will have little respect for themselves and may take up destructive habits. Parents, especially the Idealists and Guardians, must therefore steel themselves to permit more risk than they feel comfortable with in order to validate boldness in their Artisan children.

Like adult Artisans, youthful Artisans are self-confident in the degree they see themselves as being adaptable. This certainly does not mean conforming; rather, it means that young, self-confident SPs see themselves as able to fit smoothly into any situation that they care to enter, whether with their peer groups or with adults in charge (teachers, coaches, authorities, and so on). Young Artisans gradually become more and more sophisticated in interacting with others, so that by the time they are teenagers they have learned to turn on the charm or play it cool and get their way more easily than the rest. Again, this is not going along with your agenda as much as it is giving you the impression that they are on the same wave length as you, that they know, as they say, "where you're coming from."

In their own families, however, Artisans from infancy on can be seen testing the limits of their immediate environment—and not being very charming about it. If, for example, parents say "no" to something their two-year-old SP does, then the two-year-old must do it again, to see if he or she can get away with it. The little SP's self-confidence depends on it. Of course, other types in early childhood will test the limits too, but not with the recklessness and persistency of Artisans. Like colts in a corral, SPs have to kick each and every rail in the fence to see if it will give way. And so there are two sides to the development of self-confidence in Artisan children: they want to be smooth and sophisticated outside the home, but are often defiant and contrary with their parents.

Recall that Zuckerman installed the "Sensation Seeking Personality" in the research agenda of many psychologists in the 1950s. The Artisan's search for sensation, or better, for stimulation, does not wait for adolescence, since even very young Artisans seek it, some with vigor. As children they are not content to be confined in a play pen or backyard, but want to be free to roam where the impulse take them. Little SPs respond to sensory details, noting vividness and variety of colors, sounds, tastes, and so on, which means they are apt to enjoy coloring books, music, and to be what are called "good eaters." They are also likely to enjoy animals, although they will often be rough with them, just as they are usually rather hard on their toys and clothes, and should be given sturdy, well-made objects that can stand a lot of wear and tear.

As they get older, Artisan kids keep their eyes peeled for something exciting to do, something to arouse their senses, something to get the adrenaline flowing. This search, by the way, explains in part why Artisans go for wheeled toys of all sorts so early in life, and why they never really give up their wheels. For example, they are the first to go for skateboards and the last to stop using them, just as their childhood tricycles and bicycles turn into the dirt bikes and motorcycles of their adult years. Wheels bring them the enjoyable sensation of going elsewhere fast. Indeed, of all the types, the Artisans are most likely to leave home early in search of thrills, and in some cases they run away from home in pre-adolescence. SPs are also more likely than the other types to seek the stimulating pleasures they see adults indulging in, which helps to explain why so many of them get into drugs and sex much earlier than the other types.

Most children, even some of the Guardians, are impulsive when they are very young. But Artisan children are far more impulsive than any of the other types, and that impulsivity rarely declines, but in some cases even increases with age. For this reason many psychologists have come to see impulsivity as the most distinguishing characteristic of this type. Artisans act on their impulses because they trust them. We are all told to look before we leap, but looking takes time and requires us to quell our impulse until we see a safe line of movement. Looking before leaping is for those who do not trust their impulses. It certainly is not for Artisans, who will go headlong into dangerous situations, often resulting in close shaves, scrapes, and even serious accidents.

To show off is gratifying to some of the other types of children, but it is more than gratifying to Artisans—it is exhilarating to them. They hunger for chances to stand out, to make a big splash, to hot dog it, and they are more likely to brag about their accomplishments than others. Not that the other types, when young, do not brag, but Artisans can keep on bragging clear up into their adult lives. They seem to have a yearning to impress others, to influence others, to have impact on them.

Oriented as they are to the here and now, Artisans must have fun every day and all day long. In a sense enjoyment is compulsive with them. Other types can sometimes forgo immediate pleasures for later ones. But not Artisans. This day, this hour, this moment must be spent in joyful action. They insist on it, they demand it, and they press their parents for it without regard to the trouble it causes their parents; indeed, it is the trouble their parents have in denying them their immediate gratification that they count on to get them what they want.

The fun of living in the moment means not paying attention to schedules or planning for the future. Thus Artisan children may seem unconcerned about whether, for instance, they are on time for school, and they may have to be reminded to get dressed, to come to dinner, to take out the trash, to do their homework, and so on. Having a good time for an SP child also means getting into messes—leave one of these children in the yard even for a moment and he or she somehow manages to get dirty. And Artisans are less likely than other types to understand demands for clean rooms or neat and orderly closets. Their rooms are likely to be a jumble of toys, clothes, and valued objects, collected from here and there, all in a rat's nest; but, to these children, just as they want it. They are too busy having fun to want to take time to hang and fold their clothes just so, and, anyway, "What difference does it make?" they ask. Such nonsense is a waste of time when a person could be off having fun. This carefree, hedonic attitude often leads to a scolding from exasperated parents, but usually to no avail. Early on SP children learn to be indifferent to such reprimands, which usually come too many and too soon.

This press for enjoyment in the moment may be fueled by the optimistic nature with which Artisans seem to be endowed. So sure are they that what they are about to do will be fun that it is difficult for them to wait. They seem to feel lucky, so that they look forward to the next move with eager anticipation. This will be a winning shot, a great ride, a thrilling leap. The story of the twin boys, a pessimist and an optimist, may illustrate the point. On Christmas day each year the pessimist can find nothing good about his presents, his brother nothing bad. The parents are fed up with this, so they pull all stops to make it impossible for their pessimist to be disappointed and their optimist to be greatly pleased: the pessimist is given a gilded bicycle, the optimist only a pile of horse manure. Yet the parents fail in their intent. The pessimist cries uncontrollably when he finds a grease spot on his bike; the optimist is found excitedly digging into the pile of manure while repeating delightedly "there's gotta be a horse here somewhere!"

The Guardian Child

I loved going to school at Ashley Hall, where I grew up quite a bit. I was a true square, making good marks and never breaking the rules....[That year] my friends and I eased very gently into traveling in a group with both boys and girls. It was so much easier than it is now. Drugs, sex, and violence were not constantly thrust at us by television.
—Barbara Bush

Galen called Plato's Guardians the "Melancholics" no doubt because of their prevailing mood of serious concern. SJ children are concerned about many things, keeping their toys nice, picking up their rooms, helping around the house, pleasing their parents and teachers, and at times this concern can turn to worry and fear that they aren't being responsible enough. Presumably Guardians are born that way, to be the so-called "good little girls and boys," which makes their concerned temperament the foundation for the maturation of all their traits of character.

Guardian children, even very young ones, are busy beavers, taking upon themselves the role of Conservator in their home and family, and of Administrator of their friends' activities and productions—the two sides of what I have called "logistical reliability." Fortunately, there is plenty of role modeling around for this kind of behavior since these are the very things that many of their parents, relatives, and teachers are engaged in. And it is quite natural for SJ children to copy their elders in these actions, so that by the time they start school they are already well versed in these logistical roles. There is no point in providing models for the other kinds of roles—tactical, diplomatic, strategic—because Guardian children won't take to them very well, and are likely to feel bad about themselves if expected to practice them successfully. It would be wiser to wait until these children make themselves comfortable in the logistical role variants of Supervisor, Inspector, Provider, and Protector before introducing other kinds of role practice.

Guardian children are proud of themselves when they show their elders that they can be depended on to do what is expected of them, that they are trustworthy and accountable for all that they should or should not do. In school, those teachers, even pre-school teachers, who are sensitive to personality differences find that SJ children are their helpers, siding with them in advancing the teachers' agendas, and helping them keep control of class proceedings. Indeed, most teachers (most teachers are Guardians) can count on their Guardian students to be good examples for the other kids in class, who are usually less cooperative. In kindergarten, for example, the little SJs (often nearly half the class) will sit quietly and wait for instructions when their teacher asks them to, whereas the little SPs (also nearly half the class) are busy discharging their irresistible impulses by tussling or chatting or roaming around. And the Guardians' dependable attitude lasts all through school, with these students most likely becoming hall monitors, crossing guards, student aids, class officers, team managers, and the like.

In the home, Guardian children also build their self-esteem on their dependability. Little SJs usually respond well to the assignment of specific responsibilities, such as emptying the wastebaskets, setting the table, shoveling snow, doing yardwork, sorting wash, and so on. Of course, they need tasks within their ability to perform, but they tend to enjoy routine maintenance chores, and their source of pride is the approval given by adults for performing these activities reliably. SJ children thus respond well to praise, such as "You did that just the way I wanted," or "Your work is very neat." Doing their best loses appeal if adult approval is not forthcoming. By the way, and far more than the other three types, SJ children will respond to scolding and negative criticism, which can make them try all the more.

Guardian self-respect seems to be enhanced when they are serving others. Even as young as five, Guardians can be seen doing good deeds, not only for their parents and teachers, but also for their siblings and friends. At home they are quick to ask their mother to let them lend a hand with preparing the meals, with doing household chores, and with helping bathe or feed a little brother or sister. And in school Guardian children vie with each other to see who can be of more service to the teacher or the other students, something that little Artisans and Rationals would rarely, if ever, think of doing. On the other hand, Guardian self-respect can fade away rapidly and be replaced by guilt feelings if they have been less than helpful. It is usually plain to see from the outset that SJ children are far more prone to such guilt feelings than others, particularly the SPs, who seem to feel no compunction at all about not pitching in. No doubt the Guardians' beneficent attitude stabilizes parent-child and teacher-pupil interactions, and with SJs making up, on average, nearly half the student body at school, and half the children at home, teachers and parents need not ask for a more solidifying and stabilizing social force.

Self-confidence in Guardian children grows when their elders award them visible signs of approval. Guardian elementary school teachers, wanting to build self-confidence, paste or stamp all sorts of insignias on their students' papers and folders, not to mention on their faces, hands, and arms. It is doubtful whether their Artisan and Rational students are honored by such laurels, but most Guardian children are. For example, SJ first graders are delighted with a gold star on their forehead for never being tardy, say, or for doing their homework neatly. However, just as these signs of praise increase their self-confidence, signs of censure such as demerits can plant in Guardian youngsters seeds of self doubt and fear. It is very different with utilitarian Artisans and Rationals, who are largely oblivious to others' criticism of their deportment. For that matter, SP kids are not averse to being seen as mischievous, as rowdies and cutups, and NT kids don't mind being considered wits and nerds. But self-confidence in little Guardians depends in great part on being commended for good behavior, so that by their teen years they covet their respectability even more, while the Artisans and Rationals care about it even less.

Guardian children do not seek stimulation the way Artisan children do. After all, there are risks involved in getting into highly stimulating circumstances—the greater the stimulation, the greater the risk. What Guardians are looking for, as soon as they have sufficient mobility to seek anything, is security, and for this reason I have called the Guardians the "Security Seeking Personality." Thus, if Artisan children are the most impetuous of the four temperaments, Guardian children are the most cautious, looking twice and even thrice before they leap, and therefore seldom leaping. Where Artisan children are drawn to the exciting (and often elicit) places in their neighborhood, and of course to their school's athletic field, Guardian children tend to play in their own yards or in safely supervised public places such as city parks and recreation centers, the YMCA, or in and around their home rooms at school. In the same way, the speedy wheeled toys that so capture Artisan children are less attractive to Guardian children, who prefer to work on home crafts, cooking, sewing, and making objects from wood, cloth, and yarn.

Guardians of any age just can't seem to get enough security, no matter how much of it they have amassed during their lifetimes. So the question arises, how early in their lives does this search begin? The answer is, very early in life. Two-year-old Guardians, even the more gregarious ones, are already far more cautious than their siblings and playmates of other type, and they seem to worry and fret more than the rest. Also, they prefer to stay closer to home. There's no place like home for Guardian children, and if they go on some sort of trip they are likely to feel homesick more quickly than the rest, and to want to cut the vacation short. Even those SJ boys with athletic build, no matter how physically powerful they are, are prone to homesickness.

Like Dorothy in *The Wizard of Oz*, Guardians see home as a haven where they can be safe, the establishment where ceremonies, rituals, and traditions are most carefully observed. Guardian children are likely to enjoy social gatherings at home with their parents and relatives, and they get a lot of enjoyment from the traditional holidays, such as Christmas and Thanksgiving. SJ children also respond happily to well-established, clearly-defined routines that bring them predictability. They like tidy closets, their bureau drawers are apt to contain neatly folded clothes, and their toys are arranged carefully on shelves. Basically, knowing the familiar agenda at home or school and not being asked to deviate from it gives SJ children a feeling of safety, whereas constant changes, confusion, and crises can cause them distress and arouse feelings of insecurity. Because of this, and more than the other types, Guardian children need to know that what is so today will be so tomorrow. For example, these children need the steadiness of parental firmness and agreement. Parental expectations need not make sense, but they must be clear and constant. To be caught between a strict parent and a lenient one can upset them. In the same way, frequent residential changes can be especially unsettling to little SJs; they do better when raised in the same neighborhood, school system, and community, and with friends who grew up with them. Contrast this attitude with that of SPs of the same age, who not only resist situational constancy, but are eager for changes and surprises. Thus, changing teachers at midyear can be difficult for an SJ child, while an SP might well perk up with the new opportunities.

Guardian children put their trust in authority, and this trust never wanes. While the other types might trust their impulses, their intuition, or their reason, Guardian children seem to want to trust authority, and they expect their parents, principals, teachers, coaches, even their den mothers and troop leaders, baby-sitters and chaperones, to be in charge and to say what's right and wrong. SJ children are most comfortable following the rules, doing what they're told, meeting the expectations and the demands of those in authority. Indeed, and even more than the Idealists, Guardian children want their actions and attitudes to be authorized, sanctioned, stamped with approval—in a word, "legitimate." And, like their continual, purposive movement toward security, it is difficult for Guardian children to get enough legitimacy, enough sense that they have permission to act and are pleasing those adults above them.

More than being secure and legitimate, Guardians, of any age, must belong. There are few loners among Guardian children. Indeed, SJs seem to have a lifelong hunger for belonging, and the more memberships—and the more recognized status in their social groups—they can collect along their path to maturity, the better. SJ children begin early on to satisfy this hunger, joining school clubs, scout troops, youth fellowship groups, and the like. Of course, the first social group for any of us is the family, and Guardian children to take to family life like ducks to water. They get along well with large numbers of brothers and sisters, and they greatly enjoy relating to their extended family, their aunts, uncles, grandparents, and cousins. They also enjoy stories of family history and remember these stories when they have grown up. To be a member of a family is important to all children, certainly, but to Guardian children it can be a matter of survival. Divorce is particularly devastating to them, and teenage and pre-teenage suicides are far more prevalent among Guardians than all the other types combined. Very likely this is because when SJ children feel abandoned, whether or not they are really abandoned, their despair is so great that they abandon themselves, not to self-destructive behavior as do many Artisans, but to literal self-destruction.

Although such extreme measures are rare, SJ children are quite often the family's worry warts. They start out pretty early in life expecting bad things to happen. Seeking security as they do, they seem to have an inborn sense of the boy scout's motto—"Be Prepared"—and so feel it better to expect the worst than to be caught off guard. And when bad things do actually occur, as they will in anyone's life, they but confirm the Guardians' faith in pessimism as the safest attitude to cling to. Now this gloomy outlook is understandable in those cases in which a child is subjected to a number of serious setbacks, but not when setbacks are normal and infrequent. And even though the latter is the case for most Guardian children, they tend to anticipate all sorts of things going wrong.

However, pessimism is usually not apparent in Guardian children because they are likely to keep their fears to themselves. They are quick to learn that showing willingness to bear up under adversity is more likely to gain sympathy, reassurance, and service than complaining. Little SJs happily let their siblings do the griping, vaguely aware that griping gets them nothing but parental disgust. SJ kids have troubles, too, and want sympathetic attention from their parents, but they go after it by letting their parents know that they can put up with being in pain or sad or worried without complaint. Such stoicism can show up at remarkably early ages in Guardians, who find out that the squeaky wheel gets the grease, provided that the squeaks are not too loud and the wheel keeps on turning.

The Idealist Child

I was a madly gay little girl: I had fits of rage during which my face turned purple....I have often wondered what were the causes of these outbursts and what significance they had. I believe they can be partly explained by an impetuous vitality and by a lack of all moderation which I have never grown out of completely....An unbridgeable chasm separated the things I loved from the things I hated.

—Simone de Beauvoir

Plato's Idealist children are the enthusiastic ones, those whom Galen spoke of as "Choleric" because their feelings, whether positive or negative, are easily aroused and sometimes expressed with surprising vehemence. Even at an early age Idealist children seem to be fired with a passionate intensity, and are hardly able to keep quiet about their thoughts and feelings. Indeed, NFs are likely to begin to talk early, and expressive NFs may seem to their parents never to stop talking. Reserved NFs have these same strong feelings, but tend to be more shy about expressing them, and may have some difficulty communicating, especially outside the home. In either case, however, the highly enthusiastic nature of Idealist children is clear, and forms the temperamental basis of their adult actions and attitudes.

Although Idealist children can occasionally be irascible, they also can be charming—not the smooth charm of the Artisan, but a personal warmth that communicates sincere interest in understanding others, both peers and adults. NF children seem to have a natural talent for relating intimately with others, or for what I have called "diplomatic empathy." These children, even very young ones, like to play at being Teachers and Counselors, Champions and Healers, and such interest in the diplomatic role variants may be inborn, since it shows up so early in the lives of NF children, and will lead to endless practice if encouraged by their parents. Unfortunately, there is in most cases very little modeling of such behavior for them to copy. Few parents, or relatives—or even teachers, for that matter—are very skilled in diplomacy, so Idealist children must usually learn on their own rather than by taking after a good role model. But in the degree that they do become fluent in the two diplomatic roles—the Mentor and the Advocate—Idealist children develop a positive self-image. In addition, they can benefit from adult modeling in the tactical, logistical, or strategic roles, since Idealist kids are usually eager to try all sorts of things and look forward to learning in school with keen anticipation.

Showing themselves to be artistic like the Artisans, dependable like the Guardians, or ingenious like the Rationals enhances but little the self-esteem of the Idealists. What they take pride in, and from a very early age, is their ability to maintain and enhance empathic relationships with their friends and loved ones. There is no way of determining how early in their lives their empathic response to others becomes strong. Doubtless much depends upon circumstances within the family. NF children are apt to be almost hypersensitive to the feelings of those closest to them, and when their family members are in harmony they feel at peace with themselves, just as when their parents or siblings are distressed they are distressed right along with them. Thus, in a loving and supportive family self-esteem in the Idealist child can grow early and fast owing to the strong empathic bonding they are free to maintain.

On the other hand, in a dysfunctional and distantiated family Idealist children can run into serious problems. These children, especially if reserved, lack defenses against things the other types take in stride. For example, these children are devastated by conflict, and if reared in a home where the parents quarrel a good deal, they are apt to become withdrawn and insecure. Or if their parents spank them, NF children can be deeply hurt, and far more by the cruelty of the punishment than by the pain inflicted. Even if their brothers or sisters are spanked, NFs will feel the hurt; they, far more than the rest, cannot bear to see other children being treated harshly. In the same way, if competition among family members is encouraged by their parents, NF youngsters can feel a shameful sense of division. In such a competitive atmosphere, there may develop a strong bond between the Idealist child and one parent, while rifts may open with the other parent or the siblings. And in competitive games, little Idealists (particularly boys) can be badly torn between a fierce desire to win and a sharp guilt for wanting to outdo a loved one. For this reason, cooperative family games and competition against themselves are more likely to appeal to and be healthy for NF children. In all other cases they will have a hard time developing much self-esteem.

Idealist children base their self-respect on their capacity for feeling benevolent toward others. Although both NFs and SJs seem to be intent on helping others while still very young, the NFs' helpfulness is usually a different kind, more of an attempt to show their good intentions than to meet the concrete needs of others. Idealist children seem born with a high moral expectation of themselves, and want to be perfect—blameless, virtuous, perhaps even saintly—in their attitudes and actions towards others. And on those occasions when Idealist children do in fact have bad intentions, or act in a devilish way, they feel guilty about it, as if they are the worst of criminals. Such intense moral idealism is quite a burden for them to bear, particularly as they begin to develop sexually, and for this reason NF kids harbor as many good intentions as they can imagine and hold strongly to them as long as they can, at the same time suppressing as best they can those pesky bad intentions that keep welling up from within.

Idealist children are not comfortable when deliberately playing a role with others, and they seldom seek applause. Of course, they try to fit in with people (thereby avoiding conflict and rejection), and they like to be praised by adults; but they do not base their self-confidence on such things. Quite the opposite: Idealist children, even as young as five, build their self-confidence on being authentic. Authenticity, of course, is not in any way visible, even though NF kids appear to have a sincerity and open-heartedness—perhaps an innocence—about them that sets them apart from the other types. But the wish to be authentic is there, and can be deduced by watching how they behave on those occasions when they are deceitful. On such occasions their fear and self-doubt is far greater and longer lasting than that of deceitful Artisans, Guardians, or Rationals. Particularly of Artisans, who are the diametric opposites of Idealists in most respects: SPs actually get a kick out of guile or trickery—it is, after all, artfulness—and certainly do not experience even a whisper of anxiety from such behavior.

But even more than being seen as authentic, Idealist children want to be recognized as unique individuals. This search for identity begins so early in life for Idealists that I have called them the "Identity Seeking Personality," much as Maslow called them the "Self-Actualizing Personality." In school, they are apt to have the same experience as Rational children, which is that they often find themselves out of step with their classmates. They feel the difference between themselves and others, without realizing what that difference is. After all, Idealists are such a small minority (less than ten percent of the population) that until they reach college they are unlikely to find more than one or two others like themselves. Both NF and NT children can feel some estrangement, but while NTs simply go their own way, NFs actually take some comfort in feeling that they are like no one else, one of a kind, as if special or singled out. Some NF children might even try too hard in school to be different or exceptional in their actions and attitudes, so important to them is their unique personal identity.

The same in the family. Although all children are subject to sibling rivalry and to feelings of demotion when a new member is added to the family, this transition needs to be very carefully handled with Idealist children, who are never fully certain of their sense of self, and are always looking to define their special position in the family system. Not autonomous like the NTs, NF youngsters need their parents to recognize their uniqueness and to personally acknowledge their significance in order to feel they are a valuable family member in their own right. NF kids thrive on an abundance of personalized attention, and the messages they need most are those which say, "You are special; I value you; you are important to me."

Idealist children are the most trusting of all the types. They trust their impulses to a certain degree, at least their good impulses (to show affection, for example, or to help others), though it must be said that, unlike the Artisans, their negative impulses (to lie, to show spite, to retaliate) tend to frighten them and inhibit them. Idealist kids also trust authority to a great extent, resembling the Guardians in their regard for the ceremonies, rituals, and traditions of home and school, though their participation tends to be personal and enthusiastic, while that of the SJs is more dutiful and solemn. And Idealist children trust reason in some part and will, like the Rationals, ponder the sense of doing this instead of that, but they will give far more weight to what their heart tells them about their feelings and the feelings of others. In short, Idealist kids trust the voice of their intuition more than any of the other guides to action, and by adolescence their trust in intuition is deep-seated and heartfelt. Such intuitions come to them from who knows where, but they are sometimes uncanny, and always inexplicable. No matter: NF children know, though they don't know how they know.

It may seem strange to describe Idealist children as "romantic," but they certainly are romantic in the sense that, as they look for their unique qualities, they are apt to identify with characters in stories. When very young, NFs, like NTs, usually enjoy being read stories which are beyond their own reading capabilities, but which fire their imagination. Fairy tales and children's stories such as the *Winnie the Pooh, Mary Poppins,* and *James and the Giant Peach* are all real for the Idealist child to a degree not shared by other types. And, also like NTs, NF children may want the same story read over and over. They will even make up stories and recount them with vivid imagery. At times, indeed, they may be accused of lying when in fact they are only exercising their romantic imagination. In elementary school, NF kids love stories of the medieval era, of knights and their ladies, of princes and princesses, of dragons and wizards. The symbolism in such stories can be quite emotionally powerful to Idealist children, and can make them dream of taking off on romantic quests. Indeed, some caution should be exercised in monitoring the reading material of NF children, who can easily become over-stimulated by the disturbing imagery in stories of dragons, witches, ogres, and monsters—all of which can resurface in their nightmares. Isabel Myers said of NFs that harmonious human relations are more important to them than anything else. And so parents should try to steer their little Idealists toward stories that have happy endings, with heroes winning, and even villains having a change of heart in the end. Such happily-ever-after stories capture Idealist kids from the very beginning and never let go of them, however much their hopes and dreams are defied by reality.

Idealist children also project this sort of romantic make-believe onto their toys. Although (and like the NTs) they are apt to play with all their toys as fantasy objects, NFs are more likely to weave stories around them rather than to try to understand how they work. Also, NF kids are apt to enjoy non-mechanical toys—soft hand puppets, dolls, stuffed animals—to which they can attach a human personality, and these treasured toys become very much a part of their fantasy life. A teddy bear or a ceramic figurine can be unbelievably dear to NF children, and a lost toy friend, or, worse, one accidentally thrown away by a parent, is a real tragedy to them. Moreover, Idealists are more likely than the other types to have an invisible companion. And certainly the rejection or ridicule of this imaginary friend by others would especially crush an NF child, who would feel personally rejected.

For their part, Idealist children would like to think well of everyone and everything, and to give of themselves for the good of others. The group of children singing "I'd like to teach the world to sing in perfect harmony" nicely reveals the NFs' inherent altruism: the belief, even as children, that the world can be made a better place through their selfless actions. The altruism of NF children can be global in this way, but more often it focuses on their own communities, families, and friends. Idealist children become tutors for younger students and they volunteer to help the physically and mentally handicapped, and the elderly; they are also peace-makers within their peer groups, and when need be they will take on the difficult responsibility of mediating family conflicts. I call Idealist parents the "Harmonizers" in their families, but Idealist children also instinctively take up the very same role in all their social groups.

If Rationals have a precocious skepticism about what grown-ups tell them is true, Idealists have a precocious interest in finding some doctrine or philosophy of life to believe in. Many NFs become interested in religion, for example, when still quite young. Some even know as children that they want to enter the ministry or priesthood, and will train to be acolytes and altar boys and girls. Such religious exploration is sincere in these children; they go to church not because their parents make them or because they want more social life, but because they begin wondering about the meaning of life long before the other types. Idealist teenagers will also investigate other belief systems, ethical, political, and artistic, and don't mind appearing seriously philosophical to their friends. Often they flit from creed to creed, now believing one thing, now another, contradicting themselves without concern. But regardless of what system they embrace, nor for how long, NF children passionately seek out something to believe in.

The Rational Child

There was a salt-marsh...on the edge of which we used to stand to fish for minnows. My proposal was to build a wharf there...and I showed my comrades a large heap of stones, which were intended for a new house near the marsh, and which would very well suit our purpose. Accordingly, in the evening...I assembled a number of my play-fellows, and working with them diligently...we brought them all away and built our little wharf. The next morning the workmen were surprised at missing the stones....Inquiries were made; we were discovered and complained of; several of us were corrected by our fathers; and though I pleaded the usefulness of the work, mine convinced me that nothing was useful which was not honest.
—Benjamin Franklin

Galen called Plato's Rationals the "Phlegmatics" no doubt because of the four temperaments they are the calm ones, the tranquil ones. And this calm, cool, and collected nature shows up right from the start. NT infants often appear rather still and self-contained, and can be a puzzle to parents of other type. Moreover, Rational children, especially reserved ones, can seem distant and detached, as if unable or at least reluctant to express affection. But this does not mean that these children are unemotional, for behind their quiet self-possession can be mounting tension from the effort to control their emotions.

Rationals also feel tension from their intense desire to predict and control events. NTs are born to play strategic roles, but only a few of them have anyone that show them how to act like a Coordinator or an Engineer. Something less than six percent of the population, NTs only rarely have even one parent or teacher to be a role model, so they're mostly on their own in learning the role variants of Fieldmarshal, Mastermind, Inventor and Architect, with whatever progress they make coming from their own experimentation and speculation. However, Artisan adults can help their Rationals kids by providing models for tactical roles, because little Rationals are usually eager to add concrete techniques to their skills repertoire. On the other hand, Guardian parents who model logistical roles are usually disappointed with their Rational child's indifference. No matter how often they are reminded to clean up, NT children are erratic about the way they maintain their room and clothes. They may at one time keep order and at another let disorder reign. Probably the most frequent condition of their room is one of apparent chaos, but little Rationals will be likely to know where each and every treasure is placed. They are apt to have extensive collections: rocks, animal artifacts, coins, stamps, butterflies, and the like.

Anything which can be collected and which requires technical documentation and classification is apt to have appeal for the NT child.

Rationals start very young, some at the tender age of three or four, in exercising their ingenuity, and it is on their cleverness and inventiveness that they base their self-esteem. But not just any kind of ingenuity will do; Rational children, like their adult counterparts, have to be bright in technological matters—after all, these are the children of Prometheus, the bringer of technology. Little NTs have a special fondness for busy boards, for construction sets of all kinds (building blocks, Lincoln logs, Legos, and the like), and the males will turn almost any object into a weapon of some sort. As they get a bit older, NT children want chemistry sets, electronics sets, and Erector sets with which they can experiment with different structures and functions; they begin to play strategic games such as chess and Mastermind; and they turn to new weapons, showing an interest in archery or karate. And, of course, the video game player and the computer reach out and grab Rational children, and never let them go. NTs will spend days learning the maps and defeating the enemies in the latest Nintendo adventure, or in learning computer animation. Witness how proud NT children are of themselves when they have mastered any of these strategic operations. But also observe their total frustration when they find one of these high-tech activities beyond their grasp. How ashamed they feel, already blaming themselves for their stupidity.

Because of this, parents and teachers are unwise to set Rational children tasks which are beyond them, or to criticize their failures. More than all the other types, NT kids are self-doubting, and for them to feel proud of themselves they must feel smart. They are particularly vulnerable here, with too much failure undermining their self-esteem. Language development can be a special source of both feelings of self-worth and inadequacy. Some Rational children can be linguistically precocious, learning to read long before they go to school, and talking very early with a large vocabulary. But just as many can appear slow in this matter—Einstein, for example, refused to talk until he was able to say whole sentences, and his parents worried about his intelligence. Parents and teachers must thus take care: helping NT children when they ask for help, offering them encouragement (not praise), giving them play activities and materials appropriate to their developmental level, these allow them to grow up with self-esteem intact.

Rational children usually have many fears and sometimes recurring nightmares. Such fears spring from their vivid imagination, an imagination which taunts them with all manner of terrible consequences that might follow on the heals of any incompetent action. So, unlike their utilitarian cousins, the SPs, NT children certainly cannot base their self-respect on their boldness. Theirs is an entirely different base of self-respect: they must be autonomous. Rational children don't like to be governed or directed by others—told how to think, or act, or feel—and they will stubbornly oppose parents or older siblings who try to manipulate them. This is why being spanked is so deeply violating to Rationals; they see this abuse of their body as an unforgivable assault on their autonomy, and their indignation is extreme and permanent. To be sure, dignity is unusually important to NT children, and they are often described as "prideful" or "arrogant," an attitude which others can find offensive, and which can make them want to knock NTs off their high horse. However, the issue is not pride but autonomy. Rational kids want to think, act, feel for themselves, to be independent and self-sufficient, to figure things out for themselves, to go their own way. Even by the age of two this is the case, and their requirement for autonomy increases geometrically as the years go by, so that by the late teens even their financial dependency on their parents is irksome to them. There's no way around it: Rational self-respect is diminished as long as they feel such dependency, and they experience a growing sense of guilt the longer they remain dependent.

Rational children are individuals in every sense from birth on, and the concern of many parents is how to get this little individualist to join the family in its routines, that is, its rituals, ceremonies, and customs. Family routines simply exist; they are there simply because they are there, and no amount of discussion will reveal their underlying rationale, because there isn't any underlying rationale. Family routines are arbitrary and as such are bound to be questioned by the budding Rational. Particularly as a child, the NT wants to know the reason for doing something; if none is forthcoming, the child is at least hesitant, if not reluctant, to do it. So routinizing a Rational child is not a task to take on lightly, because such a little individual will never become completely routinized. This does not mean that NT children will refuse to go along with family routines, but it does mean that they are going along with them only to avoid displeasing their parents and for no other reason. Rationals will never see a reason for such conduct. Take table manners, for instance. These ways of acting are totally arbitrary and as such are puzzling to NT children, though they will not usually express their puzzlement. But because manners make no sense it takes more time for NT kids to catch on to how eating is supposed to be done. As a rule routinizing NT children takes longer than for the other types, so NTs can profit from coaching in the social niceties.

Nor do insignia, badges, and titles make much sense to them. Rational kids don't see, for instance, what a gold star on their work sheet has to do with them, or anyone else for that matter. And being in receipt of such trifles does not bolster their self-confidence in the least. But strength of will does, and it can show up in NT children very early in their lives. By the way, resolution is not to be confused with stubbornness. All types of very young children can be stubborn in insisting on their demands, and of course all types of children can develop willpower, but that does not mean that they all base their self-confidence on their willpower. Only Rational children feel confident in the degree that when they resolve to do something they are able to hold to their resolve. Other types of children can be irresolute and not be bothered by it, but not Rationals. Their self-doubt increases directly as their resolution decreases.

More than anything else, Rational children wish to learn how things work. They start their logical investigations early and continue them throughout life. NT kids, even as early as the age of two, give the things that interest them a functional definition—a switch is to flip, a button is to push, a door is to open, a wheel is to turn—and they will manipulate whatever they can get their hands on to determine what can be done with it. Let a little NT of two stand in the driver's seat of a car, and watch as every button, lever, switch, and knob is activated and deactivated time and again. If the manipulation of a switch or button is accompanied by a sight or sound or movement of any kind, the little manipulator can be entertained for long periods of time, learning how to control these intriguing causes of predictable response.

How things work, that's the issue that Rational children would settle by experimentation. For this is what I call the "Knowledge Seeking Personality," with know-how at first more important than know-about, but both more important than anything else. These are the children who must take things apart and then must put them back together again. These are the children who have to think before they act, who deliberate on what they are to do, especially if they have been asked or advised or commanded by an adult. These are the children who require of themselves that what they do is informed by their own knowledge. And these are the children with the endless "why?" questions: "Why does the sun come up here and not there?" "Why can't I fly like a bird?" "Why can't I have dessert before my vegetables if I eat both?" Just as Artisans pursue stimulation, so do Rationals pursue knowledge, wondering "What would happen if ...?" and attempting to find the answer, whether their parents approve or not. "What would happen if I pull this drawer all the way out?" "What would happen if I put my bread in the water pitcher?" "What would happen if I push all the numbers on the phone?" None of these explorations are designed to annoy their parents, but to satisfy their desire to find out. In fact, NT children are not the least bit interested in grappling with others, although, if this happens as a result of their investigations, they accept this as a natural consequence.

Parents do well to be patient and to provide their Rational children with answers to their questions, but also to give them abundant opportunities to experiment, to find out, to develop their own answers. Shutting off investigation is likely to occasion disobedience, whether overt or covert. To encourage logical investigation, parents should furnish the NT child with a variety of toys, but only a few at any one time, since the Rational tends to concentrate fully on one thing, explore it to his or her satisfaction, and then move on to the next. Thus the NT child is likely to become intensely involved with a new toy, playing with it for hours, investigating its properties—and then abandon it. Once the toy's function and operation are understood, it is no longer interesting.

Most important of all, parents would do well to read to their Rational child. NTs are fascinated by stories—science fiction, tales of magic and sorcery, and epics of heroism and achievement are their favorites. And the fascination lasts long after children of other types have turned their attention elsewhere. The Rationals' enjoyment in being read to is probably a function of their curiosity, since through stories they encounter complex ideas which stimulate their imagination well beyond their own reading level.

Where Guardian children, and later Guardian adults, trust authority, despite its occasional deficiency, Rational children remember every instance in which authority fails to be trustworthy, so that by their teens there has grown in many of them an active and permanent distrust in authority, and in some cases a large measure of contempt. Neither do Rational children put much trust in their intuition, as do Idealists, nor in their impulses, as do Artisans. For their part, Rationals learn to have more and more trust in reason as the basis of action. Watch a little NT and you will see that every action must be reasoned—that is, must be considered, deliberated, pondered to determine if it's worth doing. By adolescence trust in reason has become an absolute in the case of any thorough-going Rational. "Do it if, and only if, it makes sense" is the motto of the NT, acquired in youth and never abandoned. Admittedly, such an attitude is often a source of annoyance to their parents and teachers. Rational children will go along with a parent or teacher only if their demands makes sense, and they quickly lose respect for those who are not reasonable in their rules and reprimands.

From early on NT children seem calm and contemplative, leading an observer to suppose them without strong desires. But the calm exterior conceals a yearning for achievement that all too often can turn into obsession. As is the case with adult Rationals, all else becomes unimportant to these children once in the pursuit of achievement, once caught in the grip of accomplishing some goal. Unfortunately, this obsessiveness can make NT kids demand more of themselves than they can deliver, so that tension builds as they struggle to rid themselves of error. Also, once they achieve something, that level of achievement immediately becomes standard for them. Yesterday's triumph is today's expectation, and the escalation of standards makes Rational children vulnerable to fear of failure even when they are succeeding in the eyes of others. Once calm and focused, they now become overly tense and high-strung, impatient with everything and everyone around them. It may well be that the early onset of achievement hunger follows in the wake of the NT child's excessive and obsessive reading of stories about the great exploits of heroic figures, such as goodguy gunslingers, triumphant warriors, reluctant duelists, successful explorers, brilliant scientists, and ingenious inventors. As they grow older their collection of heroes steadily increases, and even those whose exploits are not in the fields of science and technology are seldom forgotten.

The pragmatic outlook shows up in Rational children even when very young. We can see them studiously experimenting with the relationship between means and ends and between structure and function. Already they like nothing better than tinkering and experimenting with any and all devices—anything that can be activated, anything that stores energy which can be released by a touch or a turn or a yank or a pull. Already they seem to want to spend as little effort as possible in getting the desired result, already they seem to be frustrated by wasted effort. What they do must work and work efficiently, and they will keep at whatever they're doing until they have eliminated all errors.

Although they will listen to the ideas of those who clearly know what they are talking about, young Rationals are invariably skeptical about proposed ways and means of doing things. Scrupulously aware as they are of their own mistakes, NT children have their doubts about almost everything told them, and must look critically at any plan of action, particularly if based on custom or tradition. By taking nothing for granted, nothing on faith, nothing on authority, these children position themselves early on as researchers and developers, and so get the jump on the rest in making technological progress. But this skepticism can also make them appear to be intellectual snobs, looking down on others who are perhaps less intelligent, or more gullible, and therefore judged to be inferior. Rational children need help in understanding that customs and traditions are important to other people, and to the smooth operation of society.

Parent and Child

So: the first task of parents is to recognize the different characters of their children. But parents must also recognize the role their own character plays in their way of bringing up their children. All types of parents—Artisans, Guardians, Idealists, Rationals—have a different view of the correct way to raise children, one that reflects their own personality, and one that is often unexamined and unquestioned.

Let's turn now to a brief discussion of the four styles of parenting and some of the strengths and weaknesses that each style has with the four types of children.

The Artisan Liberator

Artisan parents instinctively play a hands-off role, giving their children wide latitude in what they get to do. They are usually more permissive with their children than other types, and prone to overindulgence more than to overprotection, and to under-supervision more than to over-supervision. Their children must have leeway to test the limits of their environment, experimenting on their own and learning the hard way those important lessons about the consequences of impetuous or intemperate action. Those who are not allowed to fail are also not allowed to succeed, say the Artisans. Too stringent controls on children will reinforce their natural timidity, and timidity on the part of children is something SP parents find hard to accept. The bad news about such permissiveness is that it can be a kind of unhealthy neglect that sometimes, and with certain types of children, gives them more freedom than they can handle and fewer limits than they need. But the good news is that such a lenient, live and let live parenting style can be just the thing for other kinds of children, especially in suburban and rural contexts, letting them spread their wings and fly gracefully away to an adventurous, exciting, and creative life.

Of the two main types of Artisans, Operators (ESTPs & ISTPs) pay less attention to their children's decorum and physical and safety needs, and more attention to their fun and games and adventures. At times they can be over-extravagant with their children, quite unpredictably showering them with expensive toys and taking them on pleasure trips. At other times (and like their Administrator Guardian cousins), they can be very strict, and on occasion even harsh with their children, particularly when they tell them to do something—they want no questions asked and will tolerate no back talk.

Entertainers (ESFPs & ISFPs), in contrast, are usually obliging and easygoing with their children, themselves very much like children in wanting to have fun now and getting down to business later on. It is hard for them to be strict with their children, but they can compensate for this by being very clever in managing them so that they do not get too far out of line. Their children soon learn that they are not as clever as their parents and have a hard time fooling them, whereas they find it much easier to hoodwink adults of other type.

Artisan Parent—Artisan Child: When Artisan parents beget Artisan children they find their offspring more than ready to grab their freedom and run with it. SP children need no encouragement to be bold and adventurous and to take up sports of all kinds. They need no urging to try their hand at music, dance, acting, and other arts and crafts. Nor do they need to be taught how to have fun and be popular with their friends. Because they share so many traits of attitude and action, Artisan parents can be great pals with their Artisan kids, delighting in their toughness or their charm, their way with tools or their fashion sense, their craftiness or their gracefulness. Indeed, Artisan children can easily be the apple of their Artisan parents' eye—if boys, they are all boy, if girls, they are sure to break hearts. On the down side, Artisan parents can be so taken with their Artisan children that they can fail to give them sufficient limits, reinforcing instead their children's natural impulsiveness and insubordination. As a result, their children might push too close to the edge and get into jams; or they might come to expect indulgence and lenience from adults, and thus have trouble with authority.

Artisan Parent—Guardian Child: Artisan parents have little or no difficulty in rearing Guardian children. They enjoy encouraging their Guardian children to get into all sorts of sports and arts and adventures, hoping to help loosen them up and show them that life is for living here and now.

With such modeling on how to have fun Guardian children can overcome their natural caution and seriousness, and can thrive both at home and school. There is a danger that highly aggressive Artisan parents can communicate dissatisfaction with their Guardian child's over-concerned attitude, letting it be known they aren't happy with a goody-goody child of either gender—teasing them about being a mama's boy or a little pris. If SP parents expect (or demand) boldness and impetuosity from their SJ children, they will only frighten and inhibit them, and teach them they are a failure. Fortunately, it is unusual for both parents to be Artisans, and quite usual for the other parent to be a Guardian. So the Guardian child often has the best of both worlds: someone to show the way to joy, and someone to show the way to duty.

Artisan Parent—Idealist Child: Although they can have some trouble understanding each other, Artisan parents can be valuable models for their Idealist children. NF kids tend to get lost in abstraction and a self-absorbed search for meanings and portents, and the SP's warm embrace of immediacy can be an important lesson for them. Artisans are in touch with reality, free in physical action, comfortable with their bodies, easy-going about moral absolutes, not worried about who they are—they don't sweat the small stuff—and all of these attitudes and actions can help give balance to the soulful, emotional, self-examining Idealist child. On the other hand, such differences can be a problem. Artisan parents tend not to value in their Idealist children such important traits as authenticity, empathy, and altruism, and in the worst case the parent might show impatience with the child for being so soul-searching, so head-in-the-clouds, or so lost in fantasy, and might want the child to toughen up and take hold of reality. In the main, though, Artisan parents are easygoing with people they don't understand, and so most often they model for their Idealist children lenience, tolerance, and a spirit of fun.

Artisan Parent—Rational Child: The relationship between Artisan parents and Rational children can be, and often is, happy and productive. The SP parents' hands-off style is perfect for NT children, who, after all, want to be independent—to have no hands put on them. Moreover, both parent and child share in a strong and ever-present desire to function usefully and to increase their powers, however much their reasons for doing so differ. Rational children need no encouragement to learn new skills and know-how; they'll do that on their own. But they do need encouragement to put down their books and to enjoy themselves—even to risk themselves—now and then. And this is what SP parents can give them: in modeling artistry, boldness, and adaptability, they make it much easier for budding NTs to overcome their fear of failure and to come to see themselves as ingenious, autonomous, and resolute. As with the Idealist child, the Rational child can be a puzzle to Artisan parents, who often cannot understanding the child's interest in logical investigation and technological development. The Artisan parent's attitude is often "why not get your nose out of that book and have some fun?" or "why not get out in the world and make some money?" But such misunderstandings as Artisan parents and Rational children have are usually overlooked in their mutual interest in effective action.

The Guardian Socializer

Guardian parents are mainly concerned with socializing their children. They would teach them the customs and conventions of their society, and would pass on the attitudes of good citizenship, most of which can be neatly summarized in the twelve points of Boy and Girl Scout Law. Scouts are to be: trustworthy, loyal, helpful, friendly, courteous, kind, obedient, cheerful, thrifty, clean, brave, and reverent. Guardian parents want their children (whether they join Scouts or not) to do their best to do their duty, and thus to be increasingly helpful and productive at school, at church, at social functions, and certainly at gatherings of the extended family—to become fully a part of their communities. But Guardian parents also want their children to value their duty and to want to obey. Dutifulness and obedience for the wrong reasons are not acceptable. SJ parents are far more concerned with this project than they are with the concerns of other types, that is, with fostering their children's venturesomeness, their positive self-image, or their individuality. Indeed, the way they usually see it is that fully socialized children are in a much better position to become venturesome, to feel increasingly good about themselves, or to establish their independence than those who are not well socialized, a point made abundantly clear by Alfred Adler and his disciple Rudolf Dreikurs.

Among the Guardians, Administrators (ESTJs & ISTJs) tend to be strict parents because their main concern is that their children do what is right and not do what is wrong. They regard it as their obligation to the family and the community to keep their children under their watchful eye lest they stray from the fold. Their children must behave in a seemly manner and must not do things that reflect badly on the family. These are the parents who believe that punishment is the best way to keep their kids in line, and they will at times resort to corporal punishment to get their point across—to spare the rod, they believe, is to spoil the child.

Conservators (ESFJs & ISFJs) are usually less strict than Administrators, and this because they are more concerned with looking after their children than they are in keeping them on the straight and narrow. First their children are to be well fed, clothed, and sheltered, and only then held to a strict standard of acceptable conduct. So conscientious are these parents in providing for the physical and safety needs of their children that they can sometimes be overprotective, willing to sacrifice their own comforts to safeguard their children from the world of hard knocks. For this reason Conservator Guardian parents are not given to spanking their children, though they are very likely to scold them when their conduct is improper or they are disobedient. If they do spank their kids (and often they believe they must, to be good parents), they will say "this hurts me worse than it hurts you," with the little culprits wondering what on earth they mean by that.

Guardian Parent—Artisan Child: It is a rare Artisan child who does not have at least one Guardian parent, since the two types together make up well over eighty percent of the population, and since SJs are more prone to marriage and family than the rest. In most cases SJ parents and their SP children get along famously, especially while the kids are young, a short leash being just the thing for the normally impetuous little Artisan puppies. But the picture can change quickly. When their adventurous children get into their teens, Guardian parents can find their methods of control not working as well as before. Scoldings and spankings usually backfire, sometimes with disastrous consequences. Artisan children want to be excited and bold, sensual and impulsive, yet here they are expected by their parents to be concerned, reliable, respectable, and obedient. Perhaps it is in this relationship, the SJ parent and the SP child, where the Pygmalion Project can takes its worst turn. Young Artisans, in their rebellion against an authoritarian parent, may get into serious trouble, with drugs, say, or with the law. This is especially the case when tough Administrator fathers try to come down hard on equally tough Operator teenagers. Such children can retaliate vigorously, bent on getting even with the old man no matter how long it takes. Much of this antagonism can be avoided if SJ parents can support their SP children in productive activities—playing sports, forming a rock band, using tools—that allow them to shine in action.

Guardian Parent—Guardian Child: With offspring of their own temperament, Guardian parents have a relatively easy time of it. Guardian children rarely have a rebellious period, but seem born to trust in authority, to follow the rules, to be responsible, and so fit with their Guardian parents hand-in-glove. However, such easy agreement between parent and child can have its negatives. Guardian children are naturally cautious and prone to worry, and Guardian parents tend to reinforce these fears and concerns. SJ kids would do well with a more carefree and optimistic model from at least one of their parents. Also, traditional, conservative Guardian parents often want their children to be quiet and in their place—to be seen and not heard—as if their children's obedience and modesty reflect on them as parents and show a proper upbringing. But such humility can only serve to further inhibit SJ children, who are over-controlled to begin with, and who often need encouragement to develop venturesomeness.

Guardian Parent—Idealist Child: Guardian parents have few overt problems with their Idealist children. NF kids are naturally moral and eminently cooperative—they care about right and wrong, and they like to serve the needs of others, an attitude and a way of acting which SJ parents go to great lengths to instill in all their children. But little do Guardian parents know how much their well-meant but unnecessary admonitions and instructions bother their little NFs. Idealist children are good children, at home, at school, and in the community. They are good because they want to be good, because they need to be good, because they must see themselves and be seen by others as authentic, as benevolent, and as empathic. And it can be irritating when their SJ parents come along and remind them to be reliable (which NFs naturally are), to do good deeds (which NFs do because they have good intentions), and to be respectable (which NFs are because they are naturally cooperative). The unintended result of such intrusion is that the SJ parent, and not the NF child, takes credit for the child's good behavior, which can make the little Idealist feel dominated and manipulated. This sort of parenting is not always bad for Idealist children, but it often weakens the relationship between parent and child, causing alienation and, in extreme cases, pushing the child into rebellious behavior, just to establish a unique identity.

Guardian Parent—Rational Child: Guardian parents admire their Rational children's seriousness and will-to-achieve, and this relationship works out quite well when SJ parents show regard for their little NTs' fierce sense of autonomy. However, discipline can be a knotty problem. If the SJ parent tries to admonish or punish the NT child into obedience, the child will feel personally violated and will likely respond with growing contempt. Remember that NTs, at any age, must have a reason for doing anything, and when a parent is not forthcoming with a rationale for action other than convention or authority, the little NTs will do what they are told only reluctantly and with little respect. More specifically, it is the tough-minded Administrator Guardian that the Rational child is most likely to run afoul of, the child wanting to be free to choose, and the parent conscientiously trying to arbitrate choice. The probing Engineer Rationals usually manage, like their Artisan cousins, to steer clear of an arbitrary parent most of the time, but the schedule-minded Coordinator Rationals tend to meet such a parent head on. In extreme cases, the effect of such a clash can be lasting estrangement. Fortunately, Guardians marry Artisans most frequently, and having this live-and-let-live parent in the mix often saves the Rational child from the worst consequences of the Guardian parent's authoritarian style.

The Idealist Harmonizer

In their role as parents, Idealists seek to form close, harmonious relationships with their children. NF parents want to be intimately involved in their children's lives and the growth of a positive self-image, and so make every effort to keep themselves in touch and *en rapport* with their children, even into adult life. Physical bonding is surprisingly important for such abstract types. If Artisans tend to be hands off parents, Idealists are literally hands on—hugs, pats, back rubs, head scratches, and other signs of physical affection are very dear to Idealists, and make them the original touchy-feely parents. But even more important is mental and emotional bonding. Idealist parents will talk with their children from a very early age, especially about their dreams and fantasies, and they will read to their children book after book of make-believe and fairy tale. In times of sadness, NFs often try to act as counselors for their children or, at the very least, as patient, understanding listeners, always hoping to help their children feel good about themselves.

Idealist parents also extend their bonding efforts to harmonize the whole family. With their cooperative natures, NFs care about promoting mutual consideration in the family, asking that their children avoid arguing, and not only care about but work to meet the needs of their siblings and other family members. The Idealists' need for harmony in the family sometimes makes them take on the role of family diplomat or peacekeeper, wanting to make sure that all in the family are happy and fulfilled, that all emotional needs are being met, and that kindness prevails—an impossible and largely thankless task that can cause the NF a good deal of grief. Fortunately, the Idealists' love for their children is boundless, and they will overcome every difficulty with renewed enthusiasm.

For their part, Mentor Idealists (ENFJs & INFJs) tend to take on an active teaching and counseling role with their children, and can be quite energetic in encouraging them to develop in all three aspects of self-image—self-esteem, self-respect, and self-confidence. Searching for the most enriching pre-school, providing travel experiences for their children, arranging art and music lessons, taking their children to plays and concerts, urging the discussion of books and ideas, talking with their children about how to get along with their friends: these and many other personal growth producing activities come readily to mind for these Idealists.

Advocates (ENFPs & INFPs) are also determined to foster a healthy self-image in their children, and are ever alert for opportunities for cognitive and social growth. But these Idealists, perhaps more intensely than their counterparts, concern themselves with their children's moral and spiritual development, and so work to establish an even closer bond of understanding with them, hoping to instill in their children the purity of their own ideals.

Idealist Parent—Artisan Child: Idealist parents tend to be puzzled by the Artisan child's disinterest in fantasy and heart-to-heart sharing, and by the accompanying paucity of empathy for other members of the family. Wanting their relationship with their child to be deep and meaningful, they can be disappointed when the relationship does not grow in that direction, but continues to be what they regard as somewhat shallow and uninspiring. This as long as they persist in their Pygmalion Project, trying to turn the child into an Idealist like themselves. Once they see that their child is not like them at all, but is bent on racing from one concrete action to another, with hardly a trace of intuition or altruism, then they are quite able to give up their project and encourage the child's thrust toward artistry and optimism, if not the accompanying impulsivity, bravado, and tactical cleverness.

Idealist Parent—Guardian Child: Unlike Artisan children, whose strengths show up bright and early, positive traits of character are slow to emerge in Guardian children, so that, at first, it is easier to say what they are not—not bold, for example, not independent, not adaptable, not light-hearted, not eager to learn new things, and so on. Unable to figure out the child's nature, Idealist parents keep looking for signs of Idealism, convinced that the child is going to value what they value. For example, the SJ child is naturally cooperative with others, and this desirable trait makes the Idealist parent think that it might be the beginning of empathy and intuition and a deep identification with the parent. But this identification never quite materializes, and the deep and meaningful relationship sought by the parent remains just out of reach. Also, NF parents may well put some Pygmalion pressure on their little SJs to follow the NF path. Often Idealist parents have favorite books they want to read to their Guardian child, hoping to develop the child's interest in fantasy and fairy tales, but whatever interest that does appear under the urging of the parents gradually fades away as the child gets older. Eventually, Idealist parents catch on that their Guardian child is a both-feet-on-the-ground little person who is unusually concerned about responsibility, security, authority, and belonging, but who displays little of the parents' romanticism or enthusiasm. At this point the Pygmalion Project ceases and the Idealist parent sets about encouraging the child to be what he or she was bound to be from the beginning.

Idealist Parent—Idealist Child: Idealist parents find fertile soil for the care and nurturing of their Idealist child's unique self-image. Here it is well to be reminded of the constituents of Idealist self-image. First there is self-esteem based on empathy; then self-respect based on benevolence; and last there is self-confidence based on authenticity. Idealist parents want to enhance these traits in all their offspring, and their Idealist children are happy to meet them more than half way. NF kids are born with empathy for others, with benevolent feelings toward others, and they know exactly what their parents mean when they speak of being authentic. While it might puzzle the other three types, the idea of having inner unity, of being wholly, genuinely themselves is perfectly understandable to Idealists—parent and child—and they do not hesitate to support each other in the quest to get in touch with their true Self. At the same time, NF kids and NF parents can easily rub each other the wrong way. Both tend to be touchy and prickly in their relations with others, and when their ideals come into conflict they can hardly avoid irritating each other.

Idealist Parent—Rational Child: There are many reported cases attesting to the strong tie that can form between Rational children and their Idealist parent. After all, the NF parent, male or female, is bent on bonding with the child, searching for growth potentials, and beckoning to them to come out of hiding. The NT child, inherently eager to enlarge his or her meager collection of skills, can only flower given such ever-present appreciation and encouragement. And yet this relationship is not quite made in heaven. Idealist parents can be dismayed by their Rational child's sometimes ruthless pragmatism and calm autonomy. These traits show up quite early in NT children, but can seem cruel to NFs, who prefer warm, friendly, cooperative relations with others, and who will sometimes start up Pygmalion Projects to help their NT youngsters learn to be agreeable and considerate of others. Needless to say, Rational children aren't about to change their ways, and Idealist parents soon learn that they need to let their little Rationals be, and value them for what they admire in them, their ingenuity, imagination, curiosity, and calm reasonableness.

The Rational Individuator

Rational parents encourage an ever-increasing individuality in their children and do not impose unreasonable rules on them. It is of paramount importance to NT parents that each and every child in the family progressively increases his or her repertoire of capabilities, and is ever more self-reliant in conducting his or her life. And thus children are to be, and to be treated as, individuals, responsible to themselves alone to develop in their own direction whatever is in them to develop. NT parents are reluctant to interfere with their children and shape up their behavior, even if they see them foundering a bit. Rational parents stand ready to assist their children in reaching their potential, whatever it might be, but they will neither nag their children nor shield them from the consequences of putting off the task of individual development.

Natural pragmatists, Rational parents happen quite instinctively upon Alfred Adler's principle of "logical consequences" as a way of handling their children, and practice what I call the "abuse-it-lose-it" method of discipline increasingly as the years go by. NTs seem to understand better than other parents that most of the things their children get to do are privileges rather than rights: eating with the family, talking to adult family members, being in a given room, playing with toys, playing with the family pet, and more. Even as young parents, many Rationals figure out that, when their children abuse one of these privileges, instead of scolding, admonishing, hitting, or even reasoning with them, all they need do is simply remove the abused privilege immediately and unconditionally for a set period of time, making sure not to comment about their child's behavior. Now this is the pragmatic thing to do, but it is not very easy, even for Rationals, while for the other types it is nearly impossible, particularly going against the grain of the cooperative Guardians and Idealists.

On the one hand, Coordinator Rationals (ENTJs & INTJs) leave nothing to chance when it comes to watching over the maturation of their children. The parenting books have been read, the parenting magazines have been subscribed to, the parenting techniques have been researched and considered—the whole thing is planned out well in advance with all important contingencies factored in. After all, many of these NTs are capable of running large organizations, so running a family is done with little difficulty and with little doubt as to the right course to take.

On the other hand, Engineers (ENTPs & INTPs) are more puzzled by their children than they are certain of what to do with them. Unlike the other Rationals, they have few if any set plans for raising their children, but simply wonder how it is with each of them, and try to find out by watching them and asking questions of them. These NTs are the least given to Pygmalion Projects of all the types—the only thing they expect of their children is that their children expect things of themselves. They figure that if they are reasonable with their children and do their best to help them grow they will turn out OK in the long run.

Rational Parent—Artisan Child: The pragmatic perspective of Rational parents serves them well in overseeing the maturation of an Artisan child. Their objectivity keeps them from expecting things of their children, so that there is no disappointment when they note that their little SP is stimulus bound, impulsive, going headlong and gleefully into any activity that is exciting—and thus is not going to become a little scientist buried in technical books. Rational parents follow along in the trail of their Artisan child's impetuous doings and try their best to corral the child with firm limits which can stand up to the child's inevitable and vigorous testing. It is in the case of the Artisan child that Rational parents can most effectively apply the principle of logical consequences and the method of immediate and unconditional removal of any privilege that the child abuses, however accidentally. The naturally practical and adaptable Artisan child does not fight the reality of such firm limits, and soon plays happily within the boundaries. But this is not all that Rational parents can do for the maturation of Artisan children. They are also surprised and pleased by the show of artistry so many of the Artisan children display, if given the chance, so NT parents systematically, and as a matter of principle, encourage the development of any art that beckons the child, whether it be entertaining, athletic, or constructive.

Rational Parent—Guardian Child: Rationals find their relationship to Guardian children somewhat problematic and sometimes frustrating. They really don't know how to act, don't know what they might do to help SJ children develop their ingenuity, become more independent, and increase their strength of will, none of which are of particular interest to the child. Rational parents are, in fact, bothered by their Guardian child's attempts to fit in socially. SJ children tend to go along with their social groups, and it can distress Rational parents to see little SJs doing things because the other kids are doing it. And Rational parents are disappointed by their Guardian child's wanting always to feel secure. Why can't their SJ child be bold or enthusiastic or curious like their SP, NF, or NT siblings? Why must their child report every pain, every disappointment, every wrong, every fear? Such children make Rational parents feel inadequate and helpless, because they cannot appeal to their children's reason, nor to their courage, nor to their hopes, nor to any desire to strike out on their own. Yet here are their SJ children trying in every way they can think of to please their baffled and uncertain NT parents, by being helpful, by serving, by doing good deeds, by conforming to all the social rules. It is well that Rational parents step aside and let their mate oversee the maturation of the Guardian child into the pillar of society he or she is meant to become.

Rational Parent—Idealist Child: Rational parents, pragmatists one and all, are quick to catch on that what works with most kids does not work with NF kids. For a Rational parent, it can be disconcerting to confront an emotional, thin-skinned Idealist child who is quite impervious to logical explanation and persuasion. Even imposing logical consequences does not impress the sometimes irritable Idealist child, even though such measures may curb the child's excesses in the end. Given neither to scolding nor to spanking their children, Rational parents quickly learn that the thing to do with irritability is to back off and quietly observe what transpires, thus adding no fuel to the fire of temper. In the meantime, NT parents are both fascinated and delighted with the enthusiasm, imaginativeness, and fancifulness that their NF children continuously display. Indeed, such mutual delight in imagination is usually the basis of a strong bond of affection between Rational parent and Idealist child, one that is rarely severed.

Rational Parent—Rational Child: Most little kids are seldom reasonable in their requirements and expectations, and reasoning with them is like shouting into the wind. But Rational children will listen to reason, and the older they get the more they will listen. So Rational parents have little, if any, difficulty in dealing with their Rational children, confident in the belief that, if they are reasonable in their requirements and expectations, their children will live up to them. Also, NT parents delight in many of their NT children's traits, but particularly in their strong sense of autonomy and their drive to gain knowledge and skills. NT children are born insisting on their independence, and (like their NT parents) they can become almost single-minded in their efforts to enlarge their storehouse of knowledge, and to sharpen and enlarge their repertoire of skills. Now, Rational parents might enjoy seeing their own characteristics mirrored in their offspring, but they must also recognize their Rational child's need for social development. Better for NT children to have at least one SP, SJ, or NF parent to help show them how to get along smoothly and productively with others.

—In Conclusion—

Without a doubt, increasing our success as parents requires us to understand both our children and ourselves, at least in outline. In the degree that we understand our children's personalities, as well as our own pre-set ideas and intentions in raising them, we stand a good chance of being effective or functional as parents, that is, we can succeed in our function of promoting a positive self-image in our children. If both parents are functional in this sense, then the family system becomes functional, with children having no difficulty in acquiring a self-image positive enough to enable them to become independent and self-affirming adults.

9

Leading and Intelligence

I have often reflected that the causes of success or failure of men depend upon their...character and nature, and [are] not a matter of choice.
— Niccolò Machiavelli

Winston Churchill and Mahatma Gandhi, two giants of the 20th century. Churchill was the virtuoso of political maneuvering, wheeling and dealing in unending political skirmishes; and Gandhi was the sage of interpersonal diplomacy, seeking freedom and justice for his people by appealing to the conscience of his oppressors. The tactician and the diplomat, diametric opposites in leadership style, yet each able to do for his country something that men of other character could not possibly have done—deliver it from bondage. Equally brilliant leaders, but brilliant in radically different ways.

George Washington and Abraham Lincoln, two giants of earlier centuries, each crucial to the survival of the United States of America. Except for a large measure of kindness and great physical strength, these two men had nothing important in common. Washington was a superb logistical commander who, faced with obstacles of incredible proportion and tenure, put in his way by his Congress, his generals, and his fellow citizens, freed his country from colonial bondage. And Lincoln was a superb political and military strategist who, despite the long continued blunders of a train of ill-chosen generals, the weakness of the Congress, and the intrigues of many of his fellow citizens, saved the United States from national dissolution. The logistical leader and the strategic leader, diametric opposites in both attitude and action, yet each achieving the same end, and earning his country's eternal gratitude.

Why would these four men—Churchill, Gandhi, Washington, and Lincoln—go about leading their people in such fundamentally different ways? The answer is: temperament. It takes a certain kind of temperament to achieve certain ends. The steadfast Guardian Washington had precisely the kind of temperament that the War of Independence and the establishment of a republic required, and the pragmatic Rational Lincoln precisely the kind of temperament the Civil War, and the Reconstruction, had he lived, required. Similarly, only an indomitable Artisan like Churchill could have rallied the English people during the dark days of World War II and convinced his wily friend Franklin Roosevelt to throw in with him before it was too late; and only a benevolent and altruistic Idealist like Gandhi could have inspired the Indian people to the swell of passive resistance that ultimately set them free from British dominion.

Temperament and Intelligence

The leader's objective, whatever his or her temperament, is to execute a plan of operations in the pursuit of a specified goal. However, since implementing any goal requires a certain kind and degree of intellectual development on the part of the personnel assigned to it, all types of leaders must take intelligence—their own and that of their employees—into account if they are to lead well.

What is the relationship between temperament and intelligence? The kind of intelligent role enacted by a leader or follower is determined by temperament, and the degree of skill in that role is determined by practice. Thus Churchill saved his country by relying heavily on his well-practiced tactical intelligence, Gandhi on his well-practiced diplomatic intelligence, Washington on his well-practiced logistical intelligence, and Lincoln on his well-practiced strategic intelligence. Without holding to their own highly developed intelligent roles in their great and desperate enterprises, it is doubtful whether any of these men would have succeeded. ·

Of course, most enterprises are multi-faceted, and therefore leaders would do well to understand that different kinds of intelligent roles are necessary for implementing different goals. Leaders can stay on top of things by studying the many forms of intelligence just in case they are called on to implement a new goal calling for unfamiliar operations. Indeed, it appears that nothing has greater payoff for the effective leader than recognizing the kind and degree of intelligent operations needed for getting a variety of jobs done. The best policy for a leader of any temperament is to look for intelligence and put it to work where it is most effective. *The leader's first job is to match talent to task.*

But it is not enough that leaders recognize the intellectual strengths of their followers. They would also profit a great deal by learning to appreciate their employees for the different skills they contribute to the enterprise.

The Importance of Appreciation

Bear in mind that we are leaders only insofar as we attract and keep followers. If we want our assistants to adopt certain methods and they do not do so, then, plainly, they have not followed our lead. Likewise, if we want our employees to work toward certain results, quite apart from how they go about it, and they do not do so, then, again they have not followed our lead. Now these are the only two ways that we can be leaders: we can encourage certain methods and we can encourage certain results. The degree to which we get what we're after is the measure of our leadership.

On the other hand, a follower is a follower only insofar as he or she does what a leader requests. And the surprising thing is that followers do what the leader wants primarily to please the leader. Whatever our type we are all social creatures, and so want to please the boss. We grow up for our parents, learn for our teacher, win for our coach—and we work for the boss. Even the most independent among us presents his or her work as a gift to the boss, which makes the boss rather imprudent if he or she fails to say, in some manner, "I appreciate what you are doing for our cause."

Is not the paycheck and the satisfaction of doing a good job enough? Apparently not. This is not to say that pay and satisfaction are not important; of course they are. Rather, it is to say that they are not enough. We all want appreciation, and we want it from the person in charge.

We not only want our contribution to be appreciated, we also want the appreciation to be proportional to our contribution. The greater the contribution the greater the desire for appreciation. It seems that big contributors have more appetite for appreciation than small contributors! Achievement generates appreciation hunger.

Watch those who strive to achieve. They do their thing, and if the boss fails to notice, they hightail it over to their private appreciator, stashed somewhere close by in the organizational bushes. Their appreciator strokes them with their warm fuzzies in a manner precisely fitting their private conception of their achievement, and their thirst for appreciation is assuaged, at least temporarily. They return to work with renewed energy.

Now, watch those high achievers whose boss fails to show appreciation for their contribution. Sooner or later they'll leave the job in search of a place where their work is appreciated.

Since leadership is getting people to achieve what the leader wants them to because the leader wants them to, and since achievement creates a desire for appreciation from the leader, then it follows that: *The leader's second job is appreciation.*

Progress Reports

To this end, effective leaders are wise to hold frequent conferences with assistants in order to acknowledge progress in skills development, and to express appreciation for progress in getting results. The effective leader is on the lookout for increase in skill and in attainment of results, so these two things are usually the focus of the conference. If the conference strays from progress, it is up to the leader to steer the conversation back to progress. If there is no progress to report on, the leader asks the assistant what the leader might do to help the assistant make progress. The frequency and length of conferences are the assistant's measures of his or her worth in the eyes of the leader. The more time invested in the assistant the more the worth of the assistant. If this means that the leader invests more time in his or hers more productive followers, so be it.

It works best if the leader holds conference at the assistant's workplace, for the reason that it is there that the assistant can best give an accounting of methods and results. The leader is wise to show avid interest in the assistant's work by looking and listening carefully and by asking pertinent questions that show insight into what is shown or said. This is called "active listening," a method of interviewing that can be learned by any leader regardless of temperament. In active listening leaders repeat what their assistant says about method and ask if they have got it right. And when they don't get it, which has to happen frequently, they ask for clarification and for examples. It is imperative that they do not let up on their search for method until they fully understand it. This not only proves that they are vitally interested in useful methods (methods that get results), but also vitally interested in the person who possesses useful methods. Time spent in discussing useful methods with one's followers is time well spent. Or better, time so invested is time well invested. The effective leader invests heavily in his or her followers.

Appreciating Intelligence

Theoretically, then, the motor of effective leadership consists in matching assistants' talents to tasks and in consistently expressing appreciation for their best efforts, thus encouraging them to be entrepreneurs contributing their talents to a shared enterprise. The major advantage of having a bevy of entrepreneurs working together is that each of them becomes committed to the success of the enterprise, and so not only applies all of his or her skills to the desired results, but also seeks to improve those skills by continuously learning on the job. Entrepreneurs will always outdo wage workers because entrepreneurs have their intelligence—their skill, their ability, their talent—engaged in the enterprise, while wage workers are merely punching the clock.

So appreciative leaders get interest on their investment, interest they do well to share with their more ambitious personnel, those who can be observed striving to become ever more skilled in their work. Those with ambition of any kind, whether it be to increase their logistical, tactical, strategic, or diplomatic methods, are the ones to confer with at length and to thank. In the discussion of results-producing methods instances of desired results are bound to surface. By discussing in detail how the employee gets results leaders have the opportunity to show their appreciation for their employee's intelligent operations. Such opportunity should never be missed, for it is the exact time to say, simply and pointedly, "thank you." Douglas MacGregor in his book *The Human Side of Enterprise* was very clear on this point: leaders are wise to show appreciation for their employees' contribution of means and ends. Again, the pay check is not enough, not, at any rate, for the high-achieving entrepreneurs.

Imagine that! Thanking employees for doing something they're supposed to do and something they're payed to do! That sticks in the craw of some leaders. Even so, they had best swallow the medicine or their team is going to lose, and the owners are quite rightly going to get a new coach.

But there's a catch. Leaders of different temperament have difficulty appreciating those intelligent roles that they have not practiced very much and therefore have not developed very well. Artisan leaders, for instance, tend to be skillful tacticians, but much less skillful as logisticians and strategists, while as diplomats they are likely to be even less than mediocre. And so it goes with other types of leaders, all of whom are very much aware of their long suit, moderately aware of their second or third suits, but largely unaware of their short suit. Thus, even if leaders grant that appreciating their assistants' intelligence is one of their main tasks, they are very likely to foul up by unconsciously evaluating their assistants in light of their own type of intelligence, failing to note when their assistants are intelligent in those roles that the leaders have neglected to practice.

And so, if leaders accept the idea of appreciation being the prime motivator in the workplace, then they would do well to learn about their own best intellectual roles and those of their assistants. For one thing, they could assign those tasks that require their own less-developed roles to the appropriate lieutenants; for another, they might avoid the mistake of showing appreciation for the kind of intelligence they value and not showing it for those kinds they do not value—or may not even be aware of.

Identifying Intelligence

To be worthwhile to our employer we must be skillful in some ways and willing to contribute our repertoire of skills to the enterprise we join. And if we apply our skills at work, then the enterprise will profit from our contribution; if we don't, then it won't. Of course, when we bring our particular skills to the workplace, we want our boss to see them for what they are and to appreciate us for the function we perform in the enterprise. Smart employers will be aware of our skills and will pay us for them, not only in money, but by acknowledging and appreciating that we are smart in ways that benefit the enterprise. If they're smart leaders they will thank us for our contribution. Remember, money is not enough for those who are proud of their repertoire of skills.

Now, this rule holds true up and down the organizational hierarchy. Chairmen of the Board are ill-advised if they do not appreciate the varied skills of their Directors. Presidents who are unaware of variations of talent, and who therefore fail to comment on the talents of their Vice Presidents, are not a good example for their Vice Presidents. Task force Chiefs who pick their operations managers for reasons other than their particular skills will not only have little to appreciate, but will also have little to show for their own efforts, since the task force is likely to be derailed and the mission aborted. And crew foremen or team coaches who lack a keen eye for the varied abilities of the crew or the team members are at best going to muddle along with minimal results. In short, leaders at any level are wise to study variations of talent so that they will know them when they see them, and so be in a position to appreciate them. Leaders who appreciate what I like to call the "SmartWork" of followers are smart leaders. So let's take another look at a graph shown in Chapters 3, 4, 5, and 6:

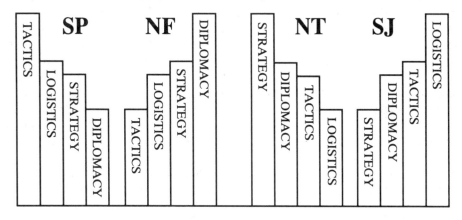

Note first of all that SP Artisans, in the role of leader, are the mirror image of the NF Idealists, and that NT Rationals are the mirror image of SJ Guardians. Predictably the most developed skill of the Artisan leader is tactics, and the least developed is diplomacy, with strategy and logistics in between and often nearly equal. The Idealist leader is the reverse, with diplomacy relatively high and tactics relatively low, the others in between. In the case of Guardians, logistics is their best skill, strategy least, with tactics and diplomacy middling and nearly equal; while Rationals are usually best at strategy, worst at logistics, with tactics and diplomacy in the middle.

As I have said, leaders of whatever type are wise to consider their major function to be that of matching talent to task—matching Smarts to Works to produce SmartWork. This done, the leader then checks on results and shows appreciation for his or her talented followers being smart enough to get the results they were hired to get.

Of course, it takes going back and forth between concrete operations (tactics and logistics) and abstract operations (diplomacy and strategy) to get work done. It's very likely impossible to get anywhere by continuing to perform either sort of operation exclusively over a long period of time. The abstractionist, whether diplomat or strategist (NF or NT), had better check on reality now and again; and the concretionist, whether tactician or logistician (SP or SJ), had better give an eye to plans and personnel every so often. Thus NT engineers have to try out their mechanisms to see how they work, then back to the drawing board armed with their observations.

In the same way, SP carpenters have to refer to the construction blueprints, then back to their hammers and power saws. The abstract and the concrete side of operations are opposites, but you can't have one without the other, if, that is, you want get the job done well.

The following diagram aligns the various intelligent roles and role variants so that they face their opposites:

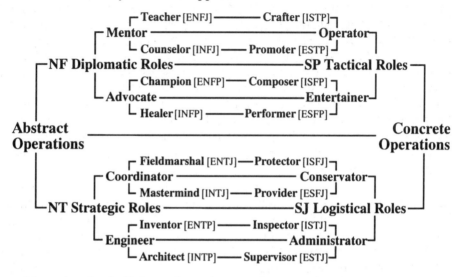

Note that both diplomatic and strategic operations and the roles they generate are abstract, while both tactical and logistical operations and their accompanying roles are concrete. This is the first and most important opposition to observe. Next, following the branching lines in from the left and from the right, we see that diplomatic roles and tactical roles are opposites, as are strategic roles and logistical roles. My guess is that the development of each kind of intelligent role largely inhibits or precludes the development of its opposite, even though some skill in both roles is needed to get work done. Thus a Mentor of personal development, at least in theory, will not be very good as an Operator of enterprises and machinery; an Advocate involved in personal mediation will not excel as an Entertainer improvising works of art; a Coordinator of efficient plans will not shine as a Conservator ensuring logistical support; and an Engineer of technological organization will not do well as an Administrator enforcing regulations. Whether such mutual exclusion extends to the sixteen role variants is a question that I cannot answer, though I suspect that it does. For example (looking at the top of the diagram), a brilliant classroom Teacher is not likely also to be a brilliant workbench Crafter. And (at the bottom of the diagram) a brilliant design Architect would surely find it hard to be a brilliant floor Supervisor. And vice versa. In any of these cases, an individual might perhaps become adequate at a given role, but not brilliant.

Why not? Because it takes continuous practice to become highly proficient in doing anything, and continuous practice is done only by someone who is interested in and enjoys a particular kind of work. For instance, someone interested in engineering usually has little interest in administering and so manages to practice it as little as possible, just as someone who finds satisfaction in administering finds little time to practice engineering. Thus, when an Administrator Guardian is hired to do engineering work, that person will very likely look for promotion to some form of administration in the engineering department. On the other hand, when an Engineer Rational is promoted to administrative work in the engineering department, he or she is very likely, sooner or later, to lose interest in such work and long to go back to engineering, even for less pay. The rightly famous Peter Principle nicely accounts for this case where a competent engineer is promoted to his "level of incompetence," with both employee and employer losing by the promotion (see *The Peter Principle* by Larry Peter.) Incidentally, Peter was wrong in speaking of different *levels* of competence; what happens to many employees highly competent in their job is that they are promoted to a different *kind* of job, one in which they prove to be less competent.

But this is not the occasion to spell out just how the eight kinds of intelligent roles preclude each other, even if it were possible to do so. That, after all, is a very large task to be accomplished down the line in a work devoted exclusively to defining, describing, explaining, and possibly evaluating the differing categories of intelligence. For now I claim only that these eight different kinds of work roles are observable—in other words, that it is possible to watch people doing these things, granting that some are easier to observe than others.

The reason I present the theory of operational preclusion in outline is that it may enable leaders to see the relations between the varying kinds of intelligent roles, to see the intellect-as-a-whole, so to speak. Whether or not this hypothetical construct proves to be useful remains to be seen. I hope it will take some of the obscurity out of the problem of intelligence and put the problem itself into of the hands of business leaders. Saying that intelligence is smart work rather than smart thought—doing work rather than thinking thoughts—may prove to be a step in the right direction toward solving the terribly complex problem of intelligence.

Whatever their temperament, the more leaders are able to get a grip on the different kinds of intelligent work roles, the more they will be able to observe such work and to estimate how well it is done. In a way the leader's role is like that of parents and spouses: there's no choice but to play the role in character. It has to be enacted consistently with the abiding self-image, interests, and values of the leader.

But especially the role must be played from a position of strength. It will not do, for instance, for Guardians to present themselves as strategic leaders, or Rationals as logistical leaders. Nor is it prudent for Artisans to pose as diplomatic leaders, or for Idealists as tactical leaders.

Recall British General Bernard Montgomery's folly in trying to roll up the German flank at the north end of the Allied line of battle in World War II (the film *One Bridge Too Far* dramatized this disastrous maneuver). Here was a great logistical leader who diminished his reputation by failing to understand that his strategic capabilities fell far short of his logistical capabilities. Or consider the American President Woodrow Wilson vying with the English Prime Minister Lloyd George and the French Premier Clemenceau in crafting the Versailles treaty after World War I. This was a case of a brilliant logistical leader being outmaneuvered by two wily tactical leaders, thus setting the stage for the eruption of World War II but one generation later.

Then of course great tactical leaders have been known to stumble badly when they attempted strategic planning. For instance, Admiral William "Bull" Halsey, having proven himself a superb tactical leader in the South Pacific naval campaign against the overwhelmingly superior Japanese forces, made a nearly catastrophic strategic blunder in leaving his post in the battle of Leyte Gulf. Halsey's Third Fleet was to guard the entry into Leyte Gulf, so that General MacArthur's ground forces could invade Leyte safely. Here was a remarkable case in which a Japanese Admiral (Osawa) based his strategy on Halsey's notoriously impulsive character. Upon studying Halsey's character Osawa prepared to sacrifice six (nearly empty) carriers by dangling them north of Halsey's Third Fleet to lure Halsey away from his guardpost. He succeeded. Halsey swallowed the bait and headed north with his entire fleet, battle ships, carriers, cruisers, and destroyers, leaving nothing to stand at the entrance to Leyte Gulf. This strategic blunder left MacArthur's ground forces vulnerable to the awesome power of Admiral Kurita's central task force. Had not Kurita then blundered just as badly as Halsey, the consensus of historians is that MacArthur's forces, receiving little protection from the Seventh fleet of Admiral Kincaid, would in all probability have been wiped out. The brilliant tactician, Halsey, faced with a crucial strategic decision, muffed it.

Then there was General Robert E. Lee's disastrous adventure into Gettysburg, Pennsylvania in the spring of 1863, in the vain hope, some believe, of drawing General Ulysses S. Grant away from his siege of Vicksburg. This adventure showed that Lee's strategic intelligence was far less developed than his well-honed tactical intelligence. In the same way, General Grant, a strategic wizard by the end of the war, was totally eclipsed by General McLelland in the logistical matter of preparing an army for battle, and who knows but what we would find on investigation that great diplomatic leaders have blundered when they essayed tactical maneuvers.

The point not to miss is that intelligence cannot be evenly developed across the board, and that defeat and loss ensue when leaders fail to understand their own abilities and that of their opponents. The intellect, after all, is a many splendored thing, and those who do not understand this fact of life will sooner or later pay the piper for their failure to do so.

It is without doubt a tall order to understand intelligence. And 20th century psychologists have not been helpful in this, most of them going along with the Binet-Spearman notion that intelligence is correlated primarily with abstract thought, and in any event is "cognitive ability" (see Sternberg's massive *Handbook of Human Intelligence*). But the bottom line is that concrete tactical Artisans are just as smart as abstract diplomatic Idealists—but in quite different ways. Likewise, concrete logistical Guardians are just as smart as abstract strategic Rationals—though again in quite different ways. The myth that intelligence depends on abstract thought has left in its wake a great deal of misunderstanding on the part of both leaders and followers.

Please understand me on this point if on nothing else: any of us, whatever our temperamental makeup, can be effective leaders, provided that we come to understand our own strengths and weaknesses as well as those of our followers, and provided that we show our appreciation whenever we note our followers contributing their intelligence to our mutual enterprise.

Now let us turn to the four patterns of intellectual development, beginning with the tactical Artisans.

Tactical Intelligence

The tactical intelligence of Artisans (SPs) can be defined as making smart moves that better one's position, whether those moves are made by Operators expediting their enterprises, or by Entertainers improvising their presentations. Artisans, like everyone else, want their leaders to appreciate their talents, and observing their roles is not at all difficult. Indeed, tactical intelligence is easily the most visible of the four kinds of intelligence, even more visible than logistical intelligence. The reason is that tactics are maneuvers in the field, on stage—where the action is—and as such are very immediate and concrete, while diplomacy and strategy are abstract, usually taking place, as it were, behind the scenes. The following diagram from Chapter 3 mirrors the Artisans' tactical roles and role variants and the kinds of work they do exceptionally well.

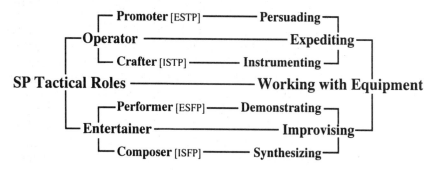

Tactical Operators

Operators work on the expediting side of tactical intelligence. They are the tough-minded Artisans, those SPs who are smart at working with people and machinery in order to advance their interests, and who are directive or quick to tell others what to do. Operators outdistance all the other Artisans in two of the sixteen role variants: the expressive Promoter and the reserved Crafter.

Promoters (ESTPs) are able to do whatever it takes to gain others' confidence in them and their enterprises. These are the so-called "smooth operators" who excel in all the forms of persuasion: assurance, belief, confidence, faith, positiveness, surety, and trust. Promoters are outgoing, conspicuous people, calling attention to themselves by their charm and wit, and by the ease with which their promotional activities win over other employees to go along with whatever they have in mind, whether recreational or productive in intent. And finding occasions for appreciating the Promoters' skill is also easy, since they are usually eager to impress leaders and peers alike, and so are always available to discuss their promotional activities.

Crafters (ISTPs) are just as easy to observe because of the remarkably graceful way these quiet Operators work with instruments, implements, machinery, and other tools, in order to accomplish the task at hand. Though not as spectacular as, say, surfing on the twenty-five foot waves at Sunset Beach on the shores of Oahu, still the Crafters' virtuosity with, for instance, a giant skip loader or backhoe or crane can be awesome, if the observer has any idea at all of how much skill is required to operate these machines. Leaders should not let such feats of skill go unsung, or unrewarded, since they are artistry just as surely, and for the same reasons, as playing first violin in a symphony orchestra.

The graph below shows a theoretical curve of the most likely role development profile of those Artisans who become smart Operators.

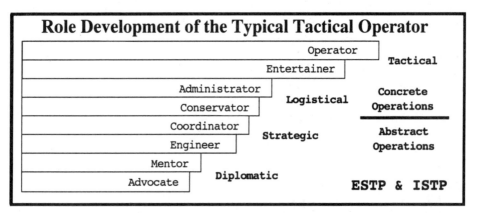

Note that the other tactical role, that of Entertainer, will usually lag slightly behind for the simple reason that it gets slightly less practice.

Second, note that the logistical and strategic roles are rarely on a par with the tactical roles, and for the same reason, only random and indifferent practice, with scant checking on results. Still, since logistics is a concrete operation, there is some likelihood that it will be more interesting to Operators than strategy, which is abstract, and so the typical Operator tends to be a little smarter at logistics than strategy. Then there is diplomacy. Compared to tactics, it is, in the eyes of most Artisans, a very dull sort of activity, and consequently when it comes to acting in diplomatic roles, Operator Artisans are not nearly as smart as when they are acting tactically.

Tactical Entertainers

Drawn to the improvising side of tactical intelligence, Entertainers are the friendly, fond-hearted Artisans, those SPs who want to amuse or to charm others, and whose first impulse is to inform those around them by making or showing them something beautiful or exciting. Entertainers shine as two of the sixteen role variants: the expressive Performer and the reserved Composer.

Performers (ESFPs) love to demonstrate their talents, to display, to exhibit, to present, to put on a show. Because they are so naturally outgoing, Performers are easy to spot in a work force, though their contribution to the enterprise may not always be so obvious, unless they are employed to advertise products or company image. In that case the improvising abilities of the Performer can be unleashed to full advantage. But these talents need not be confined to presentations to customers. They can just as well be used in displays and demonstrations to company personnel of new techniques and their relationship to the objectives of the company. Performers are entertainers at heart, and this being so, it is well that the leader of such individuals applaud them.

Composers (ISFPs) find joy in bringing into entertaining form any aspect of the world of the senses. Composers seem to have an uncanny sense of synthesis, that is, an ability to see what fits and what doesn't fit in any work of art. Who, we might ask, are the best interior decorators or fashion designers? Surely it is Composers. In this kind of art the composition speaks for itself, while the skill creating the composition is often hidden from sight. For example, consider what the film director does to get just the right camera shot. It is not at all clear to observers why the shot is taken from here rather than from there, or at this time of day rather than that, or why the background sounds are this rather than that. Directors such as Orson Welles, Federico Fellini, Steven Spielberg, and many others are obvious virtuosos of tactical improvisation, just as are musical prodigies like Mozart, Chopin, and Tchaikovsky. And yet less obvious, and far less dramatic compositions are being made daily in many businesses and enterprises. Think of it, computer graphics, video presentations, and company newsletters have to be composed, as do book jackets, posters, and pamphlets, and of course decorations and ornamentations of all kinds. Though not as visible as the others SPs, ISFPs are smart at all of these acts of composition—mingling, blending, combining—and need to be recognized for the beauty they bring to the job at hand.

The graph below shows a theoretical curve of the most likely role development profile of those Artisans who become smart Entertainers.

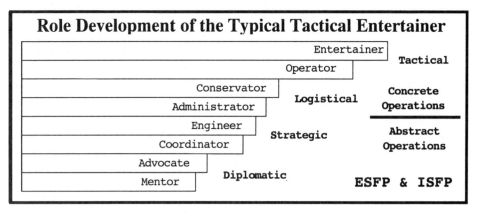

Note that the other tactical role, that of Operator, will usually lag a little behind for the simple reason that it tends to get a little less practice. Second, note that logistical and strategic roles are rarely on a par with tactical roles, and for the same reason, only infrequent and careless practice, with scant checking on results. Still, since logistics is a concrete operation, there is some likelihood that it will be more interesting to the Improvisers than strategy, which is abstract, and so ordinary Entertainers tend to be a little smarter doing logistics than strategy. And what about diplomacy? Compared to tactics, it is, in the eyes of most Artisans, a very boring sort of activity, and so when it comes to acting the diplomat, Entertainers Artisans are not nearly as smart as when they are acting tactically.

Without a doubt, types of personality other than Artisans can, by dint of practice, become fairly smart Operators and Entertainers, and of course it is not imprudent to assign them to this kind of work. But if the employer is looking for virtuosity in the tactical roles it is a much better bet to find an Artisan, however young, to fill the position. Then the leader's appreciation for such an employee's contribution can be genuine and oft-spoken.

Leaders need to identify and appreciate their Artisan followers' tactical intelligence, but the SmartWork characteristics of Artisan leaders are just as vital to an organization.

The Tactical Leader

[Churchill] never feared taking responsibility nor was he wont to lay blame on others when events wore an ugly aspect....He knew that he had great aptitudes for leadership and he always grasped the opportunity to

exercise it. If there was a battle he always aspired to be in the front line, even if not in actual command
— Randolph S. Churchill

The boldness and opportunism of Winston Churchill are rare in British politics, but certainly not in American. Indeed, the American Presidency gives us an illuminating way of looking at Artisan leaders, since thirteen of the forty-one Presidents of the United States (those holding office until the turn of the 21st century) were Artisans. Six of these were tough-minded and highly directive Operators—Andrew Jackson, Martin Van Buren, Theodore and Franklin Roosevelt, John Kennedy, and Lyndon Johnson. The other seven were more friendly and informative Entertainers—Zachary Taylor, Franklin Pierce, James Garfield, Chester Arthur, Warren Harding, Ronald Reagan, and Bill Clinton. The leadership of the Operator Presidents was clearly different from that of the Entertainers, yet quite similar in its tactical form. The tough Operators, especially the Roosevelts and Lyndon Johnson, were far more capable than the friendly Entertainers of pushing their programs, both in the sense of drumming up support and crafting political tactics. But the Entertainers were the best speech-makers, especially Garfield, Reagan, and Clinton, these three able to forward their agendas by chatting pleasantly with ordinary people, by speaking extemporaneously, and by delivering their composed speeches with a captivating flair.

Biographies and other accounts of the American Civil War give us another way of looking at Artisan leaders. The most prominent Artisan commander was General Robert E. Lee of the Confederacy. His tactical virtuosity on the battlefield remained unmatched by any other SP commander until George Patton and Erwin Rommel in World War II. But other notorious Artisan leaders were J.E.B. Stuart and Nathan Forrest on the Confederate side, and Philip Sheridan and George Custer on the Union side.

As discussed above, the most practiced and therefore most developed intelligent roles of Artisans are those of Operator and Entertainer. Artisan leaders feel alive—"having fun" they call it—when they are playing these tactical roles, or their variants, and thus feel they are using their talents and keeping their organization on the move.

Because of their tactical adaptability, Artisan leaders negotiate with ease and, of all the types, have the highest sense of immediate reality. Thus they can be called natural "Negotiators," but other names which might capture their style are "Troubleshooters" and "Beachmasters." They're good at putting out fires, at untangling snarls, and at responding to crises in a way which the other types can match only belatedly and with great effort. Running through this style is a note of tactical utilitarianism—whatever needs to be done to solve a problem is done, and is done now. Ties to the past and ties to the future are negotiable and even expendable.

Some large corporations make efficient use of the skills of this group when they buy another company which is in the red, but which they want to acquire for personnel, patents, securities, and tax write-offs. The corporation sends in an Artisan Troubleshooter to take over the smaller company, with directions to implement the take-over, that is, to incorporate it into the body of the larger company. The Troubleshooter is empowered with the authority to do whatever has to be done to make this new acquisition a part of the parent organization. And this can happen rather quickly, for somehow these SPs are capable of getting others to cooperate with them and with each other on the basis of expediency. Troubleshooters have an attitude of certainty and self-confidence that causes others to go along with their decisions and directions. If these kinds of leaders experience self-doubt, they do not transmit it to those around them.

Some of this confidence seems to stem from the Artisan's strong sense of reality. Somehow this character is more sharp-eyed or present to reality than the other types, who often go into a trouble spot with several sets of glasses firmly placed over their views of the situation. Others filter what needs to be done through fixed lenses—customs, procedures, personal sympathies, the need to be liked—all of which obscure a clear view of what is immediate, what is right here, and what is right now. Negotiating SPs wear none of these lenses. They go into a difficult situation, not like a babe in the woods, but more like a fox, with a sharp eye for opportunity. They are not saddled with rules and regulations, with policies and contracts, with personal cares and old relationships. In other words, to the Negotiator everything—and everybody—is negotiable!

Other types who sit down at the bargaining table reserve some of the things they own or the things they have done as non-negotiable. They take their places with a tiny bit of something in mind which they intend to negotiate with, like bargaining chips. They plan to give up a pittance in exchange for whatever they can get. SP Negotiators, however, do not consider anything on either side as sacred or untouchable. They go back and look in closets, and say, "Hey, look at all that gold. Let's bring it out and negotiate it!" This keen sense of reality gives this type a big edge over others, making others seem like amateurs in the art of give and take.

Artisans also make everyone else look like amateurs when it comes to improvising survival tactics. Consider the military beachmasters, who function in a shooting war. They are the leaders who go in with the second wave of troops invading an island or a continent. With all the men and material on the beach, the beachmaster has but one objective—to get the men off the beach and safely into the bushes—and he has absolute authority to shove anything into the sea. No one can say a word to the beachmaster about what goes and what does not. Beachmasters have to have a split-second sense of timing, an overwhelming sense of what is right here, right now, and in an instant decide what has to be pushed into the ditch, into the sea, or under the ground. So when a commander has men stacking up on a beachhead and needs a beachmaster, he does not send in someone who is laden with traditions and the rules of warfare, or who is acutely aware of the future, or the penalties of failure, or who is overconcerned with the meaning of death. Survival is the issue. All other considerations are expendable. Nothing counts on that beachhead but getting off the beach and surviving to attack and secure the objective.

Of course the Beachmaster brand of leadership is not restricted to war. This type is outstanding in rising to the occasion in any crisis. For instance, I remember well an ailing high school notorious as a graveyard for principals. A principal would be assigned to that school and the faculty would send him packing within a few months. The faculty was made up of two hostile factions, each battling the other; but each side knew how to dismantle a principal, and did so with unfailing regularity. No one could deal with the situation: the faculty became more and more at odds, the students were learning less and less, parents were up in arms. Finally, the superintendent told the assistant superintendent to "take over that school and straighten it out." In three months the war had ceased, and the faculty was pulling together as unit, with mutually facilitative transactions. Needless to say, the assistant superintendent was an Artisan Beachmaster with an unerring instinct for getting people to work with each other in an emergency situation. If there had been a different staff at that school, in all probability they would have been able to function just as effectively. These Beachmasters are so immediate, so unfettered with things of the past, that they can see the opportunities current in each new situation.

Artisan leaders are practical in every sense of the word. They deal with concrete problems, and will do whatever it takes to solve them. They usually know what is really going on in an organization, for they have keen and untiring powers of observation. They can observe social networks close-up and see how they work—day to day, hour by hour, minute by minute—and they can spot where breakdowns and mismatches occur, and then rapidly improvise corrections. Under their leadership things happen expeditiously, and with an economy of motion. SP leaders do not fight the system but use what is immediately at hand to get operations back on line.

Artisans can spur action in a leadership team as can no other type. Things are sure to happen with this type around. They're at their best in verbal planning and on-the-spot decision making, while they may not enjoy and are loath to produce routine paperwork. Operations are apt to run smoothly with these Troubleshooters in charge, since they will detect early signs of trouble and can prevent small problems from becoming large ones through inattention. Their productivity is apt to be high, and they are usually aware of the comfort and working conditions of employees. SP leaders are not likely to allow unnecessarily bad working conditions to exist for employees without attempting to do something about them. They verbalize appreciation easily, once they learn that there is a payoff in this sort of action; indeed, they can over-praise when such praise is not earned, and they are known to voice appreciation before their subordinates have accomplished anything, in order to encourage greater efforts.

Artisans don't like being told how to work; standard operating procedures make them restless and impatient—they would rather fly by the seat of their pants. Such impulsiveness can annoy fellow workers when Artisans forget to follow through on agreements and fail to inform others of the oversight. Artisans also may be careless about details and this may irritate others, or they can be unprepared at times when preparation is called for, and can spring the unexpected on colleagues now and then. At times they make commitments for others without getting an OK, behavior which understandably can upset the person on whose behalf a commitment was made. SP leaders can be reluctant to attend to kid-glove diplomatic issues, and may react negatively to change they have not wrought themselves. They live so fully in the moment that they may have difficulty remembering prior commitments and decisions. Yesterday is quickly gone and just as quickly forgotten. Current demands preempt anything else. This here-and-now orientation leaves Artisan leaders in a position of being somewhat unpredictable to their colleagues and subordinates. On the other hand, when there is no crisis to manage, such leaders can become rigid and entirely too predictable.

Beachmasters tend to be impatient with writing goal statements and statements of philosophy, claiming these are only exercises in futility. They themselves are the very essence of flexibility—flexible with themselves and flexible in their expectations of others. They are open-minded and can change positions easily, responding readily to the ideas of others if they are specific. With SPs in charge, institutional change is usually smooth and easy, for they can adapt easily to new situations. They welcome and seek change, but they do not waste their time and effort in worrying about changing what cannot be changed. Things that can be changed—procedures, regulations, personnel—are all in their hands in a crisis. They love to take risks, love to gamble, love to intervene in crises. When Artisans are getting a school out of trouble, rescuing a business from going under, or getting an industry out of the red, they are excited and energetic.

But consider the situation if the negotiating and troubleshooting SPs are asked to stay and consolidate an organization. Suppose they are asked to head up an enterprise that is now in the black. Suppose they are asked to maintain an organization, establishing goals, administrative regulations, and employee morale. What are they going to do? Some of them are going to make mischief to give themselves the opportunity to operate in a manner that exercises their tactical skills. They are like firemen who, having nothing to do, set fires so that they can put them out. That is the penalty of having Troubleshooters stay on as Stabilizers. They don't get their jollies from stabilizing because in trying to do so, they feel that they're not using their skills, and have nothing worthwhile to do, and so are bored—and it's then that they are likely to go looking for trouble to shoot. The moral of this story is that, for an organization of any size, Artisans are needed for crisis situations, but they should neither be required nor allowed to stay in a situation once it is unsnarled. Leaving them to do the work of another temperament is a disservice to the Artisan and to the organization. These leaders ought to be kept mobile and used only in emergencies that call for their amazing tactical skills.

Those Artisan leaders who for whatever reason remain in charge of a given enterprise are well-advised to select a support team comprised of: 1) schedule-oriented Guardians for regulation and support of material resources, people who reliably provide reminders of appointments and deadlines, and who carefully set times and places for the routine tasks often forgotten by their Artisan leader; 2) Idealists for personnel development and mediation, people who know how to maintain smooth relations and high morale in the work force; and 3) Rationals for arranging and constructing in research and development of technology, people who consider those long-term issues that can so easily be put off for some other time, and who can capture in writing the endless flow of projects for future reference. With such support there is no reason that Artisan Negotiator-Troubleshooter-Beachmaster leaders cannot continue exercising and improving their tactical skills, to the benefit of the organization as well as their own personal fulfillment.

In summary, Artisan leaders are usually flexible, patient, open-minded, easy to get along with, and adaptable in working with others. These Negotiators are not threatened by the possibility of failure in themselves or others, so they are likely to take risks and to encourage others to do the same. They change their position easily as new facts and new situations arise, seldom finding this shift in position a threat to their self-image. Artisan leaders are matter-of-fact about things as they are and do not chafe about what might have been. They do not trouble themselves or others seeking to understand underlying motives or hidden meanings. And they do not judge their employees, accepting their actions as realistically as they do changing circumstances.

Logistical Intelligence

The intelligence of Guardians (SJs) comes to the fore in their logistical reliability, that is, in their smart handling of goods and services, whether in the role of Administrator of regulations or Conservator of support measures. Like the other temperaments, Guardians want to have their own pattern of intelligence appreciated by their leaders, and, fortunately, spotting logistical intelligence is almost as easy as spotting the Artisan's tactical intelligence, and far easier than spotting either the Idealist's diplomatic or the Rational's strategic intelligence. This is because logistics has to do with concrete, down-to-earth, everyday matters of materiel, while diplomacy and strategy are abstract operations dealing with the subtleties of personal interactions and the hypotheticals of complex systems. To get a better picture of the overall pattern of logistical intelligence, consider the diagram on the next page (first presented in Chapter 4) which parallels the Guardians' logistical roles and variants with their most skillful intelligent operations in the work place:

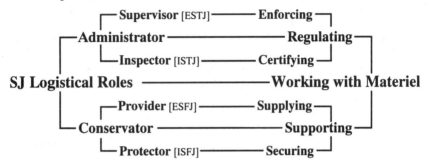

Logistical Administrators

Administrators work on the regulatory side of logistics. These are the tough-minded Guardians, those SJs who run their organizations by applying and enforcing administrative regulations. Administrators know what an institution's established policies and measurements are, and they keep their eyes peeled for compliance—and they are quite comfortable directing others to shape up or ship out. Two of the sixteen role variants find real satisfaction in the Administrator's duties: the expressive Supervisor and the reserved Inspector.

Supervisors (ESTJs) manage their people by enforcing standards of behavior and pointing out whenever their behavior crosses or fails to cross some agreed-upon line. Both in manufacturing and in services most operations become standardized, and that is the time to employ a tough Supervisor who knows the standard operating procedures, who will apply them to the operations of a staff, or crew, or team—someone who not only doesn't mind directing employees to toe the line and come up to snuff, but feels good about doing this sort of thing. Perhaps because calling workers out of line is unpleasant to those who err, ESTJs are the least likely of all to be praised for their contribution. And yet Supervisors are of immense value to companies, and leaders would do well to let them know how important they are by telling this to them face to face.

Inspectors (ISTJs) look more at products and accounts than at procedures, and so rarely have the visibility of Supervisors. After examining a product, the Inspector judges the degree to which it meets the standard, setting it aside as a second or a discard if it doesn't measure up. So if the Inspector falsely reject too many products, then he or she is not very good at the job. If on the other hand each and every reject is justifiably set aside, then the Inspector must be judged competent in this line of work, and wisely commended for being so. ISTJs are unbelievably hard-working and thorough in their inspections, though (unlike the ESTJs) they prefer simply to note and report discrepancies and not confront the violators. As in the case of smart Supervisors, smart Inspectors are of enormous value to any enterprise in which quality control and cost effectiveness are to be maintained at a high level of accuracy. For example, actuaries, accountants, brokers, corporate and tax attorneys, people who can competently detect discrepancies and glitches in fiscal reports, contracts, leases, and the like, are indispensable in financial matters, so their largely unseen contribution to enterprise ought not be taken for granted.

The graph below shows a theoretical curve of the most likely role development profile of those Guardians who become smart Administrators.

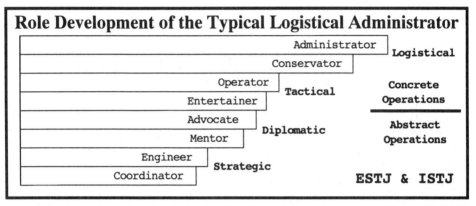

Role Development of the Typical Logistical Administrator

Note that the other logistical role, that of Conservator, will usually lag a little behind for the simple reason that it gets a little less practice. Second, note that diplomatic and tactical roles are rarely on a par with logistical roles, and for the same reason, only irregular and cursory practice, with scant checking on results. Still, since tactics is a concrete operation, there is some likelihood that it will be more interesting to Administrators than diplomacy, which is abstract, and so ordinary Administrators tend to be a bit smarter taking on tactical roles than diplomatic roles. Then there is strategy. Compared to logistics, strategy is pretty uninteresting in the view of most Guardians, so is largely ignored, and consequently when it comes to acting in strategic roles, Administrator Guardians are not nearly as smart as when they are acting logistically.

Logistical Conservators

Conservators are the friendly and informative Guardians, those SJs who prefer the task of logistical support to logistical command, and who take pride in ensuring a steady flow of materiel to an organization, and the security of the people and property in their charge. Two of the sixteen role variants surpass all others in doing the Conservator's job: the expressive Providers and the reserved Protectors.

Providers (ESFJs) work to furnish their office or company with whatever supplies are needed to get the job done. Providers are usually outgoing and seem to enjoy supporting others, making sure that they are well stocked with provisions. Look at the smart purchasing agent in business or the smart supply officer in the military: they do whatever they can to keep warehouses full with all necessary stores, so that there is no interruption in the pace of operations. Bear in mind that George Washington, the most famous and beloved of all ESFJs, not only provided the wherewithal for his army's continued existence for eight desperate years, but also protected his new nation from anarchy on the one hand and monarchy on the other, for another eight trying years. Although logistical conserving is a concrete operation, Providers can be just as creative in their own way as Fieldmarshal Rationals (ENTJs), their opposites, who are busy with the abstract operation of coordinating forces in the field.

Protectors (ISFJs) see to it that safeguards are in place and preventive measures are observed, all to secure the safety of the people and property they care about. Protectors are much like Providers in being naturally concerned about the welfare of others. Of course, all Guardians are naturally cautious and security minded, but none of them are so devoted and committed to security and maintenance as the Protectors. For them security is the highest priority, so they practice it early on and continuously, becoming the very best security guards, custodians, timekeepers, doorkeepers, wardens, defenders, screening officials, patrollers, sergeants-at-arms, curators, and so on. Protectors are quiet and can often be taken for granted, coming to be noticed only when security has been breached, or when equipment breaks down, so leaders need to take special care to appreciate this type even when things are safe and sound.

The graph below shows a theoretical curve of the most likely intellectual profile of those Guardians who become smart Conservators.

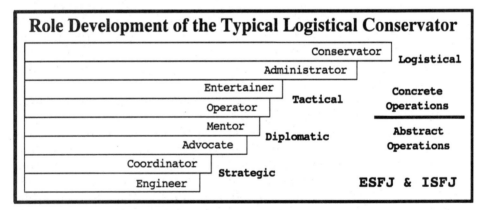

Note that the other logistical role, that of Administrator, typically lags a bit behind, for the reason that it gets a bit less practice. Then note that the diplomatic and tactical roles are rarely on a par with the logistical roles, and for the same reason, only sporadic and half-hearted practice, with not much attention to results. Still, since tactics is a concrete operation, there is some likelihood that it will be more interesting to Conservators than diplomacy, which is abstract, and so ordinary Conservators tend to be a little smarter as tacticians than as diplomats. As for strategy, the view of most Guardians is that strategy, compared to logistics, is rather uninteresting, so is mostly ignored, and consequently when called upon to act in strategic roles, Conservator Guardians are not nearly as smart as when they are acting logistically.

The characteristics of logistical intelligence need to be identified and valued in leaders just as much as in followers.

The Logistical Leader

Perhaps the strongest feature in [Washington's] character was prudence, never acting until every circumstance, every consideration, was maturely weighed; refraining when he saw a doubt, but, when once decided, going through with his purpose whatever obstacles opposed.
—Thomas Jefferson

Of the forty-one Presidents of the United States, twenty were Guardians. Thirteen of these were tough-minded, directive Administrators: James Monroe, William Henry Harrison, John Tyler, James Polk, James Buchanan, Andrew Johnson, Grover Cleveland, Benjamin Harrison, Woodrow Wilson, Calvin Coolidge, Harry Truman, Richard Nixon, and Jimmy Carter. And several of these Administrators—Monroe, Polk, Cleveland, Wilson, Truman—were outstanding chief executives, extremely capable in conducting the business of government. The other seven Guardian Presidents were more fond-hearted, informative Conservators—George Washington, Millard Fillmore, Rutherford Hayes, William McKinley, William Taft, Gerald Ford, and George Bush. As for outstanding executive leadership, only one or possibly two of these Conservators come to mind, with Washington overshadowing all others in administrative performance, and Bush coming in a distant second.

But politics is not the only work where Guardians can excel as leaders. The military also provides a place where logistical intelligence is highly useful and highly sought after. As in the case of the Artisans, the American Civil War yielded a great many highly effective Guardian commanders. George McLelland of the Union Army and James Longstreet of the Confederate Army come to mind. McLelland was a brilliant logistical leader, and that is precisely (though belatedly) how Lincoln used him, setting him the task of refurbishing the defeated and demoralized Army of the Potomac. Longstreet too was a brilliant logistician, and Robert E. Lee used him often for crucial defensive functions. In World War II many superb logistical leaders, mostly Guardians, surfaced. The most famous of these were Omar Bradley and Bernard Montgomery, both answering to Dwight Eisenhower. Incidentally, Eisenhower, the great Rational strategist, like the Rational Commander-in-Chief Lincoln eighty years earlier, soon learned how to make use of the differences in his top commanders. Thus Eisenhower gave the flamboyant Artisan Patton the assignment of flanking enemy forces, while he asked the steady Guardian Bradley to slog it out across opposing battle lines, and gave the equally steady Montgomery the task of staying put as fulcrum for the Allied sweep through France into Germany.

Also, the contrast between the leadership of Elizabeth I and her father Henry VIII is as striking as it is instructive. Henry was a blazing Artisan who, owing to his many adventures, got his country into all sorts of troubles and debts, which his successors and their ministers failed to relieve. So when Elizabeth took the throne her Guardian temperament guided her unerringly to avoid the pitfalls of intemperate action. First of all, and most importantly, she took extreme care in selecting her cabinet of ministers, making sure to have a majority of those who understood business and finance, and offsetting those of conservative bent with those of radical bent. In a way she did for England what George Washington did for America; Washington stabilized the economy by permitting the war between Jefferson and Hamilton on fiscal policy to go on for eight years, while he steered down the middle between urban and agrarian interests. Elizabeth, too, within a mere eight years had the English ship of state holding a steady course toward prosperity, the debt relieved, the currency stabilized, and foreign entanglements all but eliminated.

As outlined above, the most practiced and therefore most developed intelligent roles of Guardians are those of Administrator and Conservator. When their occupation calls for them to enact these logistical roles, or their variants, Guardians feel dependable, knowing that they are serving their organization well and thus earning their salary.

Guardian leaders at work tend to have a stabilizing and consolidating effect on the organization that employs them, and thus might be called the "Stabilizers." Their abilities lie in establishing schedules, routines, rules, and protocols. They are good at drawing up lines of communication, and at following through on jobs until completion. They are patient, thorough, steady, reliable, orderly. They value contracts, administrative regulations, and standard operating procedures. People under SJ leaders know that they can count on things remaining constant and familiar. They know that personnel and materiel and business agreements will all be kept in good order under the sensible guidance of the Guardian. Stabilizers are careful to identify their own duties and just as careful to point out the duties of their subordinates. The dutiful worker is prized—and rewarded—by the Guardian leader.

These SJ leaders also answer to the name of "Traditionalists," for, in keeping with the name, they carefully (and quite sentimentally) preserve and nurture the traditions of the institutions they belong to. They know better than most that strong traditions give comfort, a sense of belonging, and a sense of permanence to employees and clients alike. Should the organization lack traditions, the Guardian leader is likely to see to it that they are created, moving quickly to establish a basic schedule of rituals, customs, and ceremonies—a gold watch for the retiring septuagenarian, a welcoming luncheon for new employees, the annual office Christmas party, the Fourth of July picnic for employees and their families, and so on—all in an effort to solidify the organization.

Stabilization is a necessary stage in the life of any organization, but there is a tendency, after a time, for stability to go too far, and for organizations to fall victim to Parkinson's Law—the law of "the hegemony of means over ends." This law informs us that in any organization operational costs increase without a corresponding increase in production, which is to say, the organization gradually becomes more bureaucratic. And this increase of input without a corresponding increase in output seems to be a function of time alone, with older institutions usually being more bureaucratic than younger ones. Now, Guardian leaders, interested as they are in institutional stability, are more prone to fall victim to Parkinson's Law than the other types. To solve persistent problems of production they are more likely to add personnel to operate in customary ways than to redesign operations.

Paradoxically, uniformity of production can only be ensured by variation in operation. The same operations cannot continue to get the same results because situations change over time—parts and suppliers change, personnel changes, customers change. Indeed, the only thing that is surely constant is situational inconstancy; the only thing that doesn't change is the inevitability of change. So to continue to get the same results leaders have to make changes in operations, something Guardians are reluctant to do. Certainly SJs can learn to make the necessary changes, if, that is, they are alerted to the stalking of Parkinson's Law—or at least to the implications of a law they are more comfortable with, Murphy's Law, which states that "things that can go wrong will go wrong," and that "everything costs more and takes longer." Even Murphy's Law advises that Guardian leaders temper their built-in traditionalism and develop their flexibility.

As Traditionalists, SJ leaders have a tendency to resist change and so must regulate their own behavior to make sure that, in their earnest wish for rules, regulations, and standard operations, they do not overshoot the mark and attain stagnation instead of progress. If they do, they may set up a roadblock to necessary and healthy organizational growth, wasting much of their own and others' efforts. Their employees will be dutifully doing things just because they did them previously. Or a budget item will be adopted only because it was adopted on the previous budget. Guardian leaders tend to watch operational costs more than they do results costs. They should, therefore, periodically take a look at the effects of operations and eliminate those that are no longer useful. Guardian leaders lead well when they keep a sharp eye out for the silent and steady creep and domination of ways and means over goals and ends.

Given that appreciation of their subordinates' contributions is a powerful tool for any leader, how do Guardian leaders show their appreciation?

How do they give strokes? How do they give feedback to their employees (and superiors) that they have noticed what they are doing and know about what they have contributed?

Here character will out. Guardians must serve, must be needed, must do their duty. They feel responsible and obligated seemingly from birth, believing that they must always earn their keep, each and every day. They feel that, somehow, they are indebted to society and must always work at paying what they owe. And they tend to project onto others their own need to prove themselves worthy, so that they see only the very hardest workers as deserving of appreciation. Since SJs must always earn their keep, including the earning of appreciation, only those employees who have been most hard-working should be appreciated. Otherwise (the unconscious belief dictates) employees might become less industrious. Giving credit where credit isn't most deserved would be bad for morale; therefore, only the winner can receive the grand prize. Those in second and third place may receive a blue and green ribbon, but no other player gets anything.

Traditionalist leaders would do well to examine their implicit belief that only the truly deserving may be shown appreciation, and that these can be only the outstanding few. To be most effective, SJ leaders must train themselves to pay attention to the least achievement and deliberately reward those achievements just because they were achieved. They need to experiment with finding something, no matter how trifling, the least productive employee has contributed, and to express appreciation for that.

In discussing issues Guardian leaders want their colleagues to get to the point quickly, make a decision, and get on to the next item on the agenda. They want lots of facts and little theory. Although quite at home in handling data, they are less at home in handling people, especially those who are less stable, less sensible, and less reliable than they are. And when it comes to handling their diametric opposites, the Rationals, they are often at a loss. Guardians will try to be clear-cut in their dealings with colleagues and, if they feel that they are not observing agreed-upon procedures and regulations, will call this to their attention. But they may do this publicly rather than privately, and occasionally with words which are unnecessarily critical. Also Guardians may find it easier to comment on others' weaknesses than on their strengths, tending to take strengths as obvious and expected—and therefore not needing comment. They may withhold appreciation unless they believe it is fully deserved, and they may have difficulty in accepting appreciation from others. SJs may find that conferring honors, trophies, titles, appointments to coveted positions, and so on, is easier for them than saying that they appreciate an employee's skills and achievements.

SJs themselves are orderly and want others to be the same, and they are determined to be on time and on schedule. Guardian leaders are happiest when they can schedule their work and follow through on the schedule. They like to get things clear, settled, and wrapped up, and may be restless until a decision is reached on materiel, personnel, and the calendar of events. Others with whom they work will know where they stand on procedural issues. Guardian leaders want their organization to be run on solid facts. They can maintain an effective data flow up and down the company hierarchy so that staff are well informed. Guardian leaders are able to survey, remember, and apply a great amount of detail. They can be superdependable leaders and extraordinarily hard workers. A good day's work for a good day's pay makes sense to them. Their superiors can count on them, as can their subordinates, to know, respect, and follow the rules, expecting them to apply equally to all. Guardian leaders will run orderly meetings, and will establish a formal, official style in dealing with colleagues until they are well acquainted. They are thorough about the business of the organization, are loyal to its purpose and personnel, and keep themselves briefed to the last detail.

While pleased to do their duty and be respected for it, Guardians are irritated by any who brush aside their responsibilities and disregard standard operating procedures long observed at work. They simply do not understand people who are ignorant of or indifferent to schedules. Deadlines for SJs are important, and they are impatient when these deadlines are ignored. They may even annoy fellow workers by admonishing them for minor delinquencies, just as they are prone to commend only the most respectful, obedient employees and to overlook the contributions of those who question authority. Guardians can also irritate others by letting their occasional periods of fatigue and worry show.

Guardian leaders may be somewhat impatient with projects that get delayed by unforeseen complications. They may be inclined to decide issues too quickly and, at times, may not notice new things which need to be done. Also they are likely to hold that some people are good and some people are bad—and that the latter should be told of it. From this position, they can fall into relationships that create tensions, caused by their being, at times, given to scolding and criticizing. As they become overtired and discouraged, they may get in the habit of focusing on the negative characteristics of people. If SJs do not make a conscious effort, they may slip without awareness from thinking "this is a bad act" to "this is a bad person." Thus these Guardian Stabilizers would do well to have an Idealist Catalyst on their management team, someone who brings a strong focus on personnel development and management-employee relations.

On the other hand, if an organization does not have an SJ on the leadership team, important details may be missed. Plant utilization may be poor. There may be poor control in materiel and personnel divisions, and far-reaching decisions may be made at inappropriate levels—by clerical personnel, for example. Without SJ controls, waste in effort and supplies can increase. An organization without a Guardian-Stabilizer-Traditionalist leader may find itself in a constant state of change without a sound base of rules and regulations.

To summarize, Guardian leaders naturally and easily do those things which stabilize and consolidate an organization. They are decisive and take satisfaction in settling things. They have a no-nonsense understanding of the values of an organization and do their best to conserve these values. They understand institutional policies and honor their intent. They are persevering, patient, and work steadily with a realistic idea of how long a task will take. They seldom make errors of fact, do very well with painstaking work, and can be counted on to follow through on commitments. Before they take action, Guardians will weigh the consequences and will try to see the practical effect of such action. They always look before they leap, and base what they decide to do on common sense.

Diplomatic Intelligence

The diplomatic intelligence of Idealists (NFs) shows itself in their natural gift for working with people, whether as a Mentor involved in personal development or an Advocate involved in personal mediation. Idealists are like other types in wanting to have their own brand of intelligence appreciated by their leaders, but diplomatic intelligence is not easy to observe, since it is abstract in nature and particularly hard to define. Even so, it pays leaders, whatever their temperament, to learn how to identify their followers who are skilled in the diplomatic roles, and to express how much they value them. To help leaders spot diplomatic intelligence, let's look again at a diagram (first presented in Chapter 5) that juxtaposes the Idealists' diplomatic roles and role variants with their most highly developed intelligent operations:

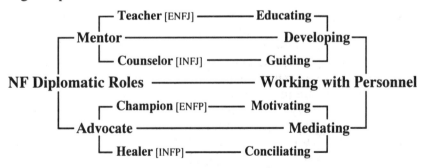

Idealists are keenly aware of their diplomatic efforts, in whatever role they take, and of any success they achieve with personnel. Of all the types, NFs are the most sensitive to appreciation or lack of it on the part of their leaders. The slightest disapproval is devastating to them, so leaders are well advised always to be encouraging and positive in conferring with these thin-skinned employees, gently focusing on method and results, and ever-grateful for the progress shown.

As indicated above, the Idealist's diplomatic intelligence shows most clearly in two SmartRoles, which I call the "Mentor" and the "Advocate."

Diplomatic Mentors

Mentors use their talents on the developmental side of diplomatic intelligence. These are the scheduling or agenda-minded Idealists, those NFs who care deeply about helping others achieve their potential, and who are so enthusiastic about personal growth that they seem almost unable to keep from stepping in to offer directions and suggestions. Two of the sixteen role variants seem born to be Mentors: the expressive Teachers and the reserved Counselors.

Teachers (ENFJs) are personally committed to the task of educating others, literally "leading out" the best that is in others, by broadening, edifying, enlightening, illuminating, improving, and refining the attitudes and actions of their learners. Teachers naturally identify with their students, drawing them out, individualizing instruction so that each lesson is personal, and each and every learner feels attached to and involved with the Teacher. This type seems to be the most positively charged of all the Idealists, playing their Mentor role with enthusiasm and charisma. Indeed, the learner is, if anything, inspired by this dynamic force and would not dream of resisting. These Teachers are rare in the workplace, and so employers should consider themselves lucky when they have one in charge of personnel, and they should show their appreciation whenever possible.

Counselors (INFJs) are the more private Mentors. These are quiet, sensitive people who work intensely with their clients, guiding their personal growth and directing them into activities that fulfill them more deeply than the phrase 'job satisfaction' can express. INFJs have an uncanny awareness of the needs and abilities of others, and they exert their influence on an almost unconscious level, facilitating their learners to discover themselves and to explore their talents. Just as rare as Teachers, and less likely to put themselves forward, Counselors are even harder to find in an organization, but are worth their weight in gold in personnel deployment and development.

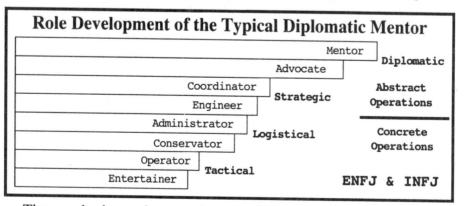

The graph above shows a theoretical curve of the most likely role development profile of those Idealists who become smart Mentors. Note that the other diplomatic role, that of Advocate, will usually lag a little behind simply because it gets a little less practice. Second, note that logistical and strategic roles are rarely on a par with diplomatic roles, and for the same reason, only occasional and unenthusiastic practice, without much attention to results. Still, since strategy is an abstract operation, there is some likelihood that it will be more interesting to Mentors than logistics, which is concrete, and so the typical Mentor tends to be a little smarter as strategist than logistician. In the eyes of most Idealists, tactics, compared to diplomacy, is a negative and even distasteful sort of activity, so is mainly ignored and even regarded as counterproductive. Consequently when it comes to the tactical roles, Mentor Idealists are not nearly as smart as when they are acting diplomatically.

Let me add that schools and counseling centers tend to be in short supply of skillful Mentor personnel, since the schools that ostensibly train them are also in short supply of role models. It is extremely rare, for example, that professors of psychology—academicians rather than practitioners—have even one method of corrective intervention that they can teach their student counselors. And, oddly enough, professors of education, also mainly academicians, are usually not well practiced in instructional technology, so they have little in the way of method to offer their student teachers. The truth of the matter is that most teachers and counselors learn their trade after leaving college, either by emulating models from their own past experience, or by locating individuals who are willing to demonstrate the methods that they have found useful in practice.

Diplomatic Advocates
Advocates find their calling on the mediational side of diplomatic intelligence. These are the probing Idealists, those NFs who are more inclined to nourish personal growth by exploring the pathways of faith and philosophy than by implementing an agenda, and who naturally offer information rather than issue directives. Advocates are devoted to the spiritual journey and will take up romantic causes with passionate intensity, searching for the core of unity or integrity in themselves and their groups, and hoping to nurture sympathy and understanding. Two of the sixteen role variants show exceptional aptitude as Advocates: the expressive Champions and the reserved Healers.

Champions (ENFPs) are the most vivacious Idealists and are so filled with conviction that they can easily motivate those around them. Champions are quick to embrace an ideal and then set about to instill their belief in others, working to kindle, to rouse, to encourage, even to inspire those close to them with their enthusiasm. In Carl Rogers' phrase, ENFPs are more "client centered" than all of the other types, and so can interview others with consummate skill, by entering another's frame of reference and empathizing with his or her feelings. Champions are not often to be seen in any organization, but are irreplaceable in recruiting personnel and building team morale.

Healers (INFPs) take as their task the wholeness or health of others. The word 'heal' has the same root as 'whole' and 'holism,' and indeed Healers encourage others to "pull themselves together," to moderate their inner conflicts, to reconcile their warring values, or to temper their opposing desires. Thus INFPs specialize in bringing about conciliation in all its forms—accommodation, adjustment, compromise, personal or interpersonal harmony, unity, or resolution—all in the interest of bringing together a divided staff or a troubled self. To be called "shaman," "witch doctor," or "medicine man" is not in the least offensive to the Healers. Some will even describe themselves as "spiritual healers" or "ordained healers." Quiet and reserved themselves, INFPs make excellent child counselors and tutors, especially in the case of shy, withdrawn, and defeated children. But in any workplace, leaders are wise to take the time to appreciate these rare individuals.

The graph below shows a theoretical curve of the most likely role development profile of those Idealists who become smart Advocates.

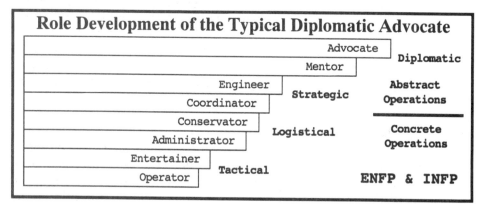

Note that the other diplomatic role, that of Mentor, will usually lag slightly behind simply because it gets slightly less practice. Second, note that logistical and strategic roles are rarely on a par with diplomatic roles, and for the same reason, only periodic and uninterested practice, with scant checking on results. Still, since strategy is an abstract operation, there is some likelihood that it will be more interesting to Advocates than logistics, which is concrete, and so ordinary Advocates tend to be a little smarter as strategists than logisticians. As for tactics, in the view of most Idealists it compares very poorly with diplomacy, and is seen as a negative and perhaps a distasteful sort of activity, so it is more often than not ignored and even regarded as counterproductive. Consequently when it comes to the tactical roles, Advocate Idealists are not nearly as smart as when they are acting diplomatically.

Appreciating diplomatic intelligence in followers is one thing, but let us look now at the characteristics of diplomatic leaders.

The Diplomatic Leader

I count the days with Gandhi the most fruitful of my life. No other experience was as inspiring and as meaningful and as lasting. No other so shook me out of the rut of banal existence and opened my ordinary mind and spirit...to some conception of the meaning of life on this perplexing earth.

—William L. Shirer

Idealists almost never take the forefront as political or military leaders—Gandhi (a directive Mentor) and Joan of Arc (an informative Advocate) being the rare exceptions. Indeed, biographical research shows that no Idealist has ever been President of the United States, with Eleanor Roosevelt the Idealist coming closest to that seat of power. Idealists make dynamic, enthusiastic leaders, but in other fields: Pope John XXIII convening the ecumenical council, Susan B. Anthony leading the fight for women's rights, Martin Luther leading the protestant reformation, Maria Montessori founding a network of schools for self-expressive children's education, and doubtless many more.

As presented above, Idealists tend to practice and develop the diplomatic roles—Mentor and Advocate—more than the other kinds. Idealists feel a sense of professional accomplishment and personal fulfillment when engaged in these diplomatic roles, or their variants; they feel they are helping others and thus keeping their organization running smoothly.

With a natural aptitude for working with people, Idealist leaders are appropriately called the "Catalysts," because their talents as Mentor and Advocate enable them to energize productive human relations. They can draw out the best in people, and they are first and foremost people-oriented. That is, their focus is on the individuals within the organization regardless of their status. They are very personal in their transactions and tend to become committed to the progress of those around them, forever alert to possibilities in both career development and personal growth. In this they are like a chemical catalyst, which acts as a reagent in a chemical mixture, catalyzing or activating otherwise latent potentials. The individual who encounters such a leader is likely to be motivated, animated, even inspired to do his or her very best work.

When in charge of personnel, Catalyst leaders demonstrate an interest in personal development, and thus their focus is primarily on the potentialities of their staff, with the development of the institution being secondary. Idealists are natural democratic and participative leaders. Their ideal is a harmonious, people-oriented work place, with documents and products a fallout rather than a primary target. NFs are comfortable working in a climate where everyone has a vote, and they are sympathetic to their people, generous with their willingness to listen to employee troubles, and sincerely concerned with their personal problems.

Sometimes, however, Idealist leaders find that their involvement with employees takes too high a toll on their time and energy, so that they have little left for themselves. Because they are so responsive to others' priorities—and, indeed, seek them out—NFs can allow other people's priorities to eat up much of their work day. They tend to be very generous with their time, even to the point of neglecting their own family or community obligations outside the organization, and of forgetting necessary recreational time. They sorely need to schedule renewal time for themselves if they are not to have their energies drained to the point where they are emotionally exhausted.

With the proper balance of professional and private time, Idealist leaders are enthusiastic spokesmen for their organization. They are forever looking for and reacting to the best in their company, office, school, church, and so on, and they are happy to communicate the fact that they are seeing this goodness. NFs are outstanding as personal appreciators. They listen carefully, intently, and with an abundance of verbal and nonverbal feedback, so that their colleagues are aware that they are being carefully and completely attended to—and that they are valued. With their gift of empathy, Idealists seem to know how to say the right things at the right time to express their appreciation.

Focusing as they do on human growth, Catalyst leaders value encouragement and acceptance, both for themselves and for their administrative unit. They have trouble communicating anything negative, anything that denies, disapproves, or that seems to impede progress or development. They can, in the process, subordinate their own wants and needs to the wants and needs of others, sometimes to the degree that the wishes of others almost erase those they hold themselves. Here again, other people's priorities can very quickly take over because of the NFs' tendency to place the needs of others before their own. Like Guardian leaders, Idealist leaders can then get overtired and come to a point where they find little personal reward in their work. The way to avoid this, of course, is for Idealists to review periodically their goals, priorities, and purposes to see if they are moving in a desired direction.

Idealist leaders can see, better than others, how a liability can be turned into an asset, particularly when dealing with personnel problems. They forget very easily yesterday's negative, disagreeable events and tend to remember the positive and agreeable—they are always the romantic about both the future and the past, and always the cheerful dreamer in their public presentation of self. They often have an unusual store of energies, although these seem to come in bursts powered by a new enthusiasm. Yesterday's projects, at that point, may not receive needed attention. Generally NFs hide their despondent moments, wanting to spare others any discomfort that might spill over from these down times.

Catalyst leaders appreciate others instinctively, and so their expressions of appreciation are quite spontaneously given, without forethought or effort. They listen with enthusiasm and approval, so that others feel fully received and validated. Because Idealists give so much, they themselves need to be replenished by having others, in turn, offer them expressions of recognition and approval. They value—and long remember—words of appreciation from their colleagues, their superiors, and their subordinates, and they can appreciate the intentions of the giver even when the approval is oblique. NFs tend to be motivated themselves by positive comments rather than negative ones, just as they tend to see the positive in others and events. If they receive this affirmative support they can continue contributing at their very high degree of productivity. If they do not, if they are met with continual disapproval, they can become discouraged and may look outside the organization for the kind of recognition they feel they deserve.

Idealists are also pleased by being recognized as unique persons making unique contributions, and not only do they need this acknowledgment by their leaders, but also by colleagues and subordinates. It should be added that the other three kinds of temperament can handle negative criticism more easily than can the NFs, who may become dejected, even immobilized, when met with negatives, including comments in fitness reports about "need for improvement," no matter how accurate the comments are, nor how kindly they are put. It is important to Idealists that their feelings as well as their thoughts are appreciated by others, and they want constant feedback concerning both as verification.

Sometimes Catalysts may feel it necessary to make administrative decisions on the basis of personal likes and dislikes, rather than on the basis of what might be best for the organization. They may also find themselves torn between the needs of their subordinates and the requests of their superiors, since they are so sensitive both to helping those under them and to pleasing those above them. They can find themselves viewed as the champion of two opposing groups because they have listened to both sides sympathetically and have communicated understanding. All too often both factions conclude that the Idealist leader, because of his or her empathic feedback, subscribes to their position. In truth, NFs are so in tune with the feelings of others that they are vulnerable to finding themselves wanting to please all of the people all of the time.

Idealists become irritated when treated impersonally, as if they were only their job or office. They do not wish to hide behind their uniform any more than they wish to be confined by it. Whatever they do is done by them personally, not by their office, badge, or title, and is so to be seen. NFs may actually irritate their superiors and fellow workers by taking things personally no matter how impersonal the context, and even when cautioned not to. They can also annoy others by playing favorites and being particularly charmed with one person, only to turn to another tomorrow, seemingly abandoning the first without an explanation. Idealists may give offense by insisting on expressing their feelings in situations where thoughts are more appropriate for exploration. They can take the side of a supposed underdog and in the process imply that others present are hard-hearted and unsympathetic to the needs of others. Idealists also can be over-helpful, giving help that is neither wanted nor needed.

Catalysts are able to create a climate where people in their administrative unit have considerable autonomy. This usually enables healthy growth for the unit, but, at times, as a result of members' freedom to act on their own initiative, mandated operations do not get carried out. Idealist leaders have to bear the responsibility for this—which may limit career opportunities. Nor does it bolster their self-image. If their unit is under criticism from superiors, or if things do not go well within their unit, they may quickly lose self-confidence, internalizing what may be the failures of others as their own failures.

Another hazard for Idealist leaders is that they have a tendency to avoid unpleasantness, perhaps hoping that, if they can delay facing problems, the problems may somehow disappear. Sometimes, then, they find that they have taken what was a temporarily easy way out, only to find that larger difficulties have resulted. Also, NFs may find themselves rescuing those they regard as "victims" of the system and this may lead them into conflicts between their loyalty to the institution and their loyalty to personnel. In spite of their best efforts to avoid this, Catalyst leaders may find themselves creating dependency relationships. Others will tend to lean on them for support, seeking direction, perhaps excessively, and generally draining their energies by bids for attention. Usually the Idealist will be at a loss as to how this happens, and mystified how to prevent it from developing again and again with a variety of people.

For the most part, however, Idealist leaders relate well and are popular with their colleagues. They enjoy personal contacts, and expressive Idealists in particular go out of their way to seek these connections. Idealists in positions of authority are sociable and like being with their staff, whether socializing or working. They touch base frequently with their staff and know a great deal about their problems, their feelings, and their pleasures. They tend to seek close, personal relationships with their colleagues and find their job a source of social satisfaction as well as a place to be productive.

Idealists are outstanding in public relations, and make excellent advocates for an organization, for they have facility in communicating their abundant enthusiasm. They work well with all types of people and can sincerely sell an organization to its clients. If they are given freedom to create and to manage, they can really produce; conversely, if they have too many arbitrary standard operating procedures to follow, they may become frustrated, and even resentful. Those around Idealist leaders may tend to be loyal to them personally, at times at the expense of seeing organizational needs, priorities, and issues.

On a leadership team, other members are apt to enjoy working with Idealists and find them supportive and attentive to their points of view. They have the characteristic, as do Artisans, of being able to make business a pleasure. Also, NFs add a personalized, people-centered point of view to a leadership team and can speak with more insight than the other types about the social consequences of a proposed change. If an organization does not have an Idealist on a team, members of the organization may find the environment cold, sterile, inhuman, joyless, dull, and complain about the decline of morale. *Esprit de corps* may be low and enthusiasm minimal. Although excellent data systems may exist, the people handling the data may not feel good about the organization and about their place in it. Many a troubled water can be calmed when an Idealist-Catalyst leader is present to pour on the necessary oils.

All in all, the leadership style of Idealists is marked by personal charisma and commitment to the people they lead. They usually have a tongue of silver and communicate through speech their caring and enthusiasm. They are often gifted in seeing the possibilities of both the institution and the people they work with, focusing intuitively on their strengths. They excel in working with and through people and, as the head of a democratically-run organization, they allow the contributions of all members of that organization to surface. NFs usually are comfortable in unstructured meetings. More often than not, they are accurate about the organizational climate. They tend to be patient with complicated situations and can wait for the right time to move forward. The Idealist can be extraordinary as the head of an organization, the visible leader who speaks well for the organization itself and for the people in it.

Strategic Intelligence

The strategic intelligence of Rationals (NTs) is shown in their ability to work with systems, that is, to figure out complex ways and means to accomplish well-defined goals, whether as a Coordinator formulating complex orders, or as an Engineer constructing complex organizations. Observing strategic operations is more difficult than observing tactical and logistical operations, because tactics and logistics are concrete and thus more visible and in-the-world than the abstract stratagems of NTs. Although Rationals are like others in wanting to have their own pattern of intelligence appreciated by their superiors, subordinates, and peers, most of them doubt that these others can understand strategic intelligence.

Of course Rationals who have joined some sort of think-tank, or some Technical Institute, or a computer company in Silicon Valley (places in which most employees are Rationals of one kind or another), find their brand of intelligence is commonplace and taken for granted. Far more likely, however, is that there are only one or two NTs on any given job site, and so they must have their doubts about others being able to imagine, let alone observe, their strategic capabilities. Those Rationals who are lucky enough to be assigned strategic work must be content to pat themselves on the back now and then and take pleasure in doing what they love to do.

Not only do other types of personality have trouble understanding the Rationals' strategic intelligence, it is quite unlikely that Rationals understand it themselves, no doubt because there are so many interlocking concepts which define that sort if intellect. By way of review, let us be reminded of the four role variants that NTs are enabled to play given their strategic intelligence: Fieldmarshals focus on hierarchical order, Masterminds focus on sequential order, Inventors focus on functional organization, and Architects focus on configurational organization. To make it easier to remember this NT intellectual pattern, let us review a diagram that was presented in Chapter 6, showing the strategic roles and role variants, and their corresponding intelligent operations:

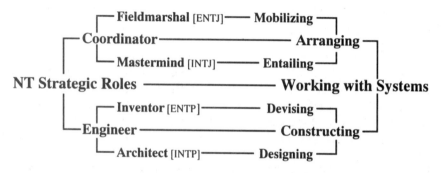

As indicated above, Rational strategic intelligence is most powerfully in evidence in two SmartRoles which I call the "Coordinator" and the "Engineer."

Strategic Coordinators

Coordinators concern themselves more with order in systemic work than with organization. These are the scheduling Rationals, those NTs who know what they want done and when it is to be done, and who are not shy about directing others to follow their plans of operation. By far the most competent Coordinators come from the ranks of two of the sixteen role variants: the expressive Fieldmarshal and the reserved Mastermind.

Fieldmarshals (ENTJs) are the best of all the Rationals at arranging hierarchical order, which means they naturally commandeer whatever human capabilities and material resources are required to execute a strategic plan, and then form a chain of command to make sure the object is accomplished. Isabel Myers referred to this type as "the leaders of leaders," and indeed in the military Fieldmarshals do extremely well in mobilizing their forces and in getting campaigns up and running. But in business as well these

ENTJs are quick in designating tasks to be accomplished, and then in selecting the personnel and resources that will most efficiently achieve the desired ends. Although few and far between in any work force, Fieldmarshals are the most visible of all the Rationals, for they are not at all shy about stepping forward and taking charge of operations.

Masterminds (INTJs) are the masters of sequential order, that is, entailing successive operations in a complex project so that all probable contingencies are anticipated and all appropriate measures are taken to keep the project on course. INTJs see the whole picture with eagle-eyed clarity and when put in charge begin immediately formulating their strategies, arranging their priorities, and making their flow charts in order to achieve their goals with a minimum waste of time and resources. Consider Thomas Edison, the wizard of Menlo Park, holder of countless patents for devices he invented during his long career. While certainly not as brilliant an inventor as his rival Nicola Tesla, Edison was far superior to Tesla in his ability to coordinate an incredible array of contingent efforts on the part of his team of engineers. In other words, Masterminds are smart at making contingency plans, which show what is to happen if certain things do or do not happen, but less smart at making architectural plans, which show all of the interrelated parts of a complex structure. In architectural plans there are no contingencies, no ifs, while in contingency plans there are no parts. Masterminds are not as conspicuous as Fieldmarshals in the work force; they would just as soon assist a competent leader as take command themselves. But when those in charge show confusion about coming up with efficient means to achieve clear-cut ends, Masterminds feel compelled to take over and get things back on track.

The graph below shows a theoretical curve of the most likely role development profile of those Rationals who become smart Coordinators.

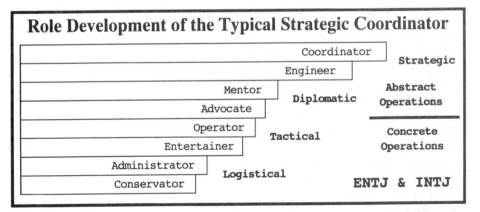

It is worthwhile noting that the other strategic role, that of Engineer, usually lags a bit behind, mainly because it gets a bit less practice. Second, note that the diplomatic and tactical roles are rarely on a par with strategic roles, and for the same reason, namely, rather sporadic and indifferent practice, with little attention to results. All the same, since diplomacy is abstract like strategy, there is some likelihood that it will be more interesting to Coordinators than tactics, which is concrete, and thus the typical Coordinator tends to be somewhat smarter at diplomacy than tactics. Then there is logistics. Compared to strategy, few Rationals are able to find much interest in logistics, so it is largely ignored and only rarely practiced. As a result, when it comes to acting in the logistical roles, Coordinator Rationals are not nearly as smart as when they are acting strategically.

Strategic Engineers

Engineers do their SmartWork on the organizational side of strategic intelligence. These are the probing Rationals, those NTs who are drawn to the harnessing of scientific principles to practical ends, in the construction of useful prototypes and models. These are also the informative Rationals, preferring to report on their project and progress rather than to direct others to follow orders. Two of the sixteen role variants are especially gifted in the role of Engineer: the expressive, outgoing Inventors and the attentive, reserved Architects.

Inventors (ENTPs) devise mechanisms with a definite function in mind. Civilization rests on an accumulation of hundreds of thousands of inventions made by many thousands of inventors, most of whom go unheralded for their achievements. A large invention, like the steam engine, makes its inventor (James Watt) immortal. But smaller ones, such as the handshake linking device holding train cars together, are taken for granted, their inventors known only by a handful of men. Unlike the Masterminds, who might start out in engineering but end up coordinating operations, Inventors have little desire to be in command of others and are quite content to go on engineering in their labs and workshops for the rest of their lives. Thus, even though their prototypes are directed out into the world, and in this sense they can be said to be "outgoing," ENTPs can go unappreciated by their leaders and unsung by the public at large. Fortunately, these inventive engineers are interested only in adapting the technology and building the prototype, and then in moving on to tackle the next problem that intrigues them.

Architects (INTPs) design the structural plans for the many tools that surround us, not only individual buildings but entire cities, not only single planes but whole airline companies, not only particular weapons but complex strategic weapons systems. Thomas Jefferson was just such an INTP, designing not only the buildings of the University of Virginia, but the overall layout of the campus, and then designing the academic curriculum to boot. Architecture and invention go hand-in-hand, the same person playing the two roles reciprocally, now devising the prototype, now redesigning it, back and forth until the fully functioning device is completed. As in the case of prototypes, models are quite visible for inspection, while the operations that produced them remain largely invisible, and thus INTPs are known more for their products than for their engineering skills. Fortunately, to these often solitary Architects the model's all that matters, the matrix of factors, the structural blueprint, and they can easily let the more visible Fieldmarshals and Masterminds get the applause. Not that they are incapable of coordinating operations. For example, Lincoln, when forced to take over the Coordinator's role by the inertia of a paralyzed Congress and inexperienced commanders, did quite well in command of Federal forces. Indeed, he kept pace with his best commanders, Grant and Sherman, in learning how to coordinate the vast military forces from the industrial north. But, in general, Architects are happy to do the work of systems design, defining the parts of a structure, and the relation between the parts, in order to map out the most efficient organization.

The graph below shows a theoretical curve of the most likely role development profile of those Rationals who become smart Engineers.

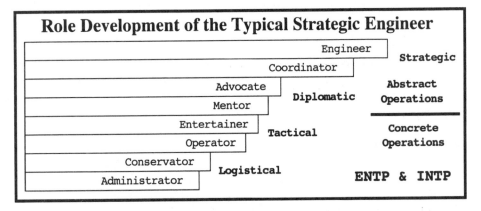

Note well that the other strategic role, that of Coordinator, typically lags slightly behind, mainly because it gets less practice. Also note that the diplomatic and strategic roles rarely even come close to the strategic roles in development, the reason again being that practice in these roles tends to be haphazard and lacking dedication, with results not often checked out. Even so, since diplomacy is an abstract operation like strategy, there is some likelihood that it will be more interesting to Engineers than tactics, which is concrete, and thus the typical Engineer tends to be somewhat smarter in diplomacy than tactics. As far as logistics is concerned, it is a most unusual Rational who shows more than passing interest in logistics, so most of them do little of it and hope that someone else will take care of such matters. The consequence of this neglect is that when it comes to playing the logistical roles, Engineer Rationals end up not nearly as smart as when they are acting strategically.

Employees with any sort of strategic intelligence are extremely rare in a work force, and need to be identified and appreciated, but the same can be said of strategic leaders.

The Strategic Leader

[Lincoln] came out in the end, on the issues most difficult for all politicians of his time, at solutions not only expedient but right—so right that, once started, they seemed to have the persuasive power of the simplest axiom.
—Rexford Tugwell

The government and the military of the United States have had their share of Rational leaders. Of the forty-one Presidents of the United States (up to 1998), eight were Rationals, which is twice the number that might be expected based on their small percentage of the population. Thomas Jefferson, James Madison, and Abraham Lincoln were probing, informative, and adaptable Engineers and unusually capable in architectural design and technological invention. John Adams, John Quincy Adams, Ulysses S. Grant, Herbert Hoover, and Dwight Eisenhower were decisive, directive Coordinators and highly skilled in mobilizing forces and contingency planning. All eight were extremely able leaders.

As for Rational military leadership, Douglas MacArthur and George Marshall were already four star generals when World War II broke out. At the time Marshall was chairman of the Joint Chiefs of Staff, and MacArthur was in command of army forces in the Philippines. But both had had Major Dwight Eisenhower working for them as their staff officer in planning strategy, tactics, and logistics. They both knew that nobody in the U.S. Army had studied the pragmatics and technology of war as continuously, as comprehensively, and as astutely as Eisenhower. Marshall's choice of Eisenhower to head the attack on North Africa, Sicily, and later on Northern Europe, was unhesitating and final, even though it was necessary to catapult him into top command over the heads of countless officers of superior rank and greater seniority.

As defined above, the most practiced and therefore most developed intelligent roles of Rationals are those of Coordinator and Engineer. NT leaders feel competent when they are playing such strategic roles or their variants; they are applying their reason and their know-how and thus contributing to their organization.

Rational leaders might be called "Visionary" leaders because they have the ability to envision the goals of the organization, and then to conceive strategic plans to implement those goals efficiently. NTs pride themselves on their ingenuity and technical know-how (including managerial technology), and want to use their innate understanding of factors to reduce the complex to the simple, to get models onto paper, to rise to challenges of design for increased efficiency. When called upon to come up with a strategy, NTs go happily to work. When called upon to devise something new—a prototype—they are all the more happy, since they are doing that which, in their view, is most worthwhile.

Lincoln on Leadership, written by Donald Phillips in 1992, is an extraordinary treatise on leadership as intuitively practiced by Rationals. It demonstrates coherently and comprehensively how Abraham Lincoln, himself a brilliant Visionary leader, sought to manage those who helped him preserve the United States through the perilous and agonizing years of the Civil War. Consider the principles of leadership that Lincoln spoke of and consistently used to govern his managerial conduct:

- Advocate a VISION and continually reaffirm it
- CIRCULATE among followers continuously
- Build strong ALLIANCES
- Search for INTELLIGENT assistants
- Encourage INNOVATION
- PERSUADE rather than coerce
- Influence people through STORIES
- Be RESULTS oriented

Were we to adopt Lincoln's style of leadership, whatever our character type, we would keep telling our followers about the end state of affairs we have in mind; would keep in constant contact with our followers, seeking to strengthen our relationship with them; would keep looking for intelligent behavior on their part; would always show our appreciation for useful changes in operations our followers come up with; would keep giving our followers convincing reasons for their actions; would keep regaling them with anecdotes that are analogous to their concerns; and, last, would keep checking on their results. It would appear that it was Lincoln, in the mid-19th century, who gave us the first intelligible model of what was to be called "results management" or "management by objectives" in the latter half of the 20th century.

Lincoln thus demonstrated the natural actions and attitudes of the Rational leader, and a hundred years later both Douglas MacGregor, in *The Human Side of Enterprise,* and Peter Drucker, in *The Effective Executive,* defined and explained his implicit model. This is the kind of leadership other Rationals, such as Jefferson, Madison, Grant, Eisenhower, and Hoover, displayed, and it is also the sort of leadership that came to be known as "results management" or "management by objectives." By the way, those NTs who in the 1970s tried to peddle the results management model to business soon found that it was not so warmly embraced by leaders of different temperament. Puzzled by this cool reception, many management consultants made a switch from a focus on objectives to a focus on operations, and began to speak of "operational objectives," the switch amounting to an abandonment of management by objectives.

Undoubtedly results management is a fine leadership model—for Rationals, who put long-range strategy before tactics, logistics, and diplomacy.

Indeed, the Visionary leader's far-reaching and all-inclusive plans, with all relevant constants and variables considered in recursively updated matrices and flow charts, try to anticipate the tactical, logistical, and diplomatic operations needed in any enterprise, so that personnel with these different skills can be deployed to do the things that are necessary and sufficient to get the job done.

Logistical regulation and support, tactical expediency and improvisation, and diplomatic development and mediation can be well provided for by Guardians, Artisans, and Idealists. But not strategic arrangement and construction, the strengths of the Rational, especially in larger enterprises where so many factors must be considered. Multivariate analysis and flow-charting are quickly and easily accomplished by NTs, while they are time-consuming and difficult for other types. Using such analytical tools the Visionary leader provides an eagle-eye view of things to come together with a contingency plan for implementing goals. Without such a leader on board, sooner or later goals and objectives are lost in the shuffle, and ways and means unrelated to the lost ends will spring up and multiply. Parkinson's law—"the hegemony of means over ends"—inexorably and inevitably takes hold of that organization which does not keep means rigorously harnessed to ends. It is the Rational's strategic intellect and well-developed pragmatism that keeps the organization on course.

With their scientific, technological, and systemic perspectives, these Visionary leaders keep their eyes open to new possibilities, and so value and support research and development efforts. What exists presently can be changed, and often is, since it is a mere remnant of the past. All rules, procedures, and offices are questioned, and only those that answer to the Rational's utilitarian criteria are allowed to survive. Any lingering or creeping bureaucracy is quickly discovered and surgically removed whenever and wherever an NT leader is in charge. While Guardian and Idealist leaders are now and then victimized by Parkinson's law, it is invariably and sometimes ruthlessly countered by Rational leaders. They will not put up with bureaucracy in any form or in any place in the system they are running, so that practices that do not efficiently serve the goals of the organization are pruned as fast as they sprout.

Even though Visionary leaders can envision how an organization might look ten years in the future, and blueprint that ten-year condition, they can have difficulty communicating their vision. People follow such leaders because they find their visions of the future intriguing; but they sometimes get lost because of the NT's tendency to avoid redundancy. When it comes to displaying their ideas, Rationals prefer not to say anything twice and assume thorough understanding on minimal information; that is, if something is only implied, that suffices. They do not believe it necessary to verbalize implications. They exercise an economy of communication, being reluctant to state the obvious lest they appear naive on the one hand, or insulting to their listeners on the other.

Visionaries, with their love of abstract strategic analysis, may also become too technical in the way they talk, using highly specialized terminology and presenting enormously complex matrices and flow-charts that show the relationship between means and ends—and naturally expecting their followers to grasp at once what seems so obvious to them. Often their would-be followers despair of following them at all in their detailed, precise, and complicated analyses.

Nor are Rationals natural appreciators, and part of their difficulty in the art of appreciation stems from their reluctance to state the obvious. They unwittingly assume that if a person has done a good job, then that fact is obvious—obvious to them and obvious to all others—and therefore they, the NT leaders, need say nothing. If they do, the person who made the contribution and who is the recipient of the appreciation might think, "Why is my boss saying this? Is it not perfectly obvious that I have done a good job? What's the boss up to?" And so Visionaries are hesitant to express appreciation for fear of being seen as manipulative.

At least that is one rationalization. Probably part of the truth is that NTs themselves are embarrassed when told by their boss that they have done a good job, and are likewise embarrassed when they express appreciation for their followers' contributions. So with these rationalizations—that others would find verbal appreciation either devious or too personal—Rationals tend not to say anything to their subordinates or superiors about their efforts and achievements.

Certainly Rational leaders understand the idea of appreciation that was so well articulated in the group therapy movement: that, if people are not told overtly and clearly that they are appreciated, they will conclude that they are not. In other words, people, regardless of character type, never take for granted that they are appreciated unless they are told that they are. If an employee accomplishes something, be it ever so small, he or she needs to be told by the leader that the accomplishment is recognized, is approved, and that it matters. The fact that the employee is paid in dollars for this accomplishment is beside the issue. If the organization is to get all the employee's commitment, the employee will have to be paid in a currency over and above dollars, one that responds to the basic need of that employee's personality. And the leader has no substitute: the leader, and only the leader, is in a position to express appreciation officially, in the name of the organization. Thus, if an employee is to be made aware that the organization appreciates his or her contributions, then the spokesman for that organization, the voice of the corporate body, must be the one who holds the office of leader. Even so, while Rational leaders might grasp the need for expressing personal appreciation, they have difficulty with this interaction and should study the behavior of an Idealist leader in this area.

When Visionary leaders are first involved in creating a model they have enormous drive; but once their model is constructed, they are more than willing to allow someone else to take over. As a result, they may find that their designs and plans were not carried out to their satisfaction. They seldom blame others for this failure, only themselves—but in the next situation they will tend to repeat their premature loss of interest. This is particularly true with Engineer Rationals, the Inventors and Architects. The Coordinator Rationals, the Fieldmarshals and the Masterminds, are apt to do the same thing but usually at a later stage.

Another weak spot for Rational leaders is that, because of their focus on long-range strategies and the big picture, they may, at times, be unaware of the feelings of others, whether good feelings or bad feelings. Their subordinates, therefore, may regard them as distant and even cold, and be hesitant to approach them. Colleagues may not feel comfortable in commenting on the domestic events in their lives, and thus the NT leader can become isolated from the after-hours activities of people within the organization. Not much good at small talk in the first place, their single-minded, all-business attitude makes it difficult for them to chat with their subordinates about what the NTs think of as trivia.

Aspiring as they do to technological wizardry, Rationals in leadership positions can give the impression that they value only their brightest subordinates, colleagues, or superiors. These Visionaries expect a great deal of themselves and others, often more than can be delivered, and they might do well to remind themselves of Drucker's rule that people with great strengths also have great weaknesses. Because NTs tend to escalate standards for themselves, they typically feel restless and unfulfilled. This restlessness sometimes takes the form of verbalized impatience with errors, and, at times, an impatience with finding it necessary to cover ground already traversed. Visionaries have little patience with snarled and tangled situations, especially in logistical or tactical matters. They cannot bear for either themselves or others to make the same mistake twice. One error is forgivable but not forgettable; recurrence of the same error, unthinkable.

Rationals can become irritated when asked to do something—like offering unearned appreciation—that defies logic and is inefficient if not ineffective. They insist on getting maximum effect with minimum effort and are bothered when custom and the need for diplomacy get in their way. Rational leaders can be adamant and stand on principle against all opponents, no matter what the price. NTs also can hurt others, not with admonition (like the SJs), but with irony and ill-concealed contempt, given their usual doubt about others' capabilities. And they can irritate others by what seems to be an unwarranted insistence on making so many fine distinctions that others forget the point at issue. Also some Rationals are seen as using a vocabulary which their listeners find pretentious and pedantic.

Visionaries prefer observers who will take the trouble to follow the complexities of their work. Seldom do the Rationals enjoy comments of a personal nature; rather, they respond to recognition of their strategic intelligence. Appreciation by a leader of a routine task well done does not delight them; indeed, it might even make them suspicious of the leader.

Only the competency of the appreciator is significant to NTs. The fact that the person expressing appreciation holds a high office means nothing if he or she does not also possess competency in the area being appreciated. Just as Rationals have difficulty appreciating others verbally, they have difficulty accepting appreciation.

But if nothing else, please remember these two characteristics of Rational leadership: First, Rational leaders are consistently pragmatic, which means that they are carefully studious of the relationship between means and ends. Goals must be defined clearly so that operations likely to reach those goals can be identified, acquired, and applied. And second, Rational leaders are consistently skeptical and error activated. All ways and means must be scrutinized for their potential inefficiency. Traditional ways and means are not automatically applied, but must compete with new ones in the crucible of strategic analysis.

—In Conclusion—

Whatever our personality type, to be effective leaders we must continually search for talent; we must nurture the talents of followers we already have; we must make sure that our followers engage in massed and distributed practice of those skills that they contribute; and we must see to it that our followers get timely feedback on the results of their intelligent operations, as well as frequent appreciation for and acknowledgment of their smart methods.

SmartPeople do SmartWork if they have a SmartBoss.

Chapter 1 Notes

1 Extraversion or Introversion

While Jung considered the distinction between extraversion (E) and introversion (I) as the most important of his dimensions of personality, I think of it as least useful in understanding people and predicting what they'll do. Indeed, in my view it borders on the trivial compared to S-N, and is much less useful than T-F and J-P. Presumably extreme extraverts and extreme introverts are easy to spot, and that may be the reason the Jungians and therefore the Myersians consider the concept to be so important.

Important or not, Myers's E-I scale is badly flawed because she inherited Jung's error of confusing extraversion with observation (S) and introversion with introspection (N). And so to make the E-I distinction useful at all, we must define the two concepts, not in terms of mental focus or interest, but in terms of social address or social attitude. Thus when someone is observed to be talkative and sociable (the so-called "extravert") he or she can be described as "expressive." In contrast, people who are more quiet and private (the so-called "introverts") can be described as "reserved." Interestingly, because Reserved persons tend to hold their fire verbally, they tend to listen carefully to what others say, while Expressive persons tend not to listen very well, so eager are they to tell others of what they have on their minds. So in general, the Expressive are quick to speak and slow to listen, while the Reserved are quick to listen and slow to speak.

Of course, everyone is expressive in some degree, but not in the same degree. Those who are more expressive appear more comfortable around groups of people than they are when alone. Thus they can also be thought of as socially gregarious or outgoing. On the other hand, those who are more reserved seem to be more comfortable when alone than when in a crowd. And thus they can be thought of as socially seclusive or retiring. Remember, however, that these distinctions are not clear cut: each individual surely varies from time to time in his or her desire to be expressive and in company or reserved and in seclusion.

A metaphor might shed light on this difference. Imagine that a person's energy is powered by batteries. Given this, then Expressive persons (ESTPs, ENFJs, etc.) appear to be energized, charged up, by contact with other people. Owing to the surge they get when in company, they are quick to approach others, even strangers, and talk to them, finding this an easy and pleasant thing to do, and something they don't want to do without. Such interaction apparently charges their batteries and makes them feel alive. Thus, when they leave a lively party at two o'clock in the morning, they might well be ready to go on to another one. Their batteries are almost overcharged, having received so much stimulation from the social interaction. In fact, quiet and seclusion actually exhaust Expressive persons, and they report feelings of loneliness (or power drain) when not in contact with others. For example, if an Expressive person goes to a library to do research in the stacks, he or she may, after fifteen minutes or so, feel bored and tired, and have to exercise strong will-power to keep from taking a short brain break and striking up a conversation with the librarian.

On the other hand, Reserved persons (ISFJs, INTJs, etc.) can be said to draw energy from a different source. They prefer to pursue solitary activities, working quietly alone with their favored project or hobby, however simple or complicated it may be, and such isolated activities are what seem to charge their batteries. Indeed, Reserved persons can remain only so long in contact with others before their energies are depleted. If required by their job, family, or social responsibilities to be expressive or outgoing—to make a great interpersonal effort—they are soon exhausted and need alone time in quiet places to rest and to restore their depleted energy. Thus, if Reserved persons go to a noisy cocktail party, after a short period of time—say, half an hour—they are ready to go home. For them, the party is over, their batteries are drained. This is not to say that Reserved persons do not like to be around people. They enjoy socializing with others, but at large social gatherings or professional meetings they tend to seek out a quiet corner where they can chat with one or two other persons.

There is some social bias toward expressiveness in American social life, but Reserved persons have no reason to feel that there is anything wrong with them, and should be sure to provide adequately for their legitimate desire for quiet time to themselves.

2 Sensation or Intuition

Carl Jung used the words 'sensation' and 'sensing' (S) to mean paying attention to what is going on outside ourselves, that is, external attention. Thus 'sensation' may be used synonymously with three words pertaining to external attention, 'observation,' 'externalization,' and 'exteroception.'

In contrast, Jung gave us two engaging metaphors to convey how he used the word 'intuition' (N). Intuition, he said, is "listening to the inner voice" or "heeding the promptings from within." The word 'intuition' is engaging because it literally means "internal attention." We pay attention to what is going on inside ourselves with our mind's eye and our mind's ear, these promptings coming as thoughts and feelings. Thus 'intuition' can be used synonymously with three other terms pertaining to internal attention, 'introspection,' 'internalization,' and 'interoception.' So we can contrast 'introspection' with 'observation,' 'internalization' with 'external-ization,' and 'interoception' with 'exteroception.'

For the purposes of describing personality types, I have found the easiest and most accurate terms to be 'introspection' and 'observation.'

Very simply, we observe objects through our senses. Thus we look at objects to see them, listen to sounds to hear them, touch surfaces to feel them, sniff odors to smell them, and mouth substances to taste them. We can observe what is present, but not what isn't present. Whatever isn't present to our senses we can only imagine by means of introspection.

Naturally, all of us do both observation and introspection, but it is a rare individual who does an equal amount of each. The vast majority of us, maybe 85%, spend most of our waking hours looking at, listening to, and touching objects in our immediate presence, and very little of our time introspecting, that is, making inferences, imagining, daydreaming, musing, or wondering about things not in our presence.

The point not to be missed is that we cannot do these things simultaneously. When we observe what's going on around us, we cannot at the same time observe what's going on within us. We may alternate our attention, but we cannot divide it. Some of us, from infancy on, seem to be more raptly attentive to inner promptings, others, to outer promptings. The reason for this difference in attention is not at all clear, and certainly it is a matter of conjecture. But if the reason for this preference in attention is obscure, the consequences of it are not. Those of us who attend inwardly much of the time as children strengthen that preference, our inner voice becoming louder and clearer, our inner promptings more vivid and complex. Likewise, those of us who heed the external much of the time come to see and hear objects in more detail and with greater specificity.

Now, if we look at Myers's type descriptions, people are either more observant than introspective, or more introspective than observant. Observers (SPs and SJs) seem more at home when looking after the particulars of everyday living, attending to concrete things —food, clothing, shelter, transportation—and to practical matters such as recreation and safety, and are likely to leave the more abstract issues to others. In turn, Introspectors (NTs and NFs) tend to be more content when these concrete concerns are handled by someone else and they are left free to consider the more abstract world of ideas. This does not mean, of course, that Observer types are without an inner life—far from it—but simply that their introspection takes a back seat to their observation. Nor does this mean that Introspector types are unaware of the objects around them—not at all—but simply that they are more inclined to become absorbed in their ideas.

To put this difference another way, Observers might be called "earthlings" or "terrestrials," concrete, down-to-earth beings who keep their feet on the ground. These persons see what is in front of them and are usually accurate in catching details. It is said that "they don't miss much." Observers want facts, trust facts, and remember facts, and they want to deal with the facts of a situation as they are, either in the here and now, or as recorded in the past. They focus on what is happening, or what has happened, rather than anticipating what might be, what would happen if, or what might occur in the future.

In contrast, Introspectors might be called "extraterrestrials," abstract beings who live with their head in the clouds, strangers in a strange land who wonder about the curious antics of the earthlings. Absorbed as they often are in their internal world, Inspectors tend miss a great deal of what's right around them—current reality is merely a problem to be solved, or a stage of development toward some future ideal. Not only can they miss details, they can also lose track of where they are, and for instance drive right past their highway turn-off. "It's only reality" they sometimes say, to register their relative disinterest in the merely concrete. But more than disinterest, Introspectors can be discontent with reality, even bothered by it, and speculate about possible ways of improving it.

Because of their tenuous grasp of reality, Introspectors can appear to Observers as flighty, impractical, and unrealistic—the dreamer or absent-minded professor who can't be bothered with the nitty-gritty of living. For their part, Observers can seem to Introspectors as unimaginative, concerned only with trivial pursuits, and exasperatingly slow to consider implications and possibilities. Both views are exaggerations. Indeed, both kinds of people are capable and even creative in their own way—it's just that they attend to very different sides of life, with the other side getting short-changed.

Thus Observers can manage the material world with skill, but the penalty they pay for ignoring the promptings from within is that these promptings can gradually fade away, and they may end up with relatively undeveloped introspective abilities. They may now and then introspect, but not for long and with little pleasure. On the other hand, Introspectors practice introspection much of their time, and with pleasure, but the penalty they pay for this is that they can end up with relatively undeveloped observational abilities.

The two ways are not mutually exclusive. Introspectors have no choice but to turn outward at times and concern themselves with the business of everyday living, while Observers do occasionally look inward to ponder, and dream, and make inferences. Such excursions can even be stimulating and satisfying, but neither type can be in both worlds at once, and each will usually show a strong preference for one over the other. For both types, the vitality, the immediacy, and the significance of life is found more easily in their own world, while what is central to the other's world seems relatively foreign, uninteresting, and unimportant.

3 Thinking or Feeling

Everybody has thoughts (T) and feelings (F) but some pay more attention to their thoughts than to their feelings while others pay more attention to their feelings than to their thoughts. Those who attend mainly to their thoughts are said to govern themselves with their head, their concepts and percepts being their guides to action. In contrast, those who pay more attention to their feelings are said to follow their heart, which means that much of what they do is based on emotion or desire. If we use a distinction made by the great pragmatist William James, some people are more "tough-minded" and others more "tender-minded." But if we note the words Myers used in her type portraits, we see that her distinction is between those who can be called "tough-minded" and those who can be called "friendly."

There is some criticism exchanged between these types. The Tough-minded are often accused of being "inhuman," "heartless," "stony-hearted," "remote," of having "ice in their veins," and of living "without the milk of human kindness." In the same way, the Friendly are chided for being "too soft-hearted," "too emotional," "bleeding-hearts," "muddleheaded," "fuzzy-thinkers," and for "wearing their heart on their sleeve."

Such accusations can be vehement and damaging, particularly in marriages and other family relationships, when two people of different orientation are in conflict over an important decision. An ENFP wife, for example, might want her INTP husband to open up emotionally and "let his feelings show," while he might wish she "would be logical for once." Or an ESTJ father might want his ISFP son to straighten up and "use his head" for a change, while the son might wish his father could "lighten up" and be more understanding of what he really is and can do.

Another polarizing (and inaccurate) stereotype is that the Friendly types have more and deeper emotions than the Tough-minded types—one side is seen as sensitive and warm-hearted, and the other seen as insensitive and cold-hearted. Here again, however, the truth is that both react emotionally with similar frequency and intensity, the difference being a matter of display. The Friendly tend to make their emotions and wishes quite visible and audible, so others see them as capable of deep feelings. To be sure, when they show their feelings, others cannot help being affected, their own emotions even aroused by the display. The Tough-minded, in contrast, are embarrassed by an exhibition of intense feeling, and will hide their feelings rather than be seen as losing self-control. Because of this, they are often described as "cold" and "indifferent," when in fact they are feeling something quite strongly—only working hard to contain themselves.

When they can get past the stereotypes, these two orientations usually find they can complement each other quite well, whether in business or in marriage, with the Tough-minded partner providing a source of clarity and toughness, and the Friendly partner providing a source of compassion and personal consideration.

4 Judgment or Perception

Myers claimed that she confined her usage of the word 'judgment' (J) to mean "coming to a conclusion," but again and again she used 'judgment' to describe people who make and keep schedules in their daily lives. Myers also used the word 'perception' (P) to describe people who prefer to probe for options and thus not be tied to a schedule.

In other words, Schedulers are judicious about schedules, Probers perceptive of options. Schedulers make agendas, timetables, programs, lists, syllabi, calendars, outlines, registers, and so on, for themselves and others to follow; Probers keep their eyes open for chances to do things they want to do, for opportunities and alternatives that might be available to them. Each orientation has problems. By committing themselves to a set agenda, Schedulers tend to stop looking for alternatives and options and so may never know what they're missing. By keeping their options open Probers are reluctant to commit themselves to schedules and so are inclined to deadlines and leave tasks unfinished.

Unfortunately, the difference between Schedulers and Probers can be a source of irritation in personal relationships, both in the home and the workplace, the latter where opposites must work together to accomplish a task. Schedulers, whether observant or introspective, tend to believe that one's work comes before all else, and must be finished before one rests or plays. This strict work ethic has a marked effect on what they will to do to get the job done. They tend to establish deadlines and to take them seriously, expecting others to do the same. And they are willing to do all sorts of preparation, maintenance, and cleaning up afterwards—just because these are necessary to see the job through to its conclusion.

Not so with Probers, who seem more playful about their work. The job doesn't have to be finished before play or rest begins, and they tend to look upon deadlines as mere alarm clocks which buzz at a given time, easily turned off or ignored while they catch an extra forty winks, almost as if the deadline were used more as a signal to start than to complete a project. Also, Probers are much more insistent that the work be enjoyable and to the purpose. Indeed, if the given task is not directly instrumental (is mere preparation, maintenance, or clean up), then they may balk at doing it, or wander off and leave it to someone else.

This difference extends to the physical environment as well. Schedulers tend to be neat and orderly. They like their desk at work to be tidy, and their house picked up—dishes done, bed made, car washed, and so on. Not that they always manage all of these chores, but they are unhappy when their personal space is a mess, and straightening things up is often near the top of their list. Probers, in contrast, have a much greater tolerance for disorder in their physical environment. They seem absorbed in whatever they're doing or thinking about at the moment, and are somewhat oblivious to the details of housekeeping. And so their personal spaces—office, house, garage, car—are often cluttered with a variety of objects they have picked up, used, and then dropped when they have finished with them.

These two styles—Oscar and Felix in *The Odd Couple*—can get on each other's nerves. Schedulers can become impatient with Probers for what seems their passiveness and playfulness, and can be heard to describe them as "indecisive" and "foot-dragging," as "aimless" and "lazy," as "uncooperative," "quibbling," and a "roadblock," as "sloppy" and even "slovenly." On the other hand, Probers can become impatient with Schedulers because of their pressure and urgency, and will describe them as "in too big a hurry" and "too rule-bound," as "driven" and "wearing blinders," as "uptight," "stressed-out," and "slave-driving," as "arbitrary," "rigid and inflexible," and even as "neat-freaks."

Usually, such irritation and name-calling will subside when the two study each other's behavior. Many become fascinated and entertained by their differences, and with further understanding find it easy to make allowances for the other's way. Some can actually come to see that the two styles are complementary in turning in a job well done: Probers to spot opportunities and lay out alternatives, and Schedulers to be timely and press for closure.

Chapter 2 Notes

1 Galen
A Roman physician and writer (130-200 A.D.) also known as Galenus. His theories formed the basis of European medicine until the Renaissance. He extolled and expanded the writings of Hippocrates and was second in a line of methods-hungry Faustian healers—Hippocrates, Galen, Agrippa, Selsus, Paracelsus, Maxwell, Mesmer, Bernheim, Erickson. See Siegel's *Galen on Psychology, Psychopathology, and Function.*

2 Plato
Greek philosopher (427-347 B.C.). A follower of Socrates, Plato founded the Academy (386 B.C.), where he taught—Aristotle was one of his students—and wrote for much of the rest of his life. Plato presented his ideas in the form of dramatic dialogues, as in *The Republic.* Studies in philosophy through the centuries are regarded by many philosophers as mere "footnotes on Plato," so highly prized are his works. Many see him as the originator of the view that ideas are eternal and the essence of reality, hence more real than people and things. It is in *The Republic* that Plato defined Utopia, or the perfect society, in which different types of character serve different social functions: artisans, guardians, idealists, and rationals.

3 Aristotle
Greek philosopher (384-322 B.C.). A pupil of Plato, tutor of Alexander the Great, and author of works on logic, metaphysics, ethics, natural sciences, politics, and poetics. He profoundly influenced Western thought with his philosophical system in which theory follows empirical observation, and logic is based on the syllogism, the essential method of rational inquiry. Aristotle said logic consists in three rules: Identity, Excluded Middle, and Contradiction. Simply put, the rule of Identity is that anything that is identifiable in a given context has an identity in that context, which is to say that it's unique even though it may be difficult to distinguish it from things that seem identical to it. The rule of Excluded Middle says that a thing identified in a given context is either one thing or another. And the rule of Contradiction says such a thing cannot be both one thing and another. (Bertrand Russell's rule of logical types was added to Aristotle's rules in the 20th century, the rule being that a thing identified in a given context cannot be part of itself.) To sum up, things identified in a given context are unique, are either one thing or another, and aren't one thing

338   *Chapter 2 Notes*

and another (nor part of themselves, says Russell). Most books on logic spell out the implications of these rules of how to talk sense and avoid talking nonsense.

4 Editor's Note on Biblical References:

There are tantalizing hints of the four temperaments in the Judeo-Christian tradition just as in the Græco-Roman. For instance, Ezekiel (writing in the Old Testament around 590 B.C.) imagined mankind as embodied in the shape of "four living creatures....And every one had four faces" symbolizing four types of character: "the face of an ox...the face of an eagle...the face of a man, and the face of a lion" [Ezekiel 6:10]. Likewise in the New Testament, Saint John (writing around 96 A.D.) beheld mankind in the form of four beasts arrayed around the throne of heaven: one beast had the face of "a lion," one the face of "a calf," one the face of "a man," and one the face of "a flying eagle" [Revelation 4:7].

And what did the four beasts bid St. John witness? Not only "four angels standing on the four corners of the earth, holding the four winds of the earth" [7:1], but also the Four Horsemen of the Apocalypse [6:1-8], four symbolic figures representing four terrible sufferings to be visited on Christians. The first (the Sanguine?) rides a red horse, carries a great sword, and brings the scourge of war. The second (the Melancholic?) rides a black horse, holds a grain scale, and brings the bane of scarcity and famine. The third (the Phlegmatic?) rides a pale or gray horse and wields the power to turn nature against man in the form of pestilence and plague. And the fourth (the Choleric?) rides a white horse, shoulders a bow (like Apollo, the Archer god), and represents the threat of foreign conquest.

The notion that mankind has four faces is thus clearly in evidence in the Bible, and perhaps this helps to explain why the New Testament has four Gospels, written in four different styles by four very different personalities. The Gospel according to Mark, for example, is an eye-witness version of Jesus's story, loosely organized, full of vivid details and physical action, as if thrown together by a man of impulsive Artisan character (also, the Lion was Mark's symbol in Medieval art). The Gospel according to Matthew, on the other hand, is a historical or traditional account of Jesus, and is likely the work of a Guardian (Matthew was a customs house official and tax collector, a student of Hebrew Law and the scribal tradition). In turn, the Gospel according to Luke is a scholarly explication of the Jesus story, written in a technical and classical style, probably the work of a Rational (Luke was the most learned of the Gospel writers, with a broad Græco-Roman education, and was also thought to be a trained physician). Lastly, the Gospel according to John is a wholly spiritual interpretation of the story, full of symbolism and metaphor, miracles and mysterious meanings, written to inspire faith in Jesus as the supernatural Son of God—and unmistakably penned by a soulful, even mystical Idealist.

The question of why the early Church included four separate Gospels in the New Testament has been debated by Biblical scholars for nearly two thousand years. Why didn't the Church fathers integrate the various accounts of Jesus into one narrative? Of course, we can never know for certain, but Irenaeus, Bishop of Lyon, based his explanation (in 185 A.D.) on what appears to be the common assumption of early Christian theology: that since "Living Creatures are quadriform,...the Gospel also is quadriform" [*Adversus Haereses*, iii,II,8].

5 Paracelsus

The book *Nymphs, Sylphs, Gnomes, and Salamanders,* written around 1540, displayed Paracelsus's view that healing is both enabled and constrained by the mental health of people who are ill in some manner. He conceived of four kinds of temperament: those inspirited by Salamanders, by Gnomes, by Nymphs, or by Sylphs. His name was Theophrastus Bombastus von Hohenheim, but this Viennese physician called himself "Paracelsus," meaning by this "better than Celsus," the latter a Roman physician famous for his curative powers. Paracelsus, like Galen, was one of a line of methods-hungry Faustian healers obsessed with developing the technology of physical and mental therapy—Hippocrates, Galen, Agrippa, Celsus, Paracelsus, Maxwell, Mesmer, Bernheim, Erickson. The story of Faust tells of the Faustian healers' eternal hunger for the pragmatics of healing. Just as Faust sold his soul to Mephistopheles (Lucifer) for know-how, so too did Odin (Wotan), chief of Valhalla, give his right eye for know-how. Incidentally, the word 'Lucifer' means "bearer of light", i.e. the one who enlightens, thus the one who gave mankind the means of survival, as did Prometheus. Note too that both Lucifer and Prometheus payed dearly for their gift to mankind: Lucifer was thrown out of heaven to rule on Earth and Prometheus was thrown off Mt. Olympus, chained to a rock, and made to suffer having his liver eaten daily by giant vultures. Fortunately, he was released by his powerful brother Atlas (another Titan), so that he could go on forever enlightening his creature, just as Lucifer, ruling Earth as he is said to do, continues to enlighten mankind such that it is understood that there are natural consequences for messing up.

6 Eric Adickes

A German scientist who in 1905 wrote *Charakter und Weltanschauung,* a treatise on the Græco-Roman theory of the four temperaments (not that he was aware of either Plato's or Aristotle's contribution). He called the Artisans "innovative," the Guardians "traditional," the Idealists "dogmatic," and the Rationals "agnostic." Like Spränger he had the four types paired, but on a different basis than Spränger—Spränger distinguishing between "political" and "social" types, Adickes between "autonomous" and "heteronomous" types. Thus for Adickes the Innovatives (Artisans) and Traditionals (Guardians) are both "heteronomous" types, concerned mainly with how they are seen by others, while Agnostics (Rationals) and Dogmatics (Idealists) are both "autonomous" types, mainly concerned with how they see themselves. The distinction between "autonomy" and "heteronomy" correlates rather well with a similar distinction made by David Riesman in his *Individualism Reconsidered* and *The Lonely Crowd.* Therein he distinguished between "outer-centered" and "inner-centered" types, his metaphor for the latter doing social navigation by gyro, the former by radar. Both of these views are similar to the distinction between introspective types (Rationals and Idealists) and observant types (Artisans and Guardians).

7 Eduard Spränger

German psychologist who wrote *Lebensformen* (1914) which was translated into English in 1920 as *Types of Men.* Spränger was a precursor of the organismic wholism school of psychology as presented later by Bühler, Hartmann, Katz, Koehler, Koffka, Lewin, Wertheimer, and Wheeler, and like the organismic psychologists he was a strong advocate of organismic field theory in the behavioral sciences. Spränger paired his Theoretics (Rationals) with his Aesthetics (Artisans) on the grounds that both were "political" types concerned mainly with functional utility, and his Religious (Idealists) with his Economicals (Guardians) on the grounds that they were both "social" types concerned mainly with moral sanction. The distinction between social and political types correlates nicely with Gregory Bateson's distinction between "symmetrical" and "complementary" ways of defining roles that are to be played in a relationship (see especially Jay Haley's *Strategies in Psychotherapy,* pp. 8-19).

8 Ernst Kretschmer

A German physician prominent in psychology after World War I who achieved fame for his work on the relation between body build and personality. Two of his more influential books were *Physique and Character* and *The Psychology of Men of Genius.* William Sheldon, an American physician, achieved fame by expanding Kretschmer's work in long and careful studies of temperament and behavior (see *The Varieties of Temperament, Varieties of Delinquent Youth,* and *Atlas of Men).* Few psychologists in America paid much attention to either Kretschmer or Sheldon thereby missing their carefully crafted descriptions and definitions of temperament-determined behavior.

9 Eric Fromm

A Viennese physician who came to America in the late 1930s to escape the Nazi takeover of Austria. He wrote *Man for Himself* and *Escape from Freedom,* two seminal works on personality that influenced many psychologists during its vigorous expansion in the U.S. in the wake of World War II. Fromm, along with Abraham Maslow, Carl Rogers, Ernest Becker, and others, headed the movement called The Third Force in psychology, softening the harsh view of Man given by Behaviorism and Psychoanalysis.

10 Function Types vs Intelligence Types

What follows shows the great contrast of Jung's and Myers's four function types and their variants with my four intelligence types and their skilled action roles. In considering the contrasts please bear in mind that Jung and Myers were trying to figure out what the different types have in mind, while I am trying to figure out what they can do well under varying circumstances.

Function Types	Intelligence Types
Thinking Types	**NT Rationals**
ESTJ—ENTJ [Extraverted Thinking]	ENTJ—INTJ [Coordinator]
ISTP—INTP [Introverted Thinking]	ENTP—INTP [Engineer]
Intuitive Types	**NF Idealists**
ENTP—ENFP [Extraverted Intuiting]	ENFJ—INFJ [Mentor]
INFJ—INTJ [Introverted Intuiting]	ENFP—INFP [Advocate]
Feeling Types	**SP Artisans**
ESFJ—ENFJ [Extraverted Feeling]	ESTP—ISTP [Operator]
ISFP—INFP [Introverted Feeling]	ESFP—ISFP [Entertainer]
Sensory Types	**SJ Guardians**
ESTP—ESFP [Extraverted Sensing]	ESTJ—ISTJ [Administrator]
ISFJ—ISTJ [Introverted Sensing]	ESFJ—ISFJ [Conservator]

The first great difference between the two schemes lies in the way function typology and intelligence typology see the ESTJs and the ENTJs. Jung and Myers call both ESTJs and ENTJs "Extraverted Thinking" types, and thus nearly identical in attitude and action. I, however, see them as light years apart. All NT Rationals, including ENTJ Coordinators, are abstract in communicating messages and utilitarian in using tools to implement their goals, while all SJ Guardians, including ESTJ Administrators, are concrete in communicating messages and cooperative in using tools.

The second major difference lies in the two typologies' view of the ISFP and the INFP. Myers and Jung put them in the same category—the "Introverted Feeling" type—very much alike and very little different, while I consider them just as far apart as the ENTJ and ESTJ. After all, the INFP Advocate is an NF Idealist, abstract in thought and speech and cooperative in implementing goals, hence diametrically opposite to the ISFP Entertainer, a concrete utilitarian SP Artisan.

The third great difference between the intelligence and function typologies is the way the two see the INTP and the ISTP. Myers and Jung see them as nearly identical, both "Introverted Thinking" types, with a few minor differences. I, however, see them as far more different. While they are both utilitarian in choosing and using tools, the INTP is an Engineer Rational, steadfastly abstract in thought and speech, and the ISTP is an Operator Artisan, just as steadfastly concrete in thought and speech.

The fourth great difference is in the two views of the ENFJ. Function typology sees the ENFJ as very little different from the ESFJ, while intelligence typology sees a much greater difference. The two have in common a cooperative attitude about ways and means of pursuing goals, but the ENFJ, a Mentor Idealist, is unmistakably abstract in thought and speech, and the ESFJ, a Conservator Guardian, is unmistakably concrete.

The other differences are great, but less important in comparison to the ones I have just discussed. Thus function theory has the INFJ quite similar to the INTJ, while intelligence theory has the INFJ a Mentor Idealist, the INTJ a Coordinator Rational, the two miles apart in what they do and what they want. And function theory sees the ENFP as much like the ENTP, while intelligence theory sees the ENFP as an Advocate Idealist, the ENTP as an Engineer Rational, the two, again, very different in their behavior and corresponding attitudes. Admittedly ENFPs and ENTPs can be hard to tell apart, at least on short acquaintance, but watch for any length of time and their differences show up one by one until it is abundantly clear that the resemblance is at best superficial.

Bibliographies on Human Nature and Organismic Psychology

Human Nature: Temperament, Character, & Personality

Adams P 1973—*Obsessive Children*
Adickes E 1907—*Charakter und Weltanschauung*
Alexander F 1948—*Studies in Psychosomatic Medicine*
Allport G 1955—*Becoming*
Ansbacher H 1956—*The Individual Psychology of Alfred Adler*
Ansbacher H 1958—*The Social Psychology of Alfred Adler*
Angyal A 1965—*Neurosis and Treatment*
Bateson G, Ruesch J 1951—*Communication: The Social Matrix of Psychiatry*
Bateson G 1972—*Steps to an Ecology of Mind*
Bateson G 1979—*Mind and Nature*
Chess S, Thomas A 1986—*Temperament in Clinical Practice*
Choiniere R, Keirsey D 1992—*Presidential Temperament*
Christie 1970—*Studies in Machiavellianism*
Cleckley H 1964—*The Mask of Sanity*
Drucker P—*The Effective Executive*
Fromm E 1947—*Man for Himself*
Hartl E et al 1982—*Physique and Delinquent Behavior*
Hippocrates 450BC—*Human Nature*
Hunt J [ed] 1944—*Personality and the Behavior Disorders*
Jackson H 1931—*Selected Writings of John Hughlings Jackson*
Janet P 1903—*Obsessions and Psychasthenia*
Janet P 1907—*The Major Symptoms of Hysteria*
Jung C 1920—*Psychological Types*
Kagan J 1994—*Galen's Prophecy: Temperament in Human Nature*
Keirsey D 1949—*Personality in Essential Hypertension*
Keirsey D 1967—*The Polarization of Intelligence*
Keirsey D, Bates M 1978—*Please Understand Me*
Keirsey D 1987—*Portraits of Temperament*
Kelley G 1955—*The Psychology of Personal Constructs*
Kipnis D 1971—*Character Structure and Impulsiveness*
Kretschmer E 1920—*Physique and Character*
Kretschmer E 1931—*Psychology of Men of Genius*
Laing R 1960—*The Divided Self*
Lecky P 1968—*Self-consistency*
Lewin K 1935—*A Dynamic Theory of Personality*
Maslow A 1954—*Motivation and Personality*
MacGregor D—*The Human Side of Enterprise*
Montgomery S 1989—*The Pygmalion Project I: The Artisan*
Montgomery S 1990—*The Pygmalion Project II: The Guardian*

Montgomery S 1993—*The Pygmalion Project III: The Idealist*
Montgomery S 2000—*The Pygmalion Project IV: The Rational*
Myers I 1962—*The Myers-Briggs Type Indicator*
Myers I 1980—*Gifts Differing*
Paracelsus 1540—*Nymphs, Gnomes, Sylphs, and Salamanders*
Ruesch J 1957—*Disturbed Communication*
Roback A 1927—*The Psychology of Character*
Roback A 1927—*A Bibliography of Character and Personality*
Shapiro D 1965—*Neurotic Styles*
Sheldon W 1942 —*Varieties of Temperament*
Sheldon W 1949—*Varieties of Delinquent Youth*
Sheldon W 1954—*Atlas of Men*
Siegal R 1973—*Galen on Psychology, Psychopathology, and Function*
Snygg D, Combs A 1959—*Individual Behavior*
Sternberg R [ed] 1982—*Handbook of Human Intelligence*
Strauss E 1948—*On Obsession*
Spränger E 1920—*Types of Men*
Sullivan H 1956—*Clinical Studies in Psychiatry*
Sullivan H 1972—*Personal Psychopathology*
Vieth I 1965—*Hysteria*
Zuckerman M 1964—"The Sensation Seeking Scale," *J Consult Psych* 28: 477-482

Organismic Psychology: Wholes, Fields, Polarities

Bertalanffy L 1933—*Modern Theories of Development*
Blanshard B 1939—*The Nature of Thought*
Bühler K 1924—*The Mental Development of Children*
Cannon W 1939—*The Wisdom of the Body*
Cassirer E 1945—*Language and Myth*
Cassirer E 1948—*An Essay on Man*
Cassirer E 1950—*The Problem of Knowledge*
Child C 1924—*Physiological Foundations of Behavior*
Child C 1941—*Patterns and Problems of Development*
Coghill G 1929—*Anatomy and the Problem of Behavior*
Dewey J 1938—*Logic, the Theory of Inquiry*
Ellis W 1942—*Readings in Gestalt Psychology*
Frazer J 1922—*The Golden Bough*
Goldstein K 1939—*The Organism*
Goldstein K 1947—*Human Nature*
Goldstein K 1948—*Language and Language Disorders*
Goldstein K, Scheerer M 1948—*Abstract and Concrete Behavior*
Gurwitsch A 1964—*The Field of Consciousness*
Haldane J 1919—*The New Physiology*
Haley J 1963—*Strategies of Psychotherapy*

Hayek F 1947—*The Sensory Order*
Herrick C 1956—*The Evolution of Human Nature*
James W 1907—*Pragmatism*
Koffka K 1935—*Principles of Gestalt Psychology*
Köhler W 1947—*Gestalt Psychology*
Lewin K 1951—*Field Theory in Social Science*
Merleau-Ponty M 1962—*The Phenomenology of Perception*
Norris L 1956—*Polarity*
Przywara P 1935—*Polarity*
Sainsbury G 1927—*The Theory of Polarity*
Strauss E 1963—*The Primary World of the Senses*
Wiener N 1950—*Cybernetics*
Werner H 1957—*Comparative Psychology of Mental Development*
Wertheimer M 1954—*Productive Thinking*
Wheeler R, Perkins F 1933—*The Principles of Mental Development*
Wheeler R 1934—*The Laws of Human Nature*
Wheeler R 1935—"Organismic vs Mechanistic Logic," *Psych Review,* 335

Enter a check mark for each answer in the column for **a** or **b**.

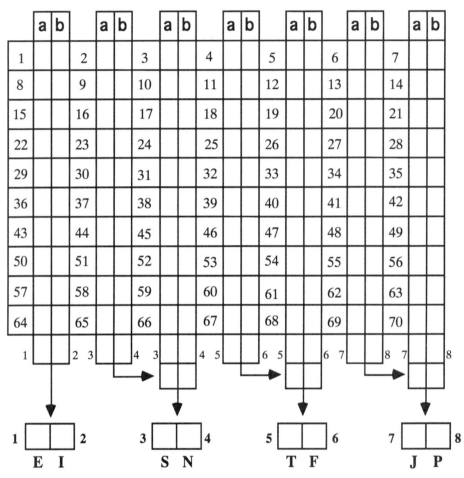

Directions for Scoring

• **First,** add down so that the total number of a answers is written in the box at the bottom of each column. Do the same for the b answers you have checked. Each of the 14 boxes should have a number in it.

• **Second,** transfer the number in box No. 1 of the answer grid to box No. 1 below the answer grid. Do this for box No. 2 as well. Note, however, that you have two numbers for boxes 3 through 8. Bring down the first number for each box beneath the second, as indicated by the arrows. Now add all the pairs of numbers and enter the total in the boxes below the answer grid, so each box has only one number.

• **Third,** you now have four pairs of numbers. Circle the letter below the larger numbers of each pair (see sample answer sheet on page 11). If the two numbers of any pair are equal, then circle neither, but put a large X below them and circle it. Then follow the directions on pages 11 and 12.

Enter a check mark for each answer in the column for **a** or **b**.

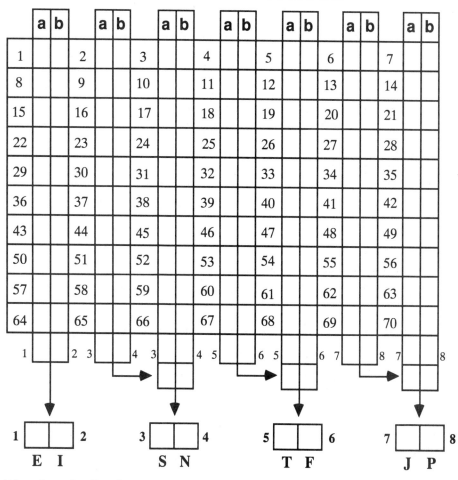

Directions for Scoring

• **First,** add down so that the total number of a answers is written in the box at the bottom of each column. Do the same for the b answers you have checked. Each of the 14 boxes should have a number in it.

• **Second,** transfer the number in box No. 1 of the answer grid to box No. 1 below the answer grid. Do this for box No. 2 as well. Note, however, that you have two numbers for boxes 3 through 8. Bring down the first number for each box beneath the second, as indicated by the arrows. Now add all the pairs of numbers and enter the total in the boxes below the answer grid, so each box has only one number.

• **Third,** you now have four pairs of numbers. Circle the letter below the larger numbers of each pair (see sample answer sheet on page 11). If the two numbers of any pair are equal, then circle neither, but put a large X below them and circle it. Then follow the directions on pages 11 and 12.

348　　The Keirsey FourTypes Sorter

For each item, rank-order the four choices. Mark the response most like you as #1; less like you, #2; still less like you, #3; & least like you, #4. Put your numbers next to the corresponding letters.

1. I'd rather study
___ (a) arts & crafts
___ (b) literature & humanities
___ (c) business & finance
___ (d) science & engineering

2. I feel best about myself when
___ (a) I'm graceful in action
___ (b) I'm *en rapport* with someone
___ (c) I'm rock-solid dependable
___ (d) I exercise my ingenuity

3. In mood I'm more often
___ (a) excited & stimulated
___ (b) enthusiastic & inspired
___ (c) cautious & prudent
___ (d) calm & detached

4. I keep coming back to
___ (a) perfecting my craft
___ (b) helping others affirm themselves
___ (c) helping others do right
___ (d) figuring out how things work

5. Coming right down to it I tend to be
___ (a) practical & opportunistic
___ (b) compassionate & altruistic
___ (c) dutiful & diligent
___ (d) efficient & pragmatic

6. I respect myself more for
___ (a) being bold & adventurous
___ (b) being kind-hearted & of good will
___ (c) doing good deeds
___ (d) being autonomous & independent

7. I'm more inclined to trust
___ (a) impulses & whims
___ (b) intuitions & intimations
___ (c) customs & traditions
___ (d) pure reason & formal logic

8. I'm sometimes eager to
___ (a) make an impression & have impact
___ (b) lose myself in romantic dreams
___ (c) be a valued & legitimate member
___ (d) make a scientific breakthrough

9. I'm in a life-long search for more
___ (a) thrills & adventures
___ (b) self-understanding
___ (c) safety & security
___ (d) efficient methods of operation

10. In facing the future
___ (a) I bet something lucky will turn up
___ (b) I believe in people's innate goodness
___ (c) you just can't be too careful
___ (d) it's best to keep a wary eye

11. If it were possible I'd like to become
___ (a) an artistic virtuoso
___ (b) a wise prophet
___ (c) a chief executive
___ (d) a technological genius

12. I'd do best in a job working with
___ (a) tools & equipment
___ (b) human resources development
___ (c) materiel & services
___ (d) systems & structures

13. As a guide to action I look primarily at
___ (a) immediate advantages
___ (b) future possibilities
___ (c) past experience
___ (d) necessary & sufficient conditions

14. I'm most self-confident when I'm
___ (a) adaptable & flexible
___ (b) genuine & authentic
___ (c) honorable & respectable
___ (d) strong-willed & resolute

15. I appreciate it when others
___ (a) surprise me with generosity
___ (b) recognize my true self
___ (c) express their gratitude
___ (d) ask me for my rationale

16. When thinking about misfortune
___ (a) I usually laugh it off
___ (b) I often wonder why
___ (c) I try to make the best of it
___ (d) I view it from a wide perspective

	1	2	3	4	5	6	7	8	9	10	11	12	13	14	15	16		
a																		**A**
b																		**I**
c																		**G**
d																		**R**

Scoring Directions: First, in the numbered columns above, record your rankings (1 to 4) for each of the 16 items. **Second,** add the numbers across each of the four rows (**a, b, c, d**) & place the sums in the boxes at the far right. **Third,** circle the letter (**A, I, G,** or **R**) beside the *lowest* sum. **Fourth,** A stands for Artisan (SP), I for Idealist (NF), G for Guardian (SJ), R for Rational (NT).

For each item, rank-order the four choices. Mark the response most like you as #1; less like you, #2; still less like you, #3; & least like you, #4. Put your numbers next to the corresponding letters.

1. I'd rather study
___ (a) arts & crafts
___ (b) literature & humanities
___ (c) business & finance
___ (d) science & engineering

2. I feel best about myself when
___ (a) I'm graceful in action
___ (b) I'm *en rapport* with someone
___ (c) I'm rock-solid dependable
___ (d) I exercise my ingenuity

3. In mood I'm more often
___ (a) excited & stimulated
___ (b) enthusiastic & inspired
___ (c) cautious & prudent
___ (d) calm & detached

4. I keep coming back to
___ (a) perfecting my craft
___ (b) helping others affirm themselves
___ (c) helping others do right
___ (d) figuring out how things work

5. Coming right down to it I tend to be
___ (a) practical & opportunistic
___ (b) compassionate & altruistic
___ (c) dutiful & diligent
___ (d) efficient & pragmatic

6. I respect myself more for
___ (a) being bold & adventurous
___ (b) being kind-hearted & of good will
___ (c) doing good deeds
___ (d) being autonomous & independent

7. I'm more inclined to trust
___ (a) impulses & whims
___ (b) intuitions & intimations
___ (c) customs & traditions
___ (d) pure reason & formal logic

8. I'm sometimes eager to
___ (a) make an impression & have impact
___ (b) lose myself in romantic dreams
___ (c) be a valued & legitimate member
___ (d) make a scientific breakthrough

9. I'm in a life-long search for more
___ (a) thrills & adventures
___ (b) self-understanding
___ (c) safety & security
___ (d) efficient methods of operation

10. In facing the future
___ (a) I bet something lucky will turn up
___ (b) I believe in people's innate goodness
___ (c) you just can't be too careful
___ (d) it's best to keep a wary eye

11. If it were possible I'd like to becom
___ (a) an artistic virtuoso
___ (b) a wise prophet
___ (c) a chief executive
___ (d) a technological genius

12. I'd do best in a job working with
___ (a) tools & equipment
___ (b) human resources development
___ (c) materiel & services
___ (d) systems & structures

13. As a guide to action I look primarily at
___ (a) immediate advantages
___ (b) future possibilities
___ (c) past experience
___ (d) necessary & sufficient conditions

14. I'm most self-confident when I'm
___ (a) adaptable & flexible
___ (b) genuine & authentic
___ (c) honorable & respectable
___ (d) strong-willed & resolute

15. I appreciate it when others
___ (a) surprise me with generosity
___ (b) recognize my true self
___ (c) express their gratitude
___ (d) ask me for my rationale

16. When thinking about misfortune
___ (a) I usually laugh it off
___ (b) I often wonder why
___ (c) I try to make the best of it
___ (d) I view it from a wide perspective

	1	2	3	4	5	6	7	8	9	10	11	12	13	14	15	16		
a																		**A**
b																		**I**
c																		**G**
d																		**R**

Scoring Directions: First, in the numbered columns above, record your rankings (1 to 4) for each of the 16 items. **Second**, add the numbers across each of the four rows (**a**, **b**, **c**, **d**) & place the sums in the boxes at the far right. **Third**, circle the letter (**A**, **I**, **G**, or **R**) beside the *lowest* sum. **Fourth**, A stands for Artisan (SP), I for Idealist (NF), G for Guardian (SJ), R for Rational (NT).

For each item, rank-order the four choices. Mark the response most like you as #1; less like you, #2; still less like you, #3; & least like you, #4. Put your numbers next to the corresponding letters.

1. I'd rather study
___ (a) arts & crafts
___ (b) literature & humanities
___ (c) business & finance
___ (d) science & engineering

2. I feel best about myself when
___ (a) I'm graceful in action
___ (b) I'm *en rapport* with someone
___ (c) I'm rock-solid dependable
___ (d) I exercise my ingenuity

3. In mood I'm more often
___ (a) excited & stimulated
___ (b) enthusiastic & inspired
___ (c) cautious & prudent
___ (d) calm & detached

4. I keep coming back to
___ (a) perfecting my craft
___ (b) helping others affirm themselves
___ (c) helping others do right
___ (d) figuring out how things work

5. Coming right down to it I tend to be
___ (a) practical & opportunistic
___ (b) compassionate & altruistic
___ (c) dutiful & diligent
___ (d) efficient & pragmatic

6. I respect myself more for
___ (a) being bold & adventurous
___ (b) being kind-hearted & of good will
___ (c) doing good deeds
___ (d) being autonomous & independent

7. I'm more inclined to trust
___ (a) impulses & whims
___ (b) intuitions & intimations
___ (c) customs & traditions
___ (d) pure reason & formal logic

8. I'm sometimes eager to
___ (a) make an impression & have impact
___ (b) lose myself in romantic dreams
___ (c) be a valued & legitimate member
___ (d) make a scientific breakthrough

9. I'm in a life-long search for more
___ (a) thrills & adventures
___ (b) self-understanding
___ (c) safety & security
___ (d) efficient methods of operation

10. In facing the future
___ (a) I bet something lucky will turn up
___ (b) I believe in people's innate goodness
___ (c) you just can't be too careful
___ (d) it's best to keep a wary eye

11. If it were possible I'd like to becom
___ (a) an artistic virtuoso
___ (b) a wise prophet
___ (c) a chief executive
___ (d) a technological genius

12. I'd do best in a job working with
___ (a) tools & equipment
___ (b) human resources development
___ (c) materiel & services
___ (d) systems & structures

13. As a guide to action I look primarily at
___ (a) immediate advantages
___ (b) future possibilities
___ (c) past experience
___ (d) necessary & sufficient conditions

14. I'm most self-confident when I'm
___ (a) adaptable & flexible
___ (b) genuine & authentic
___ (c) honorable & respectable
___ (d) strong-willed & resolute

15. I appreciate it when others
___ (a) surprise me with generosity
___ (b) recognize my true self
___ (c) express their gratitude
___ (d) ask me for my rationale

16. When thinking about misfortune
___ (a) I usually laugh it off
___ (b) I often wonder why
___ (c) I try to make the best of it
___ (d) I view it from a wide perspective

	1	2	3	4	5	6	7	8	9	10	11	12	13	14	15	16		
a																		A
b																		I
c																		G
d																		R

Scoring Directions: First, in the numbered columns above, record your rankings (1 to 4) for each of the 16 items. **Second,** add the numbers across each of the four rows (**a, b, c, d**) & place the sums in the boxes at the far right. **Third,** circle the letter (**A, I, G,** or **R**) beside the *lowest* sum. **Fourth,** A stands for Artisan (SP), I for Idealist (NF), G for Guardian (SJ), R for Rational (NT).

ORDER FORM

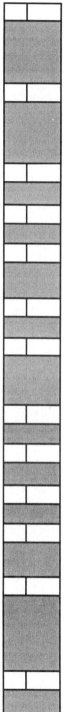

Qty $0.00

• *Please Understand Me II* Keirsey   346 pages—$15.95
An updated and greatly expanded 1998 revision of *Please Understand Me.*
Presents Keirsey's latest ideas on differences in temperament and character
in mating, parenting, leading, and SmartWork™. Comprehensive discussions
of Artisans (SPs), Guardians (SJs), Idealists (NFs), & Rationals (NTs), and
their 16 role variants. Includes *The Keirsey Temperament Sorter II.*

• *Leading and Intelligence* Keirsey   46 pages—$ 4.00
Chap. 9 from *Please Understand Me II* on leading, temperament, and intelligence. Examines different styles of leadership depending on different kinds
of intelligence—tactical, logistical, diplomatic, strategic. Useful for training
management in production, distribution, and personnel recruitment, education, and deployment. Includes *The Keirsey FourTypes Sorter.*

The Sixteen Roles Keirsey   36 pages—$5.00
All sixteen intelligent role variants reprinted from *Please Understand Me II.*
Plus *The Keirsey Temperament Sorter II* & *The Keirsey FourTypes Sorter.*

• *The FourTypes Booklets*   12 pages $1.00
Separate booklets that group the four role variants of each temperament.
Specify #: Artisan (SP)☐ Guardian (SJ)☐ Idealist (NF)☐ Rational (NT)☐

• *The Keirsey Temperament Sorter II* $.50
Self-scoring questionnaire designed to identify the sixteen variants of the
four temperaments, reprinted from *Please Understand Me II.* The best selling
personality inventory in the world.

• *The Keirsey FourTypes Sorter* $.25
Self-scoring questionnaire to identify the four temperament types, reprinted
from *Please Understand Me II.* Includes brief portraits of the four types.

• *Please Understand Me, The Videotape*   75 Minutes—$19.95
Displays many of the character traits of the Artisans (SPs), Guardians (SJs),
Idealists (NFs), and Rationals (NTs). Uses current and historical footage,
comments from Keirsey, and interviews to show the impact of attitudes and
habits of temperament and character in mating, management, and education.

• *Please Understand Me* Keirsey & Bates   208 pages—$11.95
Two million copies in print of a 40 year clinical study of four types of
temperament as they differ in mating, parenting, and leading.

• *Por Favor Compréndeme* Keirsey & Bates   238 pages—$11.95
Spanish edition of *Please Understand Me.* Includes *The Keirsey Temperament
Sorter* in Spanish.

• *Versteh Mich Bitte* Keirsey & Bates   276 pages—$11.95
German edition of *Please Understand Me.* Includes *The Keirsey Temperament
Sorter* in German.

• *Portraits of Temperament* Keirsey   124 pages—$9.95
Redefines the four temperaments as the Artisans, Guardians, Idealists, and
Rationals, each with two variant patterns of behavior based on different
kinds of ability and interest.

• *Presidential Temperament* Choiniere & Keirsey   610 pages—$9.95
Depicts the temperament-determined characters of forty U.S. Presidents,
from youth to old age. Authors found 20 Guardians (SJs), 12 Artisans (SPs),
8 Rationals (NTs), and *no* Idealists (NFs). Temperament is shown to dominate
historical and regional circumstances and situations in determining
presidential behavior—in war and peace—in depressed and prosperous
economics—in foreign and domestic politics.

• *The Pygmalion Project: 1 The Artisan* Montgomery   180 pages—$9.95
The bold, impulsive Artisan (SP) style of love with their Guardian (SJ),
Rational (NT), and Idealist (NF) mates, as illustrated by characters in novels,
plays, and films, such as Lawrence's *Lady Chatterley's Lover*, Hemingway's
The Sun Also Rises, Fitzgerald's *The Great Gatsby,* and others.

• *The Pygmalion Project: 2 The Guardian* Montgomery 258 pages—$9.95
The responsible, down-to-earth Guardian (SJ) style of love with their Artisan (SP), Idealist (NF), and Rational (NT) mates, as illustrated by characters in novels, plays, and films, such as C.S. Forester's *African Queen*, Jane Austen's *Pride and Prejudice*, Ibsen's *A Doll House*, and others.

• *The Pygmalion Project: 3 The Idealist* Montgomery 325 pages—$9.95
The enthusiastic, soulful Idealist (NF) style of love with their Artisan (SP), Guardian (SJ), and Rational (NT) mates, as illustrated by characters in novels and films such as E.M. Forster's *Howards End*, Tolstoy's *Anna Karenina*, Charlotte Brontë's *Jane Eyre*, and others.

• *Children the Challenge* Dreikurs and Soltz   335 pages—$11.95
An indispensable manual for those parents, teachers, and counselors who wish to win the cooperation of children and awaken their social interest.

• *Talk So Kids Will Listen and Listen So Kids Will Talk*   242 pgs—$12.00
The authors, Mazlish and Faber, teach interested parents, teachers, and counselors the gentle art of talking with children effectively and with mutual respect, an art that is very difficult to learn without inspired help.

• *Abuse it—Lose it* Keirsey   20 pages—$2.00
Applies the principle of logical consequences and the "abuse it—lose it" method for developing self-control in mischievous school boys who have been stigmatized as "cases" of the mythical "attention deficit hyperactivity disorder" and then drugged into obedience with cocaine-like narcotics.

• *The Evil Practice* Keirsey   4 pages—$.25
Reveals the evil of drugging school children whom teachers, parents, pharmacists, and medics falsely claim to be short on attention when in fact such children are paying lots of attention to their own agendas. Though "attention deficit" is a myth, belief in it puts *millions* of school children at risk of permanent damage to their brains and their self-regard.

• *Talking Back to Ritalin* Breggin   416 pages—$19.95
Breggin has revealed just how evil the practice is of drugging inattentive school children whose only offense is to attend to their own agenda instead of the teacher's. Breggin describes the full range of harmful effects of stimulants, including brain atrophy, weight loss, insomnia, tics, and irreparable damage to self-esteem, self-respect, and self-confidence.

Total Enclosed		Subtotal ———————
Name ————————————————		7.5% Sales Tax (CA Only) ———————
Address ————————————		Shipping ———————
City ————— State —— Zip ————		Shipping Charges

For arrival of order before four weeks call 800-754-0039 for UPS shipping charges. Mail order and check (US Dollars only) to PN Books, Box 2748, Del Mar, CA 92014. 760-632-1575; Fax 619-481-0535 or Fax 714-540-5288

Order Subtotal	USA	Abroad
$ 00.00 - $ 49.99 —	$3.00	$ 4.50
50.00 - 99.99 —	4.50	7.00
100.00 - 149.99 —	5.50	10.00
150.00 - 199.99 —	6.00	11.50